THE OLDER SCOTS VOWELS: A HISTORY OF THE STRESSED VOWELS OF OLDER SCOTS FROM THE BEGINNINGS TO THE EIGHTEENTH CENTURY

A. J. AITKEN

Edited by Caroline Macafee

The Scottish Text Society

2002

©

THE SCOTTISH TEXT SOCIETY 2002

ISBN 1 897976 186

Printed by Biddles Limited,
Guildford, Surrey, England

Distributed by Booksource
32 Finlas Street, Cowlairs Estate, Glasgow G22 5DU

TABLE OF CONTENTS

Foreword by Catherine van Buuren viii

List of Maps and Figures x

Conventions, Abbreviations and Short Titles xi

Acknowledgements xx

Editor's Introduction by Caroline Macafee xxi

PART ONE: VOWEL PHONOLOGY OF SCOTS TO 1375

1   Introduction 1

2   Preliterary Scots: general 3

OE and Early ME/Early PreSc developments

3   The PreSc stressed vowels prior to Open Syllable Lengthening 4

Vowel lengthenings and shortenings of the ME (PreSc) period

4   Open Syllable Lengthening (OSL) 11

5   Other lengthenings and shortenings of the ME (PreSc) period 16

New diphthongs and related developments

6   New diphthongs in -*i* and -*u*, especially those of native origin 18

7   The front rounded vowel (vowel 7) 39

Various combinative developments

8   The effects of palatal consonants 45

9   OF *a* before nasal combinations in OSc 54

10   OE (Anglian) *ald* in PreSc 61

| 11 | ESc /a/ and /ɛ/ before /rC/ .... | 63 |
| 12 | Smoothings of certain ESc diphthongs in particular environments .... | 66 |

Unstressed vowels

| 13 | The fully unstressed vowels .... | 69 |

PART TWO: SOURCES

| 14 | The sources of the vowels of Early Scots itemised .... | 73 |

PART THREE: VOWEL PHONOLOGY OF SCOTS FROM 1375

15	ME tonic and countertonic *i* adopted as vowel 2	97
16	Some combinative changes	98
17	l-vocalisation (LV): /a/, /ǫ/, /ṳ/ + tautosyllabic /l/ > /au/, /ǫu/, /uː/ respectively	101
18	Smoothing of /au/ vowel 12 to [aː] or [ǫː], in early MSc	105

Major developments affecting the ESc long monophthongs

19	Some comments on the testimony of *The Linguistic Atlas of Scotland* vol. III	106
20	The Great Vowel Shift (GVS)	108
21	The Scottish Vowel-Length Rule (SVLR) (Aitken's Law) ...	123

Diphthongs, particularly ESc /ai/ vowel 8

22	The diphthongs in OSc: some general remarks	131
22.1	ESc /ai/ vowel 8 and its relations in OSc with /aː/ vowel 4 and /yː/ vowel 7	131
22.2	The development of ESc vowels 4 /aː/, 7 /yː/, 8 /ai/ and 15 /ɪ/ in word-initial environments	132

22.3	The development of vowel 8, ESc /ai/, in non-initial, non-final environments	140
22.4	The development of ESc /ai/ vowel 8 in final position	146

Short vowels

23	The subsequent history of vowel 19. OSc /ụ/	150

Recapitulation

24	Recapitulation: ESc to modSc in outline	152

Notes 163

Writings Consulted 177

Glossary of Linguistic Terms 189

Index I: Source Vowels (OE, ON, OF) 191

Index II: Sound-changes 199

Index III: Selected Scots Words 201

FOREWORD

When the Scottish Text Society asked me to write the foreword to this volume I felt very honoured, but, at the same time, I was filled with a deep sense of sadness that the tribute I will now pay to Jack Aitken is, of necessity, posthumous. When he died, on 11 February 1998, an immense shock-wave came over the large circle of those of us who had been privileged to know him, though few of us could then have foreseen how intensely we would miss him, both as a fine person and as a scholar.

As early as 1954, I personally had the great good fortune of becoming acquainted with Jack Aitken through the kind offices of the historian and novelist Agnes Mure Mackenzie and David Murison of *SND* fame. Since then, my annual trips to Edinburgh have included regular visits to 27 George Square and the pleasure of an 'Aitken party', where Jack and Chandra were the perfect hosts.

Visits, letters and telephone calls became more frequent after 1957 when I had graduated and chosen to specialize in Older Scots. Jack was the instigator of and indispensable guide for my doctoral thesis, an edition of the *Buke of the Sevyne Sagis*, and, once I got going, he helped me considerably with his pioneering cyclostyled handouts and occasional reviews, which were as seminal as his later published articles. He was constantly ready to advise and gave generously of his time in assessing work done, characteristics which I found very stimulating. I, and many others, owe him a great debt of gratitude for his kind support and the prodigious energy he put into teaching.

In 1971, the publication of his article 'Variation and variety in written Middle Scots' made it clear that, in Jack Aitken, we had a torchbearer we could follow with confidence. In 1975, at the First International Conference on Scottish Language and Literature, Medieval and Renaissance, in Edinburgh, his paper 'How to pronounce Older Scots' was an eye-opener, especially to those who had thus far thought that the language of Dunbar and Henryson should sound something like Chaucer's. How fitting it was that such a lecture should have been presented at the *first* of these conferences!

The 1975 conference, of which he was the prime mover, was the beginning of a very useful and pleasant series of triennial meetings, where, for most of us, Jack was the pivotal center of both scholarly and social events. When, at the 1999 conference, he was no longer with us, his absence was keenly felt.

His outstanding work from 1948 to 1986 on the monumental *Dictionary of the Older Scottish Tongue* marks him out as a pillar of learning and as a mainstay for those who are interested in the language of Scotland. His great predecessor Sir William Craigie could not have wished

FOREWORD

for a better successor than Jack Aitken who, with great energy and utter devotion, helped to make this one of the great dictionaries of the world. After his term of office had ended, he remained active in the field, in all senses of the word, and his later articles are as full of exhortation and inspiration for new research as those of his earlier years.

And now, before us, we have Jack's final gift, yet another token of his extensive knowledge, an incomparable contribution to the study of Older Scots, as welcome as any gift could be. To have this matter so lucidly presented, so well ordered, so thorough and so complete, is the answer to a phonologist's prayer. It is the outcome of years of thought and study with the resultant insight into the developments in the language over the centuries. This book is the rewarding consequence of his many years at the workface of 'the drudgery of lexicography' (αὐτος εφη!). We would do well to stand back and admire Jack's tenacity and dedication in preparing this monument of scholarship and completing it in the face of full knowledge of the uncertainties of his physical heart condition.

Caroline Macafee deserves our appreciation and gratitude for saving this important addition to Jack's printed *oeuvre*, as does Iseabail Macleod. With great merit, they took it upon themselves to preserve his literary remains for posterity to consult. As they did before, in 1987 with *The Nuttis Schell*, they have rendered an outstanding service to scholarship on the Scots language.

Catherine van Buuren

LIST OF MAPS AND FIGURES

Map 1	The main dialect divisions of Modern Scots	xvi
Map 2	Preiotation of initial vowel 4 in SVLR-short environments, as in *yin* 'one'	135
Map 3	Modern distribution of *yae* forms of 'one' adj.	136
Figure i	Consonants	xv
Figure ii	Non-rounded vowels	xv
Figure iii	Rounded vowels	xv
Figure 1	Vowel-systems of ESc	3
Figure 2	Vowel-systems of OE	5
Figure 3	Outcome of the sME backing and rounding of OE, ON *ā*, followed by OSL	9
Figure 4	Late OE/early ME and early PreSc Short Vowel Lowering	11
Figure 5	Outcome of the lowering of the PreSc short vowels	11
Figure 6	Primary sources of ESc /ai/ vowel 8	21
Figure 7	Comparison of the PreSc and sME treatments of back vowels before /w/ and /ɣ/	28
Figure 8	Sources and outcomes of vowel 14	34-5
Figure 9	OE /ɛ/ before /ɲ/	49-50
Figure 10	AN /ɑː/, OF /a/ before nasal + C	58-60
Figure 11	OE (Anglian) *ald* in PreSc	62
Figure 12	/a/ and /ɛ/ before /rC/	65
Figure 13	The principal sources of the Early Scots vowels	89-95
Figure 14	Vowel-systems of ESc	96
Figure 15	Late sME long vowels	108
Figure 16	The ESc long monophthongs and the Great Vowel Shift	110
Figure 17	The Great Vowel Shift: changes in Scots, 14-16c	111-12
Figure 18	Lyndsay's mergers of vowel 3	121
Figure 19	Vowels 4 and 8 word-final	148
Figure 20	The later development of the ESc vowel-systems	152-9
Figure 21	Vowel systems of Scots: a rough historical outline	160-3
Additional figures		165, 174, 176

CONVENTIONS, ABBREVIATIONS AND SHORT TITLES

I have made use of many abbreviations, both those well established in tradition, such as OE (Old English) and ME (Middle English) and, for the history of Scots, ESc (Early Scots) and MSc (Middle Scots); and others which I have coined for the present work, including PreSc (pre-literary Scots) and PreStE (the Middle English or Early Modern English precursor of Standard English). The labels for the broad dialect divisions (N = Northern, NE = North-East, nEC = northern East Central, etc.) are those of *The Concise Scots Dictionary* (p. xxxi): see Map 1.

In representing the forms discussed, lexemes are given in *italics* in their traditional spellings. Traditional diacritics are added, such as macrons to indicate vowel-length, breves to indicate shortness, e.g. OE *mētan* 'meet' with *ē* or *mĕtan* 'mete' with *ĕ*. Phonemic representations are given in IPA enclosed by slants, e.g. OE /'meːtan/ 'meet' with /eː/, /'mɛtan/ 'mete', with /ɛ/. Commonly sounds are represented in the first instance by traditional graphemes in italics, such as *ē* or *ǣ* [editor's note: because italic *æ* and *ɑ* are virtually indistinguishable in the available fonts, italic *æ* has not been used, thus æ, ă̄, ǣ, ǽ]; commonly these are elucidated by accompanying phonemic representations in IPA, as e.g. *ē* /eː/, *ǣ* /ɛː/, or OE *mētan* /'meːtan/. But when the traditional grapheme might be ambiguous, the IPA symbol alone may be used. Phonetic representations employ IPA in square brackets, e.g. ESc [twaː] or [twɑː].

Citations of orthographic realisations are given in pointed brackets, as <grayting>, sometimes accompanied by the specification of the lexeme in regular spelling, as *graithing*. Citations of lexemes or orthographic realisations are commonly followed by a date, using the dating system of the CSD, as 16 (= 16c), e16 (= early 16c), la16 (= late 16c). Lexemes which coincide in form with those of modern English are usually left unglossed, as *main, plain,* but otherwise lexemes or other cited forms are identified by citing the corresponding English form and/or a gloss enclosed by quotation marks, as *layn* 'conceal', <ber> *bear* 'carry', or OSc *were* 'war'.

Below are some conventions used with IPA symbols and in formulaic representations of sound-changes or sound-change conditions:

* (before an OSc word or with IPA symbols) unattested form, reconstructed form. The *ad hoc* uses of * or ** before a word in §11.1 and of * following a word in §22.4 are explained in the text. Asterisks are also used in figures to draw attention to notes below.
C any consonant
V any vowel
( ) enclose an optional feature
{ } enclose alternative features
. syllable division

CONVENTIONS, ABBREVIATIONS AND SHORT TITLES

\# word-final, e.g. /ai#/
\+ in hiatus, e.g. /iu+/
\- (in formulae) preceding or following; a preceding or following segment (e.g. ē- or /e :-/ means this vowel followed by another segment)
/ (in formulae) in the environment of

A colon : between OSc words in italics signifies that the words rhyme with each other.

Abbreviations

In general, abbreviations are as in *The Concise Scots Dictionary* (including pre-1974 counties) or *A Dictionary of the Older Scottish Tongue*.

14-15	(e.g.) 14th-15th century
17	(e.g.) 17th century
a	(before a date) *ante*
Abd	Aberdeenshire
adj.	adjective
A-L	Anglo-Latin
AN	Anglo-Norman
Angl.	Anglian
Arg	Argyllshire
attrib.	attributive
Ayr	Ayrshire
Bnf	Banffshire
Bwk	Berwickshire
c	(before a date) *circa*
c	century
C	any consonant
C	Central (Scots)
Cai	Caithness
CF	Central French
CSD	*The Concise Scots Dictionary*
dial.	dialectal(ly)
Dmf	Dumfriesshire
DOST	*A Dictionary of the Older Scottish Tongue*
Du	Dutch
e	(before a number) early (e.g. e16 = early 16th century)
EC	East Central (Scots)
EDG	*The English Dialect Grammar* (Wright, 1905)
ELoth	East Lothian
eME	early Middle English

CONVENTIONS, ABBREVIATIONS AND SHORT TITLES

e.m.E	Early Modern English
ESc	Early Scots
F	French
Flem	Flemish
Gael	Gaelic
Gmc	Germanic
GVS	the Great Vowel Shift
HOCL	Homorganic Cluster Lengthening (pre-Cluster Lengthening)
IPA	the International Phonetic Alphabet
Kcb	Kirkcudbrightshire
L	Latin
la	(before a number) late (e.g. la16 = late 16th century)
LAS3	*The Linguistic Atlas of Scotland*, vol.III
LG	Low German
Lnk	Lanarkshire
LV	*l*-vocalisation, *l*-vocalised
MDu	Middle Dutch
ME	Middle English
MF	Middle French
MLG	Middle Low German
modSc	Modern Scots
modStE	Modern Standard English
MS, MSS	manuscript(s)
MSc	Middle Scots
n.	noun
N	Northern (Scots)
NE	North-East (Scots)
nEC	northern East Central (Scots)
neut.	neuter
nME	Northern Middle English
Norw	Norwegian
OE	Old English
OF	Old French
ON	Old Norse
ONF	Old Northern French
ONhb	Old Northumbrian
Ork	Orkney
OSc	Older Scots
OScand	Old Scandinavian
OSL	Open Syllable Lengthening
OWScand	Old West Scandinavian
Per	Perthshire
pl.	plural

CONVENTIONS, ABBREVIATIONS AND SHORT TITLES

possess.	possessive
p.p.	past participle
ppl. adj.	participial adjective
PreSc	pre-literary Scots
pres.t.	present tense
PreStE	the variety of Middle or Early Modern English ancestral to Standard English
p.t.	past tense
Rox	Roxburghshire
S	Southern (Scots)
Sc	Scots
Scand	Scandinavian
ScStE	Scottish Standard English
sEC	Southern East Central (Scots)
Sh	Shetland
sing.	singular
sME	Southumbrian (Midland and Southern) Middle English
SND	*The Scottish National Dictionary*
st.	stanza
StE	Standard English
Stlg	Stirlingshire
S.T.S.	Scottish Text Society
s.v., svv.	*sub verbo* (under the word(s) (in a dictionary))
SVL	Short Vowel Lowering
SVLR	the Scottish Vowel-Length Rule (Aitken's Law)
SW	South-West (Scots)
Uls	Ulster (Scots). Uls Scots data cited from LAS3 cover Co. Antrim and Co. Down only.
v.	verb
V	any vowel
var., varr.	variant(s)
vbl.n.	verbal noun
VL	Vulgar Latin
WC	West Central (Scots)
WGmc	West Germanic
Wgt	Wigtownshire
WS	West Saxon

	Bilabial	Labiodental	Dental	Alveolar	Postalveolar	Palatal	Velar	Glottal
Plosive	p b			t d			k g	
Nasal	m			n		ɲ	ŋ	
Trill				r				
Fricative		f v	θ ð	s z	ʃ ʒ		x ɣ	h
Approximant						j		
Lateral approximant				l		ʎ		

Where symbols appear in pairs, the one to the right represents a voiced consonant.

Figure i: Consonants

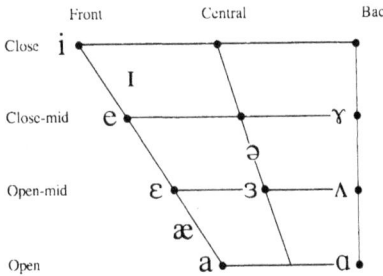

Figure ii: Non-rounded vowels

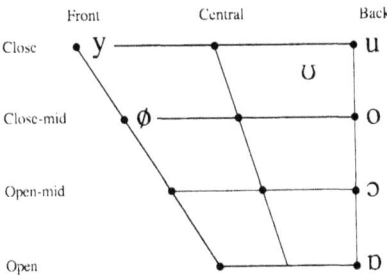

Figure iii: Rounded vowels

Map 1: The main dialect divisions of Scots, based on CSD, Map 1 and Gregg (1985), Part II: Map 1, by kind permission of the Scottish National Dictionary Association and Mrs. Gregg; artwork courtesy of Oxford University Press.

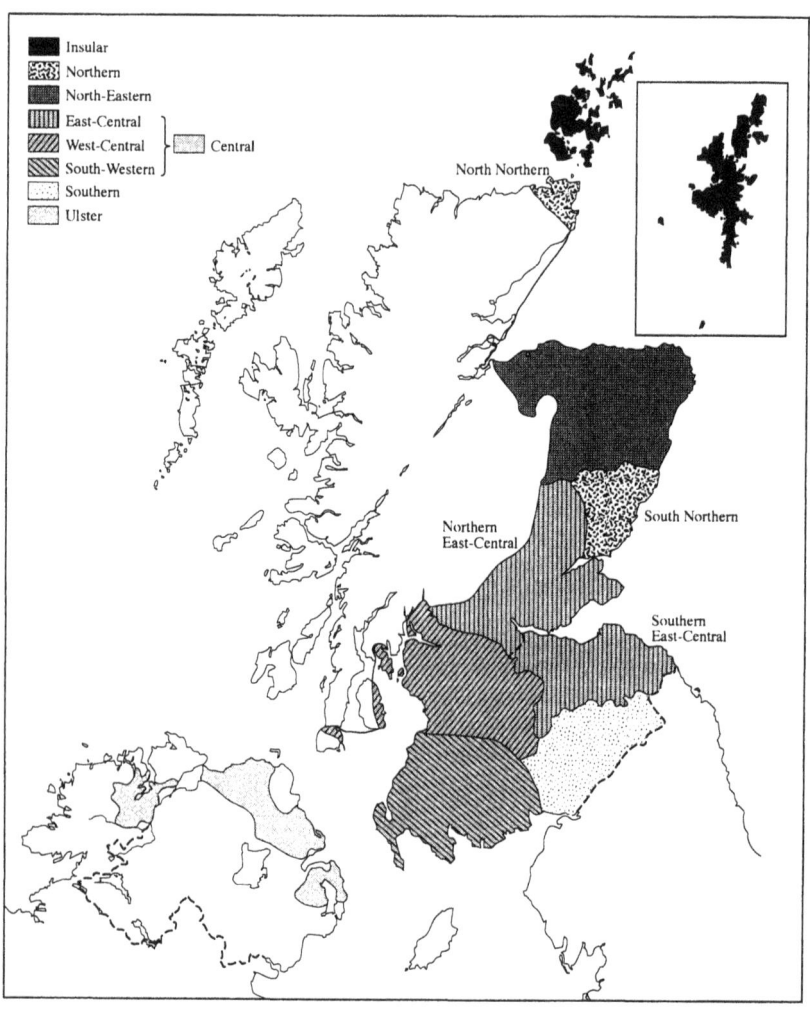

Short titles

References to Older Scots authors and abbreviated titles are mainly as in DOST. For the convenience of readers, these are listed below. In some cases AJA has referred to superior later editions, as here.

Aberd. B. Rec.	*Extracts from the Council Register of the Burgh of Aberdeen, 1398-1625*, 2 vols., Sp. C., 1844, 1848. *1625-*, 2 vols., B. R. S., 1871-2.
Æn.	[1513] *Virgil's Æneid Translated into Scottish Verse. By Gavin Douglas, Bishop of Dunkeld*, S. T. S. III. 25, 27, 28.
Alex. (Taym)	[c1460] *The Buike of King Allexander the Conqueroure, Translated by Sir Gilbert Hay*, excerpted from a transcript of the 16th c. MS. (B. M. Add. 40732) of Dr A. Macdonald. Extracts also in *The Taymouth Castle Manuscript of Sir Gilbert Hay's Buik of King Alexander the Conqueroure* by A. Herrmann, Berlin, 1898.
Allit. P.	*Scottish Alliterative Poems*, S. T. S. 27.
Asl. MS.	*The Asloan Manuscript, ... Written by John Asloan in the Reign of James the Fifth [c1515]*, 2 vols. S. T. S. II. 14, 16.
Bann. MS.	*The Bannatyne Manuscript Written in Tyme of Pest 1568 by George Bannatyne*, S. T. S. II. 22, 23, 26, III. 5.
Barb(our)	*Barbour's Bruce* S.T.S. IV. 12, 13.
Bk. Chess	[a1500] *The Buke of the Chess* in *Asl. MS.* I.
Ch. & M. Pr.	*The Chepman and Myllar Prints*, Edinburgh., c1508. (Reprinted in *Pieces from the Makculloch and the Gray MSS. together with the Chepman and Myllar Prints*, S. T. S. 65 and in facsimile, Edinb. Biblio. Soc., 1950.)
Ch. & Slae	[a1585] *The Cherrie and the Slae* in *The Poems of Alexander Montgomerie*, S. T. S. 9-11.
Christis Kirk	[15..] *Christis Kirk on the Grene* in *Maitl. F.*
Clariodus	[15..] *Clariodus; a Metrical Romance*, M. C., 1830.
Colk. Sow	[a1500] *The Tale of Colkelbie Sow*, in *Bann. MS.*
Consail Vys Man	[c1460] *Consail and Teiching at the Vys Man gaif his Sone* in *Ratis R.*
Doug(las)	*The Poetical Works of Gavin Douglas* (Edinburgh 1874).

CONVENTIONS, ABBREVIATIONS AND SHORT TITLES

Dunb(ar)	[c1500-12] *The Poems of William Dunbar*. Ed. J. Kinsley. Oxford, 1979. References by page/line.
Fab.	*The Morall Fabillis of Esope* in *The Poems of Robert Henryson*.
Facs. Nat. MSS.	*Facsimiles of the National Manuscripts of Scotland*, 3 parts. Southampton 1867-71.
Flyting	*The Flyting of Dunbar and Kennedy* in *The Poems of William Dunbar*.
Foly of Fulys	in *Ratis R.*
Fowler	[c1590] *The Works of William Fowler, Secretary to Queen Anne*, 3 vols. S. T. S. II. 6, III. 7, 13.
Gol. & Gaw.	[a1500] *The Knightly Tale of Golagros and Gawane* in *Allit P.*
Hay	[1456] *Gilbert of the Haye's Prose Manuscript*, S. T. S. 44, 62.
Henr(yson)	[a1500] *The Poems of Robert Henryson*. Ed. D. Fox. Oxford, 1981.
Howlat	[c1450-2] *The Buke of the Howlat*, by Sir Richard Holland in *Allit. P.*
Hume	[1587-99] *The Poems of Alexander Hume; Edited from the Text of Waldegrave (1599)*, S. T. S. 48.
James VI	[1581-1623] *The Poems of James VI of Scotland*, S. T. S. III. 22, 26.
Kennedy *Flyt.*	[a1508] *Kennedy's Flyting with Dunbar* in *The Poems of William Dunbar*.
Kingis Q.	[a1436] *The Kingis Quair of James Stewart*. Ed. M. McDiarmid. London, 1973.
Lanc.	[a1500] *Lancelot of the Laik*, S. T. S. II. 2.
Leg. S.	[a1400] *Legends of the Saints*, 3 vols. S. T. S. 13, 18, 23, 25, 35, 37.
Liber Calchou	*Liber S. Marie de Calchou: Registrum Cartarum Abbacie Tironensis de Kelso, 1113-1567* B. C., 82, 1846.
Lynd(say)	*The Works of Sir David Lindsay of the Mount*, S. T. S. III. 1, 2, 6, 8.
Maitl. F.	[a1570-86] *The Maitland Folio Manuscript, Containing Poems by Sir Richard Maitland, Dunbar, Douglas, Henryson, and Others*, S. T. S. II. 7, 20.
Montg(omerie)	[a1605] *The Poems of Alexander Montgomerie*, S. T. S. 9-11. Supplementary Volume, S. T. S. 59.
Orph.	*Orpheus and Eurydice* in *The Poems of Robert Henryson*.
Pal. Hon.	[1501] *The Palice of Honovr* in *The Shorter Poems of*

CONVENTIONS, ABBREVIATIONS AND SHORT TITLES

	Gavin Douglas, S. T. S. IV. 3.
Quare Jel.	[a1500] The Quare of Jelusy in Miscellany Volume, S. T. S. III. 4.
Ratis R.	[c1420] Ratis Raving, and Other Moral and Religious Pieces, in Prose and Verse, S. T. S. III. 11.
Robene and M.	[a1500] Robene & Makyne in The Poems of Robert Henryson.
Rolland	[c1550] Ane Treatise callit The Court of Venus ...: Newlie compylit be Iohne Rolland in Dalkeith, 1575. S. T. S. 3.
	[1560] The Seven Sages, in Scotish Metre, S. T. S. III. 3.
Sat.	The Satyre of the Thrie Estaitis in The Works of Sir David Lindsay of the Mount. At §20.5, reference is made to R. Lyall ed., Sir David Lindsay of the Mount, Ane Satyre of the Thrie Estaitis Edinburgh: Canongate, 1989.
Sat. P.	Satirical Poems of the Time of the Reformation [by Sempill, Davidson, J. Maitland, etc., 1567-83], S. T. S. 20, 24, 28, 30. References are by poem, line.
Seven S.	[a1500] The Buke of the Sevyne Sagis in Asl. MS. II.
J. Stewart	[c1590] Poems of John Stewart of Baldynneis, Vol. II., S. T. S. II. 5.
St. P. Henry VIII	[v.d.] Letters and Papers, foreign and domestic, of the reign of Henry VIII. 21 vols. London, 1862-1910.
Thewis Gud Women	[c1460] The Thewis off Gudwomen in Ratis R.
Troy-bk.	[c1400] Die Fragmente des Trojanerkrieges in Barbour's Legendensammlung. Ed. C. Horstmann, Heilbronn, 1882. In manuscript AJA cites c1470-1480 for the date of the MSS, but these are now thought to be c1500.
Wall.	[c1475] The Actis and Deidis of the illustere and vaileand Campioun Schir William Wallace, Knicht of Ellerslie. By Henry the Minstrel, commonly known as Blind Harry, S. T. S. 6, 7, 17.
Wynt(oun)	[c1420] The Orygynale Cronykil of Scotland, by Androw of Wyntoun, 3 vols., Edinburgh, 1872-9.

ACKNOWLEDGEMENTS

A. J. Aitken would no doubt have wished to thank everyone who contributed to this work, including the Faculty of Arts, Divinity and Music of the University of Edinburgh for funding, and the typists of the first draft, Suzanne Pender and Colin Maclean. Others who helped him in various ways will no doubt take his acknowledgement and thanks as read.

His wife Chandra needs no words of mine to remind her of the enormous contribution she made to his work by her practical and moral support. Odd as it may seem, AJA did not publish a book under his own sole authorship during his lifetime, so we cannot know what words of dedication and thanks he might have written.

For my own part, I would like to thank the Department of English and the Elphinstone Institute of the University of Aberdeen for funding, Louise Thomson for her typing, and especially the laying out of the tables, Ian Burt for artwork, Michael Shand for cartography (Map 2), Keith Williamson for Map 3, Sarah Couper for checking textual references, and Nicola Royan for seeing the book through the press. Oxford University Press kindly provided Map 1 and Figures i-iii, which appear also in DOST vol.XII. I am very grateful to everyone who assisted in the production of the book, particularly Priscilla Bawcutt, Iseabail Macleod, Sally Mapstone, Christine Robinson, Jeremy Smith and Catherine van Buuren, for their advice and meticulous comments.

I could not have completed my own part in this work without the moral support of Chandra Aitken and of Iseabail Macleod.

Finally, I am sure that AJA would have joined me in expressing gratitude to the Scottish Text Society for their willingness to publish this very technical work.

EDITOR'S INTRODUCTION

The late A. J. Aitken, 'the last native speaker of Older Scots', was working on this book at the time of his death in 1998. It has fallen to me to put the finishing touches to the work, and to prepare it for publication.

In this work, AJA returns to territory that he covered in some detail in Aitken (1977). With the wider range of evidence made available by LAS3 and by further textual studies of OSc, particularly by Catherine van Buuren and by Jonathan Glenn, as well as his own further researches, he is able to add considerable refinements to the 1977 model, and, at some points, to modify it. In particular, AJA's word-by-word examination of rhyme sets over the period has allowed him to assign a nunmber of words to vowel 2 that would seem, on etymological grounds, to belong to vowel 3, and *vice versa*. Conversely, the identification of etymological doublets of a number of vowel 8/4 words removes much of the confusion around apparent early 8/4 rhymes. There is a much fuller treatment of vowel 14 and the recognition of two additional triphthongs in the system (§6.5). Vowel 8 also receives a thorough new consideration (§22). However, AJA had not settled the chronology of the main monophthongisation of vowel 8, apart from establishing that it was too late to explain the <ai, ay> spellings of vowel 4 (as is now generally agreed), and that it preceded SVLR in some dialects and followed it in others. The undecided state of this part of the work is reflected in some small discrepancies between figures, which are pointed out to the reader at the appropriate point. The extraordinarily varied outcomes of vowel 12 in certain phonetic environments are clearly displayed (§9). The history of the development of a /j/-glide before initial vowel 4 has come in for an 'agonising reappraisal' (§22.2.4). The source of vowel 15 in words such as *mither* has been reconsidered (§16.1), and AJA no longer follows the accepted view, as he did in 1977.

It is perhaps worth mentioning that AJA's account of the Great Vowel Shift follows the traditionally accepted view, but that there is continuing debate about the origins and course of the Shift, and the relationship between developments north and south of the Humber.

There are some refinements to the notation used for the various vowel phonemes. Vowel 5 is now shown as a lowered $\bar{\varrho}$ /ǫː/. Personally (word-processing aside) I find this helpful, as it brings the account for OSc into line with the standard treatment of the same vowel in the major accounts of the history of English. AJA also shows vowels 18 and 19 as lowered ϱ /ǫ/, $\underset{\sim}{u}$ /ṳ/ (following Short Vowel Lowering), and this I find less helpful. It diverges from standard treatments of English, and seems to me to be unnecessarily narrow, as there is no contrast with any raised short /o/ and /u/ vowels. However, it does emphasise the similarity in realisation between vowels 5 and 18, which later merge, while further differentiating vowels 6 and 19, which do not.

At several points AJA drew attention to unresolved questions and to areas requiring further research. He expressed the hope that the Institute of Medieval Dialectology would throw light in the future on the dialectal distribution of the many doublets and variants in OSc. He also identified a need for a diplomatic investigation of the original manuscripts of early texts. in order to clarify such questions as the presence of a final *-e* or *-is*, and possible conditioning factors thereof, and the presence of *-ar* or *-er* or an abbreviation (§§11, 13.1, 13.3). He hoped that a full investigation of OSc rhymes would allow conclusive statements to be made about such questions as the chronology of the merger of vowels 4 and 8 (§22.3.2), the development of the vowel 8 in final position (§22.4), and the possible 15c merger of vowel 3 with vowel 2 before /r/ (§20.8.3). In some specific areas, he indicated that a fuller investigation was required than he had been able to undertake: one was the question of the chronology of the loss of final *-e* (§§4.1, 4.2.1, 7.2.2); another was the complexity of the development of the palatal consonants, *l*-mouillé and *n*-mouillé, when these remained palatal before a vowel (Treatment II) (§8.3); another was the possible alternative development of *ald* to merge with vowel 13, rather than with vowel 12 (§10). At various points he mentions aspects of phonetic environments or etymological sources which might be conditioning factors on particular developments: any of these would provide a starting point for further investigations. An interesting area that he points to, but leaves unexplored, is the possible effect of different lexical accretions and obsolescences in differentiating Scots from Standard English.

AJA gave a paper in 1997 (1997b) on the evidence for the Great Vowel Shift (GVS) in Scots and the emergence of the Scottish Vowel-Length Rule (SVLR). In the course of preparing the present work, he revised the view that he took then of the origin of preiotation of vowel 4 (see §22.2.4). AJA incorporated the GVS material into the present work. Since it seems unlikely that the 1997 paper will be published in the near future, I have incorporated some additional material from the manuscript notes of the 1997 paper into the endnotes here.

AJA was keen to see a full-scale study of OSc rhymes according to the principle of rhyming sets. In Aitken (1991) he gives the credit for the invention of this 'invaluable technique' to Heuser (1896) (possibly as an adaptation from an earlier treatise on the language of Chaucer). 'To use this method, you assemble the rhyming words as far as possible into mutually exclusive sets, rhyming only with one another ... ... in essence Heuser's approach through the rhyming sets is the same structural polysystemic approach as was devised afresh for the Phonological Survey of the Linguistic Survey of Scotland, Scots Section fifty years later'. In his notes for the conference paper which was the origin of the 1991 paper, he wrote:

EDITOR'S INTRODUCTION

For myself, I believe we still need a carefully organised examination of OSc rhyming practice using the method of rhyming sets - which could be collected and arranged very easily by a computer - as long as a merger is not totally and incontrovertibly established - so this is needed for all the early poets - and simpler assemblages of the spelling habits of individual texts. Once we have the data so organised we will be able to see how far questions of date and authorship of the earliest poems are capable of answer, if at all, and what the mutual implications of the rhyme and spelling evidence are.

[Even] a reorganisation of each of the [existing] lists of OSc rhymes and spellings into a single systematic and transparent arrangement, I would suggest by the ESc phonemes and rhyming sets, would be an important contribution. This would then need to be supplemented in various ways. So we would want frequency figures such as Heuser gives, for example we want to know whether a particular practice is normal or exceptional. And we want writers so far ignored brought in. We need much more on the 16c poets such as Lyndsay, to see the details of the merger of vowel 3 with vowel 2 or with vowel 4 (or not yet merged at all). We would want gaps in the existing record made good - Craigie on Fowler for example has nothing on the merger or failure to merge of vowels 4 and 8, and some writers treat vowels 2 and 3 as a single item.

In some cases, he thought that it would be as easy or easier to collect the data afresh, because of the disorganisation and unreliability of some of the earlier collections. Many of the rhyme lists:

> contain large amounts of redundancy, i.e. rhymes which merely re-establish what is already incontrovertible and invariable. So those which omit this redundant matter and concentrate on problematic areas are easier to use. [What is required is] a selective and full presentation of problematic points, and the remainder presented summarily thereafter, i.e. Craigie's method, roughly.

AJA was confident that, in the right circumstances, the negative evidence of the absence of certain types of rhyme was valuable and could be admitted.

AJA's purpose in writing the present work was clearly to carry out part of the agenda for OSc philology that he set out in 1991:

> Two further advances could be made. First, a much fuller overall description than the existing summary ones, with detailed and referenced statements of the evidence, and taking in the findings of the

Linguistic Atlas of Scotland, vol. 3 ... only available since 1986. Second, we need to collect the rhymes of as many OSc poems as possible, arranged ... in rhyming sets (p.27).

In his notes for the 1991 article, AJA wrote 'we could of course do with a large-scale study based on the data we presently have, but whether I will be willing to devote personally several of the few remaining years of my life to that is a moot question.' It was typical of Jack that a few years later, when he must have known or guessed how little time remained to him, he did indeed undertake this task, which probably only he could have carried out, no doubt recalling what Sir William Craigie once told him, that he was doing the work for which God had fitted him, and which it was therefore his duty to do.

This book is the culmination of decades of teaching and research on OSc, and it is perhaps worth recalling here AJA's own account of the evolution of his authoritative model of the OSc vowel system. I draw here on manuscript notes as well as on the published text of Aitken (1991):

> In 1949 Angus McIntosh invited me to give two courses on, respectively, the history of Scots, and Middle Scots, in Edinburgh University English Language Department. If you were looking for instruction on OSc phonology [at that time], this is what you had available:
>
> (1) You had two works which took in the whole of OSc and which were then, as since, regarded as standard works: Murray (1873) and Smith (1902). Neither of these offers anything approaching a comprehensive account of the history of the vowels of OSc, merely a haphazard list of some of the visible spelling peculiarities and similar, though fuller, lists for the consonants;
>
> (2) Several standard accounts of the history of English ... ... much the handiest as well as the completest being Jordan (1934). But this takes one down only to the 15c;
>
> (3) A considerable number of German PhD theses from the 1870s onwards, which deal with the phonologies of one or more OSc authors or texts ... all of them share certain defects. The history they contain stops short at the text they are dealing with. They contain a great deal of redundant material, through which one may have to wade to get at the examples bearing on matters which pose real questions. All of them have to be checked in detail [but] they are usable by a scholar who has his critical faculties well alerted: the word

identifications are sometimes mistaken, for example *deid* may be taken as the word for *dead* when it is actually the word *deed*, and likewise the word *race* from French *aracer* 'to pull out' in a rhyme in Barbour is misinterpreted by Buss (1886) as *raise* 'to lift up'. And, since the notion of phonemic systems was as yet undeveloped, none of them bothers to organise their material into rhyming sets ... their use is mostly that of data repository simply;

(4) Also important are a number of articles by Heuser (1896, 1897a, 1897b). There are numerous other minor works on individual OSc texts or groups of texts, some of these with a view to settling disputed points of authorship or dating, and some merely descriptive. The latter usually list some of the author's rhymes and spellings, sometimes without reference to or consideration of the fact that the examples listed are those of various scribes, not a single author.

Authors like Curtis (1894) and Heuser who depend on an abundance of data are more reliable than others like Girvan whose data are selective and often unreliable;

(5) Three STS editions each containing substantial sections on OSc phonology. In the first of these, Girvan (1939) on *Ratis R.*, most of the data and some of the descriptions of sound-changes were second-hand, and there are several errors in the examples quoted and the dates assigned to them. Craigie's (1939, 1941) accounts of the phonologies of William Fowler and of Hudson's *Judith* suffer, especially the first, from terminological confusion, especially the terms '$\bar{e}$ tense', '$\bar{e}$ slack' and 'long $\bar{\imath}$', which refer indifferently to ME sounds or to quite different 16c MSc ones, and they contain, as well, a fair number of errors and misunderstandings, for example in both pieces Craigie claims, as he says, long $\bar{\imath}$ (vowel in words such as *fire* and *time*) still has a pure vowel with its Middle English value in the late 16c, which cannot possibly be true.

(6) Dieth (1932) on Buchan and Zai (1942) on Morebattle are extremely useful, especially Zai, for the systematic presentation of the modern sounds and their pre-Early Scots sources, but these jump over the OSc period, and they were much too full, and for MSc incomplete, for my intended students.

How was I to put any of this stuff across to a bunch of students nearly all of whom regarded the study of English language as arid and meaningless, even more so than is the case today? Well, one answer was to minimise, as far as possible, the phonological part of the course. But I could not, it seemed to me, leave it out, because other aspects - a proper understanding of the implications of the spellings; remarks on questions of style, for example l-vocalisation and reductions - necessitated knowing something about the phonology.

Perforce, then, I set about devising my own version of the phonology of Scots, more or less on first principles, in the decade 1950-60. Since there were only a few isolated changes in some dialects in consonant pronunciations, my task was to reconstruct the history of the stressed vowels; unstressed vowels I am afraid were left to be dealt with in passing as a corollary. Though for pedagogical and other reasons it is systemic, not polysystemic, it grew up alongside the polysystemic approach to Scots dialect phonology devised by Ian Catford and others in the early 1950s. Because of its systemic layout, it is simple and certainly easier to comprehend and to use than if one had to work, say, from Luick's (1940) or Jordan's (1934) fragmented treatment of Scots. It certainly made it much easier for me to write on OSc spelling diversity, on the reading aloud of OSc and on the phonology and history of the Scottish Vowel-Length Rule than if I had had to work from the previous descriptions of, say, Luick. It provided a framework on which to base the pronunciations given in *The Concise Scots Dictionary* and enabled these to be dealt with more simply and efficiently than would have otherwise have been possible. It provides a convenient and transparent basis for presenting an OSc author's spellings and rhymes in accordance with his own system of phonemes, in preference to the clumsy, fragmented presentations based on OE or ME etymological sources formerly favoured, which do not relate in any transparent way to the author's own system.

The starting point, ESc, I took as more or less given ... between that and my goal, which was a composite version of the vowel system of Modern Scots south of the Moray Firth, I had to fit, *inter alia*, l-vocalisation, the disappearance of ESc /e/ as a separate phoneme, the Great Vowel Shift and the Scottish Vowel-Length Rule. I took a fresh look at the reconstruction evidence - rhymes and direct and reverse spellings for dating phonemic mergers, and, for the realisations, the statements of foreign commentators such as Erasmus and Sir Thomas Smith and the representations of English dramatists such as Shakespeare. The outcome of this is a series of class hand-outs from the early 1950s, including, from 1962, a short narrative history of the Scots vowels in four closely printed pages accompanied by a table. Tabular presentations seem not to have been common in the fifties and sixties (although used by Henry Sweet in 1900).

In 1976, I issued a revised version. By that time I no longer, following Kohler's (1967) work, believed in Murray's theory of the origins of *i*-digraphs, although I did not then feel able to come down firmly on a single other explanation. I have now been convinced by Veronika Kniezsa's (1989) arguments for a northern ME origin, which we ought to have investigated long ago.

The numbering of the several items ... is a device I may have got from David Abercrombie, who had his own numbered table of Modern Scottish English and RP vowels. It offers a convenient and unambiguous way of referring to any item at any chronological stage, in any dialect or idiolect, without having to specify a particular realisation. So it avoids the ambiguity of labels like, say, 'long tense $\bar{e}$ ' as used by Craigie, for example, or the clumsiness of the unambiguous label 'the 16c Scots reflex of ME long tense $\bar{e}$ '; we simply call this vowel 2. Some of the material was published in Aitken (1977), but of course all of it has always been available in hand-out form to anybody who asked for it. One of those who did was Fr Kuipers for his treatment of Quintin Kennedy's sound system in his edition (1964), which he orders phoneme by phoneme.

I think I can claim these utilities for my system: it is more easily grasped than anything before, partly because it is less complex, and the user is not presented with a confused plethora of data relating to a plethora of categories, but with a limited set of categories for reference. It is directly focussed on Scots, and is not a by-product of the history of Standard English. This enables us to see the development of Scots as a separate whole, not as occasional footnotes to RP. Likewise, it is of direct relevance to events in the later phonological history of Scots.

Use of the Aitken system does not, of course, exclude the use of other reference points, for example the OE or ME system, when necessary to make a particular point. The system has been used by several scholars of late, among whom Catherine van Buuren (1982) and Jonathan Glenn (1987) adopt a best-of-both-worlds approach by presenting their lexical lists in Vowels Systems order, but subdivided by the several etymological sources of each phoneme, thus providing very substantial enhancements to the original version of the system.

Like Aitken (1977), the present work concentrates on the stressed vowels. In a manuscript note, AJA wrote that he had:

> Regrettably not yet made time to discuss the history of the prefix and suffix syllables, albeit not all when they first appear in OSc were partially or wholly unstressed, or the consonants. Thus [he is] not able as yet to deal with the history of changing relationships between suffixes ESc /-eː/ as in *cite*, *liberte* and ESc /-iː/ as in *flatterie*, *hevy*;

or the Scots development of OF *-ée*, AN *-eie* from < L *-ata*, yielding doublets such as *cuntree, cuntray* or *journee, journay*; or any other of the innumerable prefixes and suffixes of OSc, including those in vowel 7 (*-ure, -ude*). Interesting consonantal developments not touched on include the question of *v/w* merger (in some dialects only).

In various places in manuscript notes, he mentions the unstressed vowels of OSc and expresses a wish to have investigated them further had time allowed. Without further data, he did not feel that he could improve upon the fullest account available, that of Kuipers (1964: 76-9). From his own observations:

> my general impression of contemporary Scots is that in most sentence-stress conditions there is less contrast between stressed and unstressed syllables in words than in most dialects of English.

Taken together with the phenomenon of terminal stress (see below), this suggests that 'unstressed vowel reduction may have proceeded somewhat more slowly in Scots than in Standard English'.

Two phenomena of Modern Scots unstressed vowels, he considered, may go back to the Older period: terminal stress and vowel harmony. Terminal stress, most fully described by Wettstein, is:

> an increased rhythmic or emphatic stress on final unaccented syllables ... [which] is most apparent at the end of breathgroups, where it may easily amount to a full stress or more and be coupled with a considerable reduction of a preceding accented syllable. (1942: 16-17)

> e.g. [hɛdz 'broˈkɛn]. It operates also on epenthetic vowels before certain consonants, e.g. [ðɪ 'heˑᵻ 'fʌˈwʌr]. It is a noticeable marker of modern Central Scots working-class speech, but is disallowed in middle class speech.

Vowel harmony is a predictable variation in the realisation of unstressed /ɪ/ according to the stressed vowel in the syllable preceding, e.g. in Buchan:

[spidi, dɪnɪr, doθɛr]

Today, vowel harmony is reported for Buchan (Dieth, 1932; Hill: 1963). I have myself heard it in Avoch, Denholm, Shetland and Orkney. Unfortunately, the results of the section of the Linguistic Survey of Scotland fieldwork designed to investigate this remain unpublished.

EDITOR'S INTRODUCTION

Although it is now characteristic only of some fringe dialects, vowel harmony was perhaps once more general.

As he writes in his Introduction (§1 below), AJA's approach is 'thoroughly structuralist'. It may be of interest here to include some of his lecture notes on 'theoretical principles and tenets', as given to second year English Language students in 1976:

> I operate in what is now (sometimes disparagingly) called taxonomic phonemics - what used to be called, in the 40s and 50s, structuralist phonology or traditional phonology (although structuralist phonology is more rigorous than pre-War historical phonology). Many younger scholars operate in what is called generative phonology and special developments of this, at a fairly abstract level. There are however many respected phonologists, and nearly all the Continentals ... who, like me, are unrepentant taxonomists ...
>
> Basically what I am concerned with doing is reconstructing earlier phonemic systems and specifying as well as the evidence permits the approximate realisations of the phonemes in their different phonetic environments and dialects. Often statements about realisations will be very approximate and are always likely to be much more speculative than statements about the systems. I then show how one system develops into a later one by changes resulting in phonemic mergers and splits and dialectal divergences. Essentially, the outlook and principles are those of a structural dialectologist, concerned with phonemes and their realisations and distributions and with dialectal comparisons of these, except that the comparison is done primarily in the chronological rather than in the regional and social dimension. ...
> ...
> Underlying my sort of approach is an assumption that most sound changes are ... in some sense gradual, and imperceptible while going on. This is borne out by the fact that most of those on record manifestly do involve easily explained *small* alterations in articulation, which certainly could physically occur gradually ... the experimental work of Labov and his associates in Philadelphia on vowel-shifts seems also consonant with a gradualist position, which in fact Labov holds. ... ...
>
> The representations of phonemes by phonetic symbols are, as usual, intended (1) to specify that this phoneme existed as a contrastive unit with its own lexical inventory and (2) also to say that there is some reason to suppose that it was realised with approximately the quality stated by the symbol.

The qualities stated by the symbols can of course be interpreted (if we wish to do so) as a bunch of distinctive features rather than as a phonetic identification according to, for instance, the Cardinal Vowel table ... the difference between the two methods - unitary phonetic symbol or the explicit and laborious statement of a number of distinctive features (+high, -round or the like) - seems to me analogous to the difference between the synonym definition and the genus and differentia periphrastic definition in lexicography: one has the advantage of *immediacy* but *may* - not must, may - lack some degree of precision; the other is absolutely precise and complete within its own theoretical framework, but does not immediately carry the reader to the referend - that needs rather patient elucidation and interpretation.

This work was originally commissioned as a chapter in Charles Jones ed. *The Edinburgh History of the Scots Language* (1997). Unfortunately, AJA was unable to complete the work within length and on time, and his contribution was replaced by a hasty expansion of Paul Johnston's chapter on 'OSc phonology and its regional variation', originally intended to deal only with regional variation. With all due respect to Paul Johnston, who stepped in to fill the gap at the last moment, it cannot be said that he has succeeded in doing what AJA failed to do in the available space, and it would appear that he did not have immediate access to *A Dictionary of the Older Scottish Tongue* or *The Scottish National Dictionary*. Johnston's approach is largely deductive, working from the modern dialect data, supplemented by *A Linguistic Atlas of Late Mediaeval English* (LALME). For instance, his suggestion of an early raising of Vowel 3 before /n/ (p.458) requires to be substantiated by contemporary rhyme evidence; while his suggestion that the lowering of Vowel 19 to [ʌ] and of Vowel 15 to [ɛ̈] originated in the vicinity of the Highland Line (p.478) is freely extrapolated from geography alone. Nevertheless, Johnston's is a work of great erudition, and it is reassuring that his independent reconstruction agrees at most points with AJA's. I have made occasional reference to Johnston in the endnotes.

What follows is, Johnston's work notwithstanding, the only full and detailed treatment of the vowel phonology of OSc that takes into account all of the relevant evidence, including spelling evidence, rhymes (of which AJA had a thorough knowledge, despite his modest disclaimers at some points in the work), and modern dialectal variation, as found in the SND as well as in *The Linguistic Atlas of Scotland* vol.III (with its large network of localities, but fairly limited word-list). Unlike Johnston, AJA does not make specific references to LALME (although it is listed in his 'Writings Consulted'), but it will be evident that AJA had a close acquaintance with

EDITOR'S INTRODUCTION

a much wider range of localised manuscripts than the eighteen from Scottish localities used in LALME.

In preparing this work for publication, I had before me a copy of the handwritten draft of the original chapter, kindly provided by Professor Jones, a partly corrected typescript of the same, and a partly completed enlargement and revision of the whole in manuscript and in the form of word-processed files, and other scattered notes. The revised sections incorporated word-processed phonetic symbols (sometimes inconsistent between typists), but the word-processed files of the unrevised sections substituted arbitrary symbols for unavailable phonetic ones, in many cases. A few of the many tables had been word-processed, but only in this unrevised form.

AJA preferred the traditional diacritics, e.g. ę and ẹ, for phonetic as well as orthographic representations, although he also had e.g. ę and ẹ when quoting LSS and LAS3. For ease of word-processing, as well as consistency, I have regularised e.g. ę and ẹ throughout as phonetic symbols.

In the process of revision, the endnote numbers had, of course, changed considerably; I have done my best to match the notes to the appropriate points in the text.

In preparing the work for publication, I have taken it upon myself to try to present the reader with AJA's thinking stated as clearly as possible, rather than slavishly adhering to the text of what were, particularly in some of the revised sections, quite raw first drafts. I have made some revisions (as noted in endnotes) to harmonise the text where the sense was affected by changes made elsewhere by AJA in his later drafts. I have borne in mind that I was probably only the second person, and sometimes the first, apart from AJA himself, to have read the work, and I have taken the view that if I found something difficult to follow even on a second or third reading, that others would also. I have been rather free with some of the figures, which I have redrawn, for clarity and for consistency with the revised text.

Otherwise, my role has mainly been to standardise various aspects of presentation, including the form of abbreviations, to check the typescript against manuscript, to check (and add) cross-references, and to make a few minor corrections by reference to AJA's own sources. I have not attempted to check AJA's data against the sources from which he extracted them. For ease of reference to DOST, a few (phonologically immaterial) changes have been made to the spellings AJA chose to cite in the text, mainly in relation to the last four volumes, which were not yet (fully) edited when he was writing. In a few cases where he could cite only modSc evidence, the DOST articles now provide OSc forms, which I have substituted. In other cases where he stated that there were no spellings of a certain type, and these have likewise kythed in the DOST articles, I have deleted the examples concerned from the text. I have also supplied a section on

'Conventions and Abbreviations', incorporating some preliminary material from the start of the main text, and a glossary of technical terms, and have indexed the work.

It has been a privilege to work so closely with AJA's s last writings, on which he was working only days before his death, and a consolation to know that this great man's thoughts and writings live on. I hope that the completed book does justice to his intentions.

PART ONE: VOWEL PHONOLOGY OF SCOTS TO 1375

1. Introduction[1]

This work attempts to treat in rather greater detail than hitherto the origins and subsequent development of the stressed vowels of Older Scots. As will be obvious, the treatment is thoroughly structuralist, attempting to follow the succession of systems and sub-systems of vowels from Old English onwards. The narrative centres round the system which had emerged at the stage known traditionally as Early Scots, *c*1375. In setting out this system I have assigned to its constituent phonemes the vowel numbers I have been accustomed to apply to them. This is intended to enable reference to be made to the historical phoneme and its attendant body of lexical selections without the need to specify a particular realisation at some given time and place. Thus vowel 4 means the antecedent or later reflex of the phoneme which in Early Scots is believed to have had the realisation [aː], in words derived from Old English *ā* and other sources. The Middle Scots phoneme realised as [ɛː] or [eː] in the same set of words as had contained Early Scots [aː] can likewise be referred to as vowel 4.

Some of the evidence of spellings recorded in *A Dictionary of the Older Scottish Tongue* (DOST) for the forms discussed is ambiguous, especially for identifying the vowels. Happily nearly all of the ambiguities are resolved by evidence from the modern dialects, as follows:

(a) many quasi-'phonetic' spellings in textual citations in *The Scottish National Dictionary* (SND) from many localities;
(b) intended phonetic representations of pronunciations in local grammars and dictionaries, such as those for Orkney and Shetland;
(c) pronunciations reported by Ellis (1889), Murray (1873), Watson (1923), Dieth (1932), Zai (1942), and others;
(d) pronunciations reported by SND's informants: e.g. <grunyasie> /ˈgrʌnj-/ 'ugly-faced' Ork 1955, s.v. *Grunyie*; <toolyie> /ˈtuljɪ/ 'scuffle', Abd *c*1782, Ayr 1816, Rxb 1923, s.v. *Tulyie*;
(e) information on regional distributions mostly comes from *The Linguistic Atlas of Scotland* vol. III (LAS3).

1.1 Doublets and variants

Older Scots seems to have been highly tolerant of formal variation in its vocabulary - of doublets and variants. Examples of the different sorts of these are to be found in Aitken (1971). Many of the sound-changes set out below resulted not so much in the simple replacement by a new form of a former one, but in the creation of an additional option, the old form and the new one co-existing as optional variants. In the modern dialects some of the individual members of these variant sets are separately distributed between dialects. In many cases their dialect distribution in Older Scots is much less evident, at least on a superficial inspection. It may be hoped that the more intensive investigation of the records of Older Scots by the Institute of Medieval Dialectology will reveal distribution patterns not yet apparent. Meantime, for want of knowledge, questions of regional and social distribution will often be bypassed in the present work. However, it is worth noting that the modern dialects, as displayed in LAS3, have areas of overlap in which two or more synonymous variants mingle, implying that, had more than a single informant been questioned in each locality, both the alternatives might well have been found to co-exist.

The following are examples of the variant outcomes of OE (and ON) post-vocalic *h* and *g* in OSc:

swelch n. and *swelly* v., *heich* ESc /heːx/ > MSc /hiːx/ 'high' and *he(y* ESc /heːi/ > /heː/ > MSc /hiː/ 'high', *dreich* adj. 'dreary' and *dre* v. 'endure', *laich, lauch* and *law* 'low', *law* and *lauch* 'law', *maich* and *mauch* 'son-in-law' < ON *mágr*, *ineuch* sing. and *inew* pl. 'enough', *beuch* and pl. *bewis* 'bough', *burch* and pl. *burrowis* 'burgh'.

To these add many other variant sets of other types, discussed and exemplified in Aitken (1971), especially its section 3.

1.2 The Early Scots vowel system

For convenience, I set out in Figure 1 the system of vowels I assume for Early Scots (hereafter ESc), *c*1375, with the numbers and the realisations I attribute to them at that time, and in each case a keyword in Older Scots (hereafter OSc) spelling. Here and throughout the chapter, except when otherwise specified, Scots spellings used in examples are those judged to be the least ambiguous of the ESc or Middle Scots (hereafter MSc) spellings on record.

The first section of this work deals with the history of the vowels of Scots (hereafter Sc) down to 1375, the end of the pre-literary period (hereafter PreSc) and the beginning of the much more copiously recorded and phonologically distinctive OSc period.

Figure 1: *Vowel-systems of ESc (c1375), with examples*

long vowels		diphthongs			short vowels		
1	iː *mine*	8	ai	*pain*	15	ɪ	*pin*
2	eː *sene* p.p. 'seen'	9	o̜i	*noise*	16	ɛ	*men*
3	ɛː *lene* adj. 'lean'	10	ui*	*point*	17	a	*man*
4	aː *bane* 'bone'	11	ei	*dey* 'die'	18	o̜	*fon* 'folly'
5	o̜ː *cole* 'coal'	12	au	*law*	19	u̜	*gun*
6	uː *doun* 'down'	13	o̜u	*loun* 'calm'			
7	yː *mone* 'moon'	14a	iu	*spew, grew*			
		14b	ɛu, ɛo̜u	*dew*,			
			ʔɛau	*lewté* 'loyalty'			

* [üi] (Aitken, 1991).

2 Preliterary Scots: general

The phonological development of Sc in the PreSc period largely shadowed that of ME generally, including that of Southumbrian ME (Midland and Southern, hereafter sME) as well as northern ME (hereafter nME). So PreSc shared in such developments as the smoothing of OE diphthongs and the subsequent creation of new diphthongs by native processes, supplemented by borrowings from ON, OF and other external sources. Likewise it shared in general in the succession of lengthenings and shortenings of vowels which so strikingly modified the lexical distributions of vowel sounds between OE and ME/ESc, though the effect of this on the system of the monophthongs, at least in the outcome, was less than that of the changes affecting diphthongs. There is no space here to set out *ad longum* those developments which PreSc shared with sME; for these the reader is referred to the standard text-books of Luick (1964), Jordan and Crook (1974), and others. Here will be discussed for the most part only those changes in which PreSc (and, mostly, nME) followed a different path from sME or, more often, differed in detail in the outcomes of shared trends; hitherto most of these changes have escaped discussion of any depth. In both these cases the effect was wide differences between the Northern and the Midland-Southern dialects in the lexical distributions of (mostly shared) vowel phonemes.

The great differences in the lexical inventories of the phonemes of, on the one hand, PreSc and, on the other, sME, were of course further enhanced by differences between them in vocabulary accretions and obsolescences, with Sc gaining for example words from Gael such as *reisk* 'coarse grass' vowel 2, *clachan* 'hamlet' vowel 17, *ingle* 'hearth-fire' vowel 15, or retaining from OE words obsolete in sME such as *ben* 'into the inner room' vowel 16, or *cleuch* 'a gorge' vowel 14, and so on. Vocabulary changes thus modified the token frequencies of the several phonemes in the opposed systems. No more will however be said of this cause of change in the balance of phonological elements within the lexicons of these two diverging systems.

OE and early ME/early PreSc developments

3 The PreSc stressed vowels prior to Open Syllable Lengthening

As the starting point for the history of the Scots stressed vowels I take late OE, as this has been reconstructed and described in numerous text-books, monographs and articles. Here I depend especially on Luick (1964), Wright (1905), Jordan and Crook (1974), Prins (1972), Lass (1992). The late OE vowel-system, in terms of which the OE shortenings and lengthenings about to be itemised took place, was as in Figure 2.

According to their behaviour at this time, late OE and early PreSc /aː/ vowel 4 and /a/ vowel 17 are assigned to the back vowel systems; for, in combination with following intervocalic /ɣ/ (OE *g*), as in OE *āgan* > OSc *awe* 'owe', ON **lagu* > late OE *lagu* > OSc *law*, or with following voiceless /x/ (OE *h*) as in OE *eahta* > OSc *aucht* 'eight', they yield the back diphthong /ɑu/. A little later they behave like front vowels, thus: short /a/ then operates as part of the front vowel system in merging with /æ/ by Short Vowel Lowering (§3.3 below); /aː/ merges with OF (probably front) *ā* in, e.g., PreSc (OE) *hāt* 'hot' and OF *estāt* 'estate'; and /a/ has the same outcome by Open Syllable Lengthening (OSL) in PreSc *nāme* (from OE) and *fāme* (from OF); later still /aː/ participates in the Great Vowel Shift as a front vowel. Both front and back realisations of /a/ vowel 17 occur in modSc dialects. Clearly there has been drifting back and forward across the low unrounded vowel area in the course of the centuries. For consistency's sake I use the symbol /aː, a/ or *ā, ă*, while of course varying the phonetic representations as required.

VOWEL PHONOLOGY TO 1375

Figure 2: Vowel-systems of OE (numbered as the derived ESc vowels)

(a) With traditional symbols

	front		back	
	long	short	short	long
1	ī, ȳ	15 ĭ, ȳ̆	19 ŭ	6 ū
2	ē, (ēo)	16 ĕ, (ĕo)	18 ŏ	7 ō
3	ǣ, (ēa)	17 ǣ̆, (ĕa)	17 ă	4 ā

(b) With IPA symbols

	front		back	
	long	short	short	long
1	iː, yː	15 i, y	19 u	6 uː
2	eː	16 e	18 o	7 oː
3	ɛː	17 æ	17 ɑ	4 ɑː

diphthongs

long	short
2 eːo	16 eo
3 ɛːa	17 ɛa

3.1 Vowel shortenings and lengthenings of the OE period

Here follows the succession of vowel shortenings and lengthenings in OE, as set out comprehensively in Luick (1964: §352 ff.), and summarised in Lass (1974), here with OSc examples:

(a) *Pre-Cluster Shortening I* (6-7c): OE *gōdspell* > *gŏdspell* > OSc *gospel*; OE *grēttra* > *grĕttre* > OSc *gretter* /ˈgrɛtɪr/

5

(b) *Trisyllabic Shortening I* (6-7c): OE *hlāfmæsse* > *hlăfmesse* > OSc *lammes* 'Lammas'
(c) *Pre-Cluster Lengthening* (9c): OE *cĭld* > *cīld* > ESc *child* /tʃiːld/
(d) *Pre-Cluster Shortening II* (11c): OE *fīfta* > *fĭfte* > OSc *fift*; OE *lēfte* > *lĕfte* > OSc *left*; OE *mētte* > *mĕtte* > OSc *met*; OE *īr(e)n* (*iron*) > *ĭrn* > nME and OSc *irn*
(e) *Trisyllabic Shortening II* (11c): OE *sūðerne* > *sŭðerne* > OSc *suthern, sutheron, suddren*, OE *hāligdæg* > *hăligdæg* > OSc *haliday*.

3.1.1 Pre-Cluster Lengthening (Homorganic Cluster Lengthening) in Scots

Of these changes the one in which nME behaves to some degree independently is Pre-Cluster Lengthening of OE short vowels before homorganic clusters (HOCL) ((c) above). Homorganic clusters are sequences of a sonorant consonant followed by a plosive articulated at the same point with the same tongue configuration.

Before /ld/

(1) PreSc shared the general English lengthening of OE *ĭ* and *ĕ*:

OE *cĭld* > *cīld* > OSc *child* vowel 1 (for a doublet in *ē*, vowel 2, see §5.1); OE *wĭlde* > *wīlde* > OSc *wild*; OE *fĕld* > *fēld* > OSc *feild* vowel 2; OE (Angl) *ĕldu* > *ēlde* > OSc *eild* 'old age'; OE *gĕlde* 'barren' > *gēlde* > OSc *ʒeild*, also an unlengthened doublet *ʒeld*.

(2) Unlike sME, PreSc had lengthened *ŏ*:

OE *mŏlde* 'soil' > *mōlde* > MSc *muild*, vowel 7, along with an unlengthened doublet MSc *mold*, vowel 18; OE *gŏlde* 'corn marigold' > *gōlde* > MSc *guild*, vowel 7, with doublet *guld*, vowel 19, apparently by later (? 12c) shortening (§5.3); but apparently without lengthening were *fold* (poetic: 'the earth'), *gold* (the metal) or *ʒolden* p.p. of *ʒelde* 'yield' (is it a coincidence that *molde* and *golde* had stem-final *-e*?).

(3) On the lengthening of Anglian *a + ld* and its development to *auld* and *owld*, see §10 below.

(4) The sequence *-uld* is largely lacking in OE; but *sculde* 'should' fails to lengthen in PreSc, giving OSc *suld*.

Before /nd/

(1) *i, y*

For the most part PreSc did not lengthen *ĭ* before /nd/, so OSc and modSc have /ɪ/ vowel 15 in *bind, blind, find, grind, wind*; likewise *y̆* fails to lengthen in OE *pyndan* 'to impound' > OSc *pind*, commonly spelled *poind* (see s.v. in DOST), modSc /pɪn(d)/. But lengthening did occur, yielding vowel 1, with:

OE *cy̆nde* > *cȳnde* > OSc *kind*; OE *gemy̆nd* > *gemȳnd* > OSc *mind*; OE *rĭnd(e)* > *rīnde* > OSc *rind*, vowel 1, with modSc doublet *reen*, vowel 2; OE *stry̆nd* 'generation' > *strȳnd* > OSc *strind*.

The derivation of OSc *synd* 'to rinse' vowel 1, modSc /sɛin(d)/, nME *sind*, is uncertain.

(2) *e*

As in sME, *ĕ* either did not lengthen or did not maintain length before /nd/, e.g. in OSc *bend, end, mend, send*, but lengthening did occur in OE *gehĕnde* 'handy' > OSc *heynde*, OE *lĕndan* 'to land' > OSc *leynd* 'to dwell', both rhyming as vowel 2, along with unlengthened OSc *lend*, rhyming as vowel 16, and similar doublets representing OE *lĕndenu* pl. 'buttocks' > OSc *leyndis*, vowel 2, beside unlengthened *lendis*, also the doublet *lind* rhymes with *behind*, vowel 15 (Henr.), apparently by later shortening (as in §5.3).

(3) *a*

PreSc either did not lengthen or did not maintain length with OE *ă* before /nd/ in e.g. *band, hand, sand*, except: ON *ănde* 'breath' > OSc *aynd* vowel 4; OE *făndian* 'to test' > OSc *faynde*; OE *sănd* 'messenger' > OSc *saynde*. The lengthening in *aynd* (from ON) and in the (post-OE) syncopated form *Sounday* < OE *sunnandæg*, seems to imply that some at least of these changes continued well after Luick's terminal date of the 9c.

(4) *u*

OE *ŭ* lengthened to /uː/ before /nd/, yielding vowel 6 in *stound* 'a while', *sound* adj., *sound* n. 'swim bladder', and *wound* n.; and, with unlengthened, or re-shortened, doublets in vowel 19, in e.g. OSc *bound* and *bund, bundin*, p.p., and, similarly, *found* and *fund, fundin*, p.p., *ground* n. and *grund*, and similarly with *hound* and *pound* n., *wound* and modSc /wʌn(d)/, p.p. of *wind* /wɪnd/ v. 'to turn', *houndreth* and *hundreth* and *hunder* 'hundred', and *Sounday*, with lengthening following syncope of OE *sunnandæg*. The DOST record appears to indicate that for most items the unlengthened forms were more frequent in OSc.

Before /mb/

As with *ī* before /nd/, *ī* before /mb/ shows no lengthening in OSc: modSc *clim, climb* /klɪm/. Unlike *ŭ* before /nd/, *ŭ* before /mb/ shows no lengthening in *clumbin, clummin* p.p. of *clim* 'climb', *dum* 'dumb' or *slummer* 'slumber'. As in sME, OE *ă* before /mb/ > /aː/ vowel 4, in OSc *kame, cambe* 'comb', *wame* 'belly', but not *clam* p.t. of *clim* 'climb', or *lam* 'lamb', the latter explicable as pre-cluster shortening in OE *lambru* pl.

Before *ng* /ŋg/

As in sME, no regular lengthening in PreSc: thus *bring*, etc., *sang*, etc.. *hung*, etc. But note MSc *laing* vowel 4, less common and later variant of *lang*, and OSc *doungin, doung* vowel 6, well-attested though less common variant of *dungin, dung*, p.p. of *ding* 'to beat', and *heing* la16 beside regular *hing* v. 'to hang' < ON *hengja*. On modSc *keeng*, see §§4.2.1(i) and 5.1.

Before /rd/

OE æ (*ea*) in OE *beard* yielded OSc vowel 3, ESc /ɛː/ in *beird* 'beard': OE *e* (*eo*) yielded ESc vowel 2 /eː/, according to OSc rhymes, e.g. of Henryson, *Seven S.*, Lyndsay, in *breird* 'first shoots', *eird* 'earth', *heird* 'herd', *rerde* 'uproar'. OE *ŏ* lengthened to /oː/ in PreSc before /rd/, ultimately yielding OSc vowel 7 (see §7.1) in OE *bŏrd* 'board' > *bōrd* > OSc *buird* 'board' (beside metathesised unlengthened *brod*), and similarly OSc *fuird* 'ford' and OSc *hurde* 'hoard'. On the history of OSc *hird, heird* 'herdsman', OE *hirde*, and OSc *weird* 'fate', OE *wyrd*, see §§4.2.1(i) and 5.1. The lengthened vowel in Sc *yaird* < OE *geard*, is of later (14c) origin. like that of *faird* 'paint the face' (< OF *farder*) (see §11.1).

The homorganic clusters /rn/ and /rl/ perhaps did not cause lengthening in PreSc (any more than in English generally). In most cases with lengthened vowels in these environments there are other explanations. *Cairn*, like *baird* 'bard' and *caird* 'tinker', had /aː/ by derivation from Gael /aː/ (Pődör, 1995/6: 183); on *bairn* 'child', PreSc /baːrn/, and *eirl* beside *erl* 'earl', see §4.1; *hairns* beside *harnis* 'brains' is like *faird* (above) (see §11.1). It is unclear whether the OSc variant *leirn*, modSc *leern*, i.e. /liːrn/, beside OSc *lerne*, OE *leornian* 'learn', had vowel 2 or vowel 3 in ESc. If vowel 2, this would imply a form lengthened in OE; if vowel 3, like *erl* in §4.1 (but in this case no forms with vowel epenthesis between *r* and *n* seem to occur).

3.2 Backing and rounding of OE, ON *ā* in sME

OE and ON *ā* /aː/ in e.g. *hāt* 'hot', *hām* 'home', *māre* 'more', remained common to all dialects of early ME till about 11-12c. By that date, however, in sME it had become retracted and probably rounded to something like [ɑ̞ː], while remaining unchanged as unround [ɑː] or [aː] in the north (PreSc and nME). There were thus two diaphones of early ME /aː/, [ɑ̞ː] in the south and [ɑː] or [aː] in the north. In the 13c there accrued to both these dialects a body of vocabulary containing the sound [aː], from OF *ā*, in e.g. *cās* /kaːs/, *debāt*, and by OSL of OE, OF *ă* in e.g. *nāme*, /naːmə/ *fāme*, *fāre*.

Meantime in sME the [ɑ̞ː] diaphone had undergone raising to something like [ɔ̞ː] (for the evidence see e.g. Lass, 1992: 46 f.), quite distinct from the newly introduced [aː]. In this way the sME [ɔ̞ː] diaphone achieved the status of a new low, back round phoneme /ɔ̞ː/. Around this time all dialects of English, including both PreSc and sME, acquired a new low to mid back

Figure 3: Outcome of the sME backing and rounding of OE, ON ā, followed by OSL

Sources	Examples	PreSc			sME
OF *ā*	*estāt*	aː		*fare*	aː
OE, ON, OF *a* by OSL > *ā*	*name* *fame* *fare* v.				
OE, ON *ā*	*hāt* 'hot' *hām* 'home' *māre* 'more'	aː	*mare*	*more*	ɔ̞ː (merges with)
OE, OF *o* by OSL > *ō̞* OF *ō̞*	*cǫte* 'coat' *befǫre* *estōr* 'store'	ɔ̞ː		*before*	ɔ̞ː

9

round phoneme, of rather closer quality than /ɔː/, here represented as /ǫː/, arising from OF ǭ, in e.g. *stor* /stǫːr/ 'store' < OF *estǭr*, and by OSL of OF ŏ in e.g. *rose* giving /rǫːzə/, *cote* 'coat', *before*. In due course, in some of the sME dialects, both new low back phonemes merged, as /ǫː/. PreSc and nME on the other hand did not follow sME in its treatment of OE, ON ā, but instead continued to realise it as a low unround sound /aː/, now somewhat fronted from its late OE realisation. With this established low front unround phoneme /aː/ the new [aː] in *cās, nāme*, etc. was at once merged. From this merged phoneme /aː/ the new /ǫː/ in *stor, before*, etc., remained quite separate. Thus in the outcome both these major dialects achieved the same or a similar pair of phonemes, /aː/ and /ǫː/ in both cases, but derived from distinct combinations of sources, and thus with different, though overlapping, lexical distributions, as illustrated in Figure 3. Hence in Sc vowel 4 ESc /aː/ is much more lexically prolific than is vowel 5 ESc /ǫː/, whereas in sME and PreStE this position is reversed. In comparable ways, similar disparate outcomes later came to operate at many other points in the corresponding phonological systems of these two dialects.

3.3 Short Vowel Lowering (SVL)

In the interval between the latest of the OE vowel shortenings (Trisyllabic Shortening II) (11c) and the ME and PreSc Open Syllable Lengthening (13c) a fundamental readjustment of the short-long vowel oppositions took place. It is easiest to see this as a general lowering by one height of the old short vowels, as shown in Figure 4 (Lass, 1992: 48). The outcome of the lowering of the PreSc short vowels is as in Figure 5. An alternative theory of a raising of the long vowels - anticipating by two centuries or more the 15c Great Vowel Shift - runs counter to everything else we know about the history of English sounds at this time. In this new situation vowel 15 /ɪ/ lengthens to vowel 2 /eː/ not vowel 1 /iː/ as in OE, vowel 7 /oː/ shortens to vowel 19 /ʉ/, not vowel 18 /ǫ/ as in OE, and similarly with the other new pairs of correspondences: compare the situation shown in Figure 2. But the situation in this respect of vowels 4 and 17 is unchanged, except for the addition of the inventory of OE /æ/ to that of /a/, and the fact that ă and ā, back vowels in OE, have now joined the front vowel system.

VOWEL PHONOLOGY TO 1375

Figure 4: Late OE/early ME and early PreSc Short Vowel Lowering (traditional symbols in brackets), numbered as the derived ESc vowels

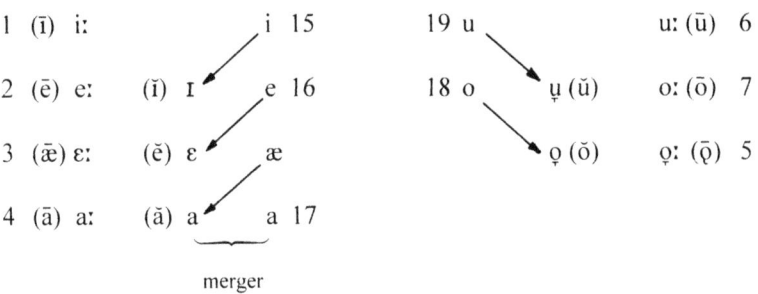

Notes: For representational convenience (to correspond with later tables, and in accordance with tradition) I employ the symbol /ʉ/ for the lowered /u/, rather than /ʊ/, which arguably more accurately represents the probable realisation at this time.

Vowel 5 /ǫː/, absent from OE, now arose as in *store* < OF *estor* and by OSL (see below) of OE, OF, etc. *ŏ* (as in *rose, cote* 'coat', *before, throte*).

Figure 5: Outcome of the lowering of the PreSc short vowels

1	iː					uː	6
2	eː	ɪ	15	19	ʉ	oː	7
3	ɛː	ɛ	16	18	ǫ	ǫː	5
4	aː		a 17				

Vowel lengthenings and shortenings of the ME (PreSc) period

4. Open Syllable Lengthening (OSL)

In terms of the vowel length oppositions of Figure 5, following SVL, this 13c sound-change lengthened short vowels in stressed syllables when a single consonant or syllable-initiating consonant sequence such as /pr/ or /st/ intervened between the stressed and a following unstressed syllable. Though the accuracy of the account of the development implied by the traditional name has recently been called into question (Minkova, 1982, 1991; Lass, 1992: 73-6), I propose to retain the traditional name here in default of any established alternative. Lengthening of the non-high vowels is believed to have taken place earlier than that of the high vowels.

4.1 The non-high vowels /e/, /a/, /o̞/

As appears from Minkova (1982), in the ME dialect underlying StE, OSL operated virtually invariably on these vowels in:

environment (1) / - Cə# e.g. *bere* (OE *bera*) 'bear, the animal',

but in 75% of the possible cases failed to occur in:

environment (2) / - CVC# (as in *hadok*),
 / - C*ig*# (as in 'body').

In PreSc likewise lengthening was all but invariable in environment (1), but considerably less frequent in environment (2). Since in both cases PreSc largely shadowed ME generally, I refer the reader to Minkova (1982) or to one of the standard ME grammars for lists of examples.

But in the case of forms that do undergo lengthening, in addition to those forms shared with PreStEng, such as *acre, bacon, labour*, etc., *even* and PreSc /ˈwɛːzəl/ 'weasel' (implied by such MSc forms as *quhasill, waizel*), MSc contained the following additional lengthened environment (2) forms:

chaipel; (stress-shifted) *chaistyce* 'to chastise'; *draigon*; *faider* 'father'; (modSc) *gaither* beside *gadder* and *gedder*; *haimer* 'hammer'; *Laitin*; (stress-shifted) *mainer* 'manner', 'cultivate', but not *maner* 'manor'; *maiter* 'matter'; *nairow* (later spelled *nairra*) 'narrow'; *saiddle; saitin; traivel; waiter* 'water'; and also *aiver* 'cart-horse'; and an underlying PreSc /ˈfaːdom/ is implied by MSc *fawdom* 'fathom'; the stress-shifted modSc *faimely*, MSc <familie, femelie, feamilie> apparently shares the same lengthening; *beisand* 'bezant'; *nevel* 'a punch' (modSc /ˈnivəl/); *seiven* 'seven'; and PreSc /ˈhɛːviː/ is implied by MSc *havy* 'heavy'; PreSc /ˈnɛːvər/ is implied by MSc *neir* (modSc /nir, ner/); and PreSc /ˈsɛːkund/ is implied by modSc /ˈsekənd/ 'second'.

Some of these have doublet lengthened and unlengthened forms, some of the latter perhaps derived from inflected forms, such as *fader, laddle, stapill, watter* < *faddres, laddles, stapples, wattres*; but other explanations sometimes apply, e.g. for *manere, matere*, the stress on the second syllable having been retained till later, as compared with the stress-shifted *mainner, maitter.*

Before clusters /rn/ and /rl/ lengthening may have been due in some cases not to Pre-Cluster Lengthening but to Open Syllable Lengthening before an epenthetic vowel forming a second syllable. These epenthetic vowels are well attested in MSc spellings in the cases of *bairn* 'child', PreSc /baːrn/ vowel 4 and /bɛːrn/ vowel 3, OSc <baren, bairen, beirin, etc.> 1572; similarly the lengthened variants *cairl* vowel 4, of *carl* <carill, cairill> 1625; *eirl* vowel 3, of *erl* <eryl, eryll, erell, earill> 1385; perhaps a similar explanation applies to OSc *eirn* and *airn* beside *erne* 'eagle', OE *earn, ærn* > /*ɛrn/ > /*'ɛrən/ > /*'ɛːr(ə)n/.

Sc also has many unlengthened forms but mostly with lengthened doublets, where the corresponding StE forms show lengthening. Some of these are explicable as due to uninflected beside inflected forms, e.g. *graff* and *grave*, *coll* and *cole* 'coal' < OE *col*. More puzzling are many verbs, such as *haf* and *have*, *mak* and *make*, *brek* and *breke*, *stell* and *stele* 'to steal', and other words in which unstressed final -*e* was part of the stem, e.g. *den* and *dene* 'valley' < OE *denu*, *dell* and *dele* 'deal, the wood' < MDu *dele*, *clok* and *cloke* 'cloak' < OF *cloke*, *cot* and *cote* 'coat' < OF *cote*, *throt* and *throte* 'throat' < OE *Þrote, Þrotu* as if in these words uncovered final -*e* had been lost before OSL; but the textual evidence does not seem to support this (see §13.1). In general, however, it seems that the PreSc non-high short vowels behaved in respect of OSL much as in PreStEng, though there were a fair number of aberrant longs and shorts in the outcome.

4.2 The high vowels /ɪ/ and /ụ/

With these vowels, which are believed to have lengthened later than the non-high vowels, environment (2) seems to be just as susceptible to lengthening as environment (1).

4.2.1 Lengthening of /ɪ/

In many cases there are doublet results. PreSc lengthened /ɪ/ to /eː/ (vowel 2) all but regularly in environment (2), and in a number of words, especially verbs or nouns with cognate verbs, in environment (1) also, almost all of these with accompanying unlengthened doublets.

Some exceptions, for which no lengthened variant appears to be recorded, are, in environment (1): *bit* < OE *bite*, *hip* < OE *hype*, *flit* v. < ON *flytja*; in environment (2), *pittance* (13c) < OF *pitance*; *rissin, rysin.* etc., p.p. of 'rise' v., but spellings <resin> and others with <e> occur, though rarely (but see §14.15 on <e> spellings for vowel 15). On the possibility of prior loss of uncovered final -*e* in the case of environment (1), see §4.1 above.

It also appears that the degemination of long consonants came too late to admit to OSL conditions such items as: *bid* < OE *biddan*, *clip* < ON *klippa*, *clip* 'to grip' < OE *clyppan*, *spit* v. < OE *spittan*, *tick* 'a mite' < OE **ticca*; equally such items as *gimmer* < ON *gimbr*, *trick* < OF *trique*, also lacked the OSL conditions. But a number of disyllabic words apparently similarly disqualified from OSL, show occasional spellings in <e, ei>, e.g. <meidle> *middil* 'middle', and *midding* 'midden' etc.

The following are either attested abundantly in OSc spellings or in rhyme or in modSc pronunciations, or in more than one of these. The apparently predominant form of a doublet is placed first; a single entry means that no doublet form is known:

(i) from OE and ON:

environment (1): *geve* and *gif* < ON *gifa;* *leve* and *live* and *lefe* and *lif* < OE *lifian; dreiwe, dreiff,* modSc *dreeve* by back formation < OE *drifon* p.t.; *frethe* 'set free' la14 < OE *friðian; methe* n. and v. 'mark a boundary, etc.' 15c and *mithe* (?/mɪð/) 1552 < ON *mið* n., *miða* v.; *clepe a*1329 and *clip* 'call' < OE *clipian; steke* and *stik* 'stitch' v. < OE *stice; swik* and *sweke,* modSc *sweek* 'deceit' < OE *swica;* modSc *feer* 'cut the first furrow' < OE *fyrian; spere* and *spyr* 'ask' < OE *spyrian; stere* < OE *styrian; spete* and *spit* 'roasting spit' < OE *spitu; wit* and *weit* 'to know' < OE *wittan; skill* and *skeill* < ON *skil* n., *skilia* v.;

environment (2): *bissy* and *besy; desy* and *dissy* 'dizzy'; *crippill* and *crepill; fickill* and *fekill; chikkin* and *chekin; mekill* 1393 and *mikel* c1300 'mickle'; *sicker* and *sekir* 'sure'; *fidill, fiddill* and *feidil* (1581; rhyming with *neidil* 'needle'); *evill* and ESc and late MSc *ivill; snevil* and *snivel; *swivel* and modSc *sweevil; river* and *rever; drevin* and *drivin* 'driven'; *revin* and *riffin,* p.p. of *rife,* 'to tear'; *littill* and *leitell* < OE **lytel,* shortened in inflected forms from *lȳtel* (from which OSc *lytil, lyitill,* etc., with vowel 1); *widow* and *wedow.*

Perhaps like *bairn,* etc. (§4.1 above) is OSc *werde, weird,* with ESc /eː/ vowel 2, < OE *wyrd,* by way of *wird,* with post-/r/ vowel epenthesis > */ˈwɪrəd/ > /weːrd/, and possibly also *heird,* variant of *hird,* OE *hirde* 'herdsman'; cf. the parallel case of *scruif,* below. A similar explanation may apply to modSc *keeng,* OSc (once) *keyng* 'king', from (conjectural) uncontracted PreSc forms from OE *cyning* (but see §5.1);

(ii) from OF

Since OF vowels were already long in tonic open syllables, we are here concerned only with stress-shifted formerly countertonic initial syllables of OSc disyllabic (and perhaps polysyllabic) words conforming to environment (2). One possible example of environment (1) is OF *giste,* in which the

14

vowel, treated as 'blocked' in OF, is 'free' (before syllable-initiating /st/) in PreSc, yielding OSc *geist, jeist* and *gist, jist* and unexplained *gest* 15c, *jest* 1501. Apparent examples of PreSc *i* /ɪ/ of OF origin > /eː/ (vowel 2) include:

> *cité, citté* and *ceté, cieté; pité, pitté* and *peté, pieté; chemer* and *chymmer* < A-L *chimera; civill* and *cevil, cewille* 1502; *figour* and *fegour*, modSc /ˈfigər/; *finis* and *feenish* 19; *phisik* and *phesik*, modSc *feesick; geigget* c1600 and *gigot* la18; *liver* n. and *lever, liver* v. 'deliver' and *le(i)ver* 17; *littar* and modSc /ˈlitər/; *licoure* and modSc *leecure* 'liquor'; *limit* and *lemit*, modSc *leemit; limon, limmon* 17 and *lemon, leimond* la16, modSc *leemon; minute* and *menwt*, modSc *meenit; mirrour* and *merour* 14-15 only; *presoun* (but see DOST) and *prisoun; serop*, modSc *seerup* 'syrup'; *sperit* and *spirit* (and *spreit*: see §15);

(iii) from MF

OSL as commonly understood is normally a phenomenon of penultimate stressed syllables, resulting, with loss of final *-e*, in monosyllables in environment (1), in disyllables in environment (2). In Sc however a substantial body of words of MF origin - *mots savants* - apparently operated OSL on original OF countertonic *i*, which yielded PreSc /eː/ vowel 2 in antepenultimate open syllables, with fronted stress. (On the separate treatment of MF tonic *i* /iː/ in 15c Sc, see §15.) Examples include:

> *citeyane* and *ceteyen; liberall, liber-,* and *leberale* la16, modSc *leeberal, leebral; library* /ˀ 'lɪb / and modSc *leebrary; livery* and *levery; minister* and *menister* 16, *meinister*, modSc /ˈminɪstər/; *miserie* and *meserie,* modSc *meeserie; miserable* and *meserable* 16, modSc *meeser-; mitigat, myttigait* and *metigate* 17; *officiale* and modSc *offeecial; officiar* and *offeiciar;* and nouns in *-itioun*, e.g. *condition* and *condecioun* 1462; *contritioun* and *contretioune* c1500; *position* and modSc *poseeshon; propositioun* and modSc *proposeeshion;* and, with following palatal consonant, *opinioun* and *openyon*, modSc *opeenion*.

4.2.2 Lengthening of /ṵ/

Roughly parallel to the lengthening of /ɪ/ to /eː/, the corresponding short back vowel /ṵ/ lengthened in the same environments to [oː]. The outcome of this shares the subsequent history of /oː/ from OE, ON *ō* and of OF *ū* /yː/, yielding ESc vowel 7 /yː/ spelled in OSc < uC-, ui, etc.> (see §7.1).

This lengthening must therefore pre-date the fronting of [oː] to [yː], as well as the loss of -e (see §13.1), since in environment (1) the change occurs only when the triggering final -e /-ə/ is part of the original stem. Examples include:

(i) from OE, ON ŭ, and OE o + f:

environment (1): OSc *cuid* 'cud' < OE *cudu;* *duik* 'duck' < OE *duce;* *duir* 'door' < OE *duru;* *huil* 'husk' < OE *hulu;* *luif* 'love' < OE *lufu;* *stuth* 'stud' < OE *studu;* *wuid* 'wood' < OE *wudu;* *umast* 'uppermost' < OE *ufemest;*

environment (2): OSc *abuin, abuve, abuif* < ME *abufan* < a (= on) + OE *bŭfan; scrufe* 'scurf'? < OE *scurf* >*scuruf* > /*scoːrf/, with metathesis thereafter; also from OE o + f in *une* 'oven' < OE *ofen; schuil* + *shovel* < OE *scofl;*

(ii) from OF u:

environment (2): modSc *cuitler* (Murray, 1873; Zai, 1942) 'cutler' < AN *cotillere;* modSc *cuisen* (Murray, 1873; Zai, 1942) and /ˈkʌzən, ˈkɪzən/; modSc *guitter* (Murray, 1873; Zai, 1942) < AN *gutere;*

also environment (1), after replacement of the OF ending accompanied by a shift of stress (see Bliss, 1969: 206, note 64): OSc *muve* 'move' < OF *muveir,* and similarly *pruve.*

In other cases this lengthening fails, and the outcome is therefore vowel 19: e.g. *cum* v., *huny, nut, ruck* 'haystack' (cf. Norw *ruka*), *somer, son; bullet, bukket, buttoun, couple, fluris, glutoun, money, sommer* 'pack-horse', *suppar, subtil;* most or all of these also have dominant or subsidiary later variants in /ɪ/ vowel 15 (*hinnie, nit,* etc.: see §16.1), by a different route. (Some of these apparently did lengthen elsewhere in ME: see Jordan and Crook (1974: §38.3).)

5 Other lengthenings and shortenings of the ME (PreSc) period

5.1 Belated pre-cluster lengthenings

OE ī, ȳ: Several words appear in 15c or later Sc with forms in vowel 2, ESc /eː/ originating from OE ī, ȳ, and thus in place of, or alternative to, expected forms either with OE HOCL yielding vowel 1, ESc /iː/, as OSc *child,* or unlengthened yielding vowel 15, as OSc *kill* v. These vowel 2 forms are *beild* 1493 'to build' < OE *byldan; chelde* beside *child* (with vowel 1) < OE *cild; kelde, keild* p.t., p.p., whence *kele* pres t., beside *kill* v. < OE *cyllan*. These have the appearance of belated HOCL before /ld/ (after SVL, §3.3). Possibly of the same derivation, and originally from the p.t. forms **pilde, *tilde*, are *pele* v. beside *pill* 'to peel' and *tele* v. beside *till*; but more likely these are by regular OSL in inflected forms. It is possible that *heird* 'herdsman', *weird* 'destiny' and OSc (rare) *keyng*, modSc *keeng*, all apparently with vowel 2, are likewise the results of belated HOCL rather than as conjectured at §4.2.1(i) above.

5.2 Miscellaneous PreSc forms with unexpected short vowels

OSc contained a number of distinctive present tense verb-forms in short /ɛ/ vowel 16, alongside sME forms with the long vowel /ɛː/. Some of these were by 'failure' of OSL such as unlengthened doublets of the verbs *brek* (beside lengthened *breke* vowel 3), *spek* 'speak', *get* 'get'. Others were back-formations from weak p.t.s and p.p.s, such as *sned* v. (also *snad)* 'lop branches of a tree' (OE *snædan*, p.t. *snædde* > ME *snădde*, also PreSc p.t. *snædde* > *snĕdde*); similarly *kned* (OE *cnedan* 'knead'), *pled* and *plede* (with vowel 3 < OF ai > *ẹ̄), len* v. 'lend' (OE *lænan*, p.t. *lænde* > PreSc. *lẹ̄nde*). A similar case is *het* adj. 'hot' (OE *gehætt*, p.p. of *hætan* 'to heat'). These shortened forms are PreSc (= early ME); but *kep* beside *kepe* 'to keep' is by Pre-Cluster Shortening in late OE (OE *cēpan*, p.t. *cēpte*). More puzzling are words such as *ʒett* v. beside *ʒete* (OE *gēotan* strong verb), *let* v. 'permit' (OE *lætan* strong verb), also *lat* (ON *láta*).

Sc did not share the PreStE (ME) tendency to shorten /ɛː/ before dentals in e.g. *breath, bread, dead, head, lead* n., *red, sweat, threat*, in all of which the vowel continued long in Sc, as vowel 3.

5.3 Shortenings of PreSc /eː/ and /oː/

Some of the shortenings of ME and PreSc /eː/ to /ɪ/ and /oː/ to /ʉ/ known in StE are missing from Sc. Thus, though *silly* (beside OSc *sely*) and *riddle* (< OE *rædels*) also occur in Sc, the regular Sc form for 'sick' is *seek* (OE *sēoc*) vowel 2, not *sick*. (ModSc forms such as /brɪks/ beside regular /briks/ *breeks*, /wɪk/ beside /wik, uk/ *week*, are local and ? late.) Likewise the regular Sc representations of OE *blōd* and *flōd* are *bluid* and *fluid* vowel 7, not vowel 19 as in StE. However, the following display shortening after Short Vowel Lowering in terms of Figure 5:

17

(i) /eː/ > /ɪ/ vowel 15:

hicht /hɪxt/ 'height' < OE *hēhþu* (the doublet *hecht* < vowel 16 is by Pre-Cluster Shortening II in OE); *licht* < OE *lēoht*; *lipper* < *lēper* vowel 2 < OF *lēpre* 'leprosy'; the ballad-word *lilly* < OE *lēofīc*; and Henryson's form *lind* 'buttocks', rhymes with *behind* (beside *leynd*) < OE *lendu*, may also belong here.

But OSc *leippie* 'a quarter of a peck', whence *lippie* 1542, and *mesell*, whence *misell* 'leprous', apparently contained vowel 3, PreSc /ɛː/, so these shortenings are perhaps later (? by SVLR);

(ii) /oː/ > /u̜/ vowel 19:

OSc *futher* 1400, *fudder* 15 'cart-load' < OE *fōđer*; *guld* 'corn marigold', modSc /gʌl/, beside OSc *guild* vowel 7 < OE *golde* (see §3.1.1(2)); OSc *fut* spelled <fout, fowt, futte>, modSc (nEC and Uls) /fʌt/ < OE *fōt*, beside the more widespread modSc /føt/ vowel 7 and /fɪt/ vowel 15; and, as in ME, OSc *munth* < OE *mōnđ* 'month'.

New diphthongs and related developments in PreSc

Following Open Syllable Lengthening, the next major event in the system of monophthongs was the fronting of PreSc /oː/. Before I describe this, the evolution of the new PreSc diphthong system falls to be narrated, parallel to, but not identical with, similar events in sME.

6 New Diphthongs in *-i* and *-u*, especially those of native origin

6.0 General

In general PreSc shared in the late OE and early ME monophthonging of the OE diphthongs: *ēo* > *ē*; *ĕo* > *ĕ*, *ēa* > *ǣ*, *ĕa* > *ǣ*. As in sME, new diphthongs arose:

(1) by adoption from external, mainly ON and OF, sources:

(a) OF *ai* in e.g. *gay, aid, faith*, yielding ESc /ai/ vowel 8;
(b) OF *oi* in e.g. *joy, voice*, yielding ESc /ǫi/ vowel 9;
(c) OF *ǫi*, AN *ui*, in e.g. *point, vois* 'voice', yielding ESc /ui/ vowel 10;
(d) OF *au* in e.g. *caus, faut* 'fault', yielding ESc /au/ vowel 12;
(e) OWScand *au* in e.g. ON *gauk-r* > OSc *gowk* 'cuckoo', and OF *ou* /ǫu/ in *couper* 'to strike' > OSc *cowp* 'to overturn', yielding ESc /ǫu/ vowel 13

(thus it appears that the first element of OWScand *au* was of backer and/or more rounded quality than that of OF *au*);

(f) OF *ū* /y:/ in final and hiatical environments, in e.g. OF *crüel*, yielding ESc /i:u/ vowel 14a.

In most cases, loanwords containing these diphthongs already existed in the language before the creation of new diphthongs by native development, as described below; merging of the new natively created diphthongs with corresponding borrowed diphthongs then followed:

(2) by development of the new native diphthongs out of various combinations of vowels and OE, ON *g* (as palatal /j/ after front vowels, velar /ɣ/ after back vowels), or OE *w*; yielding the PreSc diphthongs /ai/, /e:i/, /a:u/, /o̯:u/, /i:u/, /e:u/, /ɛ:u/. When the vowels *ī*, *ī* or *ū*, *ū* were followed by *g* or *w*, the outcome was, respectively, long /i:/ or long /u:/;

(3) For a summary survey of certain other developments and sources contributing to ESc vowels 8 /ai/, 12 /au/, 13 /o̯u/, see §§14.8, 14.12, 14.13 respectively.

There follow some general observations on the developments leading to the creation of new diphthongs from native (OE, ON) sources, (2) above.

The native sources of ESc vowel 8 /ai/ consisted of combinations of OE and ON front vowels with following *g* /j/. In most cases, the post-vocalic glide /j/ in these combinations occurred in word-final or pre-consonantal environments, thus in the same syllable as the preceding front vowel. The glide was thus readily subject to vocalisation, combining with its preceding vowel to form a diphthong in -*i*, and this occurred in late OE or early ME and PreSc.

If, however, the diphthong-forming glide was intervocalic, either /j/ in the case of vowel 11 (§6.3.2) or /w/ or /ɣ/ in the case of the diphthongs in -*u* (§§6.4 and 6.5), so that it initiated a second syllable, and thus belonged to a separate syllable from the stressed vowel, conditions for the formation of diphthongs did not exist; for these no doubt required that both elements of the future diphthong should occupy the same syllable. In these cases, diphthong-formation must have been delayed till, with the loss of unstressed final -*e* or the covered inflectional vowel in -*is* /-ɪs/, in the late 13c (§§13.1, 13.2), the glide, becoming word-final or pre-consonantal, fell within the same syllable as the stressed vowel providing the other element of the diphthong: thus in the case of vowel 11:

$$/\text{e:.j} \begin{Bmatrix} \text{VC} \\ \text{ə\#} \end{Bmatrix} / > /\text{e:j} \begin{Bmatrix} \text{C} \\ \text{\#} \end{Bmatrix} /$$

and in the case of the -*u* diphthongs:

/eː.w/ $\begin{Bmatrix} VC \\ ə\# \end{Bmatrix}$ / > /eːw/ $\begin{Bmatrix} C \\ \# \end{Bmatrix}$ /

followed by vocalisation of the glide consonant and creation of the diphthong.

This situation applied, by definition, to vowel 11. This was also the case with the more lexically prolific of the native sources of the -*u* diphthongs, vowels 12 and 13, and of many instances of vowel 14. It is true that, in a minority of the items making up the lexicons of these vowels, the -*w* providing the diphthongal second elements was word-final or pre-consonantal already in OE: e.g. OE *hlāw* > OSc *law* 'hill', OE *snāw* > OSc *snaw* 'snow', vowel 12; OE *treōwþ* > OSc *trowth* /trǫuθ/ 'truth', vowel 13; OE *cnēow* > OSc *knew* vowel 14a; OE *dēaw* > OSc *dew* vowel 14b. It is possible, as noted above, that in these cases the vocalisation of the post-vocalic glide resulting in the creation of diphthongs may have taken place somewhat earlier than when the glide was followed by a second vowel. Even so, this seems not to have been before the late 12c, since it post-dated the sME change of *ā* to [ǫː]: see §6.4.1.

It also seems probable that the natively-derived PreSc diphthongs yielding ESc vowels 11, 12, 13 and 14 had, to begin with, a trimoric structure with long first element. This would be the case when, as in many instances, the first element was already long in OE, as e.g. *hlāw* 'hill', *cnāwan* 'know', *lāg-* 'low' in inflected forms > OSc *law* adj. It would also be the case when in OE or ON the first element was short but fell in an open syllable, as OE *clăwu* 'claw', *lăgu* 'law', *bŏga* 'bow', ON *lŏgn* 'calm', in which cases the long first element arose by OSL: e.g. OE *clăwu* 'claw', PreSc /kla.wə/ > /klaː.wə/.

With vowels 12 /aːu/ and 13 /ǫːu/ the shortening of the long first elements may have taken place quite soon after the latter events, i.e. around the late 13c, early 14c. The grounds for supposing this are as follows.

There are no indications that any of the other sources of these diphthongs had long first elements or were of other than bimoric duration: e.g. OE *eahta* > OSc *aucht* 'eight', PreSc /auld/ > ESc *auld*, OE *dohtor* > OSc *douchter*, and see §§14.12 and 14.13. The l-vocalised combinations /al/ and /ǫl/ with which PreSc /aːu/ and /ǫːu/ later merged (§17) had as their first elements, by definition, short vowels in final and pre-consonantal positions, so the mergers must have been under /au/ and /ǫu/ respectively.

However, the first elements of vowels 11 /eːi/ and 14 /iːu/, /ɛːu/ may have remained long well into or, in the case of vowel 14, beyond the ESc period. Or it is possible to speculate that there was a PreSc intermediate stage of adjustment towards a regular bimoric duration for long monophthongs and diphthongs at which these first elements shortened to

VOWEL PHONOLOGY TO 1375

half-long rather than fully long. But in what follows, I have assumed full length in the first elements and trimoric duration for the diphthongs. On all this, see the specific accounts at §§6.3.2, 6.4.3 and 6.5 below. These remarks also apply to the diphthong, eventually merging with vowel 14a, arising from PreSc *ōg*- /oːɣ/ (see §7.2.1).

Structurally the outcomes of these events roughly correspond to those reached from the same inputs in sME. But there were considerable differences in lexical incidence, especially consequent on (1) the sME permanent transfer of OE, ON *ā* to the back round vowel system, as against the unround, and eventually fronted, PreSc /aː/, (2) the PreSc (and nME) fronting of /oː/, (3) the Sc (and nME) treatment of /oː/ before velars.

6.1 Front vowels before OE word-final and pre-consonantal *g*

6.1.1 The native sources of ESc /ai/ vowel 8

After the front vowels *ē, ĕ, ǣ, ӕ̆,* OE, ON *g* was realised as the palatal glide [j], forming diphthongs in -*i* in word final and pre-consonantal position. These diphthongs eventually yielded ESc vowel 8: e.g. OE *hēg*; OE *wĕg, rĕgn,* ON *hĕgna*; OE *clǣg, grǣg, cǣg, ǣghwǣþer*; OE *dæg, mægd, hægl, fæg(e)r* > OSc *hay, way, rain, hain* 'enclose', *clay, gray, kay* (beside *key*), *aither, day, maid, hail, fair*. In addition, it seems that, anomalously, after *ĕ,* intervocalic *g* produced the same outcome: e.g. OE *wĕgan, *swĕgan* > OSc *wey* 'weigh', *swey* 'sway'. On *rain, hail, fair,* see also §22.3.2(3). For the later development of vowel 8 /ai/ and other developments from these sources, see §22.

Figure 6: Primary sources of ESc /ai/ vowel 8

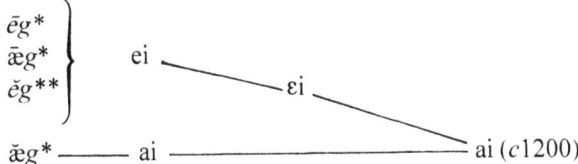

* Word-final and pre-consonantal only.
** Also with a following unstressed vowel.

6.1.2 OE *īg, ĭg*

In the same conditions OE *īg, ĭg* > *ī,* in e.g. OE *stīg(e)l, hālig* > OSc *style, haly* vowel 1. For the later diphthong /eːi/ > /eː/ vowel 11, see §6.3.2 below.

6.2 Vowels before OE word-final and pre-consonantal *h* /x/

Apart from the cases of *a* and *o* before /x/, this environment does not, except in some peripheral dialects, give rise to diphthongs. It is entered here to complete the account of vowels before velar fricatives. In word-final and pre-consonantal environments where it was not in immediate contact with a preceding front vowel, OE g /ɣ/ was devoiced and merged with OE *h* /x/, thereafter sharing the same history, cf.:

> OE *āhte*, earlier **āgte*, p.t. of *āgan* v. 'owe' and *eahta* 'eight', both > ESc /auxt/ *aucht*; OE *bōg* 'bough' and *hōh* 'heel' > OSc *beuch* /biːux/ and *heuch*; OE *swelg* 'whirlpool' and *selh* 'a seal, the animal' > OSc *swelch* /swɛlx/ and *selch*.

Before consonant clusters, regular pre-cluster shortening took place, e.g.:

> OE *āhte*, p.t. of *āgan* 'owe' > *ăhte* > OSc *aucht*, as above; OE *hēhþu* 'height' > *hĕhþu* > OSc *hecht* /hɛxt/ and (see §5.3) *hicht* (also *heicht*, ? after *heich* adj.); OE *þōhte*, p.t. of *þencan* 'think' > OSc *thocht* /θǫxt/.

6.2.1 Vowels not undergoing diphthongisation

Thereafter, the following vowels continued unchanged from OE to ESc in the several environments here exemplified:

i + h(t): e.g. OSc *dicht* v. 'array', *nicht, sich* 'sigh';
e + h(t): e.g.:

> *fecht* and *ficht* (see Jordan and Crook, 1974: §69); *hecht* 'promise, be called' < OE *heht* p.t.;

ē + h: e.g.:

> OE *hēh*, with 'Anglian smoothing' from *hēah* > OSc *heich* 'high' vowel 2, beside OSc *hey* < OE *hēge* (see §6.3.2 below); OScand *drēug-* > eME *drēh* > OSc *dreich* 'tedious', beside OSc *drey, dre* 'endure' < OE *drēogan* (see §6.3.2 below);

ā + h: e.g.:

> OE *dāg* > OSc *daich*, ESc /daːx/ > MSc /de(ː)x/ vowel 4 'dough'; and similarly ON *lág-r* > OSc *laich* 'low'.

The regular modSc outcome in this case is /e/, but in S /iu/ or /ju/, apparently vowel 14b(i): see §6.5. The latter outcome is now confined to S but in MSc was more widespread, represented by the spellings <leuch> 16, <leauch> la16, for *laich* 'low', and <dewche> la16 Fife, for *daich* 'dough'. The diphthonging must have come about after ESc /aː/ vowel 4 had been raised to /ɛː/ by the Great Vowel Shift (§20); the long vowel then developed a [u] glide onto, or was broken by influence of, the following velar, to yield /ɛːu/ or /ɛu/, thus merging with vowel 14b(i) and sharing its subsequent history (for which see §§6.5.2 and 6.5.3);

ū + *h*: e.g.:

OE *rūh* > OSc *rouch* /ruːx/ 'rough'; also by pre-/x/ shortening, *ŭ* + *h*, in *ruch* /rux̣/, *roch* /rǫx/ 'rough'; also later, in MSc, in the Flem borrowing *bucht*, MSc /bux̣t/;

e + liquid + *h*: e.g. OSc *selch* 'seal, the animal';

a + liquid + *h*: e.g. ESc *salch* 'willow';

o + liquid + *h*: e.g. OSc *borch* 'pledge';

u + liquid + *h*: e.g. OSc *burch* 'burgh'; OE *furh* > OSc *fur*, with deletion of *h*.

Except in peripheral dialects (as in the case of /laːx/ > /lɛ(ː)ux/ above), none of these develop diphthong-forming glide vowels, whether [i] or [u], as do the same sequences in some ME dialects.

6.2.2 *ă* and *ŏ* before *h* /x/

However, early PreSc *ă* and, in some dialects, *ŏ* did develop back-vowel glides onto this velar consonant /x/, yielding diphthongs /au/ and /ǫu/ respectively, more or less as in sME:

OE (Angl) *hlæhhan*, *hlæhtor* > OSc *lauch*, *lauchter* 'laugh', 'laughter', ESc /laux/, /ˈlauxtər/; OE *dōhtor* > OSc *douchter* /ˈdǫuxtər/, now found only in S, beside more common *dochter* /ˈdoxtər/ 'daughter'. Other examples are OSc *lauch*, from an early shortened form *lăh* (see DOST s.v. *Lauch*), beside *laich* 'low'; OSc *faucht*, p.t. of *fecht* v. < OE (Angl) *fæht* 'fought'; OSc *houch* /hǫux/, now found only in S, beside regular *hoch* /hǫx/ 'hough', from an early shortened form of OE *hōh* 'heel'; OSc *fowchtin*, beside *fochtin*, p.p. of *fecht* 'to fight'.

As reflexes of PreSc ă in this environment, forms derived from the diphthongised type yielding ESc /au/ vowel 12, such as *lauch* /laux/ 'to laugh', are now all but universal (as the modSc monophthong /a(:)/ or /ɑ(:)/). Conversely, however, diphthongised forms with /ǫu/ vowel 13, such as /dǫuxtər/ 'daughter', are now found only in S, the undiphthongised forms with /ǫ/ having prevailed elsewhere.

6.3 With intervocalic *g*

In words that had final -*h* /x/ in OE uninflected forms, it appears that in new inflected forms such as *hēahe*, *hēhe* 'high' (beside contracted forms such as *hē*), or **clōhas* 'ravines' (beside contracted forms such as **clōas*), the intervocalic consonant was in PreSc voiced to *g* /j/ after front vowels, /ɣ/ after back vowels, and was thereafter treated exactly as original *g* (just as, conversely, final -*g* was devoiced to *h* /x/ as described in §6.2 above).

6.3.1 Front vowels before intervocalic *g*

As noted at §6.1.1, after front vowels OE and ON *g* in final and pre-consonantal position was realised as [j], combining with certain preceding vowels to yield the diphthong /ai/. Likewise, after front vowels intervocalic or pre-vocalic *g* was similarly realised as [j].

After *ī, ĭ* and *ȳ, y̆* this resulted in *ī* /i:/: e.g. OE *hīgian* > OSc *hy* 'to hasten', OE *wīga* > OSc *wy* 'a warrior', OE *drȳge* > OSc *dry*. After liquids an epenthetic high vowel was produced, yielding [-ij-] > /i:/, producing an additional syllable: e.g. OE *byrgan* ['byrijan] > OSc *bery* 'to bury', and similarly OE *wyrgan* > OSc *wirry* 'to throttle', OE *swelgan* > OSc *swelly* 'to swallow', OE *belgas* > OSc *belly(i)s* 'bellows'.

6.3.2 *ē* before intervocalic *g*

Early ME and PreSc *ēg-* /'e:jV(C)/ > [e:j] > ESc /e:i/, vowel 11: in this environment early ME and PreSc *ē* /e:/, from the regular OE, ON sources (including OE *ǣ*[1], OE *ēo*, OE *ēa* by Anglian smoothing, ON *ǽ*), followed by intervocalic *g* /j/, yielded [e:j], ESc /e:i/ vowel 11, which then smoothed to /e:/ vowel 2, in e.g.:

> OE *drēogan* > OSc *dre(y)* 'to endure', OE *flēogan* > OSc *fle(y)* 'to fly'; and, with similar outcomes, OE *ēage* 'eye', OE *hēag-*, inflected forms of *hēah* 'high', OE *cǣge*, or *cǣg-* in inflected forms, 'key' (see also §6.1.1 above), ON *slǽg-r* 'cunning', in inflected forms > early PreSc *slēg-*; and eME *dēʒen* 'to die'; and, apparently, by-forms of OE *wĕgan* 'weigh' and **swĕgan* 'sway' (? with OSL of *ĕ* to *ę̄* /ɛ:/, thereafter merging /*ɛ:j/ with /e:j/).

This event was specially characteristic of Sc and nME. The postulated development assumes parallelism with that of /oː/ + /ɣ/ (§7.2.2). As described above (§6.0), the syllable division in these words fell between the stressed long vowel and the glide so conditions for diphthong-formation did not come about till after the loss of unstressed final -e (§13.1) or the covered inflectional vowel in -is, /-ɪz/, etc. (§13.3). Thus the sequence

was kept apart from that,

$$/eː.j\begin{Bmatrix} VC \\ ə\# \end{Bmatrix}/$$

$$/eːj\begin{Bmatrix} C \\ \# \end{Bmatrix}/$$

which produced /ei/ > /ai/ in §6.1.1, and this explains how *hēge* 'high' (modSc /hiː/) and *hēg* 'hay' (modSc /hɛi/) and *cǣge* or *cǣg-* 'key'(OSc *ke(y)*, modSc /kiː/) and *cǣg* (OSc *kay*, modSc /kɛi/) came to have such different outcomes. Eventually, with the loss of unstressed final -e and the covered inflectional vowel, the /j/ now fell within the same syllable as the preceding stressed long vowel, and the further development may have been:

$$/eː.j\begin{Bmatrix} VC \\ ə\# \end{Bmatrix}/ > /eːj\begin{Bmatrix} C \\ \# \end{Bmatrix}/$$

giving ESc /eːi/, thereafter monophthongised, after the time of Barbour (see below), to /eː/, merging with vowel 2. It does not seem necessary to suppose an intervening bimoric stage [ei] between /eːi/ and /eː/.

The usual spellings in OSc are <-ey(e), -e(e)>, later <-ie#>; the relevant nME spellings cited in Kristensson (1967: 160-4) are the same; for those of *Cursor Mundi* (Cotton Vespasian MS), see below. Barbour (1375) rhymes these words only with themselves, as *hey* 'high' with *sle* 'cunning', etc., and compare nME *Cursor Mundi* (*c*1300) rhyming *dei* with *drei* 'to endure', *sei* 'saw' p.t. of *see* with *he* 'eye' (Bennett and Smithers,1968: 191, 2). Subsequent Sc poets rhyme with /eː/ vowel 2 of any source (Buss, 1886: 7-8), showing that the monophthonging of /eːi/ to /eː/, not yet accomplished in *Cursor Mundi* and Barbour, had now taken place.

6.4.0 Back diphthongs in *-u*

Native sources:

(a) ESc /au/ vowel 12, from OE, ON *ā*, *ă* + *w* and *ā*, *ă* + intervocalic *g* /ɣ/;
(b) ESc /ǫu/ vowel 13, from OE, ON *ō*, *ŏ* + *w* and *ō* + intervocalic *g* /ɣ/ (for *ō* + intervocalic *g*, see §7.2.2).

25

The most prolific of the sources of these two diphthongs consisted of the sequence: (vowel + intervocalic -w-); for the less common cases of (vowel + final or pre-consonantal -w) (as in OE *hlāw* 'hill'), see the general description (§6.0) above. The intervocalic -w- was either original, e.g. in OE *clawu* 'claw', or arose by promotion of a labial secondary articulation of the intervocalic voiced velar fricative, /ɣ/[ɣ̃] > [w] /w/, as in OE *lagu* > OSc *law*. The latter development seems not to have taken place till the 12-13c, at least in sME, in view of the persistence into the 13c of sME spellings in <-ʒ->, e.g. Orm's <aʒhenn> 'own'; relevant PreSc spellings, if any, are not available.

The NE and other dialects' change of *āw*- to /aːv-/ later /ɑːv / (with the labial preventing GVS fronting and raising), in e.g. modSc (NE) *blyaave* 'blow' and *tyaave* 'toil'; and of *ēw*- to /eːv/ > /iːv/ by the GVS, in e.g. *thieveless* 'spiritless', must however have pre-dated the vocalisation of -w- which produced the diphthongs about to be discussed (see SND, s.v. *V*).

6.4.1 ESc /au/ vowel 12

The new diphthong, PreSc /aːu/, ESc /au/, vowel 12, was developed from:

(1) OE word-final *āw*: e.g. OE *hlāw* > OSc *law* 'hill', OE *snāw* > OSc *snaw* 'snow'; and OE pre-vocalic *āw*-: e.g. OE *cnāwan* > OSc *knaw*, OE *sceāwian* > OSc *schaw* (beside *schew* vowel 14b, with the converse diphthongal stress);

(2) OE, ON pre-vocalic *āg*- /aːɣ-/ > *āw*- /aːw-/ (see §6.4.0 above): e.g. OE *āgen* > OSc *awin* 'own', early ME and PreSc *lāg*- in inflected forms < ON *lág-r* > OSc *law* 'low' (cf. the uninflected variant *lāg* > *lāh* /laːx/ > OSc *laich*);

(3) OE *ăw*- (? chiefly or only pre-vocalic) /aw-/ > /aːw-/ by OSL: e.g. *clăwu* n., *clăwian* v. > OSc *claw*, early PreSc *lăwed* (shortened, by trisyllabic shortening, from OE *lǣwede*) > OSc *lawit* 'lay, unlearned';

(4) OE, ON pre-vocalic *ăg*- /aɣ-/ > *āg*- /aːɣ-/ by OSL, then (as in (2) above) > /aːw-/: e.g. OE *lăgu* > OSc *law* n. 'law', OE *drăgan* > OSc *draw*, OE *sceăga* > OSc *schaw* 'coppice'.

Notice that while the outcome /au/ for the short vowel combinations (3) and (4) is identical in Sc and sME, that for the long vowel combinations (1) and (2), yields /ǫːu/ in sME, e.g. sME *low* 'hill' < OE *hlāw*, *owen* 'own' < OE *āgen*, reflecting the 11-12c sME change of /aː/ [a̰ː] to [ɔː] (§3.2). It seems most likely that, at least in sME, this change preceded the creation of this diphthong.

For additional sources of ESc /au/ vowel 12, see §14.12.

6.4.2 ESc /ǫu/ vowel 13

The new diphthong, PreSc /ǫːu/, ESc /ǫu/, vowel 13, was developed from:

(1) OE pre-vocalic, also pre-consonantal, ōw-: e.g. OE grōwan > OSc grow; and, with diphthongal stress-shift, yielding PreSc /jǫːu/, in OSc ʒow 'ewe' /jǫu/, < OE eōwe; and similarly, but with early yod-absorption, in OSc chow 'chew' < OE ceōwan, four /fǫur/ < OE feōwer, trowth, modSc /trʌuθ/ 'truth' < OE treōwþ (beside OSc treuth with the converse diphthongal stress as in §6.5.1);

(2) OE, ON pre-vocalic or pre-syllabic ŏg- /ǫɣ-/ > /ǫːɣ-/ by OSL, then (see §6.4 above) > /ǫːw-/: e.g. OE bŏga > OSc bow 'the weapon', ON lŏge > OSc low 'flame', OWScand lŏgn > OSc lown 'calm', OE wantŏg(e)n > OSc wantoun 'wanton'.

It will be observed that OE, ON pre-vocalic ōg- is not treated above. This did not have the same outcome as ōw(-) or pre-vocalic ŏg-, but had the quite different outcome described at §7.2.2. It appears that ō in the sequence ōw(-), but not that in ōg-, must have undergone lowering (? by dissimilation) to /ǫː/ to yield the sequence /ǫːw(-)/, merging with that which arose by OSL from earlier ŏg- /ǫɣ-/, as above. This must have taken place before the change to /w/ of the /ɣ/ in the ōg- /oːɣ-/ sequence, or the two would have merged and shared the same outcome;

(3) When a short back vowel was followed by a liquid + w, the latter either original as in OE geolu, inflected geolw- 'yellow', or late OE arwe 'arrow', or from earlier g, as in OE galga 'gallows', OE burh, inflected burg- 'burgh'; an epenthetic vowel mostly spelled <o> was inserted between the liquid and the /w/, yielding (unstressed) /ǫu/, thus OSc yallow, arrow, gallowis, burrowis 'burghs'.

For additional sources of ESc /ǫu/ vowel 13, see §14.13.

6.4.3 ESc /uː/ vowel 6

In the same circumstances as were formed diphthongs out of the back vowels ā, ă and ō, ŏ + w and ā, ă and ŏ + g, OE, ON ū, ŭ yielded /uː/, in e.g. OE trūwian > OSc trow /truː/, OE fŭgol > OSc foul /fuː l/ 'bird', OE būgan > OSc bow /buː/, OE drūgað > OSc drouth /druːθ/ 'dryness'.
This /uː/ then merged with original OE ū as in cū > OSc cow, fūl adj. > OSc foul, vowel 6.

Figure 7 summarises these developments and compares the sME outcomes.

Figure 7: Comparison of the PreSc and sME treatments of back vowels before /w/ and /ɣ/

Sources	OSc	Examples Sc		southern	southern e.m.E	See §§
OE, ON ăg-, OE ăw	au	draw			au > ɔː	6.4.1
OE, ON āg-, OE āw(-)		knaw	know			
OE ōw-	ǫu	grow			ǫu	4.2
OE, ON ōg-		bow n.				
OE, ON āg#	aːx > eːx	daich	dough			6.2.1
OE, ON ōk, ōh, ōg-	iu	pleuch, plewis	plough		uː > au	7.2
OE, ON ūw, ŭg-, ūg-	uː	trow v. bow v.				6.4.3

6.5.1 ESc /iːu/ vowel 14a

The principal PreSc sources of this ESc phoneme were:

(i) 14a(i): early PreSc /eːw(-)/ > PreSc /eu/:

(a) from OE ēow(-), (īow(-)):

>(1) crēow p.t. 'of a cock: crowed', grēow p.t. 'grew', hēow n. 'hue', hēow p.t. 'hewed', trēowþ 'truth', þrēow p.t. 'threw' > OSc crew, grew, hew, hew, treuth (beside trowth < OE tr(e)ōwþ, with the converse diphthongal stress, as in §6.4.2), threw;

>(2) brēowan 'to brew', hrēowan 'to rue', nēowe 'new', trēowe 'true' > OSc brew, rew, new, trew;

(b) probably accruing to PreSc /eːw(-)/ > /eːu/ was OE ĭw-, in sĭwan 'to sew'. PreSc /ɪw-/ > /eːw-/ by OSL;
(c) OF eu in e.g. OF bleu 'blue', deu 'due', AN jeuel, OF neveu, yielding OSc blew etc.;

(ii) 14a(ii) /iːu/

Coalescing with PreSc /eːu/, apparently by the late 13c, was a diphthong /iːu/, of the following origins:

(a) OF *iu* < earlier OF *ęu* in *griu* 'Greek', *riule* 'rule', *iw-* in *ensiw-* 'ensue' and in AN *pursiwer* 'pursue' > OSc *Grew, rewle, ensew, persew;* (b) OE *īw-* in OE *spīwan* 'to spew' and, with puzzling re-analysis and thus re-syllabification of the compound, OE *stigward* > *stīward* 'steward', /stiː.ward/ reanalysed as /stiːw.ard/, followed by vocalisation of the [w] and diphthong formation.

The merger of vowel 14a(ii) with vowel 14a(i) is well-evidenced latterly in such rhymes as:

Grewe 'Greece' : *persewe* (Henr. *Orph.* 15 f.); *knew* : *persew* 'pursue' : *dew* 'dawned' : *hew* 'hue' (*Gol. & Gaw.* 596 f.); *new* : *hew* 'hue' : *trew* 'true' : *schew* p.t. 'showed' : *grew* 'Greek' (Doug. *Pal. Hon.* 790 f.); *new* : *ensew* 'ensue' (Doug. *Æn.* 2, Prologue, 6 f.); and numerous other rhymes of *persew* v. with e.g. *blew* 'blue', *knew, new, trew,* in e.g. *Wall., Bk. Chess,* Dunbar, J. Stewart.

Earlier evidence for the merger of these two PreSc phonemes and for the date of that merger consists of ME spellings - since evidential PreSc spellings are unavailable - in <ew, eu>, which originally were appropriated to (i) /eːw(-)/ > /eːu/, applied, from the late 13c, also to (ii) /iːw(-)/ > /iːu/, of which the regular earlier spelling is <iw, iu, yu>: cf. e.g.:

(1) <brewen> 13- 'to brew' (OE *brēowan*); <bleu, blew> 13- 'blue' (OF *bleu*);

(2) <gryu> 13, <griu> 14, <greu> la13, <grew(e)> 14, <gru> 14 'Greek' (OF *Griu*); <riwle> 13, <riule> 13, <reule, rewle, rewel> all 14- 'rule' (OF *riule*); <pursiwe(n)> 13, <pursew(e)> 14- 'pursue' (AN *pursiwer*); ME <stiward> 11-, <steward> c1330, <Steuhard> (surname) 1275, also ESc (surnames) <Stiward> 1333, <Styward> 1358, <Steward> 1333.

On spellings of vowels 14a(i) and 14a(ii) with <u, ue, w>, see below.

The later history of the merged phoneme makes it certain that its realisation was [iːu] rather than [eːu] either to begin with or quite soon. This appears not only from the modern dialect outcomes, /iu/ or /juː/, the latter evidenced from the late 15c (see §6.5.3), but even more convincingly from the several ESc outcomes of PreSc /oː/ before velars and, in the N, before /r(d)/ (§§ 7.2.1, 7.2.2, 7.3), which eventually merged with vowel 14a and which must have passed through the stages [y:u] > [i:u], but hardly [e:u].

That it should have been the <ew, eu> spelling option which prevailed rather than <iw, iu, yu>, which might seem more apt for an [i:u] realisation, is perhaps a little surprising. Perhaps the explanation is the greater lexical prolificness of the /e:w/ source, to which <ew, eu> originally pertained;

(iii) OF ū final and hiatical

OF ū in general remained as [y:] in PreSc, eventually merging with the vowel /y:/, vowel 7, which resulted from the fronting of PreSc /o:/ (§7.1): thus e.g., from OF ū, OSc *cure, habitude, rude* adj., *sure* adj., *use* n. and v., with vowel 7, ESc /y:/ > MSc /ø:/. However, the word-final and hiatical (i.e. before a stressed vowel or unstressed -e) allophones of this vowel must at some early date in PreSc have split from the other allophones, apparently by the development of an intervocalic linking glide or post-vocalic off-glide of labial quality following the close lip-rounded vowel /y:/, thus [y:V] > [*y:wV] and [y:#] > [*y:w#], yielding the diphthong [*y:u], which, with unrounding of the first element, eventually merged with vowels 14a(i) and 14a(ii) above, as /i:u/.

Thus in these environments, but these environments only, the PreSc outcome of OF ū is the same as that in *all* environments 'in popular speech' (Bliss, 1969: §11) in sME, both in e.g. ME /ki:ur/ *cure*, /habi'ti:ud/ *habitude*, etc., and in e.g. /ar'gi:u/ *argue*, etc. But in Sc this outcome is confined to the latter final and hiatical allophones only, in e.g.:

OSc *argu, argew* < OF *argüer*, OSc *rew* 'street' < OF *rüe*, OSc *valew* 'value' < OF *valüe*, OSc *vertew* 'virtue' < OF *vertü*, OSc *cruel* also <crewel, crowal> < OF *crüel*, similarly OSc *continual*, also <contynewall>.

This phonemic split must have taken place before the fronting of PreSc /o:/ to /y:/ vowel 7, as described at §7.1. Otherwise, we cannot explain how the final and hiatical allophone of the PreSc derivative of OF ū /y:/ remained distinct from the [y:] resulting in similar environments from earlier native /o:/ in such words as *do* v. 'do', *scho* 'shoe', which in OSc had vowel 7 /y:/ > /ø:/, quite distinct from the vowel of say *argu* or *rew* 'street', /i:u/.

Evidence of the merger in the final and hiatical environment of the PreSc derivative of OF ū with vowels 14a(i) PreSc /e:u/, and 14a(ii) PreSc /i:u/, consists of:

(1) 14c and 15c spellings in <ew(e), eu> alongside earlier (and continuing) spellings in <u(e)>, in e.g.:

<argew(e)> la15 beside <argu(e)>; <rew>, pl. <rewis> 'street' 15 beside <ruys> pl. 15; <sewit> p.t. 'sued' 1405 beside <suys> 'sues' 1404; <valew> 1439 'value' beside <valu> 1379, <valw> 1397; <vertew> 15 beside <wertu> 1410; <crewell> 15 beside <cruel> 15, etc. (In sME similar spellings occur in these words, and also, unlike in ESc, in such words as *rude* adj., with sME <reude> 15, <rewde> 15);

(2) 14c and 15c reverse spellings with <u>, etc. for earlier <iw, iu>, <ew, eu>, in e.g.:

(sME) <stuerd> *c*1330, <stuard> ? 1425 'steward', (ESc) <stuwart> 1377-8, <stwart> 15; <nue> la16 'new'; <ruit, rwyt> la15 p. t. 'rued'; <suyt> la15 'sewed'; <trwli> 1407 'truly'; <thrue> 1516 'true'; <truth> la15 'truth'; and in numerous such spellings in sME, e.g. <cru> 13 beside <crew> p. t. 'crowed', <gru> 14 beside <grew> 'grew', etc., etc.;

(3) rhymes such as:

knewe : *wirtewe* : *argewe* : *schewe* p. t. 'showed' (*Howlat* 262 f.); *hew* 'hue' : *vertew* (Henr. *Fab.* 127 f.); *vertew* : *grew* (*Colk. Sow* 3, 45 f.); *new* : *flew* : *vertew* (Dunb. 209/36 f.); *vertew* : *schew* 'showed' p.t. (Rolland *Seven S.*, 57 f.); *vertew* : *anew* 'enough' pl. (ibid. 5660 f.); and, with vowel 14a(ii), *ensewys* 'ensues' : *rewys* 'streets' (Doug. *Æn.* 2, 11, 77 f.); *vertewis* pl. : *persewis* 'pursues' (Rolland *Seven S.* 1441 f.);

(4) the spelling and rhyme <wertuous> 'virtues' pl., rhymes with *contrarious* (*Ratis R.* 410), and <vertiou> 'virtue' 1609 Inverness.

The OSc rhymes and spellings just considered point fairly certainly to the development [y:u] > /iːu/ vowel 14a for the PreSc derivative of OF $\bar{u}$ when final or hiatical. There also exist some rhymes in several ESc poems, especially *Leg. S.* and *Troy-bk*, and a scattering of ESc and, especially, MSc spellings which indicate a different outcome:

(1) rhymes of the PreSc derivative of OF $\bar{u}\#$, $\bar{u}+$ with vowel 6, ESc /uː/:

(*Leg. S.*) *vertew* (*wertew, vertow*) 'virtue' with *now, þu* 'thou', *trow* v. 'believe', *ȝow* 'you'; *rew* n. 'street' with *now* (*Leg. S.* 2, 575 f.); *fovs* adj. 'eager' with *vertuse* pl. 'virtues' (*Leg. S.* 6, 385 f.);

(*Troy-bk.*) *waleue, walew* 'value' with *þow* 'thou'; *superflue, wertue* 'virtue' with *now*; *wirtue* 'virtue' with *trow* v. 'believe';

(*Ratis R.* 297) *wertew* with *enschew* 'eschew' /ɛ(n)'ʃuː/ (see §6.5.3 below).

These rhymes point to the outcome /uː/ as in vowel 6, for these derivatives of OF *ū*:

(2) spellings in <ou, ow>, the regular OSc spelling of vowel 6:

valew 'value' as <valow> 1399, 1405, 1434 Ayr, and thereafter apparently only NE and SW, e.g. <wailowe> 1551 Cawdor, <wallow> 1558 Aberdeen; much more rarely, *vertew* 'virtue' as <vertow> la15, <wertow> c1570; *dewté* 'duty' as <dowité> 1494 (? from AN *dūeté*, beside the commoner <dewité, duyté> from AN *deueté*); *nevew* 'nephew' as <navow> la15- (? from ONF *nevū*, beside *nevew* from OF *neveu*); *arguit* p.t. of *argew* v. 'argue', as <argoued> 1571.

Note, on the other hand, that spellings in <ow, ou> do not similarly occur for words derived as vowel 14a(i) or 14a(ii) or as in §7.2.2; thus none of the following show <ow> spellings in OSc: *blew* 'blue', *blew* p.t., *brew* v., *crew* p.t. 'crowed', *ensew* 'ensue', *flew* p.t., *glew* n. 'mirth', *Grew* adj. 'Greek', *hew* n. 'hue', *hew* p.t. 'hewed', *inew* (*anew, enew*) pl. 'enough', *knew* p.t., *new* adj.; *persew* 'pursue', *plewis*, or, before the 17c, <plow> for *plew* v. 'to plough'. On *Jow* n. 'Jew' and *eschow* 'eschew' v., see §6.5.3;

(3) also pointing in this direction: <grew> reverse spelling of *grow* /gruː/ 'to shudder' in Barbour and *Leg. S.* (both la15 MSS), and in 1571.

The above data suggest that at some date before the late 14c (and probably before the shift of stress from the second to the first syllable in such words as *argu, vertu*), PreSc /yːu#, yːu+/ from OF *ū* was in some dialects smoothed, by retraction of the first element, to /uː/ vowel 6; these dialects included those of the authors of *Leg. S.* and of *Troy-bk*, and perhaps of *Ratis R*.

This variant, the type /*ar'guː, *vɛr'tuː/, was, however, perhaps short-lived in competition with the variant /yːu/, which > /iːu/, by unrounding of the first element, yielding the type /ar'giːu, vɛr'tiːu/ (as also happened with the monophthong /yː/ in the North, and the diphthongs arising from early PreSc /oː/ before velars: on all of these, see §7). For no /uː/ outcomes for the words in question appear to be recorded for modSc dialects, except when the yod of MSc, modSc /juː/ < earlier /iːu/ has been absorbed by preceding consonants (see §6.5.3).

6.5.2 ESc /ɛːu/ vowel 14b(i), ?/ɛǫu/ vowel 14b(ii), and ?/ɛau/ vowel 14b(iii)

The sources are:

(i) OE ēaw(-), ǣw(-), > early ME and early PreSc /ɛːw-/ > /ɛːu/, e.g.:

(a) OE dēaw, þēaw, slǣwþ, yielding OSc dew, thew 'a habit', sleuth 'sloth';

(b) OE fēawe, hēawan, scēawian, scrēawa, lǣwede, yielding OSc few, hew v., schew v. 'to show' (beside schaw from sc(e)āwian, with shifted diphthongal stress), schrew 'shrew', lewed 'lewd' (beside lawd etc. from OE lǣwede > lǣwede, by trisyllablic shortening > lăwd(e));

(ii) OF eau: e.g.:

OSc bewté, beuté 'beauty', lewté 'loyalty', pewter, also <pewder>, rewm(e) 'realm'; also OSc reule with this vowel, confirmed by modSc (NE) /rʌul/, presumably from OF reule, beside OSc /riːul/ from OF riule.

The principal modSc outcomes of vowel 14b are:

(1) /iu/ or /juː/, the same as for 14a;

(2) in the NE, from the Moray Firth to Angus, along with a few further localities nearby, the sequence /jʌu/, consisting of the palatal glide [j] + /ʌu/ vowel 13 (and so rhyming with vowel 13 in e.g. grow, how 'hoe', etc.: see §14.13), in e.g.: dew (see s.v. in LAS3), few, beauty (Dieth, 1932: 58), as /djʌu, fjʌu, 'bjʌutɪ/; in the same area modSc sleuth, slouth apparently has the same development /(j)ʌu/, but with yod-absorption by the preceding liquid. This implies an earlier /ɛǫu/ vowel 14b(ii);

(3) in addition, most of the words of OF origin (ii), but apparently only these, yielded variants with some such realisation as ESc [ɛau] vowel 14b(iii), which, with regular early MSc smoothing of vowel 12 /au/ to /ɑː/ (§18.1), and presumably raising of its first element as with 14b(i) at §6.5.3, resulted in something like [iɑː], or, with diphthongal stress-shift, /jɑː/, in e.g. OSc beauté, leauté 'loyalty', reaume 'realm'; also, with yod-absorption by a preceding liquid, apparently in the course of the early 15c, lauté (first recorded 1452), rawme (1544). Forms of this type appear not to be recorded after the 18c (see e.g. Lawtie (SND)).

Figure 8: *Sources and outcomes of vowel 14*

Vowel number; see §§	Sources	Examples
14b(i/ii/iii) §§6.5.2, 6.5.3	OF *eau*	*bewté, lewté*
14b(i/ii) §§6.5.2, 6.5.3	OE *ēaw*(-)	*dew*
14a(i) §6.5.1	OE *ēow*(-) OE *īw-* OF *eu*	*crew* 'crowed' *sew* (by OSL) *blew* 'blue'
14a(ii) §6.5.1	OF *iu* OE *īw-*	*grew* 'Greek' *spew*
14a/6 §6.5.1	OF *ǖ* final and in hiatus	*argue, cruel*
7 §7.2.2	OE/o:γV(C)/ and in N /o:r(d)/	*enew* *mure, buird*
7 §§7.2.1, 7.3	OE *ō* before /k, x/	*eneuch, heuk*

VOWEL PHONOLOGY TO 1375

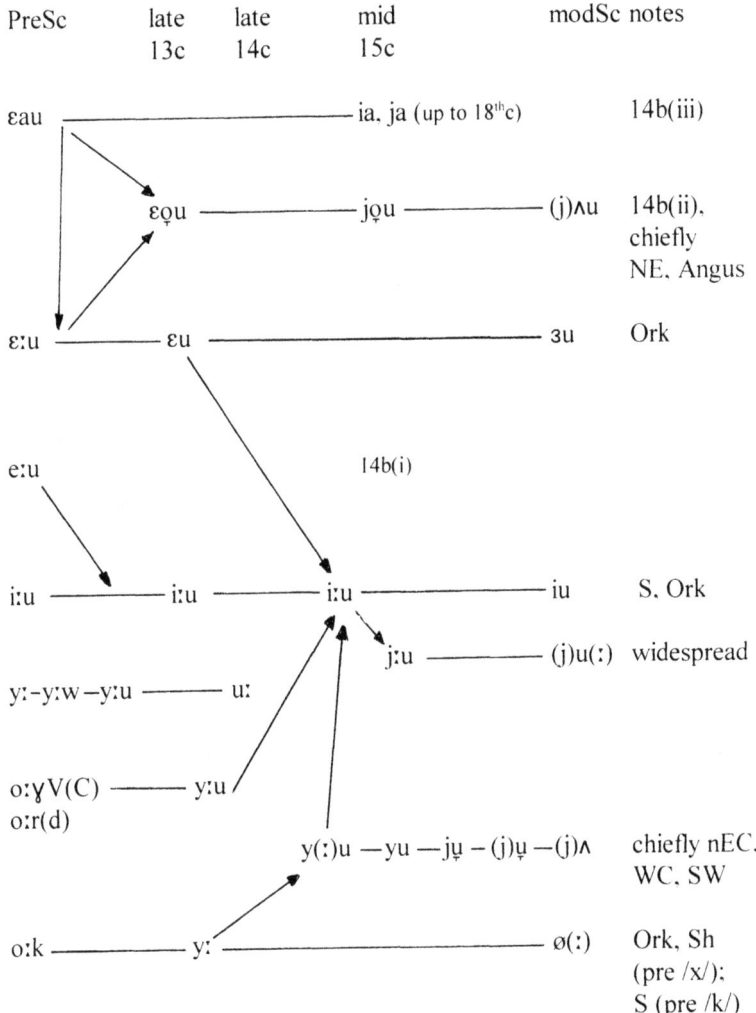

Since the several outcomes (vowels 14b(i), 14b(ii), 14b(iii)) of OE *ēaw(-)*, *ǣw(-)* and OF *eau* affect only 14b words, all of them must have been in separate existence before the merger of vowels 14b(i) and 14a described in §6.5.3, i.e. in the ESc period *c*1400. It is possible that their origin is much older than that. The speculative scenario set out in Figure 8 would account for all the so far observed results, albeit its precise early chronology remains unclear.

The regular OSc spellings of vowels 14b(i) and 14b(ii), are <ew, eu>, and in words from OF *eau* <eau, eaw> vowel 14b(iii); spellings in <u, ue>, as in the case of vowel 14a, are virtually absent. The apparent yod-deletion after a voiceless plosive seemingly implied by the spellings <pouder> 1522-3, <powder> 1550, <powter> 1562, <polter> 1589> 'pewter' is irregular. On other spellings in <ow> see §6.5.3 below.

6.5.3 Later history of ESc /iːu/ vowel 14a, /ɛːu/ vowel 14b(i), ?/ɛou̯/, vowel 14b(ii)

The merger with vowel 14a, ESc /iːu/, of the outcome of PreSc /oːɣ-/ is dealt with at §7.2.2 below, and of the outcome of PreSc /oːk, oːx/ at §7.2.1. The subsequent history of vowel 14a, now to be described, is shared by these accretions also. One event in this subsequent history is the merger with vowel 14a, ESc /iːu/, of vowel 14b(i), ESc /ɛːu/, presumably after the first element of this had undergone raising, possibly under the same impetus as produced the Great Vowel Shift (GVS) (§20). This seems however not to have been *directly* associated with, or part of, GVS, since it seemingly took place some time before ESc /ɛː/ vowel 3 began merging generally, by GVS, with ESc /eː/ vowel 2 (on which see §20.8.3).

The following rhymes by several 15c and 16c poets suggest that in their dialects vowels 14a and 14b(i) were merging or had merged, thus by the mid 15c:

> *ynewe* (vowel 14a) : *dewe* adj. (vowel 14a) : *schewe* pres. t. (vowel 14b(i)) ; *knewe* (vowel 14a) (*c*1450 *Howlat*, 575 f.); *grew* (vowel 14a) : *hew* v. (vowel 14b(i)) : *schew* pres. t. (vowel 14b(i)) : *rew* 'rue' pres. t. (vowel 14a) (15c *Gol. & Gaw*, 960 f.); *trew* 'true' (vowel 14a) : *schew* (apparently pres. t.) (vowel 14b(i)) (Doug. *Æn.* 1, Prologue, 213 f.); *hew* v. (vowel 14b(i)) : *grew* (vowel 14a) (Doug. *Æn.* 2, 10, 117 f.); *trewth* 'truth' (vowel 14a) : *slewth* 'sloth' (vowel 14b(i)) (*Clariodus* 4, 1098 f., 2341 f.); *few* (vowel 14b(i)) : *trew* (vowel 14a) (1570 *Sat. P.*, 16, 22 f.); *few* : *sew* v. (vowel 14a) (1571 ibid., 26, 59 f.); *shewe* pres. t. : *trew* (Montg. *Ch. & Slae* 1018 f.).

(On certain poets who keep vowels 14a and 14b separate in rhyme, see below.)

Somewhat later than this event, because its modern outcome is identical for all vowel 14a and 14b(i) words, came the following diaphonemic split of the merged phoneme, which we may now call simply vowel 14. In some dialects the established [iːu] realisation continued unchanged to yield modSc /iu/, surviving only in Rox as [iu] or, a little to the east, as [ɪu]. In all other dialects but those of Ork (see below), the universal outcome is /juː/, realised as [ju(ː)], occasionally [jü(ː)] or even [jy(ː)].[2] According to the following evidence, the diphthongal stress-shift, from [iːu] to [iúː] to [juː], which brought this about, took place in the first half of the 15c:

(1) <nyow> > 1503 'new', ? /njuː/;

(2) showing yod-absorption by a preceding liquid or nasal consonant, thus [Liːu] > [Ljuː] > [Luː], where L = liquid or nasal consonant:

<trowly> 1451 'truly'; <lowch> p.t. 'laughed' (*Wall.*) la15; <ynowch> la15, <enowch> 1545 'enough'; <crowall> e16 'cruel'; <nowk> e16 'nook'; <browhous> 1508 'brewhouse'; <crowk> 1552-3, <crowkit> 1588 'crook, crooked'; <loukit> 1568, <lowk> 1576 'looked, look'; <plowcht> 1583, <plouers> la16 'plough, ploughers'; <clow> 1584 'clue of yarn' (OE *cliwen*); <rouk> la16 'rook'; <row> la16, <rowit> *c*1600, 'rue(d)' v.;

(3) spellings showing yod-absorption by a preceding /s/: <sow, sowyd, -it> la15 'sew, sewed', <persow> 'pursue' 1537-8;

(4) Perhaps the development /siːu/ > /sjuː/ > /ʃuː/ followed a little later, evidenced by:

OSc *ensew* 'to follow' 1482 as <enschew> e17; OSc *persue* 1416, *persew* 1432, 'pursue' as <perschew> 1495; OSc *sew* la15 as <schew> 1566-7, <schewid> la16, <shoue> 1603, and OSc *sewing* as <scheuing> 1550, <schewing> 1572;

(5) The rhymes at *Christis Kirk* (82 f.) of *drew* p.t. : *flew* p.t. : *trew* 'true' : *anew* 'enough' pl. with *trow* v. 'believe' (usually /truː/); the spelling <schow> (if correctly read) 'show' pres. t., Aberdeen 1503 (presumably ESc /ʃɛːu/ > MSc /ʃjuː/ > /ʃuː/); and the reverse spelling <grew> la15, 1571 for *grow* 'shudder', always /gruː/, all point in the same direction.

The 15c spellings <trew, treu> 'to believe' and Barbour's rhyme of this with *rew* v. 'rue' probably reflect OE *trēow(i)an* rather than OE *trūwian*, ON *trúa*, the sources of regular OSc *trow* /truː/ 'believe'.

The apparently anomalous spellings <coukes, kowk> *c*1570 'cook', beside regular <cuke, kuke> etc., require special explanation, not attempted here.

Note: The histories of ʒou pron. 'you', *eschow* 'eschew', *Jow* 'Jew', are not evidence of this development. In all of these cases, in the course of ME and PreSc, the preceding palatal continuant absorbed the first element of the vowel 14a diphthong /iːu/, thus: OE *ēow* 'you' pron. (oblique cases) > early ME and PreSc /eːu/, then, with initial /j/ borrowed from nominative *gē* 'you' pron., /jeːu/ > /jiːu/ (§6.5.1 above), then, with diphthongal stress-shift and absoption of [i] by the palatal > /juː/, a stage already reached in 13c ME as evidenced by such 13c ME spellings as <iou>, <ʒuw>. Similarly for the pronoun *your*. Likewise /ɛˈʃiːu/ < OF *eschiver* > /ɛˈʃuː/, OSc <eschow> e16. and /ʤiːu/ (OF *giu*) > /ʤuː/, ME <Iuwe> 14, and ME and OSc <Iow> 14.

The unchanged /iːu/ phoneme, now surviving only in Rox and a little to its east, is perhaps represented in <diueties> 'duties' 1545 and <niwe> 'new' *c*1614. At one point James VI rhymes vowel 14 against vowel 6: *trew* : *dew* 'due' : *anew* 'enough' : *grew*, against *bow* : *vow* : *trow* : *now*. Presumably James used the unshifted /iːu/ phoneme. Further indications of this kind may emerge when a full study of OSc rhymes is carried out.

While in almost all dialects the vowel 14 outcome /juː/ [juː] indicates that the vowel 14b(i) with vowel 14a merger has been in that direction (14b(i) > 14a), several modern Ork dialects display an outcome which suggests the opposite direction of merger, 14a > 14b(i), in some environments at least. In these dialects the words *dew* (vowel 14b(i)) invariably, and mostly also *blue, new, spew, stew, enough, leuch* 'laughed', *tough* (all vowel 14a), yield not /juː/ but [ʒu] or, in one dialect each, [eu] and [ɪu]. Occasional co-existent [juː] forms, *stew* once, *new, spew* once, *feud* invariably, may be due to borrowing from StEng or neighbouring dialects.

The foregoing discusses the events following the merger of vowels 14b(i) and 14a. Of course, the vowel 14b(ii) phoneme, OSc /ɛǫu/ > /(j)ǫu/, modSc /(j)ʌu/, was not involved in this. And indeed some OSc poets appear (on the basis of my own scanty gleanings) to rhyme vowel 14b only with itself: *Leg. S. (scheuis* 'shows' : *thewis* 'manners', 36, 645 f.); Henryson *(few : schrew, Fab.,* 703 f.); Dunbar *(kewis* 'cues', etym. unknown : *schrewis : few is,* 209/51 f.). The S.T.S. collection of the poems of J. Stewart of Baldynneis (la16) has a total of 31 sets of rhymes of vowel 14a words, many of these with three or four rhyming words; but there is not a single instance in rhyme of a word containing vowel 14b (which would have included the words *dew* n., *few* adj., *hew* v.). Of these poets just mentioned J. Stewart at least belonged to the modern /jʌu/ area. Since the possibility exists that the 14b(ii) triphthongal variant /ɛǫu/ > modSc /(j)ʌu/ was more widespread in OSc than today, it is possible that the other three poets of this group also belonged to an /ɛǫu/ > /(j)ʌu/ area, in which case their rhyming practice is not evidence for the history of diphthongal 14b(i), ESc /ɛːu/.

Of the date at which vowel 14b(ii) shifted from a level to a rising triphthong, /ɛǫu/ > /jǫu/, I have no evidence. Meantime it is possible to presume that it took place alongside, and possibly influenced by, the parallel developments of vowel 14 (/i:u/ > /ju:/) discussed above, and of the diphthong /yu̯/ before voiceless velars > modSc /jʌ/ (§7.2.1).

As well as the regular spellings in <ew, eu> (see §6.5.2), vowel 14b is occasionally spelled with <ow, ou>:

<schow> 'show' 15, <roume> 'realm' 1490, <rowll> 'rule' Dunfermline 1534, <thowles> 'thewless, dissolute' la16, <slouth> 'sloth' la16.

These spellings apparently represent yod-deleted variants of either MSc /ju:/ (vowel 14b(i) merged with vowel 14a) or /jǫu/ (vowel 14b(ii)), but are ambiguous between these two possibilities.

7 The front rounded vowel (vowel 7)

7.1 The fronting of PreSc /o:/

The principal sources of PreSc /o:/, yielding ESc /y:/ vowel 7, were these:

(a) OE, ON ō, e.g. OE gōd 'good', dōn 'to do'; MDu, MLG ō, e.g. cōte > Sc cuit 'ankle'. Note that this included word-final incidences of these sources, as in OE dō 'to do', scō(h) 'shoe', tō 'to, too' (unlike OF ū̄ in word-final and pre-vocalic environments);
(b) OF ō following a labial, e.g. OF bōte 'boot', fōl 'fool', brō 'broth', mōld 'mould', AN pōre 'poor', contracted from OF pōvre; also in OF dōl > Sc dule 'sorrow';
(c) early PreSc /u̯/ by OSL > /o:/, e.g. OE duru > /do:rə/ 'door' (OSc duir).

In the late 13c PreSc and nME /o:/ was fronted to /y:/, merging, in pre-consonantal environments, with /y:/ mainly of OF origin (for the merger of OF ū̄ with /i:u/ vowel 14a in final and hiatical environments, see §6.5.1). This theory (o: > y:) readily explains the merger with OF ū̄, if we assume that to have been realised as [y:]. It is certainly no more unlikely than that we have to suppose that a lower front vowel first raised to merge with ū̄, then subsequently lowered again to [ø:]. The latter pronunciation underlies the realisation of vowel 7 throughout the entire Central and Southern dialects of Scotland and, in addition, Ork and Sh. Against this is only the fact that as a general rule peripheral vowels raise and non-peripheral ones lower.[5]

The sources of OF ū̄ [y:]:

(a) OF ū̄ [y:], VL ū, (Bliss, 1969: §11), e.g. OSc sure, use, -ude as in conclude and habitude, -ure as in mesure;

(b) AN ū [y:] < OF üi (Bliss, 1969: §20), e.g. OSc *fruit, June, lure*.

The fronting of PreSc /o:/ was an event of far-reaching importance in the history of the vowels of Sc, possibly the most crucial of all. As well as changing the vocalism of a numerous existing body of lexemes and providing the resultant merged phoneme with a substantially increased lexical inventory, this change, drastically altering the shape of the long vowel system, was ultimately responsible, at least in part, for the different direction taken by the Great Vowel Shift in Sc and nME from that in sME and so modern StEng. It seems possible that a contributory factor towards this occurrence may have been the prior introduction into the long back vowel area of a new open or half open vowel, OSc vowel 5 (see §3.2), thus reducing the free space in the back round part of the system.

As noted above, an immediate outcome of the fronting was the merger, in pre-consonantal environments, of the fronted vowel, presumably at the [y:] stage, with an existing /y:/ phoneme, mainly of OF origin. Kristensson (1967: 89-92) has abundant evidence of the accomplishment of this merger in nME spellings from Northumberland, Cumberland and Durham, from 1296, such as <Gudeknaue> 1296, <crucum> 'Crookham' 1296 < ON *krók-r*, <mudy> 'Moody' 1338 < OE *mōdig*, <Segistanhugh> 1342-3 < OE *hōh* 'spur of land'. And Luick (1940: §406, Anm.1) cites from the Yorkshire writer, Rolle (*a*1340), the rhymes: *use : duse* 'does', *rude : gude, fortune : sone*.

There is abundant evidence of the same kind in ESc and MSc, and a little in PreSc. Apparently reliably dated are e.g.:

<Swarthbrandkruc> (*Liber Calchou, c*1300), <crukis> 1384 < ON *krók-r*, <wyther> 'other' 1396, <furde> 1398 < OE *ford* with HOCL, <mute> 1400 < OE *mōt* 'moot' n., <hude> 'hood' 1406 < OE *hōd*, and others in Slater (1952).[3]

Mostly, PreSc and ESc spellings of original /o:/ were in <o>, e.g. <botha> 'booth' 13c, <botes> 'boots' 1378. However, except word-finally and in 'minim-rich' environments such as those with following <n, m, u>, 15c spellings of former /o:/ are now most often in <u>, also <ui, uy, wi, wy>. Conversely, former OF ū sometimes appears with such 15c reverse spellings as <oyse> beside <use>; <royde> beside <rude>; <froite>, occasionally <frote>, beside <fruit, frute>. Rhymes of former OF ū with former PreSc /o:/ are abundant from Barbour (1375) onwards, e.g. *forfur* (OE -*fōr*) : *aventure, fortone : done* (OE *gedōn*), *multytud : stud* (OE *stōd*) 'stood'.[4]

In those modSc dialects in which this vowel continues as a rounded vowel - Sh, Ork, north Angus, east Per and Southern - the predominant present realisation is half close [ø:], or sometimes now [e:], in the SVLR-long environments (on SVLR, the Scottish Vowel-length Rule, see §21.2), with [ø] in the SVLR-short environments; but here and there in all of these regions, in SVLR-short environments only, also [y] or [ɪ]. Outside this conservative area, the realisation in the N, with the exception noted below, is [i(ː)]; in nEC it is [e(ː)] in both long and short SVLR environments; in the rest of C and SW, [eː] in the long environments, and some mid front unround vowel in the short environments, mostly [ë] or [ɛ̈], but occasionally [ɪ]; in sEC and WC, but not SW, the latter is merged with vowel 15, as [ë] or [ɪ]: see LAS3's lists and relevant Word Maps (Maps 3, 4, 5, 26, 46, etc.).

So far these facts fit well enough with the value traditionally assigned to vowel 7 following the fronting, namely [ø] or [y]. The English 16c orthoepist, Sir Thomas Smith, in 1568 equates this sound in *hür, kük, güd*, etc., with 'Greek or French upsilon', which, he tells us, 'is pronounced with the lips almost closed, etc.', evidently [yː], and his contemporary, John Hart, heard a similar realisation (Kniezsa, 1991: 3). A little later the Scots grammarian, Alexander Hume (1616: 11), opines: 'If I should judge, the frensh sound is neerest the voual sound as we pronunce it in mule and muse.' The N unrounding to [i], merging with vowel 2, is evidenced in several 16c occasional spellings, in N texts, such as <rief> 'roof' 1542, <meid> 'mood' 1568, <meildis> 'mools, soil of a grave' 1596, <sein> 'soon' 1596, and others.

In the dialects immediately north of the main [i] area, however, the reflex of vowel 7 is today mostly [u] or [y], merged with vowel 6 as in *about*. These dialects are those of the north mainland excluding northern Cai (an [i] district). If these pronunciations are part of the native Scots tradition and not, as the suspicion must be, 'Highland English' adoptions from StE, they support the suggestion given below. There are also however two conservative dialects immediately south of the main [i] area, in which vowel 7 is realised with a centralised back, not front, realisation [ʊ] or [ʊə], quite distinct from vowel 6, namely Gourdon (as reported in LAS3) and Johnshaven (personal observation), both Kincardineshire, precisely between the N [i] and the Angus [ø] areas. If we regard this as an archaic or relic pronunciation, it would square rather neatly with Bliss's (1948/9: 43) suggestion for the direction taken by the change: that /oː/ was first raised to [ʊː] before shifting frontwards. Further, the diphthongisation of the fronted vowel before /x/, /k/ and /r(d)/ to [yːu] or [yu̞], a century or so after the fronting, subsequently yielding general modSc /tjux, tjʌx/ *tough* and /hjuk, hjʌk/ *hook*, and modSc (N) /bjuːrd/ *board*, seems to point to a closer vowel than the mid vowel [ø] as its starting point, see §§7.2.1, 7.3. This suggests that the path of the shifted vowel was by raising to [ʊː], then, by way of fronting to [yː], merger with OF *ū*, the presence of which may indeed have attracted the merger and consequent fronting.[6] Thereafter came first the diphthongisation before /x/, /k/ and /r(d)/, then, about the late 15c, the N unrounding to [iː], only then followed in regions other than N by the lowering to [øː], which plausibly underlies all the modSc results except those of the N. The OSc form <paig> 'puke, the fabric' 1595, 1602, suggests that the unrounding in C to merge with vowel 4 as [e(:)] had begun in the second half of the 16c.

As the fronting of /oː/ involved /u̯/ > /oː/ by OSL as well as original /oː/, it must have come after *c*1250; and the indications above place it, as far as [yː], before the late 13c. If we trust the orthoepists cited above, the lowering to [ø(ː)] may not have come about before the late 16c or early 17c, but it is not impossible that they could have heard [øː] or an intermediate [ʏː] as [yː].

7.2 Early PreSc /oː/ before velar consonants

7.2.1 /oː/ before the voiceless velars

Before clusters of *h* + consonant, mostly *-ht*, OE, ON *ō* had been shortened, e.g. in *pōhte*, (p.t. of *pencan* 'to think') > *pŏhte*. This environment is treated at §6.2. The following treats only unshortened *ō*. The sources of /oː/ before final /x/ and /k/ are:

(a) OE, ON *ō*: e.g.:

OE *bōg* > *bōh* > OSc *beuch* 'bough', OE *clōh > OSc *cleuch* 'ravine', OE *plōg* > *plōh* > OSc *pleuch* 'plough', OE *genōg* > *genōh* sing. > OSc *ineuch* 'enough'; and e.g. OE *bōc* > OSc *buke* 'book', OE *hōc* > OSc *huke* 'hook', and similarly OSc *cruke* 'crook', *luke* 'look', *nuke* 'nook';

(b) OE *ū* > /oː/ by OSL, in OE *dūce* > *dōke /doːkə/, whence OSc *duke* 'duck'.

Early PreSc /oː/ in these as in other environments remained till the late 13c, when it participated regularly in the PreSc fronting to [yː] and merger with OF etc. *ū*, as /yː/ vowel 7, as decribed in §7.1. Loan-words which already contained this phoneme were *duke* (from OF *dūc*), ESc /dyːk/, and, in a similar environment and thereafter similarly treated (see s.v. in DOST). MSc *peug* and *paig* 'puke, the cloth' (from MDu *puuc*), OSc originally /*pyːk/. This /yː/ then remained for some time till about the late 14c or early 15c.

Three different outcomes then followed:

(1) in some dialects /yː/ remained, developing thereafter as regular vowel 7. Doubtless this is the form represented by continuing OSc spellings in <u, ui, etc.>, persisting alongside those in <eu, ew> representing the new diphthongs (on which see below), e.g. <pluche> 1478 and later, <pluiche> la16, <inuche> 15 and later, and <buke, buik, bouk> 'book'. Judging from the relative frequencies of the alternative spellings, this type appears to have predominated in OSc till the 17c or later. But in the modern dialects, the

type with vowel 7 before /x/ has been superseded by one or other of two diphthongs (see below) except in Sh and a few dialects of Ork, while before /k/ the vowel 7 type remains mainly in Ork and S, as e.g. /høk/ 'hook', /nøk/ 'nook', etc.;

(2) in one outcome a glide [u] developed between the long vowel and the following velar, yielding [yːᵘ]. With unrounding of its first element, this diphthong has then joined vowel 14a /iːu/ and has shared the further development of the latter to modSc /juː/ or /iu/. This is now the most widespread outcome;

(3) in other dialects the following velar has caused breaking of the long vowel, yielding a diphthong */jʉ/ with a second element resembling vowel 19 /ʉ/, with which, either at the time of the split or later, merger occurred. (The second element of (2), on the other hand, resembled vowel 6 /uː/.) The modern representative of (3) is, by regular development of vowel 19, /jʌ/, in e.g. /ɪn(j)ʌx/ 'enough' and /hjʌk/ 'hook'. The /jʌ/ outcome is locally widespread in the environments before /x/, whereas before /k/, the /hjʌk/ type seems now to be recessive, but specially concentrated in a swathe of territory from nEC to SW. This outcome, like (1), is thus quite distinct from the /juː/ outcome of vowel 14a, and of PreSc /oːɣV/ > /yːu/ which had already joined vowel 14a (see §7.2.2).

In the modern dialects both types (2) and (3) show forms both with and without yod-absorption by preceding liquids: thus /hjuk/ and /hjʌk/ 'hook', but /luk/ and /lʌk/ 'look' and /njuk/, /njʌk/, and /nʌk/ 'nook'.

The date of the merger of (3) with vowel 19 /ʉ/ is quite uncertain: for the spelling evidence see below. The (3) diaphone must of course have been distinguished in some way from (2) when (2) but not (3) joined vowel 14a. It seems, however, to have pre-dated and thus been unconnected with SVLR. (In time, (2) had of course its own SVLR-shortened form, viz. /ju/ in e.g. /bjux, njuk/, etc.) The earliest spelling in <eu, ew> in DOST for one of these words is <clewch> 1456, whereas spellings in <u> are found from c1350 <clucht>. The earliest <eu, ew> spellings for forms in /-k/, <beuk, heuk, etc.>, appear to be late 15c. It seems moot whether these <eu, ew> spellings represent type (2) or type (3).

All three of these outcomes were widely different from the corresponding outcomes in sME, which were /uːx/, whence e.g. modStE *bough* /bʌu/ and also /ux/, whence modStE *enough* /ɪnʌf/; and /oːk/, whence e.g. modStE *book* /buk/ (Prins, 1972: §§3.24, 3.41; Jordan and Crook, 1974: §§53, 125).

7.2.2 /oː/ before intervocalic *g* /ɣ/

Early PreSc intervocalic *ōg-* /oːɣ-/ > ESc [yːu], eventually merging with vowel 14a /iːu/, in e.g. OE *bōgas* pl. > OSc *bewis* 'boughs', and similarly

OE *clōgas* pl. 'ravines', *hōgas* pl. '"heels" of land', *plōgas* pl. 'ploughs', *drōgon* p.t. pl. of *dragan* 'to draw' > OSc *drew*, *genōge* adj. pl. > OSc *inew* 'enough', pl.

The PreSc development of *ōg-* is unlike that of both PreSc *ōw* and of sME *ōg-*, both of which yield /ou/ by way of late OE or early ME *ōw* > /ou/, merging with the outcome of *ŏg-*. But it parallels the PreSc development of *ēg* > ESc /eːi/ > ESc /eː/ (§6.3.2). In the case of *ōg-* /oːɣ-/, it appears that the /ɣ/ was not opened to [w] till after the merger of original *ōw* with the /ǫːw/ which arose from original *ŏg-*, as explained at §6.4.2 (or the two sequences, *ōg-* and *ōw*, would have had the same outcome), and most probably not till after the fronting of early PreSc /oː/ to /yː/. Doubtless, as with *ēg-*, and with the sources of the later diphthongs discussed at §6.4, the syllable division remained, between the long vowel and the consonant, as /oː.ɣV(C)/, the open syllable situation, till the loss of unstressed final *-e* and the covered inflectional vowel.

Conjecturally we may envisage the further development as follows:

$$/\text{oː.ɣ} \begin{Bmatrix} \text{VC} \\ \text{ə\#} \end{Bmatrix} / > /\text{yː.ɣ} \begin{Bmatrix} \text{VC} \\ \text{ə\#} \end{Bmatrix} /$$

which, with opening of [ɣ] to [w],

$$> /\text{yː.w} \begin{Bmatrix} \text{VC} \\ \text{ə\#} \end{Bmatrix} / > /\text{yːw} \begin{Bmatrix} \text{(V)C} \\ \# \end{Bmatrix} / > /\text{yːu} \begin{Bmatrix} \text{(V)C} \\ \# \end{Bmatrix} /$$

followed by merger with vowel 14a, presumably as [iːu], and yielding, apparently by the early 15c, ESc *bewis* /'biːu(ɪ)z/, and likewise *clewis, hewis, plewis* /'pliːu(ɪ)z/, and *inew* 'enough', pl. /ɪ'niːu/, *drew* p.t. /driːu/. This assumes a somewhat later date (no earlier than late 13c) for loss of final unstressed *-e* than has sometimes been proposed for nME and PreSc.

Presently available and ascertained PreSc data on this issue are in limited supply. Meantime reliable data include nME spellings such as <how(e)> for the dative of OE *hōh* (= OSc *heuch*, pl. *hewis*) (Kristensson,1967: 89 f.), and ESc <howys> 1373; <plew> attrib. *c*1379, back-formed from <plewis> pl. 'ploughs', <plew> uninflected pl. 1428, <plvis> 1416, <plewis> 1483; <buwys> and <bewis> 'boughs', *a*1480 (Wynt.). The ESc rhymes include 'self-rhymes' (both rhyming words from OE *ōg-*): *slew* : *inew* (Barb.), *bewis* 'boughs' : *cluys* 'ravines' (Wynt.), and *hwe* 'precipice' : *slwe* 'slew' (Wynt. 8, 5736). But Barbour (*c*1375) also rhymes *withdrew* : *knew* (9, 256), and Holland (*c*1450) rhymes *ynewe* 'enough' with *adewe, dewe* 'due', *hewe* 'hue', *knewe, reskewe, trewe* 'true', *wirtewe*; and *drewe* with *ynewe, knewe, trewe*, that is with /iːu/ vowel 14a; as well as *ynewe* with *schew* pres.t. 'show' with vowel 14b. Similar rhymes with vowel 14a are very common from some time in ESc.

Like vowel 14a generally, the predominant modern outcome has been the type with the rising diphthong /juː/, with yod-absorption by the liquid in such forms as /ˈpljuː(ɪ)z/ > /ˈpluː(ɪ)z/ 'ploughs' or /drjuː/ > /druː/ 'drew', in contrast to e.g. /bjuː(ɪ)z/ 'boughs' or /ɪnjuː, ɪniu/ 'enough', pl..

7.3 Northern breaking of /yː/ before /r(d)/

In a swathe of N Scots from Cai to Aberdeen, the modSc outcome of PreSc /oː/ before /r/ and /rd/ is vowel 14a, OSc /iːu/, modSc /(j)u(ː)/, like the outcomes of PreSc /oː/ before the voiced velar (§7.2.2), perhaps by the following path. After the fronting of /oː/ to [yː], the close lip-rounding has produced a velar glide from [y] to /r/, with the following consequence: yːr(d) > yːᵘr(d) > yːur(d), merging, like [yːu] from /oːɣ-], with vowel 14a as [iːu], which later produced the rising diphthong [juː]. Words affected are mostly from OE *ō*, or from OE *ŏ* before /rd/ by HOCL, e.g. OSc *mure* 'moor', and *flure* 'floor', and *burde* 'board', *furde* 'ford', as /mjuːr, fluːr, bjuːrd, fjuːrd/ (Dieth, 1932: 36), in OSc also spelled <bourd, bowrd(e), bowird>, <flour, flowr, flowir>, etc. This must have taken place before /yː/ vowel 7 unrounded in the N to merge with vowel 2 as /iː/, i.e. before the late 15c.

Various combinative developments

8 The effects of palatal consonants

8.1 General

By adoption from OF, Gael, and to a much lesser extent MDu, early PreSc possessed the palatal consonants /ɲ/ and /ʎ/ in open syllable environments after preceding short vowels. In the course of PreSc or OSc these were succeeded by /nj/ or /ŋj/ (also forms with /ŋ#/, see §8.3(iv) below), and /lj/, which continued in common use in Sc down to recent times, though obsolescent since the late 19c. (The existence of these sounds in Gael place and personal names may have contributed to their much longer preservation in Sc than in preStE (Macafee and O' Baoill, 1997).) How long the original palatal consonants continued as such rather than the sequences with [-j] which succeeded them is not apparent.

The favoured spellings for these consonants are <nʒe, nyhe, ny(i)e, etc.>, and, less frequently but nevertheless common from at least the 16c, <ngʒe>, and similarly <lʒe, etc.>. Spellings of French origin - <(n)gn(e)> and <lle> - are markedly less common, though favoured by some scribes, e.g. the copyist of Gilbert Hay's *Prose Works* (la15).

As the above indicates, the palatal component of these consonant sequences was from the first recorded occurrences represented orthographically by <ʒ, y, yh>, either 'as an on-line diacritic to indicate a

45

preceding palatal consonant' (Benskin, 1982: 24, note 20) or simply to represent a discrete [j] element. The third of these options <yh> was disused in late MSc, but the other two continued into modSc. Of these the graph <ʒ> was used in writing from PreSc onwards for both /j/ and though mostly only word-initially, /z/, e.g. in <ʒele> 'zeal'. Sixteenth-century Scottish printed books lacked a separate <ʒ> letter.[7] Hence, just as the MSS used <ʒ> for both /j/ and /z/, the printers used <z> for both /z/ and /j/, so that e.g. *year* could be spelled <zeir>. Thus arose, originally in print, such forms as *cunzie, capercailzie, gaberlunzie,* and such name-forms as *MacKenzie, Menzies, Dalziel,* all of which in modSc, produced spelling-pronunciations in /z/, some of which tended to supersede the original forms in /j/.

The several environments in which, originally, the short vowels + the palatal consonants occurred are these:

(1) with original tonic stress on the syllable preceding the palatal:

$$/C_0^3 V \begin{Bmatrix} ʎ \\ ɲ \end{Bmatrix} (ə)\#/$$

(a) with final -*e* /-ə/ as part of the stem, e.g. OF *loigne* > OSc *lunʒe* 'loin', OF *(es)soigne* > OSc *sunʒe* 'hesitate';
(b) without original final -*e*: OF *coin* /kuɲ-/ > OSc *cunʒe,* OF *poign-* > OSc *punʒe* v. 'prick';

(2) with original tonic stress on the syllable opened by the palatal:

(a)

$$/C_0^3 V' \begin{Bmatrix} ʎ \\ ɲ \end{Bmatrix} \begin{Bmatrix} i: \\ e: \end{Bmatrix} \#/$$

as in OSc *menʒee* 'company', *ligne(e)* 'lineage';

(b)

$$/(V)C_0^3 V' \begin{Bmatrix} ʎ \\ ɲ \end{Bmatrix} VC_0^3/$$

as in OSc *palyas* 'palliasse', *opinioun* and *punʒoun* 'opinion'.

In environment (2b), /lj/ and /nj/ occur in such words as *milʒeoun* (= million) and *onʒeon* (= onion), in all varieties of English, from ME onwards. In the other environments there are sporadic occurrences in ME and e.m.E, especially in northern texts:

in environment (1): <assailʒe> *Hali Meidenhad c*1225, <asaly> 13; <cheny> nME 14, (cf. OSc <chenʒe>) 'chain'; <soyny> n. and v. nME 14; <sonyon> v. 15 (cf. OSc <sunʒe>) 'essoign'; <cully> 'caress' 1576 (beside <cull> *a*1564); <oly> 'oil' 15; <spoili> 14;

in environment (2a): <lygnee, -ye> Caxton, (cf. OSc <ligne(e)>) 'lineage'; nME <menȝe(e)> 14, (cf. OSc <menȝee>) 'company of persons'; and mod StE *rally, tally, sully.*

But only Sc continued these consonants or the palatal sequences which succeeded them as regularly and copiously exemplified constituents of the system.
Whether or not the diphthong-forming glide vowel *i* had developed before /ʎ/ and /ɲ/ in early OF as described in Pope (1934: §§ 406, 407, 408; also Kniezsa, 1986: 108), the PreSc and PreStEng outcomes are most readily understood if we assume that the OF, etc. sources consisted of one of the simple vowels *e, a, u,* or *i* (on *o,* see below), followed by the palatal consonant. Treatment of these in PreSc and PreStEng was as below.

8.2 Treatments I and II

8.2.1 Treatment I

In the regular PreStEng treatment a palatal glide [-i], forming the second element of a diphthong, was inserted between the vowel and the consonant, either in early ME, or already in OF, while the consonant itself was realised in English as the familiar native dental or alveolar /l/ or /n/. Thus the palatal element of the consonant now preceded rather than accompanied the consonant, combining with the vowel to produce in English the diphthongs /ɛi/, /ai/, /ui/ as well as, with *i*, the long monophthong /iː/. (Instances with *o* seem to be confined to environment (2b), which, because the stress at first followed the palatal, did not at first produce diphthongs.) Of these diphthongs, /ɛi/ shortly merged with /ai/ (Prins, 1972: §3.57); thus there were in ME three vocalic outcomes, in e.g. *fail* and *feign* with /ai/, *boil* with /ui/, *sign* with /iː/. Stem or inflectional final *-e* /-ə/ terminating these forms were lost as was normal with the general loss of *-e* in later ME and PreSc. This is of course the normal outcome in PreStEng and StEng. It also occurs as an option in PreSc and OSc. It will be seen that this provides sources for the ESc vowels 8, 10 and 1 respectively (see §14). Thus:

vowel 8:

OF/'faʎ-/ *faillir* > ME /'failən/, OSc <fail(l), fale> 15; OF /'baʎiː/ *bailli* > OSc <bayli> 1393, <bely> la17; OF /'feɲ-/ *feign* > ME and PreSc /'fein/ *feign-* (which then > /'fain/); OF /e'spaɲə-/ *Espagne* > OSc <Spane> 14-15 'Spain';

vowel 10:

OF /'buʎ-/ > OSc <boyl> 16, modSc *bile* /bʌil/ 'boil' v.; similarly OSc <oyll> la14, modSc *ile* 'oil'; OF /'ʤuɲ-/ > OSc <join, joyne> e16 /ʤuin/:

vowel 1:

OF /fa'miʎə/ *famille* 'family' > OSc <famyl(e)>; OF /de'siɲ-/ *designer* > OSc <desyne> 16 'design', <desynd> p.p., rhymes with *mynd*.

However, not all qualifying words in fact display in OSc these Treatment I as well as Treatment II forms. Thus OSc has *brulʒe* etc. 'to broil' by Treatment II, but there appears to be no *broil form on record. Similarly *cunʒe* 'coin' and *lunʒe* 'loin' (16c <loyne> is doubtless borrowed from Eng). For 'join', conversely, there are only the Treatment I form *join* /ʤuin/ and a variant *june* /ʤy:n/ vowel 7, of uncertain derivation.

8.2.2 Treatment II

In this treatment in PreSc, the consonant remained palatal, realised either as [ʎ, ɲ] or as [lj, nj]. When, in OF, the consonant was followed in environment (1) by a final unstressed -*e*, as in OF /luɲə/ *loigne* 'loin', this was continued in PreSc; when the consonant itself was final, as in OF /kuɲ/ 'coin', its off-glide was extended into an unstressed vowel, so that in both cases there was a final vowel, probably, as the later outcomes indicate, of [ɪ]-like quality, constituting a second syllable. Unlike unstressed final -*e* of other sources, this off-glide vowel (orthographically <-e, -ie> rarely <a> (<chenya> 1471 Peebles)) continued as an integral part of the word even when the consonant was depalatalised in MSc or modSc (or the post-consonantal [j] element was deleted). In this treatment there was no pre-consonantal vocalic glide, and the preceding vowels continued as simple vowels, which were then subject to OSL, and, as with other intervening consonants, outcomes with both lengthened and unlengthened vowels appear. This is the more common Sc outcome.

In inflected forms there are orthographic indications both of forms in which the off-glide vowel was deleted (or had never developed) before the inflectional suffix - <fal(e)ʒand> 1391, <falyhyd> 15, <failʒet> 16 - and, much more copiously, of forms maintaining the off-glide vowel in this situation - <falyheand> 15, <failʒʒeand> 1445, <falʒeit> 1448, <failyeid> 15, <faillieing> 17, <failʒieing> 17, as if both /'fa(:)ljand/ and, possibly with lengthening in the hiatical position, /'fa(:)lje:and/, and both /'fa(:)ljɪt/ and /'fa(:)lje:ɪt/ existed, i.e. both disyllabic and trisyllabic forms. But indications of disyllabic forms with the ending -*is* seem rare or non-existent: thus <chenʒeis, failʒeis>, but apparently not *<chenʒis, failʒis>.

Figure 9a: OF /ɛ/ before /ɲ/: treatment I, vowel 8

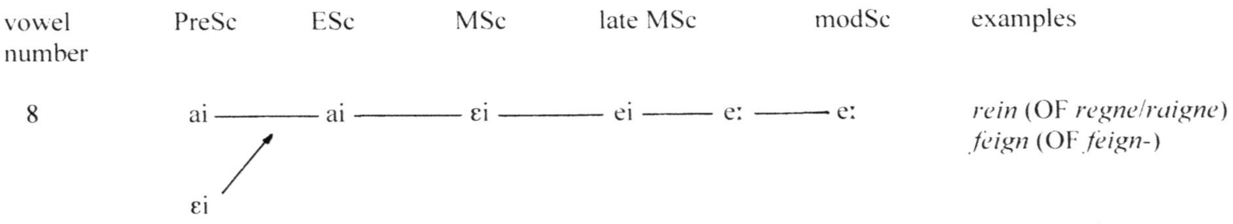

vowel number	PreSc	ESc	MSc	late MSc	modSc	examples
8	ai —— ↑ ɛi	ai ——	ɛi ——	ɛi ——	ɛ: —— e:	rein (OF regne/ruigne) feign (OF feign-)

Figure 9b: *OF /ɛ/ before /n/: treatment II, vowel 16*

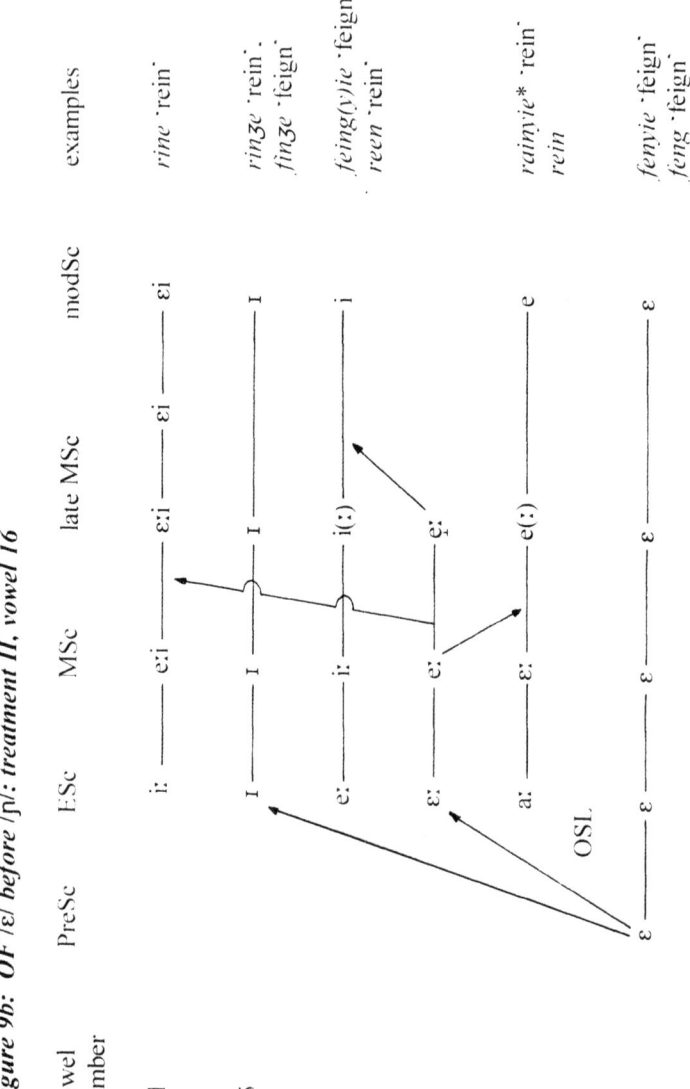

*If not a blend with Treatment 1.

8.3. Examples of Treatment II

In the following selection of examples of Treatment II by no means all the complexities are mentioned. For these a fuller study is needed.

OF *e* > OSc /ɛ/ vowel 16, and by OSL /ɛː/ vowel 3

Environment (1):

/ˈfɛnjɪ/ <fenʒe, fenyhe> 15, modSc <fenyie > Ork 19; by OSL > /ɛː/ /ˈfɛːnjɪ/ <feneyit> p.p. 16, <feinye> 16. Like *fenʒe* are *ansenʒe* 'ensign', *denʒe*, also <deigne, deyngne> 15 'deign', *plenʒe* 'complain', etc. Either by reverse spelling following GVS merger of vowel 4 with vowel 3, or by contamination from Treatment I are: <fane> la15 'feign', <rainʒ(i)e> 17, <rainie> 17 'rein'. By raising of vowel 16 (§14.15 (9)) are: <finʒe> 1563 'feign', <rinʒe> la16, <ringay> la17 'rein' (but see §8.4 below), <chinʒie> la16 'chain'.

Environment (2a):

OSc <menʒee> 'company of persons', with types /mɛˈnjeː/, /ˈmɛnjɪ/, /ˈmɛːnjɪ/, all evidenced by rhyme and modern outcome.

OF *a* and Gael /a/ > OSc /a/ vowel 17, and by OSL ESc /aː/ > MSc /eː/ vowel 4

Environment (1):

(a) vowel 17 /ˈspanjɪ/ <spanʒe> la14 'Spanish', <skanʒe> 16 'skein', <falye> 1402,[8] modSc <canally> 19 'mob';

(b) by OSL > ESc /aː/ vowel 4: modSc <spainyie> 'Spanish' (and, by 15c shortening of vowel 4, OSc <spene> la15, modSc <spengie>); <skainʒe> la16 'skein'; OSc <failyhe> 1387, <faylyhe, faylyʒand> 1396,[9] <felʒe> 16 (with vowel 4 shortening); <canaille> la16, <canailly> la18 'mob'; also <skeeny(i)e> la16, <skeenʒie> la19, and <skeenie> la18. Similarly OSc <ganʒe, gainʒe, genʒe> 'cross-bow bolt' < Gael *gainne*, <manʒe, etc.> 'maiming, maim' < OF *mahaing*, <assailʒe, etc.> 'assail', <mailʒe, etc.> 'chain-mail', <vailʒe, etc.> 'avail';

Environment (2): OSc *bailʒe* 'baillie' < OF *bailli; tailʒour* 'tailor' < AN *taillour*: ESc /ˈbaljiː/, ˈtaljuːr/ and lengthened /ˈbaːljiː/, ˈtaːljuːr/:

(a) OSc <balʒe> 1425, <ballie> 15, <ballyhie> la16, and note also, for *bailʒery*, <ballery, balry> 16;

(b) <bailʒhe, bayhly> 15, modSc <bailyea> Rox 1868 and the vowel 4 form attested by Murray (1873: 132), <bailyee> Uls 1879, <bail-ye> Uls la20; also (with vowel 4 shortening) <belʒe>, common from 1459, <bellyee> Ork 1904; OSc <tailʒour, etc.>, modSc <tailyeor>, attested with vowel 4 by Murray (1873: 116), and <tail-yer> Uls la20.

It is possible to conjecture that the modSc forms <bylie> la19, <tilor> 1705, <tyleyor> 1818, etc. /ˈbɛilɪ/, /ˈtɛil(j)ər/ derive from these Treatment II forms with vowel 4, rather than from Treatment I forms with vowel 8.[10] Like *bailʒe* was *tailʒe* 'a tax' < OF *taillié*.

OF *u* > OSc /ʉ/ vowel 19, and by OSL /y:/ vowel 7

Environment (1):

(a) vowel 19: OSc <cunʒe, cunʒhe> la14, <cungyie> la16, modSc <cunzie> /ˈkʌnjɪ,' kʌnzɪ/ 'coin'; OSc <tulʒ(i)e>, modSc <tully, tullzie> /ˈtʌljɪ, ˈtʌlzɪ/ 'brawl'. Similarly OSc <culyie> 'caress', modSc <cullie> /ˈkʌlɪ/ Moray 1925 and OSc <ully> 16, var. of <ulʒe> 'oil';

(b) by OSL, PreSc /ʉ/ > /oː/ > OSc /yː/ vowel 7: OSc /ˈtyːljɪ/ <tuilyie>, <toilʒie> la14, modSc <tuilyie>, <tüllie> Sh la19 /ˈtølɪ/; also NE *eely* /ˈilɪ/ 'oil' with the regular NE outcome of vowel 7;

Environment (2b):

<monʒealle> 16 /ˈmʉnjal/, <mungell> 17 'monial' < OF *monial, moinel;* <unʒeoun, onyon> 14 < OF *oignon;* with doublets < minʒell> la16. <ingyeoun, ingon> 16, with /ʉ/ > /ɪ/ as in §16.1(2).

Some words deriving from OF *u* have modSc variants with /uː/ vowel 6, e.g. modSc <coolye> Cai 1911 'caress', <ooly, oulie> 'oil'; 16c OSc spellings of the same words with <ou, ow> are ambiguous. The origin of these variants is uncertain.

OF *i* before /ɲ/ > OSc /ɪ/ vowel 15, and by OSL /eː/ vowel 2

In the special case of OF *i* in closed syllables, before final /ɲ/,[11] the original form may have been, and the ESc outcome certainly was, regularly /ɪŋ/, by dissimilation from the high front vowel, in e.g.:

Environment (1):

OSc <bening, -nigne> 15; <conding, -dign(e)> 15; <consing, -sign(e)>; <desing> v. la16 (<dessein(g)> n. 'design' la16 is apparently from16c French); <sign(e)> la16; <ding, digne, dingne> 15 'worthy'; <maling> adj. 'malign', <maling, malign(e)> v. (id); <resing, -sign(e)> 'resign'; <ring, rigne, ringne> 14 'reign'.[12] The spellings in <-(n)gn(e)> are often, as many rhymes show, orthographic for *-ing* /ɪŋ/;

Environment (2a):

(a) OSc /ɪ/ vowel 15: OSc <lignee, lygnie> 15 'lineage' <MF *lignée*; OSc <lignie> 15, <lygny, linʒe> 16 'slender';

(b) by OSL, PreSc /ɪ/ > /eː/ vowel 2: PreSc ?/ˈleːnjeː/, OSc <lenʒe, -ie> 16 'slender', modSc <leengyie>, cf. northern OF *ligne*, L *līneus*, but the Sc rhymes and forms seem to point to an OF *lignée*;

Environment (2b):

OSc <linyell> 17, <lingle> 17 'cobbler's thread' < OF *ligneul*; OSc <opinioun> 15, <opunyone> la14 -16 (for /ɪ/ > /ɰ/, see §14.19(9)). modSc <opingan>; (for the modSc form <opeenion> see §4.2.1(iii)).

8.4 Some further general comments

In later MSc, the forms in /-njɪ/ acquired dissimilated doublets in /ŋjɪ/, and both of these display forms in which the /j/ element was absorbed by the preceding nasal:

<feingʒe> la16, modSc <feing(y)ie> /ˈfiŋ(j)ɪ/ 19, 20; <many> 17 (= *menʒe* OSc <ringay> la17 'rein'; modSc <spaingie, spengie> 'Spain, Spanish'; OSc <cungyie> la16 'coin'; OSc <rainie> 17 'rein'; modSc <skainie> la18, <skeenie> la18 'skein'. The entire second syllable could be absorbed: OSc <fene> 15, rhymes with *complene, mene*, modSc <feng> Sh 1914, Bnf 1924 'feign'; OSc <skene> 16 'skein'. Like <fene> are <chene> 15 'chain'; <rene> la15, <rein, reyne> la15, <rean> 17 'rein'; modSc *cheen, reen* and also *streen* 'strain'.

Just as /-njɪ/ was optionally simplified to /-nɪ/, so, from late MSc, was /-ljɪ/ to /-lɪ/:

<faillie> 1644, <faili> 1677; <canally> la19, <canailly> la18, modSc <tully, tooly> 'brawl', <toillie> /ˈtølɪ/ Sh 1949; /ˈkʌlɪ/ Mry 1925 'caress'; modSc (NE) *eely* 'oil'.

The common (and earlier occurring) OSc form <ballie> 'baillie' 1473-1653 is perhaps a Treatment I form with the vowel from Treatment II.

In many cases the number of variants arising from these developments is further enhanced by some of the following:

(1) doublet or multiple forms of the etymon, as in the case of *chenȝe* and *chanȝe* 'chain', apparently *regne* and *ring* 'rein', *appill oreynȝe* < OF and *apill oranȝe* < MDu 'an orange', and others;

(2) mixed forms with the vowel of Treatment I but the consonantism of Treatment II, or, as Kohler (1967: 41) conjectures, conversely; by the emergence of alternative forms arising later.

In the course of the 16c vowel 3 underwent a further development in the words *cheen, reen, streen,* noted above. The controlling environments are /tʃVn/ and /(st)rVn/ (as well as /tʃVndʒ/ and /(st)rVndʒ/: see §9.3(2)). In these environments the resultant allophone of vowel 3 acquired a diphthongal realisation approximating that reached by vowel 1, by which it was then captured (see the fuller discussion at §9.3(2)), resulting in late MSc and modSc *chyne* 'chain' 17, *rine* /rɛin/ 'rein' la18, which in modSc is widespread as far north as the Moray Firth (see LAS3: Map W146), and *stryn* /strɛin/ 'strain' 1893.[13]

9 OF *a* before nasal combinations in OSc

For an account of the history of OF *a* in nasal combinations in AN and ME, see especially Bliss (1969: §§29-32 and §34). In brief, OF *a* was retracted in AN to [ɑ] before a following nasal, and this was then (like AN *u* to [uː] in the same environment) lengthened to [ɑː], which was then borrowed into ME and PreSc. In ME (and PreSc) 'in the early thirteenth century' this was broken by the following nasal to [ɑu] which was then levelled with existing ME and PreSc /au/ vowel 12 of other origins. The OSc consequences of these events were as follows.

9.1 Before nasal + single consonant

Before nasal + single consonant as /nt/, /nd/, /nk/, /ns/, /mb/, /mp/ in e.g. *grant, grand, plank, dance, amble, ensampill* 'example', there were, as in sME, two principal outcomes:

(1) OSc /a/ vowel 17. In OSc, from the late 15c, spellings of these words in simple <a> greatly outnumber these in <au, aw>, and modSc has similar spellings in <dant> 'daunt', <hant> 'haunt', <pand> 'pawn'. Furthermore, in WC dialects which keep vowels 12 and 17 unmerged, LAS3 reports, for *grand*, forms in vowel 17 not vowel 12. Thus it looks as though such items as those listed above, and also e.g. *ant* 'aunt', *command, land* 'clearing', *avance, ancester, chance,* had OSc and modSc forms in /a/, either by earlier

shortening of AN [ɑː] or by direct adoption from CF [a].[14] OSc /a/ of this origin merged with /a/ of other origins in e.g. *band, hand, sand, gant* 'yawn', *want*;

(2) ESc /au/ vowel 12, from [ɑu] as above, with numerous and early OSc spellings in <au, aw> and, for *grand* in LAS3, vowel 12 outcomes in many dialects of Fife, Ork and elsewhere: in e.g.:

OSc <aunt, awnt> 15-17, <graunt, grawnt> 15-16, <graunde, grawnde> 1400-, <pawnd, paund> 'pledge' 1431-, <chaunce, chawnce> 15, <ensaumpill> 15; and the predominant OSc and modSc form of *chamber* <chaumer, chawmer> la14, <chawmbyre> 15, later, with the reverse spelling <al> for <au>, <chalmer> 1473;

(3) There are also rare OSc spellings in <ay> of *dant* <daynt> 15, *plant* <playnt> 15, and *ant* <aynt> la16, conceivably representing survivals of unbroken ME and PreSc [ɑː], from AN, surviving as ESc [aː] vowel 4. Such forms are not known to survive today, and the absence of any <ai, ay> spellings of OSc *chamer, chamber* tells against the existence of an ESc /*'tʃaːm(b)ər/ > MSc /*'tʃeːm(b)ər/ vowel 4, like StE *chamber*.

9.2 Before alveolar nasal + affricate

More distinctively Sc is the treatment of ME/PreSc /au/, from the breaking of AN [ɑː], as described above, before alveolar nasal + affricate /n(t)ʃ/, /n(d)ʒ/, with later reduction of the affricate to simple fricative /ʃ/, /ʒ/, in e.g. *branch, danger*. In part this overlaps with the history of ESc /ai/ < OF *ai* + /nt/, in e.g. *faint, paint* (see (4) below). All of the words of these patterns are of OF origin. The OSc outcomes are:

(1) ESc /au/ vowel 12 is attested by spellings in <au, aw> from 1263 (<plaunch> 'plank'), thereafter <brawnche> 15, < haunche> e16, <chawnge> 'change' 15-17, <daunger, dawngere> 15-16. There is no presently accessible evidence that such forms survived into modSc (e.g. *paunch* beside Sc *painch, pench* is just as likely to be a borrowing from StE);

(2) ESc /aː/ vowel 4: despite the relative paucity of obvious direct evidence, there is no doubt of the existence of Sc forms in vowel 4, either by merging of AN /ɑː/ with PreSc /aː/ vowel 4, or by smoothing to /aː/ of /au/, as before labials[15] and affricates (see §12.1 and cf. Bliss, 1969: §30). In six of the eleven localities surveyed in Sh for LAS3, *change* is reported with vowel 4 ([e] or the like). In other Sh dialects it has vowel 3 (as regularly exemplified by *lean* adj., an invariable vowel 3 word) merged with vowel 2, as [i], an

outcome which presupposes a preceding vowel 4 (as in note 13). It is likely that some of the common OSc spellings in

$$<aC^4_2(e), aC^4_2->$$

such as <bran(s)che, change>, <manger> also <maneger> la16, <plan(s)chour> represented vowel 4 rather than vowel 17 forms (see (5) below).

(3) ESc /ai/ vowel 8: just as [ɑu], the source of /au/ in (1) above, originally arose by breaking before a nasal of the earlier back vowel [ɑː], so in the nasal + affricate environments, there arose a new front diphthong [ai] by breaking of what was now a front vowel /aː/ as in (2), or its fronted and raised successor by the Great Vowel Shift (on which see §20). Since OSc spellings in <ai, ay> which might represent this diphthong could equally represent the monophthong vowel 4, e.g. <hainch> la16, <playnscheour> 16, <chaynge> 1473, <dayngere> *a*1470, <dayingere> 1577, and many more. this change can only be dated from its subsequent outcomes, discussed in (4), (5) and (6) below, the earliest of which in evidence is <chenge> 'change' 1495. It appears that this breaking may have been a 15c sound-change. Its outcome [ai] then merged with existing /ai/ vowel 8 of other sources and in particular with /ai/ in such words as *faint, paint*, with which it shared the subsequent development to /ɛ/ as in (4) below. In addition to this last point, the existence of this diphthong in OSc is confirmed by the following. The only word of this type surveyed for LAS3 was *change*. Except in Sh (see (2) above) and in Cellardyke, Fife, in all localities other than those displaying the forms to be discussed below, and in which vowels 4 and 8 remain unmerged, *change* has the vowel of such words as *hain* 'save', *main, pain* and *own* (viz. *ain*), i.e. vowel 8, ESc /ai/:

(4) OSc /ɛ/ vowel 16: from about the same time or a little later than the <ai, ay> spellings mentioned in (3), there appear for the same group of words spellings in <e>, such as <chenge> 1495, <denger> 16, <grenge> 16, etc., and <brench> 16, <hench> la16, <plenschour> la16, <stenchel> la16, etc. So too do <e> spellings for words with ESc /ai/ vowel 8 + /nt/, alongside earlier spellings in <ai, ay> and <a>: <fent> la16, <pent> la16, <plent> 16, <mentene> la16, <mentenance>, earlier <faint> 15, <paynt> 15, <playnt> 1389, <mainteigne> 1389, <maintene> 15, <mainteinance> 1477, <man(e)-> 1420. Some of these words have widely current surviving variants in /ɛ/ in modSc, such as /hɛnʃ/ 'haunch', /ˈdɛntɪ/ 'dainty', /fɛnt/ 'faint', /pɛnt/ 'paint', and LAS3 reports several occurrences of *change* with vowel 16 ([ɛ], etc.), e.g. in Longside and Peterhead, Abd.

Since this change is shared by such words as *paint* with pre-existent /ai/ it is evident that in all of these cases the /ɛ/ outcomes derive from vowel 8 antecedents and not, as might have been supposed if only the /ntʃ/ and /ndʒ/

forms were involved, from vowel 4 as in (2). What happened, one supposes, is that once /ai/ had been raised to /ɛi/, about the second half of the fifteenth century, the second element, [ɪ] or [i], of the diphthong was absorbed into the following front nasal with its following stop or affricate, thus reducing the weight of a 'super-heavy' syllable (Lass, 1992: 68 f.) leaving as residue [ɛ], which readily merged with /ɛ/ vowel 16;

(5) OSc /a/ vowel 17: It seems possible that a type with /a/, derived as in §9.1(1), may have persisted in this group of words in Sc in the environment preceding /ntʃ/ but not preceding /ndʒ/. This is suggested by certain occasional modSc spellings cited in SND: <panch> 1706, <planching> 1914 Arg. These are less ambiguous than the very common OSc spellings <branch, hanch, panch, planching>, etc. But there is nothing to suggest any corresponding forms in /a/ for *angel, brainge, change,* etc.

9.3 After /tʃ/ or /r/

The following outcomes apparently affected only a subset of this group of words, all with /tʃ-/ or /r-/ before the vowel, viz *change, range, strange* and modSc *brainge, breenge* 'to dash'. With identical outcomes was a group of words from OF *e* + /n/ with the same pre-vocalic consonants, *chain, rein, strain* (see §8.4(2)):

(1) ESc /ɛː/ vowel 3, later merging with vowel 2 as /iː/: the MSc spelling <cheinge, cheynge> occurs several times in la16, and *cheenge* is well-attested in modSc, as is *breenge* 19; but <streenge> only Sh 1898 (modSc *reenge* 19, also well-attested, may be partly of different derivation from *range*). LAS3 reports *change* with /i/ in 22 localities: 3 in Sh, the rest compactly from south Abd to Fife. In all but four of these localities *lean* adj., vowel 3, also has /i/; in one of the excepted localities *lean* is not recorded, in the other three (in the southern part of the relevant area) it has the vowel of merged vowels 4 and 7 (to be explained away as due to inter-dialect borrowing). Thus the origin of /i/ in *cheenge* and the other words in consideration may be like that of NE /i/ in words with original vowel 4 + /n/, *ane, bane, stane* etc. (as *een, been, steen,* etc.) (Macafee, 1989: 433-6); that is, it derives from /aː/ vowel 4, as in §9.2(2), vowel 4 in this environment having in the course of the Great Vowel Shift caught up with vowel 3, pre-existing in e.g. *lean* adj., with the ultimate outcome being that of vowel 3 merged with vowel 2 in late MSc;

THE OLDER SCOTS VOWELS

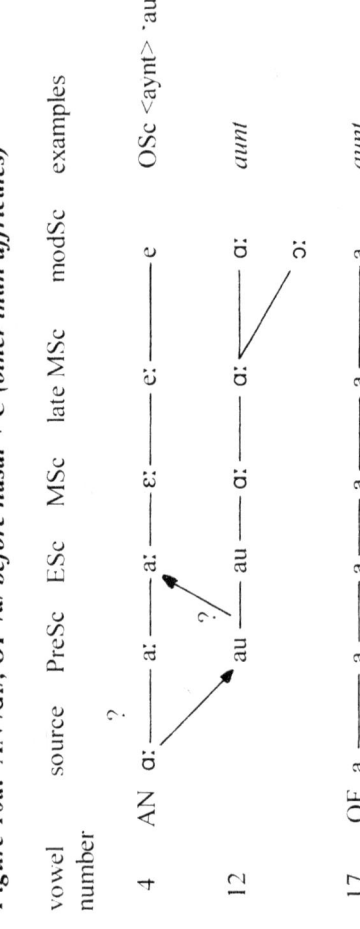

Figure 10a: AN /ɑː/, OF /a/ before nasal + C (other than affricates)

vowel number	source	PreSc	ESc	MSc	late MSc	modSc	examples
4	AN ɑː	——— aː ———	——— aː ———	——— ɛː ———	——— eː ———	——— e	OSc <aynt> 'aunt'
12		au	au ——— ɑː ———	ɑː ———	ɑː ———	ɑː / ɔː	*aunt*
17	OF a	——— a ———	——— a ———	——— a ———	——— a ———	a	*aunt*

58

Figure 10b: *AN /ɑː/, OF /a/ before nasal + affricate*

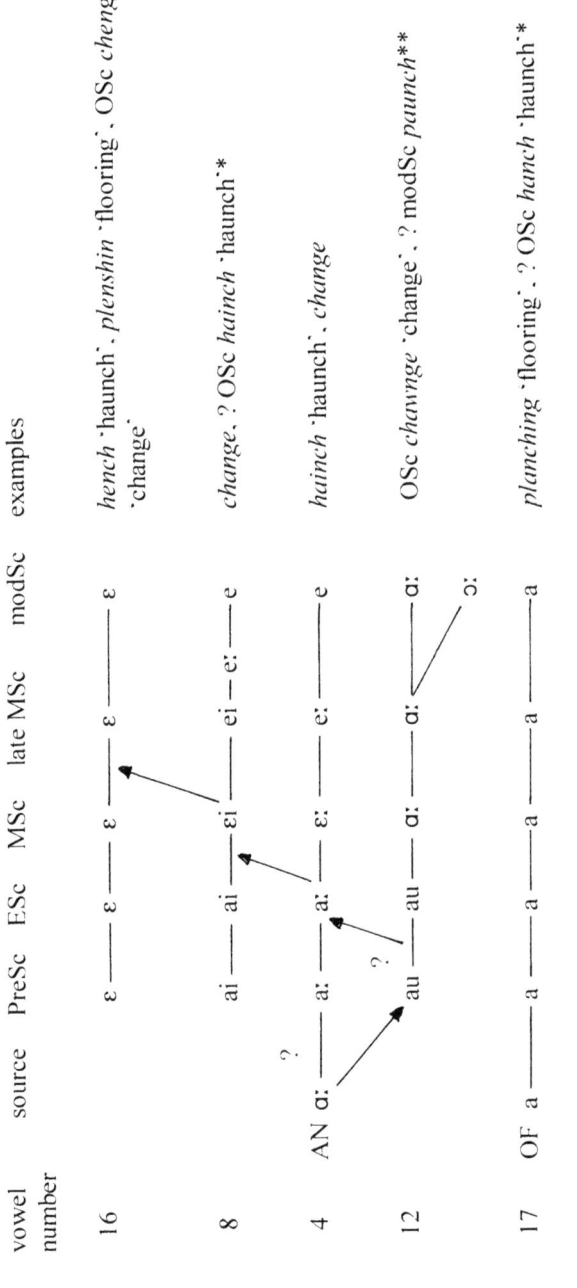

* OSc spellings inconclusive.
** If not StE.

Figure 10c: AN /ɑː/ before nasal + affricate: additional outcomes following /tʃ, r/

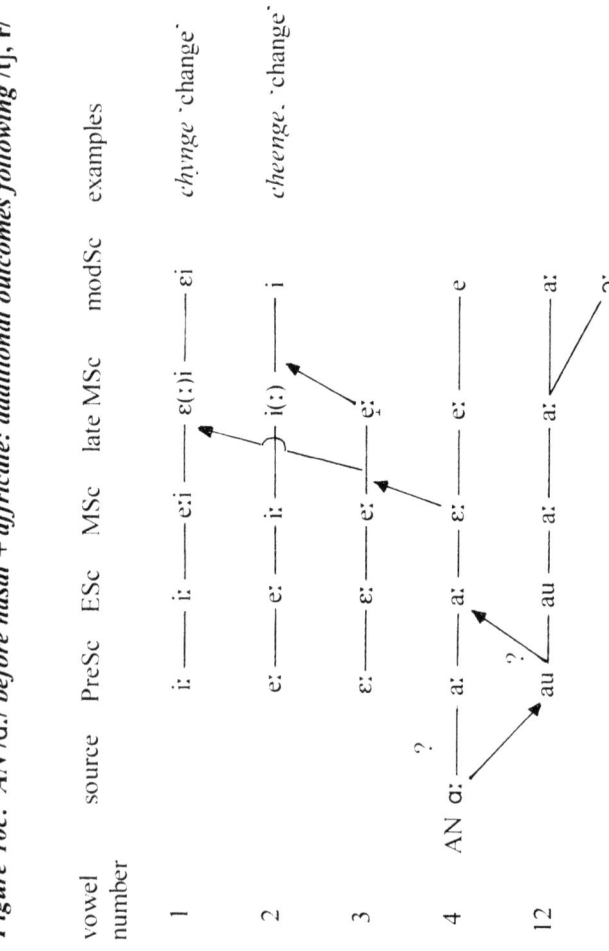

(2) MSc /eːi/ > /ɛ(ː)i/ (< ESc /iː/) vowel 1: orthographic indications for forms of the type MSc /tʃɛindʒ/ for *change* with vowel 1 are scarce and late: <chynge> la16, <rynge> la16, <strynge> 19: and there are 19 and 20c spellings for *range* in <y, i, ei>, which, *pace* SND, doubtless represent the same phoneme. In modSc, according to LAS3, this form of *change* has a distribution similar to but less wide than that of /rɛin/ for *rein* (see §8.4 (2)), with two occurrences in north Cai, others along the coast of the Moray Firth, in central Fife, sEC, WC and SW, but with no instances recorded for Uls; and SND's examples of <rynge, etc.> and <strynge> fall within the same region. Taken together these several indications suggest a period in the 16c for the emergence of the vowel 1-like form /tʃɛindʒ/ for *change*, as for the vowel 1-like form /rɛin/ for *rein*. In view of the wide distribution of these forms today, they are far from recent, the negative indication of the absence of occurrences in Uls notwithstanding.

As with *chain, rein, strain* (as *chyne, ryne, stryne*) (§8.4.2), the capture of the vowel 3 forms by vowel 1 perhaps took place when vowel 3 had reached by GVS a quality in the [e] area. It seems that an allophone of vowel 3 had its onset lowered by influence of the preceding /r/ or /tʃ/ and its coda raised by the following alveolar nasal in the environment before /n(d)ʒ/. The quality of the resultant diphthong must have approached that which had by then been reached by the corresponding allophone of the diphthongised vowel 1, ESc /iː/ > MSc /eːi/ > /ɛ(ː)i/, and the capture of the words under consideration readily followed.

10 OE (Anglian) *ald* in PreSc

Pending more exhaustive dialectological study, the following seems to be the likeliest reconstruction of the development of OE *ald* in PreSc:

OE (Angl) /ald/ > /aːld/ by HOCL > (14c) /auld/ or /ǫuld/.

Like sME, PreSc lengthened OE (Angl) *ă* before /ld/, *ăld* > *āld* /aːld/, except in environments which did not tolerate lengthening, as in OE (Angl) *aldorman* (with antepenultimate stress) > OSc *aldirman*, with /a/ vowel 17. In early sME the resultant /aː/ was regularly rounded to [ɔː] (§3.2), yielding sME *ǫld, cǫld*, etc. In PreSc the unrounded /aː/ remained, perhaps till the early 14c, when it underwent breaking before what we may suppose was then a velarised /ld/ sequence (by anticipating the movement to the velar position while the long vowel was still being articulated). This resulted in something like [ɑᵘ] or [aᵘ]: quite likely the precise realisation varied locally. In the first instance the backer diaphone of the diphthong so created was merged with the existing diphthong /ǫu/ vowel 13. This seems certain, for in the modern dialects, in Sc at least, the latter outcome occupies what are clearly fringe areas (N, Ork, around the Beauly Firth, Arg, single localities in Renfr and Wgt, and Uls, where this form predominates), as a relic form alongside the alternative vowel 12 form. which occupies the main Sc dialect area. In other localities, perhaps where the fronter realisation of the first element of the diphthong existed, as [aᵘ], and perhaps somewhat later, the merger was with vowel 12 /au/, and this form then spread at the expense of /ǫu/.

The above is postulated on the basis of the modern dialect evidence, e.g. LAS3, Map W137. The OSc orthographic evidence is meagre. PreSc has <a> spellings from c1190, e.g.<Kalde welle>, and <fald> c1200. According to DOST, <au> spellings appear from 1329 (s.v. *Ald*). Kristensson (1967) has no <au> spellings for his nME areas (down to 1332), but has <old> spellings from 1327, and earlier <ald> spellings. OSc generally has predominantly <ald>, less often <auld, awld>. DOST's rare <ai> spellings might indicate surviving undiphthongised vowel 4 /aː/ (> /eː/) forms; if so these have not survived into modSc.

Figure 11: OE (Anglian) ald in PreSc

vowel number	OE source	1300	1400	1500	modSc
12	*āw(-), āw-, āg-, ăg-*	au ——————— au – aː ——————— aː				ɔː
4	*ald > āld* by HOCL	aː —— aᵘ —— au ↘ aᵘ ↘				
13	*ōw-, ŏw-, ŏg-*	ou ——————— ou ——————— ʌu				

OSc orthographic evidence for a type /ǫuld/ is even more scanty: <old> 'old'1447 Abd, <ould> the anglicised *Troy-bk.*, and a few 16c instances, including some from the Edinburgh-born William Fowler (1560-1612), who also has <hould> 'hold'. It is far from certain that any of these represent the type in question. The earliest examples of <cowld> on record appear to be those of the late 19c, and <cold> 17 is of course just as likely to be a normal 'anglicisation'.[16]

The irregular OSc and modSc *haud*, ESc /haud/, modSc /haːd/ vowel 12, beside regular *hauld* 'to hold' is perhaps due to a syntactically shortened /haːld/ > /hald/ with subsequent *l*-vocalisation.

11 ESc /a/ and /ɛ/ before /rC/

11.1 /a/ vowel 17 lengthened before /r/ + consonant; /aːrC/ > /ɛːrC/ vowel 4, shortened to /ɛ/ vowel 16

Some time in the PreSc period, perhaps just before the lowering before /r/ of /ɛ/ to /a/ (§11.2), PreSc /a/ was lengthened before /r/ followed by any consonant, but apparently not /r/ final (as in, e.g., *bar*, *car* 'left(-hand)', *dar* v. 'dare'). In most cases the outcome seems to have been doublet unlengthened and lengthened forms and both variants are represented in modSc as /a/ vowel 17 and /eː/ vowel 4, also sometimes /ɛ/ vowel 16: e.g. OE *scearn* 'dung' > *sharn* 17, modern Sh, Ork, N /ʃarn/; and *shairn*, modSc /ʃeːrn/; *shearn* la16, modSc *shern* e18, /ʃɛrn/. For the evidence (OSc and later spellings in <ai, ay> and modern pronunciations in /eː/ vowel 4) see the lists of examples below. The /aːrC/ outcome of this merged with already existing /aːrC/, as in *laird*, earlier /ˈlaːvərd/, OE *hlāford*; *bairn* 'child' and perhaps *cairl* beside *carl* 'churl'; and, from Gael /aː/, *baird* 'bard', *caird* 'tinker', *cairn* (Pődör, 1995/6: 183).

Some of both of these groups of words then proceeded to develop variants in /ɛ/ vowel 16, presumably by shortening of vowel 4 at the GVS [ɛː] stage;[17] e.g. OSc *cart*, *cairt*, *kert* 16, modSc /kert/, /kɛrt/; OSc *arm* and *airm*, but modSc /erm/ and /ɛrm/. Yet a further group of words, apparently qualifying for this change, has not manifested it, and present only spellings in <a> and modSc forms in /a/; it may be significant that the majority of examples of the latter seems to be in original OF countertonic syllables (see the list of examples below).

There follows the OSc and modSc orthographic evidence of these changes. (* = Items with modSc pronunciations in /eː/, vowel 4, only. ** = Items with modSc pronunciations in /eː/ and /ɛ/.) As the above would presuppose, there appear to be no instances of /ɛ/ and /a/ without also some occurrences of /eː/. Undated forms are of the late 14c or early 15c.

OSc orthographic doublets in <a> and <ai, ay>: **archer* and *airchour* la16, ** *arm* and *airm* 16, **barge* and *bairge* 16, and similar doublets of *carp* 'talk', **fard* 'paint (the face)', **gardin*, *lard* 'fat', *reward*, **ȝard*, and ***sharn*.

OSc orthographic variant sets in <a>, <ai, ay> and <e>: ** *argh* 15 and *airch* la16 and *erch* la16 'timid', modSc /arx, eːrx, ɛrx/; **armie* and *airmie* la16 and *ermé* 16; ** *cart* and *cairt* 16 and *kert* 16; **fard* and *faird* 16 and *ferd* 17 'impetus'; ***hard* and *haird* e17 and *herd* 15; ***harm* and *hairm* la16 and *herm* la16; ** *harp* and *hairp* 20 and *herp* 16; **large* and *lairge* la16 and *lerge* la16; *mart* 1328 and *mairt* 16 and *mert* 16 'fattened ox'; ** *part* and *pairt* 15 and *pert* 15; ** *scharp* and *schairpe* la16 and *scherp* 16; and modSc (Uls) has *wairm* and *werm* beside **warm.

Of the forms with original /aː/, *bairn, **carl and *laird all have <e> variants, especially well recorded for *bairn* as *bern* 14-18. Since the OSc manuscript abbreviation for <ar> and for <er> was identical, some, but hardly all, of the OSc incidences of these forms should be discounted.

Forms showing no form other than /arC/, either by OSc orthographic indications nor by modSc pronunciation:

harsk, lark; argu, argune 'argue', *artailʒe* 'artillery', *article, Arthur, ar(c)tik, cardinale, garnis, harlot, harnes* 'harness', *incarnate*.

11.2 /ɛ/ lowered before /r/

As in sME (Jordan and Crook, 1974: §§67, 270), /ɛ/ vowel 16 before tautosyllabic /r/ and, in Sc at least, also intervocalic /r/, was lowered to /a/ vowel 17 in the 14c. Forms in /a/ are attested in rhyme from Barbour onwards, e.g. with *outwart* (*Troy-bk*), with *are* verb pres. indic. (Wynt.), and in spelling from the 15c. But spellings of the 14c and earlier are apparently all in <e>: see DOST s.v. *Bern* n.[1], *Farn(e)*, *Hert* n.[2], *Merchet* n., *Mers* n[1]. This suggests a date no earlier than the late 14c for the lowering. This change was lexically very productive, but not invariable. As usual in Sc, most occurrences have doublets with unchanged forms. In nearly all cases the <a> forms are later than those in <e> (but see above on the dubiety occasioned in some cases by ambiguous manuscript abbreviations). The following is a small sample only:

certane and <sartan> 1525, *derf* and *darf*, *derth* and *darth*, *fert* and *fart*, *fernʒere* 1456 and *farn-* 1488 'last year', *gers* and *gars* 'grass', *gert* and *gart* 'great', *quert* 14 and *quart* 15 'in good health', *serk* and *sark* 'shirt', *sterk* and *stark* 'strong', *stern* and *starn* 'star', *warld* 'world', *fer* and *far*, *ger* and *gar* 'to cause', *wer* and *war* 'worse', *Erskine* and *Arskin* 1544, *pertinence* and *par-* 1489, *wersill* and *warsill* 'wrestle'; *erretike* and *arratick* 'heretic', *errasy* and *arrasie*, *Errol* and *Arrel*, *perill* and *parell* 15.

There are also many words without a recorded <a> form:

ferm n. 'farm', *ferm* adj. 'firm', *perle*, *ferter* 'enshrine', *fertil* 'fertile', *divert*, *pervert*, *serpent*, *cercle* (and *circle*).

Figure 12: /a/ and /ɛ/ before /rC/

vowel number	examples	ESc	early MSc	modSc	examples
4	ON *barn* 'child'	aː	ɛː	e	*bairn, shairn, sair*
17	OE *scearn* 'dung'	a	a	a	*sharn, sar*
16	OF *servir*	ɛ	ɛ	ɛ	*shern, hern, ser*

Since for many words the only outcomes are /ɛ/ and /a/, this change appears to come after lengthening of /a/ to /aː/ in some of the same environments. But there may also have been some chronological overlap, for a limited number of /ɛr/ forms do seem to have proceeded via /ar/ to /aːr/:

> *erlis* and *arlis* and *airles* la16 'earnest payment', *fern* 14 and *farn* 15 and *fairn* 16, *pertrick* and *partrick* and *pairtrik* 16, *quern* and *quairn* 17, *revert* and *rewarte* (rhyming with *smarte*) 16 and *rewairt* (rhyming with *depairt*) 16, *serve* and *sar* la16 and *sair* e17, *wersch* 17 and *warsch* 15 and *wairsch* la16 'insipid'.

For some of these words the vowel 4 form is confirmed by modSc variants with /eː/: e.g. *pairtrik, sair* and *wairsch*. (OSc *hart* and *hairt* 16, modSc /heːrt/ 'heart', beside *hert*, modSc /hɛrt/, may, however, be due to ONhb *hearta* beside OE *heorte*.)

This may also explain the variants in MSc and modSc /eː/ vowel 4 (ESc /aː/), with spellings from MSc onwards in <ai>, of a group of words deriving from OE *ě, ěo* or ME /ɛ/ + /rd/ and /rn/, viz.:

> *braird* beside *breird* 'first shoots'; *aird* (and modSc *yird*, presupposing MSc /#eːrd/ like *yin, ane* 'one' and *yill* 'ale') 'earth'; *raird* beside *rerde* 'uproar'; *lairn* beside *lerne* and *leirn* 'learn'.

Some of these also had forms in vowel 2, ESc /eː/ > MSc /iː/ by HOCL (§3.1.1). Their vowel 4 <ai> forms imply underlying PreSc forms in unlengthened /ɛ/, which survived on record in the cases of *erd* and *lerne*.

12 Smoothings of certain ESc diphthongs in particular environments

12.1 Smoothing of /au/ before labials and affricates

As in sME, in the late 14c the diphthong /au/ was smoothed to /aː/ before /f. v, d, ʤ, ʧ, tj > ʃ/ in *safe* (ME and OF *sauf*), *save, sage* 'the plant' (ME *sauge*, OF *salje, sauge*), *chafer* 'warming dish', *catioun*, OSc <caischoun>, modern legal Sc /'keʃn/; in all these cases except *sage*, there are persisting doublets in /au/ vowel 12 (DOST). The combinations involved occur only in words of OF origin.

12.2 The former theory of wholesale monophthonging of ESc diphthongs in -*i* discounted

Murray (1873: 52) averred that the ESc diphthongs in -*i* - /ai, oi, ui/ vowels 8, 9,10 - became monophthongs at some date not clearly specified but apparently around early to mid 15c, merging with corresponding long monophthongs (not, however, in Southern Scots or Northern English), and that a consequence was the ESc and especially MSc practice of spelling the original long monophthongs /aː, eː, ɛː, ǫː, yː/ as <ai, ei, ei, oi, ui> respectively, and conversely of spelling the original diphthongs with simple <a, e, o, etc.>. This notion was taken up in the standard textbooks of Morsbach (1896), Luick (1964) and Jordan (1934); and in e.g. Jordan and Crook (1974: §132), the supposed sound-changes /ai > aː, oi > oː, ui > uː (sic)/ are assigned a date in the late 14c. While some monophthonging of certain of the diphthongs in question did take place in particular environments about the time suggested (see for vowel 11: §6.3.2; for /ai/ > /aː/ §12.3; for /ǫːi/ > /ǫː/ §12.4), it has long been evident that, as pointed out by Heuser (1897c), Williams (1907-1910), Kohler (1967), Kniezsa (1983a and 1983b) and Mohr (1990), no wholesale monophthonging process as postulated ever took place, and none at all of */ui > uː/. The origins of the digraph-spelling for vowel 4 ESc /aː/ and similar digraph spellings for vowels 2, 3, and 7 - greatly favoured in MSc, though not unique to Sc (Kniezsa, 1983b) - have therefore been sought elsewhere: see especially Kniezsa (1983a, 1989), also Kohler (1967: 52-61).

However, while the origins of the practice of spelling long monophthongs with digraphs are to be sought earlier and elsewhere, as demonstrated by Kniezsa, yet such mergers of diphthongs and corresponding monophthongs as did take place, and the presence of etymological doublets, as pointed out in §22.3.2 below, no doubt also contributed to the tendency to treat single-letter and digraph spellings as interchangeable alternatives for either the original long vowels or their corresponding diphthongs.

A probable further contribution to the same tendency was that the inflection -*is* /ɪs > ɪz/ had its vowel absorbed by some time in the 14c (see

§13.3) after vowels in such words as ESc /hwaː/ <quha> 'who', /gaː/ <ga> 'go', /dyː/ <do> 'do'. Thus such words as OSc /hwaːz > hwɛːz, gaːz > gɛː z, dyːz > dyːz/ had their monophthongal vowels apparently represented by digraph spellings such as <quhais, gais, dois>.

12.3 Smoothing of /ai/ before front fricatives

The earlier belief was succeeded by a contrary view which turns out to be equally sweeping and oversimplified, that no monophthonging took place. On the contrary, there are strong indications of a smoothing of /ai/ to /aː/ in nME and especially in ESc, about the same time (the late 14c), as the more widespread smoothing of /au/ just described. Presumably the second (palatal) element of the diphthong was absorbed, with compensatory vowel-lengthening, by the following front voiced and perhaps also voiceless fricatives /v, f, ð, θ/, and possibly /z/ and /s/. For the first four of these environments the words affected are the verbs in *-save* (*consave* 'conceive', etc.), the noun *glave, aither* 'either', *graith* n. and v. 'equip(ment)', *faith*.[18] The nouns *consait* 'conceit', *dissait*, etc. appear to share, or follow, the same development, probably by adopting the vocalism of the corresponding verbs in *-save*.

One indication of this development is an apparent tendency for these words to manifest numerous alternative spellings in <a> almost as early as those in traditional <ai, ay>: such as <resafe> 1399 beside <resayve> 1397 'receive', <gratht> 1394 beside <grayth> 1387, <grayting> vbl.n. c1360 'preparing', from ON *greiðe* 'equipment'; for indications of the comparative frequency of these spellings, and similar indications for other relevant words, see DOST, s.vv. It is true that spellings in <a> appear alongside <ai, ay> in words in which vowel 8 pronunciations undoubtedly continued, unmerged with 4, to modSc, and they do so quite early in a few cases, but less copiously than in the group of words under consideration: e.g. <grane> 1477 beside <grayne> 1435 'grain'; < hanyng> 1472 beside <hayny[n]g> 1348 'enclosing', from ON *hegna* v.; <batit> v. p.t. 1497 'stopped for feed'. beside <bayt> n. 1473 'feed', from ON *beit*.

Much more certain evidence is the abundance of rhymes of the words in question with vowel 4: *consave, dissave, resave* etc., and *glaive*, with:

> *crave* (<crafe, craif>, etc.), *drave* 'drove', *gafe* 'gave', *lafe* (<layff> etc.) 'remainder', *save*; in e.g. Leg. S., Thewis Gud Women, Howlat, Gol. & Gaw., Wallace (very frequently), Henr., Seven S., Lynd., Rolland, etc.

In some of the same poems and others, *faith* and *graith* rhyme with *clayth* 'cloth', *rathe* 'promptly', *wraith* 'wroth', all three vowel 4. Of the nouns in *-sait* cognate with verbs in *-save (consait*, etc.), *dissait* rhymes in Leg. S. (late 14c) with *tate* (< ON *teitr*), i.e. with /ai/ vowel 8 ; but all other (later) rhymes of this set of words that I have noted are with vowel 4, with e.g. *estate, gate* 'road', *lait* 'late', *predestinat, regrate*, in e.g. *Howlat,* Dunb., Doug. However, Barbour appears to lack rhymes of these sorts, which supports the date proposed.

In contrast, other words with /ai/ before /t/ rhyme regularly with each other; thus:

bait (ON *beita*) : *lait* 'search' (ON *leita*) : *gait* pl. 'goats' (ON *geit-r*) (Henr. *Fab.* 741 f.); *plaitis* 'pleats' (ONF *pleit*) : *gaitis* 'goats' (ON *geit*), (*Christis K.* 13 f.); and compare *violate : estate : wate* 'knows' : *prelate : gate* 'road', all vowel 4 (Doug. *Pal. Hon.*, London edn, 220 f.), and *waitit* 'watched' (ONF *waitier*) : *translatit* (irregular, since vowel 4) : *slatit* 'incited' (ON **sleita*) : *batit* 'fed' (ON *beita*), (ibid., Edinburgh edn, 321 f.).

More doubtful, because of the infrequent incidence of the possible rhyming words such as *amaze, gaze, raze*, which would confirm this development, are some words or variants of words of OF origin in *-ais*, which escaped the smoothing to /ɛː/ (vowel 3) (see §14.3(9)), viz. *pais* 'weight', *praise, laisere* and *raisin*, also *abais* 'dismay' < OF *abaiss-*, and *raise* v. < ON *reisa*: note, however, <pase> 1458 beside <pais> 1434 'weight', and many other incidences of spellings in <a> from the mid 15c of this and the other words of this configuration, and the rhyme of *pase* v. 'weigh' with *brase* 'brass' and *wase* 'was' (*Gol. & Gaw.* 463 f.).

The smoothing appears not to have reached the extreme SW (see §§22.3.1, 22.3.4).

12.4 Smoothing of /ǫi/ before /s, z, ʔd/

Despite the general acceptance (following Kohler, 1967: see especially p.57 f.) that PreSc /ǫi/ and /ǫː/ were not merged as /ǫː/ (as Murray, 1873: 52 had postulated), except in the one word *jo* beside *joy* (see further §14.5(4)), there are clear indications in OSc spellings and rhymes and the modSc outcomes that such a change had indeed taken place in some words containing /ǫi/, before /s, z/ and perhaps /d/, earlier than the mid 15c or before 1375, at least in the case of the word *chose* 'choice' /tʃǫːz/, OF *chois* (which rhymes with *purpose* in Barbour). Other words that, like *chose*, clearly and copiously evidence this smoothing, though in all cases with doublets in /ǫi/, are *croce, crose*, variant of *croice* 'a cross' (OF *crois, croiz*), *jose, rejose* 'enjoy, rejoice', *voce* var. of *voice*, *vode* var. of *voyd* (for the OF *ǫi* forms of these words see Jordan and Crook, 1974: §§236, 237). For the abundant evidence of this, see the relevant entries in the several dictionaries, especially DOST. This appears to be a peculiarly nME and Sc, and especially Sc, sound-change.

Unstressed Vowels

13 The fully unstressed vowels

13.1 Unstressed final -e in PreSc

An event which influenced several of the developments described above was the deletion of earlier unstressed final -e (see below for examples). Generally reckoned to have been realised as some 'neutral' or 'colourless' vowel [ə], distinct from any stressed vowel in the system (Lass, 1992: 78), this must have persisted in PreSc till near the end of the 13c (see §§6.0, 6.3.2, 6.4, 6.5 and 7.2.2). But by the early 14c it had been deleted, apparently in all environments. For the mechanism which initiated this change, beginning seemingly in hiatical environments such as *sune and mone* (OE *sunne and mōna*), see Lass (1992: 79-80), Minkova (1991). Evidence for the early stages is not available in the scanty PreSc records.

The following evidence of early place-name forms comes from DOST. Not all of it is fully reliable, since in the dictionary entries for the earlier part of the alphabet no attention was given to the dates of the actual copies, often much later than those of the (mostly lost) originals cited (see note 3). But most of the reported forms seem to fit the dates assigned to them plausibly enough, and may be accepted as evidence, at least in the aggregate.

13.1.1 Evidence for -e#

(1) Nouns with -e# as part of the stem:

Galtunesside 1143-7 (OE *sīde*), *Kaldewelle* c1190 (OE *wella*), *Aldetuneburne* c1200 (OE *burna*), *Bradestrothirburne* c1220, *Bradewude* a1240 (OE *wudu*), *Farenyacredene* c1320 (OE *dene*); and numerous examples with <kirche, kirke> (OE *cyrice*, ON *kirkja*), s.v. *Kirk*;

(2) strong fem. nouns with inflectional -e generalised:

Holemede (OE *mǣd* fem., *mǣdwe* 'meadow') c1200 Melrose, *la blac Rode* 1291 (14c) (OE *rōd* fem.), *Redehalle* 1373-4 (OE *hall* fem.).

Contrast with both (1) and (2):

Blakepol c1190 (OE *pōl*), *Wytefeld* c1200 (OE *feld*), *Kaldestrem* c1200 (OE *strēam*), *Fitheleres flat* 1226-34 (ON *flatr* adj.);

(3) weak forms of adjectives (plurals are not available): weak forms of adjectives with monosyllabic stems are almost always spelled with <-e> in

the DOST material before the 14c, e.g. s.v. *Ald, Blake, Hare, Quhite, Rede* (see the examples cited above), and in <holleresky lech> 1214 (OE *hol* adj.) (s.v. *Lech*(*e* n.³). But after vowels, as in *resky* adj. 'overgrown with coarse grass', the *-e* had been already lost, it seems.

Apparent early 'erroneous' or 'inorganic' *-e* spellings, such as the second *-e* in <Aldetuneburne> *c*1200 or <weregehelde>? *a*1214 (OE *wergeld*) or *Caldelaue* 1218 (OE *hlāw*) are probably due to later copyists.

13.1.2 Evidence of *e*-deletion

(1) For nouns, spellings directly showing *-e* deletion include: *blod(e)wyt, bludwyt* 14c (OE *wīte*), *kyrkhalch*.

(2) Uninflected attributive adjectives, presumably formerly 'weak', become common from the late 13c: *Westfeld* 1294, *Hwytfeld* 1333, *Caldclogh* 1363, *red heuch* 1388-9, *Redhowch c*1220 (14c).

The 1317 Aberdeen Court Roll (*Aberd. B. Rec.* (S.H.S.)) shows stem *-e* deletion in the surname <wytleyir> 'fault-finder' (OE *wīte*) and the place-names <kyrcgat> (OE *cyrice*, ON *kyrkja*; ON *gata*) and <gallugat> 'gallows-road'. In the place-name <grendoun> the element <gren> represents OE *grēne* 'green'. It is perhaps merely coincidence that the nick-names <breme> (OE *brēme*) 'fierce' and <lene> (OE *hlǣne*) 'lean' appear to retain OE stem *-e*: the preceding long vowels would equally account for <-e> in these forms; contrast <red> (OE *rēad*) and <halt> (OE *halt*) in the same text.

In the *Scone Glossary* of *c*1360 (*Facs. Nat. MSS.* II. 14) the incidence of <-e> is not predictable on etymological grounds: 'organic' in <fode> (OE *fōda*), <on side> (OE *sīde*), <in yair stede> (OE *stede*), <cnaueschipe> (OE *cnafa*, OE *-scipe*), but 'inorganic' in <iere bi iere> (OE *gēar, gēr* neut.), <lauerdscape> (MDu *-schap*, ON *-skapr*), <yaime> (ON *þeim* 'them'); and verb infinitives are without ending: <grind, get, gif, cal>.

An exacter and more reliable dating for the desuetude of *-e* will no doubt one day come from the much needed fully diplomatic investigation of the vernacular material in the PreSc records.

13.2 Unstressed *-e* in 15c verse

In certain ESc and early MSc poems in iambic metre there are many instances of the juxtaposition of fully stressed syllables where regular metrical convention requires an intervening unstressed syllable. To remedy this, the editors of these poems have postulated that in such cases an unstressed vowel, usually but not always orthographically present in the text as <-e>, be supplied for pronunciation also. In some instances this is a very attractive supposition, for it regularises what would otherwise be very implausibly irregular lines: e.g. *The scharp, grene, suetë jenipere* (*Kingis Q.* st. 32); ? read: *The scharp[ë], grenë, suetë jenipere*, where *ë* indicates that an unstressed vowel is inserted in pronunciation.

This option is most regularly resorted to in the strongly English-influenced *Kingis Q.*, just quoted, most commonly for adjectives, mostly 'weak', attributively preceding a noun with an initial stressed syllable, thus we could read *ʒongë* in *The fairest or the freshest ʒong floure* (st. 40), but also in other functions, often with no etymological justification: *The pryncë than the page* (st. 9), *The rypënesse of resoune lakkit I* (st. 6), *bot fourë greis evin* (st. 21), *Nere by the space of ʒeris twisë nyne* (st. 25). Other poems in which this feature has been plausibly detected are *Quare Jel., Lanc., Bk. Chess,* and *Seven S.*, and there are rare apparent instances in Dunbar (the *ë* is the present writer's in both of the following examples): *With that annone scho send the swyftë ro* (Dunb. 143/78); *Off lusty May upone the nyntë morrow* (146/189). But there are no evident grounds for assuming this phenomenon in most other OSc verse, from Barbour onwards, in which in the main the circumstances calling for the added /-ə/ are seemingly avoided. Nor are there any grounds whatever for assuming anything of the sort in OSc prose. We are probably justified in seeing in these belated 'schwa-supplemented' forms a further 'Chaucerian' 'anglicised' feature of some OSc verse (Aitken, 1983: 26 f.), perhaps first introduced in *Kingis Q.*[18a]

13.3 The covered inflectional vowel in ESc

The covered inflectional vowel occurred in ESc (14c) *-is* /ɪs/ > /-ɪz/[19] (verb pres. t., noun possess. and pl.), and in *-it* /-ɪd/ > /-ɪt/[20] (verb p.t. and p.p.). The full story of the process of discarding the vowel must remain for some other occasion. Here I offer only a few remarks on the history of *-is*, since this bears on the history of certain of the new PreSc diphthongs in *-i* and *-u*.

From the treatment in verse, it appears that after secondary-stressed or fully unstressed syllables in such words as *cité* 'city', *dowcot, labour, profit, questioun, resoun*, the vowel in *-is* had been deleted some time before the ESc period, as also in sME, although the spellings (when not represented by the MS abbreviation for *-is*) invariably retain <i, y> or sometimes <e> till the late 16c: *Ye barowynys yus war at discord* (Barb. 1, 69); *Wittalis wyne and oyer thing* (ibid. 4, 451). In all OSc verse the ending in such cases is non-syllabic, except when the preceding stem syllable consists of a fully unstressed vowel + a liquid or nasal. In this case it seems that optionally the unstressed stem syllable rather than the inflection might undergo syncope: e.g. *eldris* 'elders', *noblis, watrys, lipnis* (pres. t. of *lippin* v. 'trust'); this is exemplified from the earliest ESc texts onwards.

After vowels, the inflectional vowel had been absorbed before ESc: see rhymes such as *rais* p.t. 'rose' : *gays* 'goes' (Barb. 7, 349 f.), and verse lines such as: *Yai bar all oyer-wayis on hand* (Barb. 1, 62).

After stressed syllables ending in sibilants there was never syncope: *facis, raisis, fechis, jugis* 'judges'. After consonants other than sibilants it seems that, by the time of Barbour, retention of the vowel in this ending was optional, though down to the 16c, unsyncopated forms seem to outnumber the syncopated. Apparent examples of syncopated forms in Barbour include: <Off king*is* y*at* aucht y*at* reawte> (1, 45); <For wnfayr thing*is* may fall perfay> (ibid. 123); <And yat y*at* suld be owr*is* off rycht> (ibid. 4, 523). Similar instances of both syncopated and unsyncopated forms can be found in all OSc poets down to the late 16c, when syncope becomes regular.

Much more research will be needed to determine (1) the dates at which the tendency to discard the covered inflectional vowels in these several cases first appears. (Jordan and Crook (1974) cite spellings from *Cursor Mundi* and Rolle apparently showing nME deletion *c*1300); (2) whether there were discriminatory conditions favouring e.g. post-sonorant over post-obstruent environments, or e.g. verbal over nominal inflections. Data to determine all of this have yet to be assembled.

This uncertainty extends to the environments with which we are here specially concerned, following the voiced palatal or velar fricative or [w], preceded by a long stressed vowel (§§6.0, 6.3.2, etc.). But it seems *a priori* quite likely that these environments would indeed favour absorption of the unstressed [ɪ] of this inflection and thus that the loss in this case would have taken place relatively early in the process (? early 14c).

PART TWO: SOURCES

14. The sources of the vowels of early Scots itemised

There follows a list of the principal sources of the vowels and diphthongs of Early Scots. As well as the principal sources, I have incorporated in the lists some minor earlier changes not discussed elsewhere.[21]

The long vowels

14.1 Vowel 1, ESc /iː/ > MSc /eːi/

This phoneme arose much as for sME, from:

(1) OE, ON *ī*, *ȳ*: e.g. *bite, bide, idill, mine, mile, fire, myre, knife, life, five, wise* /wiːs/, *quhy;*

(2) OE *i* before /ld/: e.g. *child, wild;*

(3) OE *y* (rarely *i*) before /nd/: e.g. *kind, mind, rind;*

(4) OE *īg, ĭg, ȳg, y̆g*: e.g. *nine, stile, dry;*

(5) the PreSc combination *-ethen* /ˈɛðən/ in *hyne*, 'hence', *quhyne* 'whence', *syne* 'afterwards', *thine* 'thence'; contracted to ?*[ɛɪə] (spelled <ey, ei> in the 14-15c), captured by vowel 1 after the latter's diphthongisation by GVS;

(6) OE suffix *īg, ĭg* in *haly, lady*; OE suffix *-līc, līce*, ON *-líg, líga*, in e.g. *frendly, gudly*; OE *ic* > *I*;

(7) as at §6.3.1: e.g. *bery, swelly*;

(8) OF *i* of various derivations in *devide, fine, cry; despite, engine, nice, price, denie; private, libel, giand, ryale;*

(9) OF pre-palatal *i* with treatment I (§8.2.1): e.g. *desyne* 'design', *famyle* 'family';

(10) OF suffix *-ie* of various derivations: e.g. *folie, flatterie, chevalry; navy; augury, remedy;*

(11) suffix *-i, -y* of OF origin: e.g. *mercy, satisfy;*

(12) PreSc /ɛː/ between /tʃ/ or /r/ and certain alveolars, e.g. *ryne* 'rein'. *chynge* 'change' (see §9.3(2)), and in *gryte* 'great' < PreSc /grɛːt/, OE *grēat;*

(13) of other origins: e.g. *styme, crine* (Gael *crion*) 'shrink', *dice, slype, sile* 'sew up the eyes of a hawk'.

14.2 Vowel 2, ESc /eː/ > MSc /iː/

(1) OE ē (WGmc ē): e.g. *here* adv., *mede* 'reward'; in L loans: e.g. *bete* 'beet', *crede;* ON é: e.g. *sere* 'separate(ly)';

(2) OE (Angl) ē (WS ǣ^1): e.g. *schepe, wete,* 'wet', *dede* 'deed', *drede, mede* 'meadow', *rede* v. 'read', *threde, hele* 'heel', ȝ*ere* 'year', *hering* 'herring', *evin* 'evening';

(3) OE ē, ON ǿ, by i-mutation of earlier ō: e.g. *kepe, fete* pl. 'feet', *stede* 'steed', *seme* 'seem', *grene* 'green', *quene* 'queen', *teith* pl. 'teeth';

(4) OE (Angl) ē (WS īe), by i-mutation of Gmc *au* (OE ēa): e.g. *eke* v., *nede* 'need', *here* v. 'hear';

(5) OE ēo, ON jú: e.g. *depe, quhele,* 'wheel', *lefe* 'dear', *ferde* 'fourth', *devill, chese* 'choose' (varying with *chuse,* from the rising diphthong), similarly ȝ*ede* varying with ȝ*ude* 'went', *frende, be, kne;*[22]

(6) OE ēa by 'Anglian smoothing': e.g. *bekin* 'beacon', *eke* 'also', *leke* 'leek', *heich* 'high';

(7) OE ē by lengthening of ĕ *(ĕo):* e.g. *felde, ? wele* adj. 'well', *leynd* 'to dwell', *eird* 'earth', *rerde* 'outcry';

(8) OE ĕ lengthened in final position in monosyllables; e.g. *he, me;*

(9) OE ǣ^2 final in *se* 'sea';

(10) OF *e* (AN ē) with unaltered stress:

(a) (from L ā): e.g. *clere* 'clear', *frere* 'friar', *pere,* 'peer', *appere, gre* 'satisfaction';
(b) (from L ē): e.g. *cautele* 'cunning', *decrete, complete, succede, extreme, decree, fee;*

(11) OF *ie* (AN *ē*): e.g. *febill, maintene, chere* 'cheer', *dangere, manere, rivere, ferse, chefe, pece* 'piece', *greve* 'grieve', *releve, sege* 'siege';

(12) OF *ue* (AN *ö*): e.g. *pepill, befe* 'beef', *quere* 'choir', *prefe* 'proof', *preve* v. 'prove' (cf. *prufe, pruve* vowel 7: see §4.2.2(ii)), and similarly OSc *meve* v. 'move';

(13) L *ē* (from the L p.t.s *exēmit*, etc.) in *exeme* 'exempt', *expreme* 'express', *redeme* 'redeem';

(14) OF *e* before *rC* (Bliss, 1969: §53): e.g. *perce, pert*;

(15) PreSc *ī* with OSL: e.g. *geve*, 'give' (from Scand *giva*, alongside variant with vowel 3, from OE, ON *ĕ*: see §14.3(1)), *spere* 'ask' < OE *spyrian, mekill* 'big', *cete* 'city', *menister*; *? weird* 'destiny';

(16) OE *i* with 'belated' HOCL: e.g. *chelde* 'child';

(17) OF *-é* (L *-ātem*): e.g. *bewte, cite, leaute* 'loyalty', *liberte*;

(18) OF *ée* (L *-āta*) (with doublets in *ay*: see §14.8 (5)): e.g. *allye, assignee, cuntre, journee*;

(19) OE *ǣ*^{2} (i-mutation of earlier *ā*, Gmc *ai*) split between vowel 2 and 3: evidence of 15c and 16c rhymes (esp. Heuser 1896,7), in most cases confirmed by the modSc dialect outcomes, shows that in PreSc the reflex of OE *ǣ*^{2} underwent an (? environmentally conditioned) split between vowel 2 and vowel 3, yielding vowel 2 before the voiced alveolars /d, n, l, r/, (Jordan and Crook, 1974: §48 Remark 2), either invariably or as an optional variant, in e.g. *brede* 'breadth', *sprede, clene, mene* v. 'intend', *mene* v. 'complain', *dele* n. 'deal, share' (whereas *dele* v. has vowel 3), *lere* 'learn'. In ESc and early MSc *lede* v. 'lead', *hete* n. 'heat', *swete* v. 'sweat', and the suffix *-hede* (all with original *ǣ*^{2}, before alveolars) rhyme with either vowel 2 or vowel 3; some poets (e.g. Henryson) rhyming these with vowel 3, others (e.g. *Leg. S.*) mostly with vowel 2, others again (e.g. *Wall.*) variably (Heuser, 1896,7: 342; Fox, 1981: 492). For the converse case of OE *ǣ*^{1} > vowel 3, see §14.3(5);

(20) OE *ēa* also yields vowel 2: OE *ēa* in *lefe, leve* 'permission' (OE *lēaf*), rhymes as vowel 2 (*Troy-bk., Wall.,* Dunb., Doug.); and on the testimony of the modSc dialects OE *bēan* > OSc *bene* 'bean' also had this vowel (the all but invariable modSc outcome (LAS3) is /bin/, i.e. vowel 2), but Dunbar rhymes this *bene* as vowel 3; in Douglas *lepe* v. 'leap' (OE *hlēapan*)

rhymes both as vowel 2 and vowel 3; in other 16c texts there are rhymes of *lepe* with vowel 2 (DOST, s.v.); Henryson rhymes *eith* 'easily' (OE *ēaðe*) with *teith* (Henr., *Fab.* 1083 f.);

(21) On the group of words in *-eche* /-tʃ/, whose vocalism is uncertain, including *fleche* 'flatter', *leche* (ǣ²) n. 'healer'and v. 'heal', and *speche* (ǣ¹), see Heuser (1896: 344).

It is an interesting question whether we should put these irregularities and inconsistencies down to dialect mixing in the period of the 12c settlements.

14.3 Vowel 3, ESc /ɛː/

Evidence of the distinction between vowel 2 and vowel 3 comes from rhymes (Heuser, 1896; Fox, 1981; van Buuren, 1982,1997), and many other rhymes collected by the present writer and others, and from the modSc outcomes. Sometimes the two sounds rhymed 'against' one another, e.g. Henr. *Fab.* 2022 f.: *leid* 'person' : *dreid* : *neid* 'need' (vowel 2) against *heid* 'head' : *deid* 'dead' (vowel 3); Dunb. 65/55 f.: *complene* : *derene* : *bene* 'bean' (vowel 3) against *ene* 'eyes' : *bene* p.p. : *splene* (vowel 2).

Vowel 3 does not occur word-finally. The most prolific source of this vowel is:

(1) PreSc *ĕ* with OSL: e.g. (from OE) *ete* 'eat', *mete* 'meat', *mele* 'meal', *stele* 'steal', *geve* 'give', *hevin* 'heaven', *sevin*, *spere* 'spear', *were* 'wear': (from ON) *gere* 'gear', *neve* 'fist'; (from OF) *apele*, *were* 'war',[23] *cese* 'cease', *prese* 'press', *decent*, *second*, *tresure*; OF *ĕ* before the palatal consonants, in e.g. *fenʒe*, *fene* 'feign', *menʒe* 'company'; OF *ĕ* in *beste*, *feste*; OF *ĕ* in *mese* 'serving of food'.

Other main sources are:

(2) OE *ēa*: e.g. OSc *bete* 'beat', *grete* 'great', *brede* 'bread', *dede* 'dead', *he(v)id* 'head', *beme* 'beam', *dreme* 'dream', *lefe* 'leaf', *refe* 'robbery', *ere* 'ear', *lese* 'lying', *este* 'east';

(3) OE *ĕa* + /rd/ in *berde* 'beard';

(4) OE *ǣ*²: e.g. *quhete* 'wheat', *gleme*, *lene* adj., *dele* v., *hele* n. and v. 'health, heal', *mele* v. 'tell', *ere* 'before', *leste* 'least', *clethe* 'clothe', *blese* 'blaze'; also ON *ǽ* in *sete* 'seat';

SOURCES

(5) OE ǣ¹: e.g. *rede* n. 'counsel', *fere* 'fear',²⁴ *brethe* 'breath';

With (2), (4) and (5), compare vowel 2's selections from the same sources: §§14.2(2), 14.2(19) and 14.2(20);

(6) OF ē (from L ē, ĕ) (in 'learned words', Bliss, 1969: §25): e.g. *repete* 'repeat', *remede* 'remedy', *concele, increse, creat*;

(7) OF *es* in *breme* 'bream', ? *rene* 'rein';

(8) OF *e* in hiatus, (Bliss, 1969: §50): e.g. *preche* 'preach';

(9) OF tonic *ai* before *t, d, s, r,* and *g*, and countertonic *ai* and *ei* similarly, also in hiatus, were smoothed in AN to ē (Jordan and Crook, 1974: §§233, 234; Bliss, 1969: §§21, 22, 48, 50). The OSc outcome is vowel 3: e.g. *nete*, 'neat', *trete* 'treat', *fede* 'feud', *ese* 'ease', *crese* 'grease', *pese* 'peace', *affere* 'bearing' (OF *afaire*), *egir* 'eager', *egill, dese* 'dais', *plese* 'please', *pleseir* 'pleasure', *sesoun* 'season', *dene* 'dean', *mene* 'means', *lele* 'legal, loyal'; *chere* 'chair'. *Pese* 'pease', appears, from its modSc outcomes, also to be from OF *peis*, not the cognate OE *pise*, L *pisa*.

(Some other words in the same environments retained diphthongal *ai*, yielding PreSc /ai/ vowel 8: e.g. *pais* 'weight', *praise, laisere* 'leisure', *plait* 'pleat', *consait, dissait, resait*; doublets in <e, ei, ey>, if any, appear only in late MSc, ? by borrowing from e.m.E. In most or all of this group of words the /ai/ was smoothed to /aː/ vowel 4: see §12.3);

(10) *were, weir* 'wire', la15 < OE *wīr* is due to capture of the originally vowel 1 item by vowel 3, the converse of the development which produced *chynge, ryne, gryte* with vowel 1 from antecedent vowel 3 forms: see §§9.3(2) and 14.1(12).

14.4 Vowel 4, ESc /aː/ > MSc /eː/

(1) OE, ON *ā*, in e.g. *hāt, stān, sār, gān*, ON *báðir* > respectively *hate* 'hot', *stane* 'stone', *sare* 'sore', *ga* 'go', *bathe* 'both';

(2) PreSc /a/ with OSL: e.g. (from OE, ON, MDu, Gael) OSc *make, gate* 'road', *wake, nakit* 'naked', *craig* 'neck', *craig* 'crag', *tale, fare;* (from OF, L) *plate, able, -able* suffix, *fame, pale, place, Pasche* 'Easter', *chaste, age;* (with shifted stress) *mater* 'matter', *labour, maner* 'manner', *mary* 'marry', *natioun, contemplatioun;* also before palatal consonants, in e.g. *falʒe* 'fail', *Spanʒe* 'Spain'.

Other sources include:

(3) OE, ON *ă* with HOCL; e.g. *aynd* 'breath', *wame* 'belly';

(4) OF *a* before a single consonant: e.g. *estate, case;*

(5) AN *a*, as in §9.2(2): e.g. *branche, change, danger;*

(6) PreSc /a/ before /rC/ (§11.1): e.g. *cairt* 'cart', *cairt* 'card', *airm;*

(7) by smoothing of /au/ before labials and affricates (§12.1), and of /ai/ before front fricatives (§12.3): e.g. *chafer, catioun, consave;*

(8) The suffix *-ale,* from L *-ālis,* as in *bestiale, cathedrale, celestiale, liberale, mortale,* etc., sometimes rhymes as vowel 4, as well as, more frequently, as vowel 17, *-all.*

14.5 Vowel 5, ESc /ǫ:/ > MSc /o:/

The chief source of this vowel is:

(1) PreSc /ǫ/ (chiefly from OE, ON *ŏ* and from OF, AN, and L *o*) with OSL: e.g. (from OE, ON) *hope, throte, gloming* (from OE *ǣfen-glōming*, with early shortening by reduction of stress), *lone* 'a lane', *thole* v., *before, love* v. 'praise', *dother* 'daughter' (beside *dochter,* with vowel 18), *lose* v. /lǫ:s/ 'lose' (from OE *lŏsian*: see DOST on the consonant devoicing), *nose, host* 'cough' (? from ON dial. **hoste,* beside ON *hóste*); (from OF, L) *cote* 'coat', *note, cloke* 'cloak', *approche, broche* and *loge, dispone* 'dispose', *glore* 'glory', *glorie* (id.), *restore, rose, dispose, nobill, pover* 'poor' (beside *pure* vowel 7), *sober, monument* (with stress shift), *odour, motioun, sojourn.*[25]

Other sources include:

(2) from OF *o,* before single final consonant and /st/: e.g. *close* n. and adj., *los* 'praise' n., *bost* 'boast', *host* 'army', *store* (OF *estor*);

(3) from PreSc /ǫ/ lengthened before /rC/, as follows: in a number of words of this configuration modSc, like ScStEng, has vowel 5 outcomes. The words which most regularly show this outcome appear to be *port, force* and the place-name *Forth.* Of the words investigated in LAS3, *north, storm* and *sort* appear most often to have the unlengthened vowel 18 outcomes. But these and the other relevant words in LAS3 - *born, corn, horn, worn* and

horse - display widely (and confusedly) varying results in the dialects. The apparent lengthening in *Forth*, and sporadically in words of OE origin, such as *worn*, and the failure of lengthening (in most dialects) in *sort* (OF *sorte*) seem to cast doubt on Bliss's (1969: §§39 (3), 41) belief that this was specifically an AN sound-change;

(4) By smoothing of /ǫi/ before alveolars e.g.: *chose* 'choice', *croce* 'cross' (§12.4): it is unclear whether or not the monophthongal forms *glore* (OF *gloire*, also *glore*) 'glory', *memore* (OF *memoire*, also *memore*) 'memory' and, but differently derived, *devore* (MF *devoir*) 'duty', and *closter* (OF *cloister*, also *closter*) 'cloister' are due to the OF monophthongal variants or to the same smoothing. (With *closter* 'cloister' cf. also L *clōstrum*, beside *claustrum*, and MDu *clooster*). The monophthongal form of *joy* was perhaps by OSL from (disyllabic) OF /ˈʤo.iə/ or /ˈʤo.jə/ > /ˈʤǫː.jə/, with the second syllable thereafter discarded, or by back-formation from OF *joios*, also with OSL.

14.6 Vowel 6, ESc /uː/ > MSc /uː/

This phoneme arose much as in sME, from:

(1) OE, ON *ū*: e.g. *clout, souk* 'suck', *schroud, thoum, doun* 'down', *foul, schour* 'shower', *mouth, roust* 'rust', *cow;*

(2) OE, ON *ūf-*: *dow* 'dove' (ON *dúfa*), *schow* 'shove' (OE *scūfan*);

(3) OE, ON *ūg-*, *ŭg-*: e.g. *bow* 'to bend', (OE *būgan*), *sow* (OE *sugu*), *foul* 'bird', *drouth* 'drought';

(4) OE *ŭ*, with HOCL before /nd/ in *ground*, etc.;

(5) OF, AN *u* of various derivations (Jordan and Crook, 1974: §229; Bliss, 1969: passim): e.g. *croun, sound; allow* v.[1] 'praise' and v.[2] 'credit', *flour* 'flower', *hour; noumer, count, fountain, abound, ounce, counsail; course, court; doute* 'doubt', *pouche, double, soupill* 'supple'; *avow, power; joug* 'jug'; and, with retained stress, the final syllables of e.g. *baroun, prisoun, resoun, natioun; cullour* 'colour', *labour; famous, jelous;*

(6) OF *ū* in *dour* (L *dūrus*) (Pope, 1934: §1142(i));

(7) MDu *ū* in *spout*, MDu, MLG *ū* in *stouk*, MLG *ō* in *stoup* 'drinking vessel';

(8) OE ŭ after w > ū in (w)ouk 'week' (OE wŭcu), (w)oull 'wool' (OE wŭll) (also (w)ou /(w)uː/ by l-vocalisation), s(w)ourd /s(w)uːrd/, woud 'wood' (OE wŭdu) (beside wuid, etc.); OE wi- > /wu-/ > /(w)uː/ in s(w)oum 'swim';

(9) OE ŏg- after /w/ > ū in swoun 'swoon', from OE geswogen p.p.;

(10) PreSc /yː/ vowel 7 produced by-forms, wouk, woush, etc., in vowel 6 /uː/ following a labial consonant: e.g. woik p.t. of wake (OE wōc p.t.); wuisch p.t. of wesch v. 'wash'; fusioun 'foison, plenty', modSc fuishen; fuist p.p. of fesh 'fetch'; and in muild (OE mŏld > mōld);

(11) PreSc /yː/ vowel 7 in N before /r/, /rd/ > [yːu, juː]: e.g. /fluːr/ 'floor', /bjuːrd/ 'board' (§7.3);

(12) ON ó > /uː/ in Ork and Sh (via Norn) in outhall 'udal';

(13) on vowel 6a (/ulC, ul#/ > /uː/), see §17 (l-vocalisation).

14.7 Vowel 7, ESc /yː/ > MSc /øː/

This vowel represents a merger of PreSc /oː/ in e.g. PreSc gōd 'good', dō, dōre 'door', bōte 'boot', and /yː/ from OF ū and üi: see §7.1. The several sources of PreSc /oː/ (examples cited in their later OSc forms) were:

(1) OE ō: e.g. gude 'good' (OE gōd), do v. (OE dōn), buke 'book' (beside beuk), blude, mune, cule, mure 'moor', stude 'stood', tuth 'tooth', wuisch 'washed' p.t.;

(2) ON ó: e.g. cruke, blume, lufe 'palm of the hand';

(3) MDu, MLG ō: e.g. cuit 'ankle';

(4) OE eō, treated as a rising diphthong: e.g. chuse v. , schute v.;

(5) OE eōw: truith 'truth' (beside treuth vowel 14a and trowth vowel 13);

(6) OE ŏ before /rd/, e.g. burde 'board';

(7) OF ō following a labial: e.g. bute 'boot', bro 'broth', fule 'fool', mulde 'mould', pure 'poor';

SOURCES

(8) PreSc /ṷ/ by OSL > /oː/: e.g. *dure* 'door', *lufe* 'love', *muve* 'move'; and before palatals e.g. *tuilyie* 'brawl', *ulʒe* 'oil';

The sources of OF *ū̄*:

(9) OF *ū̄* /yː/ (L *ū*): e.g. *duke, reduce, fuist* 'fust', *just, juge* n. and v. (with variants in /ṷ/ vowel 19), *cure, sure, use, confuse, music, stupid, curious, confusioun, fusioun* 'plenty', *attitude, habitude*;

(10) OF *üi*: e.g. *bruit* 'noise', *fruit, June.*

On the breaking of /yː/ before velar consonants, see §7.2.1; on the N breaking before /rd/, see §7.3; on pre-vocalic and final /yː/ from OF > /yːu/ prior to the fronting of /oː/, see §6.5.1. On the subsequent history of this vowel see §7.1. On OSc rhymes of vowel 7 with vowel 6 before /r/, see note 4.

The diphthongs in -*i*

14.8 Vowel 8, ESc /ai/ > MSc /ɛi/

(1) OE, ON word-final and pre-consonantal *ēg, ǣg, ĕg, ægg,* (§6.1): e.g. *hay, gray, way, day;*

(2) ON *ei, ey*, merging with late OE *ei* > *ai*, as in (1) above: e.g. ON *ei* > OSc *ay* 'always'; *eiginn* > modSc *ain* adj. 'own'; *beita* > OSc *bait; greiðe* n., *greiða* v. > OSc *graith* 'equip(ment)'; *leyna* v. > OSc *layne, lain* 'conceal'; perhaps *feig-r* > OSc *fey* 'doomed'; and the pronouns *thay, thaim, thair;*

(3) OF *ai* and *ei* (in AN > *ai*): e.g. OSc *gay, stay* v., *obey, aid, faith, aim, pain, pair, air* 'heir';

(4) by Treatment I of /ɛ/ or /a/ before palatal consonant (§8.2.1): e.g. *faine* 'feign', *faill;*

(5) in the suffix -*ay*, -*a*, from AN -*eie*, OF -*ée*, L -*āta*, (with doublets in -*e(e)* see §14.2(18)): e.g. OSc *allya* 1431 'ally'; *assignay* 1406 'assignee'; *causay* 'causeway'; *cuntray; entray; hak-, haiknay* 'hackney'; *ischa* 'egress'; *journay; liveray; valay,* etc.;

(6) also from OF -*eie* < L -*ēta* in OSc *monay;* and OF -*ai* in *verray* 'true'.

THE OLDER SCOTS VOWELS

14.9 Vowel 9, ESc /oi/ > MSc /ǫɪ/

(1) OF or AN *oi*, chiefly from L *au* + *i*: e.g. OSc *joy, joyous, nois* (OF *noise* /noizə/) 'noise'; also, with doublets in vowel 5, *croice* n. 'cross', *jois* v. 'enjoy'; and with variants also in vowel 10, *vois* 'voice', *void*;[26]

(2) in ? *moy* 'demure' (? < MDu *mooy*);

(3) in *boy*, of uncertain origin.

14.10 Vowel 10, ESc /ui/ > MSc /ṳi/

(1) OF *oi*, AN *ui*, chiefly from L *u* or *ō* + *i*: e.g. *point, vois* 'voice', *void* (OF *vuide*), *foisoun* (beside *fusioun* vowel 7), *poisoun* (beside *pusoun* vowel 7);

(2) by treatment I of /ṳ/ before a palatal consonant (§8.2.1): e.g. *boil* v., *join* v.;

(3) from MDu: MDu *duit* > OSc *doit* 'the small Dutch coin', MDu *hoei* > OSc *hoy* 'the type of boat'.

14.11 Vowel 11, ESc /eːi/ > /eː/ vowel 2 > MSc /iː/

The only source of this diphthong which, once smoothed to /eː/, merged with vowel 2 (as in *he* v., *me* pron., *cité*), was the PreSc combination *ēg*- before a vowel, e.g. *drey* 'to endure' < OE *drēogan, hey* 'high' < OE *hēag*- in inflected forms: see §6.3.2.

The diphthongs in -*u*

14.12 Vowel 12, ESc /au/ > MSc /ɑː/

(1) OE, ON *āw(-), ăw-*, and pre-vocalic *āg-, ăg-* (see §6.4.1): e.g. OSc *knaw* 'know', *awin* 'own', *law;*

(2) OE (Angl) *(-)ald* /ald/, lengthened to OE *(-)āld* /aːld/, with 14c breaking to /auld/;

(3) early PreSc *a* before *h* /x/: e.g. OSc *lauch* 'laugh'; *lauchter* 'laughter';

(4) OF *au* of various sources: OSc *baum* 'balm', *saumon* 'salmon', *caus, causé* 'causeway', *sauf* 'safe', *cautioun, maugré* 'ill will', *faut* 'fault';

(5) ME and PreSc [ɑu] < AN [ɑ:] before nasal combinations: e.g. *graund* 'grand', *chaumer* 'chamber', *daunger* 'danger' (§9);

(6) ON *mav-* > OSc *maw* 'gull'; ON *maðk-r* > OSc *mauch* 'maggot': OE *heafoc*, ON *hauk-r* > OSc *hauk;*

(7) l-vocalisation of /al/: e.g. *all, salt* (see §17).

14.13 Vowel 13, ESc /o̯u/ > MSc /o̯u/

(1) OE *ōw(-)*: e.g. OE *grōwan* > OSc *grow;*

(2) OE, ON pre-vocalic *ŏg-*: e.g. OE *bŏga* > OSc *bow* n. 'the weapon';

(3) OWScand *au*: e.g. ON *gauk-r* > OSc *gowk* 'cuckoo', *hlaupa* > OSc *loup* v. 'leap', *laus-s* > OSc *lous* 'loose', *naut* > OSc *nout* 'cattle';

(4) OF *ou* /o̯u/: e.g. *couper* 'to strike' > OSc *cowp* 'to overturn'; *houe* > OSc *how* 'a hoe'; *poulenet* > OSc *powny* 'pony'; *soudure* > OSc *souder, sowther* 'solder';

(5) OE (Angl) *(-)ăld* /ald/, lengthened to OE *(-)āld* /a:ld/, with 14c breaking to /o̯uld/ (see §10);

(6) early PreSc /o/ before *h* /x/ (see §6.2.2), e.g. *douchter* beside *dochter* 'daughter';

(7) the /ɛo̯u/ > /ju̯u/ outcome (vowel 14b(ii)) of vowel 14b (see §6.5.2), also with yod-absorption: e.g. *schow* 'show', *slouth* 'sloth';

(8) OE *o* + *f* [v], vocalised in PreSc: in *ofer* > OSc *owre* 'over';

(9) F *au* in the OSc name *Lowrence* 'Lawrence';

(10) l-vocalisation of /ol/: e.g. *gowd* (see §17).

It appears that at some point the first element of this diphthong converged in its realisation with vowel 19, OSc [y̯] > [ʌ], so that the predominant modSc outcome, in mainland Scotland, is [ʌu] or the like.

THE OLDER SCOTS VOWELS

14.14.1 Vowel 14a, ESc /iːu/, from PreSc [iːu] and [eːu]

The sources of this vowel are set out at §6.5.1 and §7.2, including OE *ēow* (e.g. OSc *knew*), OF /yː/ final and in hiatus (e.g. *crewel, cruel*) and PreSc /oː/ + velar consonant (e.g. OSc *beuch* 'bough', *beuk* 'book', *bewis* 'boughs').

14.14.2 Vowel 14b, ESc /ɛːu/ and /ɛo̯u/, early PreSc [ɛːu]

See §6.5.2 for the sources and history of this vowel, including OE *ēaw* (e.g. OE *dēaw*, OSc *dew*), OE *ǣw* (e.g. OE *slǣwþ*, OSc *sleuth* 'sloth') and OF *eau* (e.g. OF *beauté*, OSc *bewté*).

The short vowels

14.15 Vowel 15, ESc /ɪ/

The sources are much as in sME, apart from (3), (5), (7), (8) below. From:

(1) OE, ON *ĭ, ў*: e.g. *bid, bit, bitter; hill, hit; ill, kirk, big* v. 'build';

(2) late OE *ĭ* variant of *ĕ* before *-ht* (Jordan and Crook,1974: §69): e.g. *ficht, hicht* 'promise';

(3) OE *ī* + *nd*: e.g. *bind, find*; OE *ў* + *nd* in *pind* v. 'impound';

(4) OE, ON *ī, ȳ* shortened: e.g. *hiddillis* /'hɪdəlz/ 'hiding' < OE *hȳdelse*, inflected form of *hȳdels, wicht* 'valiant' < ON *vígt* neut., *fift* 'fifth' < OE *fífta*;

(5) PreSc *ī* shortened before *-k*: *lik* var. of *like* adj. and v., *dik* var. of *dyke*;

(6) OF *ĭ*: e.g. *riche, mittane*;

(7) PreSc /eː/ shortened: e.g. OE *hēhþu* > OSc *hicht* 'height';

(8) early ME and PreSc *ĕ* before alveolars and palatals, mostly with doublets in /ɛ/ vowel 16; e.g. *blis* 'bless', *gris* 'grass', *grit* 'great', *togiddir, widdir* 'weather';

(9) early ME and PreSc *ĕ* before /ŋg/, /ŋ(g)C/, /nC/: e.g. *bink* 'bench'; *fling, Inglis* 'English', *linth* 'length', *strinth, stink*.

SOURCES

The lowered and often centralised realisations of this vowel in the modern dialects, as [e, ë, ɛ, ë̞, ɜ], are perhaps anticipated in the the occasional OSc spellings, frequent in certain 'irregularly spelled' texts, as <e> (see Aitken, 1971: 202; Meurman-Solin, 1999, 2001: 33 f.).

14.16 Vowel 16, ESc /ɛ/

(1) OE, ON ĕ, ĕo: e.g. *bed, bell, end, kned* v., *fecht* 'fight', *cleg* 'horse-fly' (ON *klegge*), *mense* 'honour' (ON *mennska*);

(2) OF *e*: e.g. *det* 'debt', *pend* n., *serve*;

(3) OE ǣ, ĕa before alveolars and dentals: e.g. *esch* 'ash tree', *blether* 'bladder, talk foolishly', *bress* 'brass', *creddil* 'cradle', *erse* 'arse', *festin, gef* p.t. 'gave', *gether* 'gather', *gled* adj. 'glad', *gles* 'glass', *gres* 'grass', *helter* 'halter', *ledder* 'ladder', *mes* 'mass, the religious service', *peth* 'path', *Setterday, wesch* 'wash';

(4) PreSc *cha-* (with doublets in /a/ vowel 17): e.g. *chelder* 'chalder', *chelice* 'chalice', *chennon* 'canon', *cheplane, chepman* 1330- 'chapman', *cheppil, cheptour, cheritee*;

(5) PreSc /ɪ/ lowered, especially by following *n*, but also *l*: e.g. *ben* 'inwards', *denner* 'dinner', *melt* 'milt', *menoun* 'minnow', *senoun* 'sinew';

(6) PreSc /ɪ/ lowered (? as (5)): *prence* 'prince', *prencipall, sempill*;

(7) On /ai/ before /nt/, /ntʃ/, /ndʒ/ > /ɛ/, see §9.2(4): e.g. *denger* 'danger', *pent* 'paint'.

In many modSc dialects this phoneme is realised as long [ɛː] in SVLR-short environments (on SVLR see §21.2), often in contrast with vowel 15 realised as [ɛ].

14.17 Vowel 17, ESc /a/

(1) OE (Angl) ǣ, ă, ON ă: e.g. *bad* p.t. 'commanded', *sad, cast, graff* n. 'grave', *clam* p.t 'climbed', *hand, want, lang;*

(2) OF and AN *a*: e.g. *cattle, fasch* 'vex', *plank*.

THE OLDER SCOTS VOWELS

The following are more specially Sc:

(3) optionally for PreSc /ɛ/ before final /k/ (with doublets in vowel 16): *brak* 'break', *frak* 'bold', *rak* 'reck, heed';

(4) in the early PreSc combination *elgV(C)* > /ɛl(o)wV(C)/: *fallow* 'fellow', *ʒallow* 'yellow', *swallow* v.;

(5) PreSc /ɛ/ before /r/ (see §11.2): e.g. *sark* 'shirt';

(6) PreSc *we-* (mostly with less common doublets in /ɛ/ vowel 16): e.g. *twal* 'twelve' la16; modSc *wab* 'web'; *waddir, wathir* 'weather'; *wadge* 'wedge'; *walt* (also, with l-vocalisation, <waut> la15) 'welt'; *wast* la15 'west'; *wat* 15 'wet';[27]

(7) in *fallow* 1478 var. of *follow* v., *hallow* la16 var. of *hollow* adj. (if not reverse spellings for those examples in §14.18(6));

(8) on /ǫ/ > /a/ in labial environments, see §16.3.

14.18 Vowel 18, ESc /ǫ/

(1) OE *ŏ*: e.g. *god, lok* 'lock', *hollin* 'holly', *dochter* 'daughter', *hors*; ON *ŏ*: e.g. *toft*;

(2) OE, ON *ō* shortened (§3.1): e.g. *thocht, oxter* 'armpit' < OE *ōhsta*;

(3) OF *o*: *bonnet, joly, roche* 'rock';

(4) PreSc /ǫ/ in open syllable unlengthened before *k*: *clok* beside *cloke* 'cloak';

(5) of other origins: *tocher* 'dowry' (from Gael), *clog, clok* 'beetle';

(6) PreSc /a/:

(a) between labial consonant and /l/: *twol* 'twelve' la16, *wolter* 'toss about', *follow* 15 (var. of *fallow*) 'fellow', *swolly* (<swolɪt> p.t. e16) (var. of *swallow*) v.;

(b) between labials: *wob* 15 (var. of *wab*) 'web';

(7) PreSc /a/ before /n, ŋ/: *mony* 'many', *donk* 'dank'.

86

14.19 Vowel 19, ESc /ṳ/

(1) OE ŭ: e.g. *burch* 'burgh', *burn* 'stream', *come* /kṳm/: ON ŭ: e.g. *bus* 'bush', *rug* v. 'tear';

(2) OE ŭ before /nd/ and /ŋg/ (with doublets in /uː/ vowel 6): e.g. *grund* 'ground' (see §3.1);

(3) OE, ON ū shortened: e.g. *husband, but* 'without, outside', *clud* 'cloud';

(4) OF tonic *u* in closed syllables (varying with /uː/ vowel 6 outcomes): e.g. *bukkil* 'buckle', *nummer* 'number', *trubill* 'trouble', *abund* 'abound', *fund* 'found, establish', *hurt*;

(5) OF countertonic *u*: e.g. *bucket, buttoun, cullour* 'colour', *supper*;

(6) rarely, OF ǖ: *juge, justice,* beside variants with /yː/ vowel 7 (§14.7(9));

(7) PreSc /oː/ shortened: e.g. *futher* 'cart-load' (§5.3);

(8) PreSc /ǫː/ shortened before /tʃ/, /dʒ/: e.g. *bruche* 'brooch', *luge* 'lodge' (§16.2);

(9) PreSc /ɪ/ before or after a labial, when an unstressed syllable follows: e.g. *luffar* 1481 'one who lives' (var. of *liffar*); *luffer* (var. of *liver*); *lufré, luveray*, etc. (varr. of *liveray*); *muk(k)ill* 16 (var. of *mikill*) 'big'; *muttone, -ane* (var. of *mittan(e)*) 'mitten'; <apownʒowne> 1479, <oppunʒoun> 1528, <punʒoun> 15 (varr. of *opinioun*). (But *bussie* la16, beside *bisy* 'busy' is from e.m.E.)

14.20 General comments on the ESc vowels

The principal sources are summarised in Figure 13 and Index I. It will be seen that the ESc system now attained was as in Figure 14.

Of these phonemes, the principal realisations of vowels 5, 18 and 19 are specially open to speculation. Vowel 5 in most dialects, and vowel 18 in some, have by today acquired closer realisations than those shown for ESc. Quite possibly these closer realisations had been reached in the course of OSc. A half-close realisation is virtually universal for vowel 5 in C and S except the SW; quite likely the 15c smoothing of /au/ vowel 12 to [ɑː] or [ɔː], occupying the low back vowel slot, encouraged merger-avoiding raising of vowel 5. In some dialects, especially those of C and S, vowels 5 and 18 have merged, by SVLR, with the same half-close realisation.

In the 16-17c many words with /ʉ/ vowel 19 - e.g. *burch, burrowis, burn, culverin, cullour* 'colour', *cum* 'come', *custom, cut* - have occasional spellings in <ou, ow>, suggesting an approximation to the quality of /uː/ vowel 6, of which these are the regular spellings. Beyond this I know nothing to pinpoint the OSc realisation of vowel 19, except that a rounded realisation evidently persisted in the neighbourhood of labials and before nasals into the 18c (see §23 and note 62), as of course it does to this day in the modern northern English dialects. In view of these pointers, I represent vowel 19 as [ʉ].

Principal sources	Examples	late OE & Scandinavian			PreSc AN & OF		ESc		
		HOCL	SVL	OSL					
OE, ON ī	OE bītan 'bite'	iː					iː	1	
OE, ON ȳ	ON knif-r 'knife' OE fȳr 'fire'	yː							/iː/
OE ī + ld	ON mȳr-r 'mire' OE wilde 'wild'	iː			iː				
OE ȳ + nd	OE cȳnde 'nature' OF prīs 'price'	yː							
OF ī	OF crīer 'cry'								
OE, ON ē	OE hēr 'here'	eː					eː	2	
ON ǣ	ON sǣma 'to honour'	eː							
OE ēo, ON jú	OE dēop 'deep'	eːo							
OE ǣ¹	OE dǣd 'deed'	eː							/eː/
OE ǣ²	OE clǣne 'clean'	eː							
OE ē̆ + HOCL	OE fē̆ld 'field'	e – eː			eː				
AN ē	AN pēce 'piece'				eː				
OF ue, AN ō̄	AN bōf 'beef'								
PreSc ī + OSL	OE spyrian 'ask'	y – i	ɪ			eː			
PreSc ē̆ + OSL	OE stelan 'steal'	e	ɛ			ɛː		3	
OE ēa	OE dēad 'dead'	æːa					ɛː		
OE ǣ²	OE hlǣne 'lean'	æː	æː		ɛː				/ɛː/
OE ǣ¹	OE brǣþ 'breath'	æː							
OF ę̄ (L ē)	OF remę̄de 'remedy'				ɛː				
OF ai; AN ę̄	AN plę̄de 'plead'					ɛː			

THE OLDER SCOTS VOWELS

Principal sources	Examples	late OE & Scandinavian		PreSc AN & OF		ESc	
		HOCL	SVL	AN & OF	OSL		
OE, ON ā	OE stān 'stan'	aː⟶				aː	4
Gael. à	Gael càin 'kane'	⟵aː					
OF ā	OF estāi 'estate'		aː				
AN ā > au	PreSc chaunge 'change'			auː⟶	aː		
OE,OF etc. a + OSL	OE nama 'name', OF fame	a			aː⟵		/aː/
PreSc a + rC	PreSc cart	a			aː		
PreSc au smoothed	OF cautioun			au	⟶aː		
PreSc ai smoothed	OF conceiv-			ai	⟶aː		
OF ǭ	OF estǭr 'store'	o⟶		ǭː ⟵		ǭː	5
PreSc ǭ + OSL	OF protu 'throat'	o⟶⟶o̜		⟶o̜ː		⟵o̜ː	
PreSc /o̜i/ + s, z	OF vois 'voice'			o̜i		⟵o̜ː	/o̜ː/
OE, ON ū	OE mūþ 'mouth'	uː				uː	6
OE ū + HOCL	OE grūnd 'ground'	u—uː					
OE, ON ūg-, ūg-	OE fugol 'bird'	uγ—	uː				
OE ū after w	OE wucu 'week'	u—	uː				
OF, AN ū	OF counter 'to count'			uː			/uː/
	OF flour						
OE, ON, MDu ō	OE gōd 'good'	oː⟵		⟵oː			7
OE ō + HOCL	OE ford	o—oː					
OF ō following a labial	OF fōl 'fool'			oː		yː	
PreSc /ψ/ + OSL	OE duru 'door'	u⟶	u̜	⟶oː			/yː/
OF ū̄	OF sūr					yː	
OF ǖi, AN ü	OF frūit			yː yː		yː	

SOURCES

Principal sources	Examples	late OE & Scandinavian HOCL	SVL	PreSc AN & OF	OSL	ESc		
OE ēg#, ǣg#, ĕg	OE hēg 'hay', clǣg 'clay', regn 'rain'	ei						
OE ǣg ON eg ON ei, ey	OE hǣg(el) 'hail' ON gegna 'befit' ON eiginn 'own', ON leyna 'conceal'	ai ei ei ei	ai			ai	8	/ai/
OF ai, OF ei > AN ai	OF peine 'pain'	ei	ai	ai				
pre-palatal e or a (treatment I: §8.2.1)	OF/fɛɲ-/feigner 'feign', OF /faʎ-/faillir 'fail'		εi ai					
OF ǫi (especially L au + i)	noise		ǫi	ǫi		ǫi	9	/ǫi/
OF oi, AN ui (L ō or ŭ + i) pre-palatal u (treatment I: §8.2.1) MDu ui	AN puisoun 'poison' OF/buʎ-/boiller MDu duit (the coin)		ui ui ui			ui	10	/ui/
Early PreSc pre-vocalic ēg-	OE drēogan 'endure', OE hēag- 'high' in inflected forms	e:j-			$\begin{cases} \text{e:j\#} \\ \text{e:jV} \end{cases}$	ei	11	/ei/

Principal Sources	Examples	late OE & Scandinavian		PreSc AN & OF		ESc	
		HOCL	SVL		OSL		
OE āw-, āw(-), OE. ON āg-, āg-	OE cnāwan 'know', OE clawu 'claw', OE āgen 'own', OE lagu 'law'	āw- āw- āg- āg-		au		au	12 /au/
OF au AN ā > au*	OF caus 'cause', faut 'fault', PreSc graund 'grand', chaumer 'chamber'			au		au	
PreSc a before /x/ OE (Anglian) ă + ld	OE æhta (eahta) 'eight', OE ald 'old'	æ —— a a —— a:			aᵘ —— au aᵘ —— au		
OE ōw(-)	OE grōwan 'to grow'	o:w —— o:w		ǫu		ǫu	13 /ǫu/
OE. ON ōg + V. syllabic C	OE boga 'bow (the weapon)', ON logn 'calm weather'	oɣ- oɣ-		ǫu		ǫu	
OWScand au	OWScand gauk-r 'cuckoo'	au		ǫu		ǫu	
OF ǫu	OF soudure 'solder'	o —— ǫ		ǫᵘ		ǫu	
OE. ON ō before /x(C)/	OE dōhter 'daughter'					ǫu	
OE (Anglian) a + ld**	OE ald 'old'	a —— a:			aᵘ		

SOURCES

Principal sources	Examples	late OE & Scandinavian HOCL	SVL	PreSc AN & OF OSL	ESc	
OE īw	OE stī(e)ard 'steward'	i:w ——— i:u			i:u	14a
OF iu	OF riule 'rule'		? iu			/iu/
OF ū#	OF dū 'due'		? y:#			
OE ēow	OE cnēow 'knew'	e:ow ——— e:u				
OF eu	OF bleu 'blue'		? eu			
OE, ON ō + intervocalic g /ɣ/	OE plōgas 'ploughs'	o:ɣ ———		y:ɣ- ——— y:w ——— y:u		
OE ēaw	OE dēaw 'dew'	æ:aw ⎤ ⎥ ε:w		ε:u	εu	14b /ɛu/
OE ǣw	OE slǣwþ 'sloth'	æ:w ⎦			nɔ̞u ← εo̞u	/ɛo̞u/ /ɛau/
OF eau	OF beauté 'beauty'			εau	εau	

93

THE OLDER SCOTS VOWELS

Principal sources	Examples	late OE & Scandinavian HOCL / SVL	PreSc AN & OF / OSL	ESc		
OE ī	OE *biddan* 'bid'	i				
	OE *bisig* 'busy'	i				
OE ȳ	OE *hyll* 'hill'	y				15
ON ī	ON *kirkja* 'kirk'	i— i—ɪ	ɪ	ɪ	ɪ	/ɪ/
ON ȳ	ON *byggja* 'build'	y				
OE ī shortened	OE *fīfta* 'fifth'	i				
OF i	OF *mitaine* 'mitten'					
	OF *résister* 'resist'					
PreSc ě before alveolars	OE *græs* 'grass' OE *tōgædere* 'together'	æ — e	i			
PreSc ě before alveolar or velar nasal	OE *benc* (ON *benk-r*) 'bench', OE *englisc* 'English'	e — e	ε			
PreSc ē shortened	OE *lēoht* 'light'	eːo — eː — eː	ɪ			
OE ě, ěo	OE *bedd* 'bed', *cnedan* 'knead'	e	ε			
ON ě	ON *klegge* 'horsefly'	e	ε	ε	ε	16
OE ǣ before alveolars	OE *hælfter* 'halter', *glæs* 'glass'	æ — e	a — ε			/ε/
OF ě	OF *dette* 'debt'					
PreSc ā in /tʃap-/	OF *chapele* 'chapel'					
PreSc ī before /l. n. d. ʃ/	OE *binnan* 'within', OE *glida* 'kite (the bird)'	i	ɪ			

SOURCES

Principal sources	Examples	late OE & Scandinavian		PreSc AN & OF	OSL	ESc		
		HOCL	SVL					
OE æ̆, ā	OE græf 'grave',	a	a			a	17	/a/
	OE catt	æ				a		
ON ā	ON kasta 'cast'	a	a			a		
OF ă	ONF castel 'castle'		a	←— a		a		
PreSc /ɛ + rC/	ON serk-r 'shirt'	e	ɛ			a		
PreSc /ɛ/ after /w/	OE west	e	ɛ			a		
PreSc /ɛ/ + -l(o)w(e)	OE geolu 'yellow'	e	ɛ			a		
PreSc /ɛ + k#/	OE brecan 'break'	e	ɛ			a		
OE ŏ	OE god, OE dohtor	o	ǫ			ǫ	18	/ǫ/
ON ŏ	ON topt 'toft'	o		←— o				
OE ō shortened	OE pōht 'thought'	o: — o						
OF ŏ	OF bonet 'bonnet'							
OE ŭ	OE cuman 'to come'	u	u — ụ			ụ	19	/ụ/
ON ŭ	ON rugga 'to shake'	u		←— u				
OE ū shortened	OE clūd 'cloud'	u: — u						
OF and AN ū (tonic and countertonic)	AN buket 'bucket', OF bouton 'button'							
Early PreSc /o:/ shortened	OE fōt 'foot'	o:						
OE, ON ō before /k, x/	OE hōc 'hook', bōh 'bough'	o: ——— y: ——— yu(:) — ju(:) — ju: / jụ						

95

THE OLDER SCOTS VOWELS

Notes to Figure 13:
* For the suggestion that OSc forms such as <aynt> 'aunt' are directly derived from the AN monophthong, see Figure 10a.
** *Ould* forms (see §10).
Notes: HOCL = Homorganic Cluster Lengthening (§3.1.1)
          SVL = Short Vowel Lowering (§3.3)
          OSL = Open Syllable Lengthening (§4)
          For various other minor sound changes of more or less specific nME and PreSc or only PreSc provenance, see Part Two: Sources (§14).

Figure 14: Vowel-systems of ESc

front unround   back round

1   iː   19 ʉ   uː 6

2   eː   ɪ   15

3   ɛː   ɛ   16   18 ǫ   ǫː 5

                    4 aː   a 17

front round

7   yː

diphthongs

          8   ai   au 12

          9   ǫi   ǫu 13

         10   ui   iu 14a

         11   ei   ɛu, ɛǫu, ?ɛau 14b

Note: see also Figure 1.

PART THREE: VOWEL PHONOLOGY OF SCOTS FROM 1375

Between the system just set out and the system which in general still operates (though with considerable dialect variation in detail), there intervened several important series of changes. Two of these in particular drastically altered the phonological relations of the vowels of Scots, and greatly modified the realisations of the long front vowels (except vowel 7): the Great Vowel Shift (GVS) and the establishment of the Scottish Vowel-Length Rule (SVLR). And the GVS was accompanied by the smoothing, albeit at widely different dates, of two of the diphthongs listed above, /au/ vowel 12 and /ai/ vowel 8. Before I describe these major developments, it will be convenient to expound a series of changes of less general consequence, albeit far more visible in the record.

15 MF tonic and countertonic *i* adopted as vowel 2

OF or MF words with countertonic *i* in open syllables were discussed above (§4.2.1). Apparently differently derived is a considerable number of words in which MF tonic *ī* /iː/ with unshifted stress appears in 15c Sc or later as vowel 2, ESc /eː/ > MSc /iː/, e.g. *habeit*, in most cases with a doublet in 'regular' vowel 1, ESc /iː/ > MSc /eːi/, e.g. *habyte*; and in certain cases also, following the fronting of the stress, with a further variant with unstressed /ɪ/ vowel 15, e.g. *habitt*. The words in question are all relatively late adoptions (late 13c or later) as, no doubt, 'mots savants'. The explanation seems to be that MF /iː/ in these words was identified with Sc vowel 2 as this was being raised from [eː] to [iː] by the Great Vowel Shift (§20). A number of the resultant forms with vowel 2 are on record from the 15c, in one instance mid 15c, which would suggest that the shift of this vowel was well under way or completed by this time.

The following list of examples (of variants in vowel 1, vowel 2, and vowel 15) is not exhaustive:

baptime la15 and *bapteme* la15; *ingyne* e15 and *ingene* 1457 and *ingen* la15; *reconsile* 1532 and *reconcyl* 1567 (*reconseild* rhymes with *reweild* 'revealed' e17); *assise* e15 and *assese* 1576; *advertise* and *adverteist*, *advertesit* p.p. early 16c, *avertese* 1525; *baptise* and *baptese* la16, modSc *bapteese*; *chastise* and modSc *chasteese* la19; *rewife* c1550 'revive' and *reveif* 1568 (rhymes with *beleeue*, *releeue*, A. Hume c1590); *oblige* 1379 and *obleg(e)* 1526; *oblis* la14 and *oblys(e)* 1385 and *obleiste* p.p. 1448; *oblisch* la16 and *obleisch* 16-17; *attyre* and *atteir* 16; *retyre* ? 1548 and *retere* e16; *condyte* c1400 and *condeyt* la15 'conduct'; *contrite* la14 and *contreit*[27a] (rhymes with *sweit, compleit*, Dunb.); *elyte* 15 and *eleit* la16; *lyte* 15 and *leit* la16

(OF *elit*); *habyte* (Wynt., in rhyme, e15) and *habeit* e16 and *habitt* la14; *inveit(t)* 17 'to invite'; *profyte* la14 and *profeit* 16 and *proffet* 1391; *respyte* la14 and *respeit* 1499 and *respitt* e16; *sprete* 15 (cf. *sperit* and *spirit*, §4.2.1(ii)); *item*, *ytem* and modSc *eetim*; *title* la15 and *teetle* la19; modSc *cheenie* 'china'; *cypher* and *ceyphre* 1568, *ceepher*, *seefer* 19 (OF *cyphre*); modSc /ˈmaɪzərt/ and *meeser* 'miser'; *cite* la16 and *ceit* la16; *type* and *teep* 19.

Perhaps *gyle* 'wort' 1264, *geill* 16 /giːl/ (MDu *gijl*) was similarly treated.

But not all items which would seem to have been liable to this development in fact show it: e.g. *delite*, *descrive*, OSc *scrive* 'to inscribe' (of which modSc *scrieve* is perhaps not a direct variant: see SND), *despise*, *despite*, *divise*, *exile*, *expire*, *facile*, *paradice*.

In some other words OF or MF countertonic *i* has yielded /iː/ > /eːi/ vowel 1 in ME and OSc. and some of these too show Sc doublets in /eː/ > /iː/ vowel 2:

finale la14 and modSc *feenal*; *libel* 15 and *lebell* 1625, *leebel* 19; *licence* 1442-3 and *lecence* 1423, modSc *leesence*, *leeshence*; but not e.g. *finance*. For some further examples, see J. Craigie (1941: lxix).

16 Some combinative changes

16.1 ESc /ṷ/ > /ɪ/

A large body of words containing vowel 19 /ṷ/ in ESc displays variants in vowel 15 /ɪ/ from the 15c onwards:

(1) in some of these the /u/ is original (e.g. in OE *hnutu* 'nut'); in others it is by PreSc shortening of earlier /oː/ (e.g. in *futher* 'cart-load', *fut* 'foot') (see §5.3); both of these consequently display variants in /yː/ vowel 7 (vowel 7 arising either from original (OE etc.) *ō*, or by OSL of PreSc /ṷ/), e.g.:

uther la14 and *ud(d)er* 15-16 (vowel 19), and modSc *ither* la18 (vowel 15), and EC <aither> la19 (implying earlier /yː/ vowel 7 > /øː/ > EC /eː/); and similarly *brither* la18, earlier *bruther*, etc.; *fidder* 16 'cart-load'; *mither* la17 'mother'; *fuit* la14 'foot' and *futte* 16 and *fit* 16 (modSc /fɪt/); and similarly *nit* 17 'nut'; *pit(t)* la16 'put'; *widd* la15 and *wuid* la18 and *wudd* /wʌd/ la18; *guttar* 15 and *guit(t)er* la17 (modSc /'gøtər/) and *gitter* 19 (OF *gutere*);

(2) words deriving from /ʉ/ in an open syllable and thus potentially yielding vowel 7 (following OSL to /oː/), but with no evident indication of a vowel 7 variant, e.g.:

dusane 15 and *dousane* la15 and *dissone* la15, modSc *dizzen; huny* 15 and *hinnie* la16 'honey'; *husy* 15 and *hizzie* la16 'hussy' (reduced from *huswif* < OE *hūs-wīf*); *somir* la14 and *simmer* 16 'summer' (OE *sumor); similarly *sommer* and *simmer* 16 'pack-horse'; *sut(t)ell* la14 and *sittel* la16 'subtle'; *ingan* 16 and *onʒeon* la16 'onion'; *sone* and *sin* la18 'son' (OE *sunu*); and numerous others, such as *billet* 'bullet', *kipple* 'couple', *sipper* 'supper', *tribble* 'trouble';

(3) a smaller group of words lacking the conditions for *u* > /oː/ (vowel 7):

din e16 and *dun* (OE *dunn*), *sin* la16 and *sun* (OE *sunne*), *sinder* and *sunder, sindry* la14, *kimmer* 17 and *cummer* 'godmother' (OF *commere*), *winder* la16 'wonder'.

Sets (2) and (3) appear to disqualify Luick's (1903: 117) theory of an unrounding and shortening of PreSc /yː/ vowel 7.[28] It seems rather that the /ʉ/ doublets of set (1) are by early PreSc shortening of /oː/ to /ʉ/. The presence of the following nasals and/or preceding or following labial consonants in most, though admittedly not all, of the above suggests that the PreSc or ESc /ʉ/ in these words has been captured by nasalised or labialised allophones of vowel 15. The failure of the change to manifest itself in some words of apparently similar conditions, such as *buit* 'boot', *buist* 'box', *humill* 'humble', *money*, is perhaps to be set down to incomplete lexical diffusion. The spelling indications suggest a 15c date for this development.

16.2 /o̜ː/ vowel 5 before /tʃ/ and /dʒ/ shortened to /ʉ/ vowel 19 in ESc

Prior to the 15c, /o̜ː/ vowel 5 followed by the palato-alveolar /tʃ/ or /dʒ/ was raised and shortened to /ʉ/ in the following words of OF origin: *broche* and *bruche* 15, *crochet* and *cruchet* 15, *loge* and *luge* 1434, *motion* and *mudgeoune* la16, *sojourn* and *sudiorne* 15.

THE OLDER SCOTS VOWELS

16.3 /ǫ/ vowel 18 unrounds to /a/ vowel 17

Beginning in the first half of the 15c many words containing vowel 18 /ǫ/ acquired doublets in /a/, when a labial followed or, in some words, preceded, e.g.:

> *aff* 16 beside *off*, *aft* 1455 beside *oft*, *cap* beside *cop* 'cup' (ONhb *copp*, ON *kopp-r*, MLG and MDu *cop(p)*), and similarly *craft* 'croft' la16, *laft* la16, *saft* la16, *stamack* la18, *tap* 'top' 16, *thrapple* 'windpipe' 17, *bannet* 'bonnet' 1490, *parritch* la18, *patt* 'pot' la16.

Presumably in this environment /ǫ/ approximated to a lip-rounded allophone of /a/ and was then 'captured' by the /a/ phoneme. By no means all words apparently possessing the qualifying conditions in fact opt for this change: thus e.g. *fon, foly, mok, groff* 'coarse' show no doublets in *a*.

16.4. OSc /ǫ/ > /ǫu/ before velar stops and voiceless labials

In the course of the 15c OSc /ǫ/ vowel 18, either original or less often by shortening of vowel 5, developed a [u] glide on to following velar stops /k, g/ and voiceless labials /p, f/ (? only final), yielding vowel 13 /ǫu/:

> <choukis, cholkis> 'quinsy', 'jougs, the instrument of punishment' (var. of *chok*, itself a var., with shortened vowel, of *choke*): and similarly <louk, loug> e17 and *lok, loke* 'lock'; <rowkis, rolkis> pl. 1514 and *rok* 'rock'; <dowg> 1662, modSc /dʌug/ 'dog'; <jowggis> 1587 and *jogis, joggis* 'jougs, the instrument of punishment'; <dolp> 1513, <doup> 1641 'buttock' (MDu, LG *dop* 'egg-shell'); <grou(i)ff> 1610 and *groff* 'coarse'; <houf, holf> 1565 and *hoffe* la17 'enclosure' (Du, Flem *hof*); <houp> 1496 and *hope* n. 'expectation'; <howp> 1606 and *hop, hope* 'valley'; <howp> 1593 and *hop* 'the plant'; <houpe> 1573 and *hope, hop* 'heap'; <sowp, solp> la15 *soupe* 'to weary', f. *sopit* 'sunk (in sleep, etc.)' (L *sōpītus*); <sowp> 16 and *sop*.

16.5 Vowel 3 > /ɪ/ vowel 15 before /v/ or /z/ followed by a syllabic liquid or nasal consonant

About the first half of the 16c, and certainly before the general merger of vowel 3 with vowel 2 (§20.8.3) (or, probably, of vowel 4 with vowel 3), vowel 3 ESc /ɛː/, by then realised as approximately [eː], shortened to /ɪ/ vowel 15 (on the quality of this vowel, see §14.15) before /v/ or /z/ followed by a syllabic liquid or nasal consonant:

VOWEL PHONOLOGY FROM 1375

$$e: > \iota \ /\text{-} \ \begin{Bmatrix} v \\ z \end{Bmatrix} (\partial) \begin{Bmatrix} l \\ n \\ r \end{Bmatrix} \#$$

The words affected are:

divill, diwil 16 'devil' (doublet of OSc vowel 2 /'de:vl/ > /'di:vl/, the vowel 3 form having arisen from OE *dēofles*, inflected form of OE *dēofol*, with Pre-Cluster Shortening and later OSL of the resultant *ĕ*); *niver* 1615 (var. of *never*); *niffer* 1666 'barter' (a derivative of *neve* n. 'fist': see DOST); and the modSc forms *hivven* 'heaven', *siven* 'seven', *rizzon* 'reason', *sizzon* 'season'.

The OSc and modSc form *niv* /nɪv/ (<nive> la16, <niv(v)e> 17) is perhaps a back-formation from OSc *nevel*, modSc *nivvel* 'blow with the fist'. The outcome of this seems everywhere to have merged with vowel 15 /ɪ/. Alongside these forms, there also exist variant forms with unshortened vowels which pursue the regular development of vowel 3, merging with vowel 2 and yielding modSc /i:/, or alternatively yielding /e:/ or the like, with vowel 4: see the entries in CSD.

16.6 Localised developments

I have not here attempted to treat of the many localised developments which certainly arose in the OSc period, of NE Scots and of other dialects, such as the NE developments of allophonic sub-sets treated by Macafee (1989: 433-6); nor the NE outcome of ESc /a:/ as /jɑ:/ instead of regular /e:/ before velar consonants, /v/ (representing earlier /w/: see §6.4.0) and /rC/, apparently by breaking in this environment of the /a:/ to /au/ prior to GVS, in e.g. modSc (NE) /njɑ:kɪt/ *naked*, /bl(j)ɑ:v/ (var. of *blaw*) 'blow', /tjɑ:v/ (var. of *taw*) 'to prepare leather', /kjɑ:rn/ *cairn*: see Dieth (1932: 91).[29]

17 l-vocalisation (LV): /a/, /o̧/, /u̧/ + tautosyllabic /l/ > /au/, /o̧u/, /u:/ respectively

Though its only phonological effect was to greatly increase the lexical inventories of the diphthongs /au/ vowel 12, /o̧u/ vowel 13 and the long vowel /u:/ vowel 6, this series of changes did produce visible effects on OSc spelling practice (though these were by no means as pervasive as the digraph spellings in <-i, -y> for vowels 2, 3, 4, etc.) and some effect also on rhyming-practice. This rather common type of sound-change has occurred more than once in the history of both French and English: the alveolar-lateral consonant [l] ceases to be fully articulated, the front of the tongue failing to make contact with the alveolum, thus leaving a back vowel, commonly [u] when the [l] had been velarised. In the present case, when /l/ was preceded in a stressed syllable by one of the three short back vowels (including /a/ vowel 17 as a back vowel) - a circumstance which might well have induced velarisation of the /l/ - and followed by another consonant or by a word boundary (so that it fell within the same closed syllable as the vowel),[30] it vocalised to [u]:

$$/a, \varrho, \underset{\sim}{u} + l \left\{ \begin{matrix} \# \\ C(V)C \end{matrix} \right\} / > /au, \varrho u, u: \left\{ \begin{matrix} \# \\ C(V)C \end{matrix} \right\} /$$

(1) /al/ > /au/, merging with vowel 12: thus /fal/ > /fau/ <faw>, /halx/ > /haux/ <hauch>, etc., in e.g.:

> *all, fall, salt, hals* 'throat', *half, balk* 'beam', *calk* 'chalk', *halch* 'haugh, river-meadow', *haud* 'hold' (see §10), *almous* 'alms', *almeral* 'admiral';
>
> rhyming with /au/ vowel 12, as in *aw* 'owe, own', *knaw, faut, caus, hauk* 'hawk';

(2) similarly, /ǫl/ > /ǫu/, merging with vowel 13: thus /knǫl/ > /knǫu/ <know>, /hǫlk/ > /hǫuk/ <howk>, etc., in e.g.:

> *holl* 'hollow', *knoll, folk, holk* 'dig', *bolt, golf, colpindach* 'young cow' > *cowpendach*; also, unlike /al/, before /d/, in e.g. *gold, mold* 'earth';
>
> rhyming with /ǫu/ vowel 13, as in *bow* 'the weapon', *grow, gowk* 'cuckoo', *nout* 'cattle';

(3) /ul/ > /u:/, merging with vowel 6: thus /ful/ > /fu:/, /fulθ/ >/fu:θ/, etc., in e.g.:

> *full, pull, wolf, pulpit, culter* 'coulter', *multure, pultrie* 'poultry', *schulder, fulth* 'plenty';
>
> rhyming with /u:/ vowel 6, as in *cow, out, loud*.

The earliest reliably attested direct evidences of these changes I have found are the spellings:

> <kaw> Ayr 1438 (beside *call*); <Hawch> 'meadow' Peebles 1457; <Auche> ibid. 1464 (beside *halch*); <how> 'hollow' NE 1459;

<Sydwawdyk> 'side-wall-dyke' Peebles 1462; <bauk> 'beam' la15; <cawk> 'chalk' la15; <pow> 'pull' la15.

Reverse spellings attesting this change include:

<half> (var. of *haf*) 'to have'? 1425; <calse> 'causeway' Glasgow 1434 (beside <causay> Ayr 1448); <walle> 'the measure of weight'? *a*1434 (beside <waw>); <nolt> 'cattle' Ayr 1437 (beside <nout>) (ON *naut*); <chalmer> 1473 (beside <chawmer> 1456) 'chamber'; the place-name <Falkirk>[31] 1458, earlier <Fawkirk, Faukirk> 1298, 'variegated church'; <saulfgarde> 1473, <salue conduct> 1474; <pulder> 'powder' 1479 (beside <pouder>) (OF *poudre*); <haltyn> 1488 (beside <hautane>) 'proud'; <wall> la15 (beside <waw>) 'wave'; <bollis> 1516 (beside <bowis>) 'ox-bows';

these and other such reverse spellings are common and widespread thereafter.

Certain purportedly earlier-dated 'evidences', e.g. those advanced by Girvan (1939), are for various reasons inadmissible. The collections of early documents to 1410, by Slater (1952) and MacRae (1975), contain no such evidence.[32]

Rhymes of the type <all> : <knaw> (vowel 12), <bolt> : <nowt> 'cattle' (vowel 13), <pow> (LV variant of *pull*) : <Iesu> (vowel 14a), occur from the latter part of the 15c (in *Wall*. 15c and in Douglas and other 16c poets, especially in comic and satiric poems); Sempill (1572 *Sat. P.*, 30, 30 f.) rhymes <wais> 'walls' : <fais> 'falls' : <cais> 'cause'.

It looks therefore as if these changes became established in the late 14c or early 15c but no earlier, notwithstanding previous incidences - <hawhes> 'haughs' Kelso *c*1240, and <hafthrepland> 'half-' 1383 - perhaps casual or idiosyncratic. If their place of origin was south Scotland or, as the modern dialect reflexes would permit us to believe, northern England, they doubtless took time to spread throughout the country. This might explain why Robert Henryson, supposedly of Fifeshire origin, unlike his contemporary, Hary the Minstrel, has no rhymes consequent on these changes.

As well as the new reverse spellings just exemplified for vowels 12, 13, and 6, some words display, mostly rather later, equivalent spellings which are in effect blends of the new spellings with the original, pre-l-vocalisation, spellings: <aul> or <awl> alongside <al> and <au, aw> for vowel 12; <oul, owl> beside <ol> for vowel 13; <oul, owl> and, on the analogy of vowel 13, <ol> for vowel 6, e.g.:

<haulk> 1599 (beside <halk>), <noult, nowlt> 1527 (beside <nolt>), <nowldir> 1562 (beside <nolder>) for *nowther* 'neither', <cowlp>

1572 (beside <cowp>) 'to trade', <oulk, owlk> 1480 and <olk> 1491 (beside <ulk>) 1531 for <ouk> 1444 'week', and similar variant spellings of <bouk> 'carcass' and <pouder> 'powder'.

Reverse spellings of any of these types do not however appear in all of the 'qualifying' words: so, for example, *<schall> does not occur for the very common word *schaw* 'to show', nor *<lalte> for *lawt*é 'loyalty', nor does *<lolp> occur for *loup* 'to leap', whereas <rolp> for *roup* 'to shout' is common from the 15c.

There are discussions of the stylistic distributions of spellings directly representing LV forms, and of the occurrences of these forms in rhyme with vowels 12, 13 and 6, in Aitken (1971: 195-7; and Aitken 1983: 43-45). In brief, certain forms, including *hauch, how, fouth*, are as common as, or more common than, the older spellings with <l> - <halch, holl, fulth> - and otherwise show no specialisation of distribution; whereas others, including *faw* 'to fall', *stown, stoun* 'stolen', *pow* 'to pull', are favoured by particular texts and specific genres only, such as 'low-life' verse and 'semi-literate' prose, but in general are used less often than the older traditional spellings <fall, pull, stollin>.

Unvocalised doublets, surviving alongside some of the forms that underwent LV, are visible in many rhymes of words such as *all, fall, small, thrall* with the Latinate suffix *-all* (L *-ālis*) in such words as *bestyall, celestiall, special*, etc.: there is no indication that this suffix ever underwent LV, and the verb *sall* 'shall', which also participates in this set of rhymes, never displays a vocalised form *<saw> in OSc. One of the poets who frequently rhymes in this manner, Henryson, has no vocalised forms, in rhyme or otherwise. But others, such as Dunbar, Walter Kennedy, Douglas and Lyndsay, employ both types of rhymes, the unvocalised type especially in their more serious verse, but rhymes displaying vocalisation only in 'overtly colloquial' passages (there are four sets of rhymes of the latter type in Dunbar and Kennedy's *Flyting*, for instance).

The MSc unvocalised forms of *all*, etc. were not mere verse archaisms, useful as rhymes. Such forms survive to the present day. SND records /al/ as well as /ɑː/ *all*, in the fringe dialects, Sh, Ork, Cai, Argyll and Uls; EDG has /kal/ as well as /kɑː/ *call* in S. Ayr and Kcb; and modern Antrim Sc has both vocalised and unvocalised forms of *all, call, fall*, etc., and /kalv/ for *calf, calve*. Also /fʌl/ beside /fuː/ *full*, /pʌl/ beside /puː/ *pull*, are widespread throughout Scotland and Uls as 'free variants' in single idiolects; as noted below, of the pair /*buː/ and /bʌl/ *bull*, the animal, only /bʌl/ survives. How long other unvocalised forms survived after LV is not evident.

When the /l/ is intervocalic, a primary condition of this change is absent (that the /l/ should be in the same closed syllable as the vowel). In such cases LV does not occur: so it fails with e.g. *allay, bal(l)ance, ballet* 'ballad', *ballok* 'testicle', *bollyn* 'swollen' (but see below), *college, col(l)er* 'collar', *dolour* 'sorrow', *buller* 'bubble', *bullet, cullour*, etc. However, *boldin* beside *bollin* 'swollen', with d-epenthesis, has vocalised <bowdin> /'bǫudən/; and beside *stollin* the vocalised <stoun> /stǫun/ results from previous contraction of the suffix syllable. There are also failures when the conditions are apparently met. For some of these explanations may be conjectured: perhaps in *culverine* the fronting of the stress did not come about till after LV; some may reflect an earlier intervocalic environment, lost by syncope, e.g. *culroun* 'rascal', earlier *culleroun*; *bull* 'papal bull' had, according to rule, a doublet <bow> /buː/, whereas *bull* 'the animal', as noted above, had not, perhaps by reinforcement of the form with retained /l/ from the existing doublet <bule> /byːl/ vowel 7, and similarly *coll* influenced by *cole* 'coal'. The explanations of other cases of failure of the change are less apparent: *alderman, als, alsa, alswa* 'also', *alway, calfat* 'caulk', *bulget, bulwerk*, etc.

18 Smoothing of /au/ vowel 12 to [a̰ː] or [g̰ː], in early MSc

Shortly after vowel 12 /au/ had its lexical inventory enlarged by accretion of l-vocalised /al/ > /au/ near the beginning of the 15c, it became smoothed to [a̰ː], merging with labialised vowel 4 [a̰ː] (> [aː] in the N, etc.; [ɑː] or [ɔː] or the like elsewhere) in those dialects in which this allophone did not undergo raising by the Great Vowel Shift (see §20.9), or constituting a new low back long monophthong on its own in the remaining dialects. Apparent direct evidence of this monophthonging occurs from the late 15c, e.g. <a> 'all' 16, <badkyn> 'baudkin, embroidered cloth' 16, <crais> pl. 'crows' e16, etc. There is abundant evidence of the merger of /au/ vowel 12 with labialised vowel 4 in the shape of spellings such as <wawpyn> 'weapon' ['wa̰ːpən] (see §20.9 for a full list) in which graphemes historically appertaining to vowel 12 are appropriated by vowel 4. Since there is no reason to suppose that vowel 4, in either its labialised or unlabialised diaphones, was ever anything but a monophthong, which it was in ESc and remains everywhere today, these spellings must signify monophthonging of vowel 12 to [a̰ː] (> /ɑː/, etc.) (rather than diphthonging of vowel 4).

The modern dialects realise the outcome of vowel 12 invariably as a monophthong, as [ɑː], [ɒː] or [ɔː], or, in some dialects of N, Ork and Sh [aː], both in localities in which labialised vowel 4 is merged with it and those other localities in which vowel 4 and vowel 12 remain entirely distinct.

Major developments affecting the ESc long monophthongs

19. Some comments on the testimony of *The Linguistic Atlas of Scotland* vol. III

The following sections depend heavily on the data offered by *The Linguistic Atlas of Scotland* vol.III (LAS3). However, because what is presented in LAS3 is not invariably a straightforward reproduction of the fieldworkers' notes, the following comments bearing on the trustworthiness of LAS3's reports seem worth making.[33]

(1) In a few cases highly specific indications of vowel quality by fieldworkers have been replaced by less specific or 'broader' representations in LAS3. Some (perhaps most or all) of these are to be taken as revisions by an editor who is the same person as the fieldworker (viz. J Y Mather (JYM)). Thus for Denholm, Hounam, Teviothead, Edgerston (all fieldworker JYM) the fieldworker-reported [ëi] in *knee, key, gey,* etc. appears in LAS3 as [εi]; similarly, the fieldworker's (JYM) [i̠ᶦl] in *heel,* etc. in Kilrea appears as simply [i]. On occasion several slightly variant representations of apparently the same phoneme in the same environment are regularised to one representation: e.g. in Cromarty (fieldworker JYM) [ęᵊ], [ę̇], and [ę̇ˈ] before /l/ all appear as [εi].

None of these adjustments appears to falsify the height relations of the several phonemes, which are crucial to some of the arguments below.

(2) There is some inconsistency in the treatment of what the fieldworkers heard as epenthetic vowels before liquids: e.g. in Denholm and Hounam JYM as fieldworker heard [eᵊ] before /l/ in *pale, pail,* etc., but rendered this as [e·] in LAS3, yet for the intervening locality Oxnam (fieldworker CMacG) LAS3 shows the epenthetic vowel in [eᵊ]. Similarly in Ballywalter and Newtonards, N. Ireland, the fieldworker's [ęᵊ] and [eᵊ] appear as respectively [ę] and [e·]; Mostly, it seems, epenthetic vowels before /r/ are not shown; but there is an exception for Kirkinner, Wgt (fieldworker JSW). In Denholm, Hounam, etc., JYM has, as in the case of the pre-/l/ context, substituted for the epenthesis the length sign: so [iᵊ] appears as [i·]. On the assumption that these are considered revisions, I accept all of these LAS3 reports at face value in the discussions below.

(3) The Linguistic Survey of Scotland's fieldworkers operated with a three-term system of vowel-length: [V:] long, [V·] half-long, [V] short. As a normal rule, LAS3's editors operated a two-term system: [V·] long, [V] short. They do not tell us how they treat the fieldworkers' [V·]. Such inspection of the fieldworkers' reports as I have been able to carry out

suggests that fieldworkers more often denote vowels as fully long or fully short than half-long. Except in the case of (4) below, for the most part the fieldworkers' half-longs are represented in LAS3 as fully long (represented in LAS3 as [V·], but in my discussion as [V:]). There are however exceptions to this, many of which may be conjectured to be JYM's revisions as editor of his own fieldworker reports (perhaps as afterthoughts, or perhaps with the help of tape-recordings): so for Cromarty, in *beef*, the fieldworker's (JYM) [i·] appears as [i], but his *most* with [e] appears in LAS3 as [e· ¹]. For Newhaven (fieldworker JCC) [i·] before /l/ and /n/ is rendered in LAS3 as [i] but other vowels - [e·] etc.- are left unchanged as long. For Uptown Nairn JYM as fieldworker has [e·] in *pane, pain*, etc., but [e] in LAS3; and [ẹ·] in *gate, gait,* etc. as fieldworker, but [e] in LAS3. With slight hesitation I have accepted all of these as accurate revisions.

Cases of the representation of fieldworkers' shorts as longs in LAS3 seem to be rare. I have noted one case in Denholm, Hounam, etc., in which JYM has represented final [e] in *away, day, toe,* etc. as [e·] in LAS3.

But such cases are exceptions. It appears that in the great majority of instances LAS3 faithfully represents fieldworkers' decisions as to vowel-length, treating their half-longs as longs. It seems reasonable to treat exceptions to this as reliable revisions, except for the matter discussed in (4).

(4) Certain of the Scots diphthongs, vowel 1 especially, but also vowel 9 and occasionally vowel 8 word-final, were in many cases (in the case of SVLR-long vowel 1, possibly most cases) heard by the fieldworkers as having long or half-long first elements. Only exceptionally are the long first elements shown in LAS3: e.g. Creca's [ɑːɪ] appears as [ɑɪ], Westerkirk's [eːi] in *aye, gey, hay,* etc. (vowel 8) as [ei], but Canonbie's [ẹːi] in the same group of words as [ẹ·i] in contrast with [ẹi] in *die, eye, key,* etc. (vowel 2, originally 11), (but Canonbie's [ẹːi] in *boil, mile,* etc. as [ẹi]!). Likewise half-long first elements are generally given as short: thus [ɑ·e] in many dialects appears as [ɑe], [a·ɪ] as [aɪ], [o·ɪ] as [oɪ], and so on. This is especially relevant in considering the history of vowel 1 (see below).

A difficulty of a different kind in interpreting LAS3's results is occasioned by the rather common phenomenon which I propose to call 'lexical misplacement' - when a lexical item selects not the phoneme which one would expect from its etymology but some other. For example, in the dialect of Creca, Dmf, the word 'fruit', which etymologically one would expect to share the phoneme /y/ with 'boot' and 'root', has instead the vowel /u/ of 'about' and 'out'; in the neighbouring dialect of Gretna Green, however, it has the 'correct' phoneme /ø/ like 'boot' and 'root'. Here the explanation of the 'erroneous' /frut/ is doubtless simple 'dialect mixture' or 'interference' from a neighbouring dialect, in this case the Standard Scottish

English dialect. In Kilconquhar, Fife, with /eː/, which here would regularly represent vowel 8, we find *bait* (a regular vowel 8 word), *gait* (vowel 8), *wait* (vowel 8) but also *gate* (which etymologically belongs to vowel 4). However, in neighbouring dialects vowels 4 and 8 regularly merge before /t/. So this is an instance of borrowing into a dialect with a greater number of phonemic distinctions than the lending dialect, with the result that the speaker making the borrowing has to decide between two phonemes in his own dialect to which to allocate the borrowed item and makes the etymologically 'wrong' choice. Still another way in which apparent irregularities of lexical placement are likely to have come about is that of 'incomplete lexical diffusion', in cases of ongoing lexical split and merger, when only some of the items have as yet transferred their allegiance. In the rather broad treatment of the systemic arrangements of phonemes attempted below I have mostly ignored apparent anomalies of lexical placement of these sorts, accepting as regular either the phonemic choices of the majority of the lexical items, or, on occasion, what seems to be the normal phoneme selection for the dialect group to which the dialect in question seems to belong.

20 The Great Vowel Shift (GVS)

20.1 Outline

In late sME the sound-changes generally known as the Great Vowel Shift (GVS) affected the long stressed monophthongs in two separate but matching series, for front and back vowels. The long vowels of late sME, corresponding to the ESc long vowels, were as in Figure 15.

Figure 15: Late sME long vowels

	front			back	
ESc 1 =	iː	*time*	*about*	uː =	ESc 6
ESc 2 =	eː	*queen*	*moon*	oː =	ESc 7
ESc 3 =	ɛː	*eat*	*before*	ǫː =	ESc 5
ESc 4 =	aː	*name*	*whole*	ǫ̞ː =	ESc 4

In outline, in Midland and Southern English, the GVS, beginning in the 14-15c, raised (closed the articulation of) the three lower vowels in both the front and the back series and diphthongised the close vowels /iː/ and /uː/ respectively, so that:

(1) (a) [iː] > [ɪi] > [əi] and eventually modEng [aɪ],
(b) [eː] > [iː],
(c) [ɛː] > [eː] but thereafter merged with one or other of the neighbouring vowels,
(d) [aː] > [ɛː], and later [e(ː)];

(2) (a) [uː] > [ʊu] > [əu], and eventually modEng [ʌu],
(b) [oː] > [uː],
(c) [ɔː] and [ǫː] in PreStE merged and eventually > [oː].

The ESc system, however, lacked back vowels in the slots occupied by ME /oː/ (since PreSc vowel 7, originally /oː/, had long since fronted to /yː/, see §7.1) and ME /ɔː/ (since OE, ON, etc. /aː/ had in PreSc remained as [aː], see §3.2). There was thus ample space for minor movements of the points of articulation of the Sc back vowels, without setting up any 'push-chain' overall shift in the back vowel system. Perhaps in consequence of this, therefore, OSc (and nME) underwent no general shift of the long back vowels beyond a tendency visible in many modern dialects to a closing of vowel 5's realisation from [ɔː] > [o(ː)], and a tendency, especially in C dialects, to some fronting of the realisation of vowel 6 /uː/ > [ü(ː)], though how early the last two events took place is unclear. In the case, then, of vowel 6, Sc (and nEng) continue to this day the ancient (indeed proto-Indo-European in some words) pronunciation of such words as *house, mouse, about, down, cow* with /u/, whereas StEng now has a diphthong /ʌu/ or the like.

But just as in sME, and presumably by a shared impetus, the Shift of the long front vowels also took place in Scots through the 15th and 16th centuries. In very broad outline, the three non-high long front vowels were each raised by one or two stages, as shown in Figures 16 and 17, and vowel 1, being already fully close, could only maintain its differentiation from encroaching vowel 2 by becoming a diphthong. In Scots it seems that the general upwards (or closing) movements of vowels 2, 3 and 4 came to an end with the establishment of the Scottish Vowel-Length Rule, whereas the opening of the long form of the diphthong vowel 1, which we shall refer to as vowel 1 long continued thereafter.[34]

The evidence which follows provides indications of the qualities achieved at various stages by vowels 1, 2 and 4. For vowel 3, we depend on inferences from the mergers of this with 2 and 4, more or less dateable from rhyme evidence.

On these grounds, I conjecture that vowel 4 had been raised from /a/ in ESc to [ɛː] or [ẹː] by the mid 16c, when its realisation approximated that then reached by vowel 1 (see the pun at §20.5). Its all but universal realisation in the modern dialects (in both long and short environments) is [e(:)], and it has largely maintained its separation from vowel 16 /ɛ/ except in some N dialects. This suggests that shortening did not come about till it had reached the [e:] stage in its upward progress. Had shortening come about at the [ɛ:] stage we would have expected many more [ɛ] outcomes of vowel 4 than we actually find. Even in those N dialects in which vowels 4 and 16 have merged, the resultant merged vowel invariably has a closer realisation than simple [ɛ] - most often [ẹ], also [e] or [ɛ̣] - as if in those dialects the merger had taken place at an [ẹ:] stage of vowel 4.

Vowel 2 seems to have been raised from ESc /e:/ to near [i:] by the mid 15c (see §15, and Erasmus' remark on the Scots *i* for *e*, §20.2). About this time vowel 7, ESc /y:/, merged with it in N.

There appears to be no direct evidence as to the date at which vowel 1 began diphthongising, except that it was apparently not till after *c*1400 (§20.3). If, however, the diphthongising process was first triggered by the encroachment of vowel 2 towards [i:], which seems *a priori* likely, this would date it to before the mid-15c. Several kinds of evidence (§§20.4, 20.6, 20.7) seem to point to a diphthong with a low to mid front first element, converging with vowel 4 and vowel 8, by the second half of the 16c.

Figure 16: The ESc long monophthongs and the Great Vowel Shift

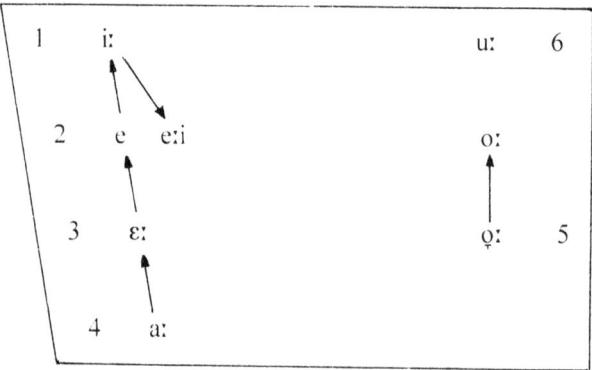

Note: see also Figures 17a-c and 19 for monophthongised vowel 8b word-finally, and see note 58.

The present-day representative of the original SVLR-short allophone of vowel 1 (which we shall refer to as vowel 1 short) is predominantly /ɛi/, with more or less retracted diaphones [ëi], [əi], [ʌi]. Though it need not follow that the SVLR-conditioned phonemic split of vowel 1, of which this is an outcome, came about immediately upon the establishment of SVLR, it is quite likely that it did so. If so, then the vowel 1 diphthong had opened to the extent of [ɛ:i] by the late 16c if our proposed dating of SVLR is correct (§21.2.3). At that point, we may assume the diphthong-opening process ceased in the new short allophone (vowel 1 short) whereas the long allophone (vowel 1 long) continued for some time to open further. The rounded long front vowel /y:/ > /ø:/ vowel 7, was protected by its rounding from involvement in the GVS of the other long front vowels.

Figure 17: The Great Vowel Shift: changes in Scots, 14-16c

(a)

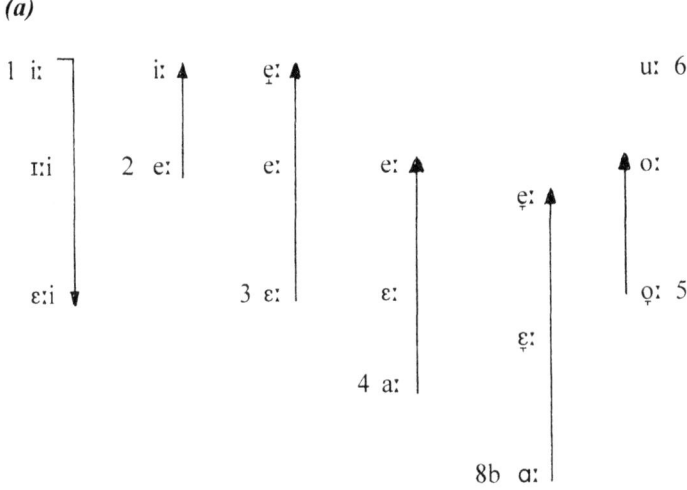

(b)

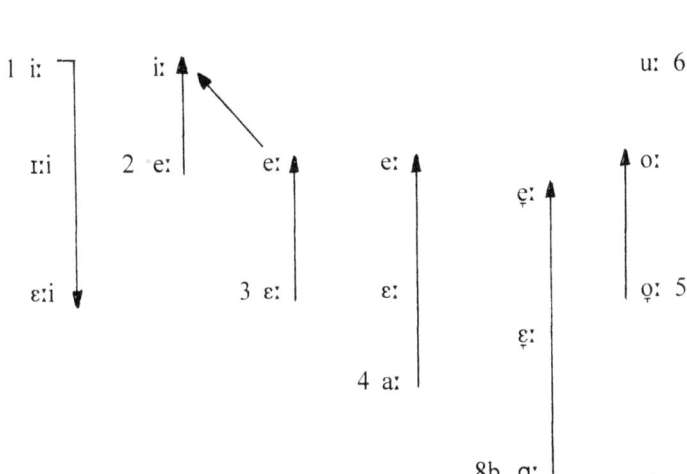

(c)

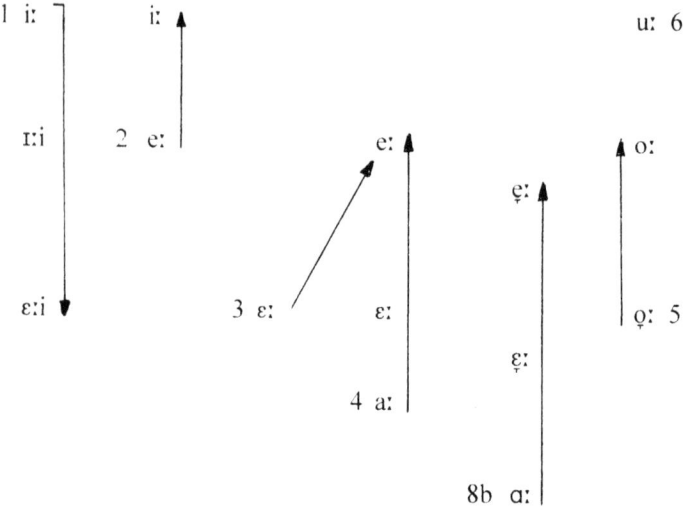

Note: For a more detailed representation of the several mergers of these vowels with one another and with others, see Figure 19 and note 36. The marginal numbers are the vowel numbers as elsewhere.

Editor's note: on vowel 8b (in final position), see §22.4 and Figure 19; on vowel 8 in non-final position, see §22.3.4 and note 58. For the suggestion that Vowel 11 was affected by the GVS, see §22.

20.2 Statements by contemporary observers

There follow several sets of evidence in support of the preceding reconstruction. Erasmus (1528) compares the pronunciation of ancient Greek η [e:] with 'the *a* heard today in Scotland and parts of Holland' (Erasmus, 1985: 411; 1973: 52), which he describes as between *a* and *e* in Italian. Later (1985: 435; 1973: 72) he says Greek η should be separated into two short *e*'s to make Scots *a*. So he is referring to the long *a*. Sc vowel 4, realised as [æ:] or [ɛ:]. Perhaps merely echoing Erasmus, in 1568 the English scholar Sir Thomas Smith (Smith, 1983 [1568]: 64-7), mentions a Scots vowel in *hän* or *hean* and *stän* or *stean* corresponding to English *o* in *bön* 'bone' and *stön* 'stone' halfway between Roman *a* and *e* which likewise must mean a low to mid front vowel realisation of vowel 4: unlike Erasmus he tells us nothing of its quantity. Also according to Erasmus (1985: 412-3) 'the Scots often pronounce an *i* instead of an *e*, saying *faciibat* instead of *faciebat*' presumably, that is, realising vowel 2 as [i:].

Erasmus presumably encountered Scots during his periods of residence in England, and in 1508 he had tutored in Siena Alexander Stewart, Archbishop of St. Andrews, illegitimate son of James IV, then fifteen years old.

20.3 Pre-GVS rhymes in ESc

The ESc rhymes of vowel 1 /iː/ and 15 /ɪ/ before /n/ and /nd/ (Buss, 1886: 20 f.; Heuser, 1897a, 1897b) suggest a tendency to neutralise the length contrast between these sounds in these environments, possibly by a lowering here of /iː/, possibly accompanied by a lengthening of /ɪ/. Examples are:

> *tharin* 'there-in' : *wyn* 'wine' and *with-in* : *tyne* 'lose' (Barb.), with similar rhymes in *Troy-bk; Leg. S.* rhymes *dekine* : *wyne* 'wine' and *hewyne* 'heaven' : *hyne* 'hence', and several times the p.p. ending *-in(e)* with words containing vowel 1; Barbour and *Leg.S.* both rhyme the vbl. n. ending *-ing* <-yng, -yne> quite freely with vowel 1 (in *syne* 'afterwards', *vyne* 'wine', etc.); *Thewis Gud Women* (? e15) has a rhyme of *syne* with *in*. Quite exceptionally, *Leg.S., Ratis R.* (? la14, ? e15) and *Thewis Gud Women*, have single rhymes of vowel 15 and vowel 1 before /nd/, of the type *fynd* v. : *kind* n. (see §3.1.1), whereas rhymes of vowel 1 words together and vowel 15 words together in these environments are quite frequent.

According to Heuser (1897a: 404) such rhymes do not occur before /nd/ in later poets; pending a thorough study of OSc rhyme-practice, I can only say I am not aware of any before /n#/ in later poets either. Barbour once rhymes *is* v. : *wys* 'wise, manner' (2, 339), and once *schyrreff* 'sheriff' (? vowel 15) : *ryve* v. 'rive' (vowel 1), (16, 551).

This suggests a situation before vowel 1 had started to diphthongise, when some approximation to the quality of vowel 15 obtained.

Leg.S. also has a few rhymes of vowel 4 ESc /aː/ with vowel 17 ESc /a/, mostly before /n/, such as *tane* 'taken' : *lemmane* '-man', and four of *hale* 'whole' : *sall* 'shall'. Perhaps this points to a date before GVS raising of vowel 4. All this suggests a *terminus post* of the late 14c for the beginning of GVS.

20.4 Rhyme and orthographic indicators: 15c and later

Fifteenth-century poets appear to rhyme the sequence vowel 4 + *s* /aːs/ with vowel 16 + *s* /ɛs/, especially in the suffix syllables *-es, -nes*: e.g. *riches* : *clathis* (*Foly of Fulys* 116); *grace* : *kyndness* (*Consail Vys Man* 129 f.), and there are similar rhymes in *Kingis Q., Howlat*, Henryson, *Wall.*, Dunbar and *Clariodus*; but such rhymes appear to be absent from Barbour and *Leg. S.*

Conventional or not (see Fox, 1981: 494), such rhymes seem hardly conceivable unless vowel 4 had moved upwards some way towards [ɛ].

Rhymes of vowels 4 with vowel 16 also occur, though less frequently, in other environments:

> *maist* 'most' : *lest* 'duration' (*Ratis R.* 685 f.), *gest* 'guest' : *traist* 'trust' (? vowel 4) (*Consail Vys Man* 357 f.), *men* : *cheften* (Wynt. 4, 971 f.), *tellis* pres. t. : *fellis* 'fails' : *sell* 'cell' *is* : *dwellis* pres.t. : *bellis* n. pl. (*Wall.* 2, 216 f.), *planait* 'planet' : *stait* (*Wall.* 7, 175 f.), *flaid* 'flayed' : *gled* 'kite' (Dunb. 81/126 f.).

Also suggestive of the same conclusion are many spellings of vowel 4 (and also vowel 8) as <e> from the mid-15c onwards, e.g.:

> <sem> 'same' 1456 Peebles, <get> *gate* 'road' 15c, <led> *lade* 'load' 1494, <gem> 'game' 1514, <greth> *graith* 'equipment' 1562, <ell> 'ail' 1586, <ell> 'ale' 1655, <ken> *cane* 'the duty' 1596, <knewschip> *knaveschip* 1610, <kell> *kale* 1614, <twe> *twa* 'two', etc., and the common 16c reverse spelling of *gest* 'guest' as <gaist>.

In the 1520's, Queen Margaret Tudor, who by that time had scotticized her speech, spells <benfyre> *banefire* 'bonfire', <get> *gate* 'road', <mer. meir> *mare* 'more', <ne> *na* adj. 'no', in her holograph writings (various documents in *St. P. Henry VIII* IV) (see Aitken, 1997a).

Less transparent are the conclusions to be drawn from five rhymes of *freind* 'friend' vowel 2 with *kynd* vowel 1, in *Consail Vys Men* and *Foly of Fulis* 15c (Girvan, 1939: lxxii-lxxiii), and the same rhyme in *Alex.* (Taym. 440 f.), but it certainly seems possible that they mark an encroachment by vowel 2 on the space of vowel 1.

The preceding indications that ESc /aː/ vowel 4 was moving towards [ɛː] and /eː/ vowel 2 towards [iː] in the early to mid 15c, whereas /iː/ had not yet started to shift around la14c, e15c, might suggest a 'push chain' rather than a 'pull chain' mechanism for GVS in OSc.

20.5 A pun

As Lyall points out in an editorial note, in Lyndsay *Sat.* (863 f. in Lyall's edn.), Falset, *alias* Sapiens, has forgotten his assumed name, remembering it only as 'Thin Drink', or (l.867, ibid.) *Sypeins* 'oozings', from *sype* v. 'to leak, ooze' (vowel 1). It seems that vowel 4 in *Sapiens* had by then, *c*1540, a mid-front realisation, ? [ɛ̝ː], ? [e̞ː], while the vowel 1 diphthong had reached some apperceptionally similar quality, ? [eːi].

20.6 Orthographic indicators for late MSc

It seems that towards the mid 16c vowel 1 was apperceptually converging on vowel 4 (and perhaps vowel 8), having reached a quality in the mid front area. This is signalled by the appearance and increasing popularity of the following spellings for vowel 1: <ay>, less often <ai>, occasionally <a>; also, less frequently, <ey>, <ei>; and, much more rarely still, but perhaps especially in nEC and NE, <oi>. These, it would seem, are borrowings of the established spellings of vowels 4 (and 8), vowel 3 (? rather than vowel 2), and vowel 9, respectively, e.g.:

<chaylde> 'child' 1544-5, <fayftlie, nayntlie> 'fifthly, ninthly' 1545, <quhait> (for *quhite, fyte*, nEC and NE varr. of *quhete* 'wheat') 1532 Dunfermline, <yai> 'thy' *c*1580, <blaith> *c*1580, <fayte> 'wheat' 1585 NE, <quhat> 'white' 1575-6 Dunfermline, <quhaytt> '*idem*' 1607 Argyll, <quhai> 'why' 1559-60, <quhay> '*idem*' 1642, <fawe> 'five' 1574 Aberdeen, <fayf> '*idem*' *c*1639 Taymouth, <dayn> 'dine' 1597-8, <dayamond> 'diamond' la16, <aydant> *idand* 'diligent' e17, <cray> 'cry' e17, <kayth> *kythe* 'make known' 1620, <dayell> 'dial' 1633, <prouayd> 'provide' *c*1633, <layttil> *lytill* (vowel 1, var. of *litill*) 'little' 1644, <blaithly> 'blithely' la17, and very many more of the same chronology;

<quheit> 'white' 1562 Inverness, <quheyt> '*idem*' 1597 Paisley, <heyr> 'hire' 1611, <heir> '*idem*' 1684, <heyd> 'hide' 1622, <feyne> 'fine' 1628, <whey> 'why' 1665-7;

<moiter> 'mitre' 1591-2 St. Andrews.

The idiosyncratic orthography of Mary Queen of Scots in her holograph writings, partly French-derived, partly English-derived (did she learn to write English before learning to write Scots?), has many spellings manifesting post-GVS vowel pronunciations: <i> for vowel 2, presumably after F *i, viz.* [i(:)], e.g.

<bi> 'be', <birar> 'bearer', <mi> 'me', <Vui> 'we', all 1568; <frind> 'friend', <hir> 'hear', 1569

and <e(e)> for vowel 4, i.e. representing [ɛ(:)] or [e(:)], e.g.

<en> *ane* 'one', <fer> 'fair', <fre> *fra* 'from', <meer> *mare* 'more', <merid> 'married'.

A very much less cursory collection and survey than I have been able to carry out will be needed to establish more detailed patterns: for example, was the <ay> spelling favoured in particular, e.g. SVLR-long over SVLR-short, environments? The appropriation to vowel 4 of spellings that originated with vowel 3, beginning in the mid 16c, must reflect some phonetic approximation, and therefore signal that vowel 4 had reached the mid front area: these include <ea> recently adopted from preStE (e.g. <meat> 'meat' 1571 with vowel 3):

(vowel 4) <heale> 'whole' 16, <kean> 'cane, the duty' 1578, <keam> 'comb' 1597, <keall> 'kale' la16, < meanis> 'mains' 1610, <mead> 'made' 1656;

and vowel 3's longer established spellings <ei>, also <ey> and <eCe>, are also now sometimes applied to vowel 4, e.g.:

<leid> *lade* 'load' 1555, <heill> *hale* 'whole' la16, <kele> 'kale' 1604, <meid> 'made' and <meie> *ma* 'more' *c*1633, <wheir> *quhare* 'where' 1666, <sheim> 'shame' 1676.

For vowel 4 (and vowel 8) spellings applied, rather earlier, to vowel 3, see §20.8.3.

20.7 English dramatists' representations

English dramatists of the time of Shakespeare (on whom see Eckhardt, 1910: 95 f.; Luick, 1896: §§29,236) similarly represent their Scottish characters' renderings of vowel 1 by <ai, ay>, and of vowel 4 (also vowel 8) by <e> (also <ea> and, once, <ei>), e.g.:

(1) vowel 1: <ais, ays> *I'se* 'I shall' (N. Woodes *Conflict of Conscience* 1581, R. Greene *James the Fourth* 1598); <aid> *I'd* 'I would' (W. Bowyer (? himself a Scot) *The Valiant Scot* 1637); <ayl> *I'll* (Greene; Shakespeare *Henry V* 1623); <faine> 'fine', <whayet> 'quiet', <year-whayle> *arequhile* 'erewhile' (Greene); <waif> 'wife' (Bowyer): and many more such examples;

(2) vowels 4 and 8: <agen> 'again', <clethes> *clathis* 'clothes', <ene> 'one', <feth> 'faith', <hely> *haly* 'holy', <whe> *quha* 'who', etc. (Woodes); <ne mere> *na mare* 'no more', <wembe> *wame* 'womb' (Greene); <feith> 'faith' (Shakespeare); <beweere> 'beware' (Bowyer);

seemingly implying a diphthong with a low to mid front first element for vowel 1, and a mid to high front vowel for vowel 4. In *Henry V, faine* 'fain' and *tway* 'two' are so spelled, and *baith* 'both' is rendered <bath>: no doubt various explanations of these inconsistencies are possible. Also in *Henry V*, SVLR-long vowel 7 in *do* is rendered both as <de> and as <do> and SVLR-short vowel 7 as <u> in <gud>. Does this mean that vowel 7, MSc /øː/, was heard as unrounded to [eː] in the SVLR-long environment, but remained a rounded [ø]-like sound when SVLR-short, as in some modern C and S dialects?

20.8 Whatever happened to vowel 3, ESc /ɛː/?

20.8.1 The modern dialect evidence

According to LAS3's word-lists, vowel 3 continues unmerged into modSc in a small number of scattered dialects N of Forth and, in one instance, in the SW (the dialect of Stoneykirk, Wgt). In several Cai dialects and in Avoch (Ross and Cromarty), it has the realisation [ɛi] and in these it is either merged, as normal N of Forth, with vowel 4, or, as far as LAS3 shows, continues unmerged before /ð, v, z/ in Brough, before /d/ in Keiss, before /l/ and perhaps /t/ in Dunbeath, before /t, d, l/ in Latheron. A likely interpretation of the Cai outcome is that there vowel 3 survived for a time as a separate phoneme, ultimately realised as [ɛi], until vowel 4 became merged with it, except for the relic instances just mentioned, with vowel 4 merging with vowel 3 rather than, as perhaps happened elsewhere, vowel 3 with vowel 4.

Other dialects presenting relic survivals of vowel 3 as a distinct phoneme in particular environments are those of Deerness (Ork), as [e] before /t/, Hopeman (Moray), as [e¹] before /d/, Drybridge (Bnf) as [e] before /t/, Dykends (Angus) as [ẹ] before /d/, Methven (Per) as [ẹː] before /t/, Newburgh (Fife) as [ëë] before /ð, f/, Pitscottie (Fife) as [ẹ] before /k/, Stoneykirk (Wgt) as [ẹ] before /d/. (In some cases the certainty of these results is affected by 'lexical misplacement' (§19)). It will be noticed that, Cai [ɛi] excepted, these realisations represent each dialect's closest vowel height below the [i(ː)] of vowel 2, as we would expect given vowel 3's starting-point between vowels 2 and 4.

In addition, in most of the dialects of Fife north of Buckhaven, vowel 3 is found in merger with vowel 7, before /t/ or /d/ or both. The first hints of the unrounding of vowel 7 to a half-close front quality like that of late MSc and modSc vowels 3 and 4, [ẹ] or [e], come around the turn of the late 16c, early 17c (see §§7.1, 21.2.3). If we assume that the merger of vowel 3 and vowel 7 took place after this, it follows that vowel 3 still survived as a distinct phoneme in these environments in the dialects of northern and eastern Fife at least into the 17c.

For example, in Dysart (Fife), pre-/t/ we have:

with [i] *beet, leet, meet, wet, wet²* (all vowel 2), plus *wheat* (vowel 3),

with [ẹ⁹] *beat, cheat, heat, meat, sweat* (vowel 3), plus *boot, fruit, root* (vowel 7) and *slate* (vowel 4).[36]

with [eːᵊ] *bait, wait* (vowel 8), plus *gate, grate, late, mate* (vowel 4).

Other than in the instances just discussed, in the nEC dialects as far as Migvie (Angus) and Gourdon (Kincardineshire), the all but regular outcome of vowel 3 in all environments is merger with vowel 4 as [ẹ(ː)] or [e(ː)], often plus vowel 7 and/or vowel 8, especially, but by no means only, in the SVLR-long environments. Exceptions to this occur in some dialects of Fife and Angus, in which, before /n/ and less regularly before /l/, merger with vowel 2 occurs (possibly by a raising effect of the following consonant). Merger with vowel 2 occurs before /r/ in Cellardyke (Fife).

So far as present observations go, there appear to be no instances of possible vowel 3 survival south of Tillicoultry (Clackmannanshire) and Blackford (Per), except in the extreme SW (see above); or in the NE heartland north of Cowie (Kincardineshire) (but see below). In these C, S and NE dialects, in all environments, vowel 3 merges regularly with vowel 2 as [i(ː)], except in western Wgt, where merger of vowel 3 with vowel 4 as [ẹ(ː)] is again the norm.[37] West of the NE heartland, in Morayshire, the nEC pattern of merger of vowels 3 and 4 as /e/ is regular. There are a few exceptions to the vowel 3+4 merger in Morayshire: Findhorn merges vowel 3 with vowel 2 before /n, d, l/ and Elgin does the same before /n, t/. In the western Wgt dialects, vowel 8 is separate from vowels 3+4 as [ẹː] in all environments, and in Morayshire it is separate, mostly as [eː] or [ẹː] in SVLR-short environments.

In Nairn and north of the Moray Firth, the picture is rather more confused, with many dialects adhering to the Morayshire pattern, but others to that of those nEC dialects in which vowel 3 merges with vowel 4 as /e/ except before /n, l/, where the merger is with vowel 2 as /i/. There are also a few Cai, Ork and Sh dialects in which vowel 3 goes with vowel 2, as /i/, before /d/ and in one or two other environments: /r/, /ð, v, z/, /m/, /k, p/.

In what follows, it will be useful to bear in mind this broad distinction between the dialects of NE, C (south of Forth) and S (except SW), where vowel 3 regularly goes with vowel 2 as /i/, and those of the rest of Scotland, including nEC, where it goes with vowel 4 (and/or vowel 7 or more rarely 8) as /e/, with exceptional merger with vowel 2 in some dialects and some environments.

20.8.2 Vowel 3 as a separate phoneme in ESc and early MSc

Evidence of an apparently much simpler ESc and early MSc situation comes from rhymes, as presented by Heuser (1896-97), Fox (1981), van Buuren (1982, 1997), and other rhymes collected by the present writer and others. According to this evidence, vowel 3 rhymes separately from vowel 2 and all other sounds, except for limited instances pre -/r/, in 15c verse generally. Among the poets/poems who/which regularly keep vowel 3 separate in rhyme are: *Howlat, Wall.*, Henryson (Heuser, 1896,7; Fox, 1981: 492), *Seven S., Bk. Chess, Christis Kirk*, and (except for one rhyme of *preist* : *breist* (both vowel 2) : *beist* (vowel 3)), Dunbar. In another instance (Dunb. 5/37 f.), Dunbar has a sequence of 15 rhymes in *-ene*, all without exception vowel 2. The clear distinction from vowel 2 is also sometimes shown when the two vowels rhyme against each other: in Henr. (*Fab.* 2022 f.) *leid* 'person' : *dreid* : *neid* 'need' (vowel 2) against *heid* 'head' : *deid* 'dead' (vowel 3); and in Dunb. (65/55 f.), *complene* : *derene* : *bene* 'bean' (vowel 3) against *ene* 'eyes' : *bene* p.p. : *splene* (vowel 2).

20.8.3 Vowel 3 merges with either vowel 2 or vowel 4 in MSc

The beginning of the loss of separate identity by vowel 3 is hinted at by a few 15c rhymes of vowel 3 with vowel 2 before /r/: in *Howlat* 327 f., *weris* 'wars' (vowel 3) : *deris* 'harms' (vowel 3) : *maneris* 'manners' (vowel 2) : *saphiris* (vowel 2); in *Wall.* 7, 821 f., *ster* 'stir' (vowel 2) : *ber* 'carry' (vowel 3); in Henr. *Robene and M.* 17 f., *leir* 'learn' (vowel 2) : *feir* 'behaviour' (vowel 3) : *deir* 'harm' (vowel 3) : *poweir* (vowel 2) (and see §14.2 (19)). Gavin Douglas (e16) no longer distinguishes vowels 2 and 3 before /r/, and he also occasionally rhymes them before /d/, while maintaining the distinction in all other environments. Are these the first indications of the now general raising of vowel 3 to merge with vowel 2, now [i(ː)], found today, as we have seen (§20.8.1), in these and all other environments in the NE, C and S dialects, and before /d, t/ (but not /r/) in Tillicoultry (Clackmannanshire) and Blackford (Per)?

The earliest rhyme evidence so far observed of the merging of vowel 3 (ESc /ɛː/ > MSc /eː/) with vowel 4 (ESc /aː/ > MSc /ɛː/ or /ẹː/) comes in the verse of Sir David Lyndsay (? 1486-1555) whom we may regard as a Fifeshire man. With the exception of one rhyme - *bair* p.t. 'bore' (vowel 4) : *mair* (= *meir*) 'female horse' (vowel 3) - Lyndsay rhymes vowel 3 before /r/ either with itself or with vowel 2, of which Heuser (1897b) cites 9 examples. Lyndsay also has a few rhymes with vowel 2 before /d/, including such vowel 3 words as *heid* 'head' and *feid* 'feud', which he also rhymes with vowel 4 (see below), e.g. *heid* (vowel 3) : *remeid* (vowel 3) : *proceid* (vowel 2) (*Mon.* 4919 f.). But before /d/ and in other environments, he has numerous rhymes of vowel 3 with vowel 4 (Heuser, 1897b: 406-7), e.g. *feid* 'feud' (vowel 3) : *heid* 'head' (vowel 3) : *raid* 'rode' (vowel 4); *dreme* 'dream' (vowel 3) : *hame* 'home' (vowel 4); *reuin* 'raven' (vowel 4) : *heuin* 'heaven' (vowel 3). Thus Lyndsay's rhyming habits with vowels 2, 3 and 4 may be depicted as in Figure 18.

The closest parallel to this outcome in the modSc dialects seems to be that of Cellardyke (Fife), where (quite exceptionally for Fife) vowels 2 and 3 are merged before /r/, except that in Cellardyke, vowel 3 has not yet merged with either vowel 2 or vowel 4 before /d/, but only with vowel 7, while in several other environments vowel 7, as well as vowel 3, is merged with vowel 4 (§20.8.1). (Except in N, vowel 7 remained unmerged with any other vowel in Lyndsay's time.)

In a later generation than that of Lyndsay, John Stewart of Baldynneis (c1540-c1605) has a pattern of mergers approximately similar to Lyndsay's. In particular, vowel 3 merges with vowel 4 in several environments including those preceding /t, d, l/, but is unmerged preceding /r/ and (unlike Lyndsay) preceding /n/. Stewart grew up in Angus, and both these poets hailed from the area which today also shows vowel 3 merging mostly with vowel 4 (§20.8.1).

While rhyme evidence of the merger of vowel 3 with vowel 4 is first known in Lyndsay, spelling indication of this seems to begin with John Ramsay's 1488 MS of *Wall.*, with such spellings as <havin> 'heaven', <havy> 'heavy', <mar> and <meir> 'female horse'. A fair number, albeit always a minority, of such spellings appear thereafter: e.g. <mait> 'meat, food' 1512; <mare> *meir* 'female horse' Selkirk 1518, Stirling 1525; <braid> 'bread' 1546; <daith> 'death' 1567; <sate>, <sait> 'seat' 16; and others. Some of these are from the nEC area, in which the effects of this merger are now most prominent, but others appear to be from localities now having merger of vowel 3 with vowel 2.

Around the mid 16c Alexander Scott's rhymes show him merging vowel 3 with vowel 4 before /s/ and /l/, but also, like Douglas earlier, with vowel 2 before /r/ and /d/. It is not easy to find a plausible modSc correspondent to this: the nearest are the dialects of Wgt, but in these vowel 3 merges with vowel 4, not vowel 2, before /d/. Near the end of the 16c, James VI's courtier, Edinburgh-born William Fowler, rhymes vowel 3 with vowel 2 before /r, t, d, k, f/, but also with 4 before /t, d/ and /s/. About the same time the Ayrshire man Alexander Montgomerie, like his contemporary Alexander Hume, of Polwarth (Bwk), and his patron, King James VI, freely rhymes vowel 3 with vowel 2 in all environments as in the modern dialects of these areas:

<heipping> 'heaping'(vowel 3) : <keiping> 'keeping' (vowel 2), <indeid> (vowel 2) : <heid> 'head' (vowel 3), <feit> 'feet' (vowel 2) : <eit> 'eat' (vowel 3), etc.

Figure 18: Lyndsay's mergers of vowel 3 as shown by his rhymes

a) before /r/

vowel number

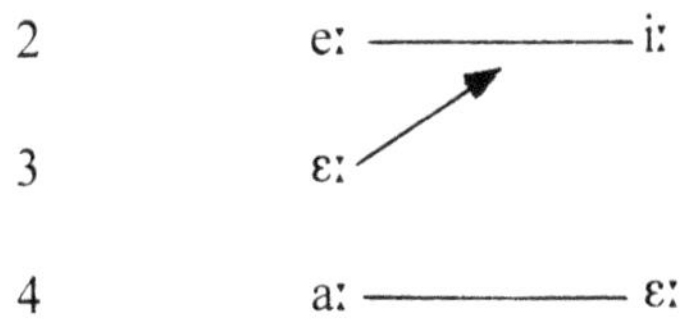

2   eː ——————— iː
3   ɛː ↗
4   aː ——————— ɛː

b) before /d/

vowel number

2   eː ——————— iː
3   ɛː ⟨
4   aː ——————— ɛː

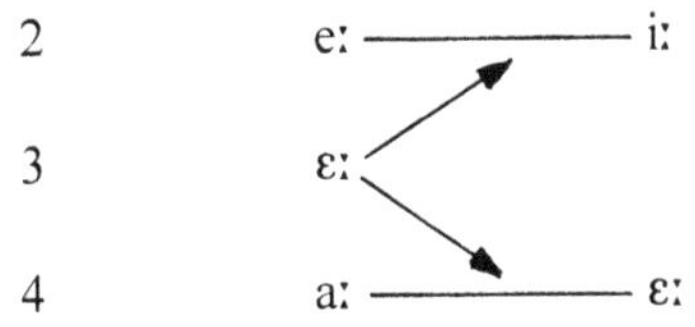

(c) *other environments*

vowel number

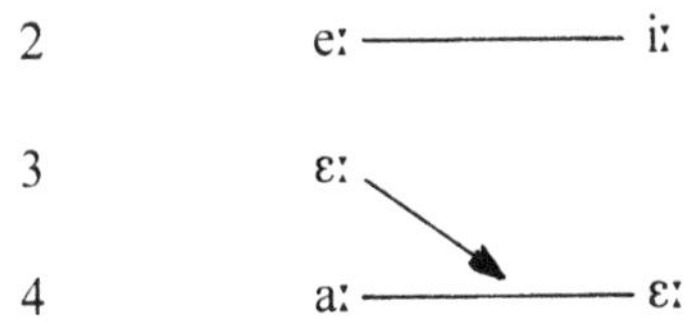

2   eː ——————— iː
3   ɛː ↘
4   aː ——————— ɛː

King James VI rhymes:

treat (vowel 3) : *heat* (vowel 2 or 3) : *weit* 'wet' (vowel 2) : *streit* (vowel 2), *seame* 'seem' (vowel 2) : *dream* (vowel 3), *tearis* (vowel 3) : *yearis* (vowel 2), *heid* 'head' (vowel 3) : *leid* 'lead' v. (?vowel 2) : *deid* 'deed' (vowel 2), etc.

By now, over part at least of C and S Scotland, it seems that vowel 3 had been raised to [i(ː)] through its whole lexical range, and was fully merged with vowel 2, as it is in this area today.

20.9 Vowel 4 in labial environments merges with smoothed vowel 12

In most dialects (the present-day exceptions are sEC, S and eastern SW) the GVS fronting and raising of vowel 4, ESc /aː/, was inhibited by an adjacent labial consonant, either:

(1) /(C)w-/ preceding, e.g. /twaː/ 'two', /waːk/ 'wake', or

(2) any labial consonant preceding or following the vowel, when an unstressed syllable followed, so that the vowel was final in an open syllable, e.g./'faːdom/ 'fathom', /'haːmər/ 'hammer',

(3) ? in *brave* > /braːv/ <brawf> 1561, whence *braw* 'fine'.[37a]

In the dialects in question, these allophones of vowel 4 did not undergo fronting and raising by the GVS, but remained unshifted as labialised [ɑː] or [ɒː] or the like. Ultimately this was merged with vowel 12 when this became a monophthong, sharing (in the dialects in question) the same subsequent history. This took place about the middle of the 15c or a little later.

As evidence of the merger of labialised vowel 4 with vowel 12, there appear from the late 15c many spellings in which the graphemes appertaining to vowels 12 and 12a <au, aw, al, aul> are now applied to labialised vowel 4:

<walk> *c*1460, 1488 (beside <wake> ESc /waːk/) 'wake', also < wawk> *a*1538, <waulk> la15, <awalk> *a*1520, and <walkyn> la15 (beside <waken>); <wawd> 1498-9 (beside <wad, wade> /waːd/) 'woad' (OE *wād*); and similarly <walter> 1491 'water'; <wawpyn> e16 'weapon', <quhals> 1485, <quhawys> 1489 (beside <quhais>) 'whose', <quhaw> 1543 (beside <quha>) 'who'; <awfald> 1487 (beside <afald>) 'one-fold'; <balhoyis> 1535-6, <bawhoy> 1539 (beside <bahuvis>) 'coffers'; <fawvoure> 1548 'favour'; <laubour> 1548 'labour'; modSc, especially NE, <awpron> 1871, <ahpron>

1881 'apron'; <Dawvid> 1871, <Dawvit> 1884 'David'; <hawmer> 1866 (beside <haimmer>) 'hammer'.

There are also, much more rarely, rhymes of *twa* 'two' with *all a*1568 and with <fa> 'fall' 1567.

In the south-eastern and southern area in which this change did not take place, /aː/ in labial environments has had the regular outcome of vowel 4, viz. /e(ː)/ in these words as in all other vowel 4 words. For localisation of the isogloss see LAS3's Maps W42 'two', W116 'waken'. The regional distribution of the outcomes of vowel 4 + labial consonant + syllable, e.g. *haimmer, hawmer* 'hammer', remains for investigation. It is my impression that the regional distributions of the competing types in OSc, as revealed in localised texts, were like those of today.

21 The Scottish Vowel-Length Rule (SVLR) (Aitken's Law)

21.1 Vowel-length contrasts no longer functional

The changes in the qualities of the vowels which had undergone GVS, along with the earlier removal of vowel 7, PreSc /oː/, from the back to the front vowel system, as (ESc /yː/, MSc /øː/) abolished the historical vowel-length oppositions between 'long' (bimoric) and 'short' (monomoric) vowels as these existed at the time of OSL.

Vowel 7, formerly opposed, as PreSc /oː/, to PreSc /u̜/ vowel 19, had lost this connection since its fronting to /yː/. After GVS, vowel 2, having progressed to /iː/, lost its correspondence with vowel 15. Vowel 3 had largely ceased to exist as a separate phoneme (see §20.8). Vowel 4 had eventually progressed to /eː/, where, however, it hardly replaced vowel 2's relationship with vowel 15. The overall effect of such new long-short oppositional arrangements as arose out of this have yet to be worked out, as these are revealed in lexical interchanges between the historical phonemes in the modern dialects. But almost certainly they will turn out to be less general than those of the PreSc oppositions.

Vowel 15 has shown no tendency to relate to either vowel 2 or vowel 4 as the 'short' of either vowel. Vowel 16 /ɛ/, it is true, did display transitory coincidence with vowel 4 as this passed on its way to its present closer realisation [e(ː)] (see ɑː §20.4). Some Ork, Cai and S dialects, and occasionally others, have merged vowel 12, early MSc /aː/ or /ɑː/ after /au/ smoothing (§18.1), with vowel 17 /a/ in most environments; but most dialects keep them quite separate.[38]

Among the back vowels, long-short relationships are no more coherent. Judging from its modern dialect outcomes, in most dialects vowel 5, which had begun as a half-open vowel /ǫː/ (§4.1) had closed to a half-close realisation /oː/ following, it may be, on the vacation by vowel 7 of the half-close long back vowel space. In some, especially WC, dialects, vowel 18 has closed and merged with vowel 5, as /o(:)/, but in most other dialects the two remain distinct, either by virtue of an opener realisation of vowel 18, [ɔ] or the like, or by virtue of maintained bimoric quantity by vowel 5 in SVLR-short environments, [oː] or the like, contrasting with [o] for vowel 18 in the same environments; or in some dialects both means of contrast operate. These last represent one case (vowel 8 in SVLR-short environments is another, see §22.3.1) in which vowel-length oppositions continue to function in modSc.

In the case of vowel 6 ESc /uː/ and vowel 19 ESc /ʉ/ we have reason to believe that at the time of OSL vowel 19 ESc /ʉ/ had a half-close realisation, [o] or [ö], rather than fully close, since when lengthened it produced vowel 7 - then /oː/ - not vowel 6 - then /uː/ - e.g. in *lufe* 'love', *dure* 'door'. But in the 15c and 16c, it often has, alongside its regular spelling in <u>, a secondary spelling <ou, ow>, the regular spelling of vowel 6,[39] and conversely vowel 6 sometimes adopts the <u> spelling of vowel 19.[40] It therefore seems possible that by the 15c vowel 19 had in its turn closed to a realisation nearer to vowel 6 (and to its own original quality prior to Short Vowel Lowering, §3.3). However, in view of its subsequent history, it is clear that vowel 19 did not then or later merge with vowel 6, then perhaps [uː], not even with the SVLR-short allophones of the latter, [u]. Thus vowel 19's realisation cannot have been any closer to that of vowel 6 than, say, [ʊ].

21.2.1 SVLR set up

Once the action of GVS had abolished for the front vowels the phonemic function of vowel quantity in favour of a system of contrast by quality only, it was open to speakers to shorten all long vowels which were by then monophthongs (but see note 41), and this also included the first element of the post-GVS diphthong vowel 1: we must suppose then that the new vowel 1 diphthong maintained a long first element (as it does in many dialects in the SVLR-long environments today). Among speakers of Scots a tendency to do this now took effect, and this was extended to include in some dialects the remaining long monophthongs, particularly vowel 6 /uː/. We can, if we wish, follow Lass (1974) in viewing this as the final act in an unconscious 'conspiracy' amongst speakers of English to reduce all vowels to a single, uniform vowel-length system, abolishing the traditional distinction between 'long' and 'short' vowels in favour of a system in which vowel duration is purely allophonic - dictated solely by the vowel's phonetic environment in any particular word. In the case of Scots the 'conspiratorial' action of shortening long vowels was indeed carried into effect, but only in part: only for the original long monophthongs[41] and only in specific phonetic environments (on which, see below). The result was a new, essentially allophonic, rule known as the Scottish Vowel-Length Rule or Aitken's Law, which determines vowel-length over part of the Scots vowel-system.[42]

21.2.2 SVLR defined

In certain environments, which we will call SVLR-short environments, vowel shortening indeed took place and in most of the modern dialects the outcome is short realisations of the original long vowels before consonants other than voiced fricatives and /r/. But in certain other environments specially conducive to longer vowel-duration - namely before voiced fricatives, /r/ and zero-consonant (i.e. before a word-boundary or in hiatus) - the tendency to shortening was resisted, no shortening took place, and in these environments, here called SVLR-long environments, the ESc long vowels remain fully long.[43] The resultant Rule, in what may have been its original form, may be thus expressed:

> The affected stressed vowels are realised long in end-stressed syllables before the voiced fricatives - /v, ð, z, ʒ/ - in most dialects /r/, before a word-boundary and in hiatus; in other environments they are realised short.

Or, in the usual formulation:

$$V > V: / - \left\{ \begin{array}{c} r \\ v\ z\ ʒ\ ð \\ \#+ \end{array} \right\}$$

Though SVLR is usually, and conveniently, expressed thus as if it were a *lengthening* rule, it in fact began, as stated above, as a *shortening* process, on the environments not specified above. These, the short environments, it will be noted, include lenis continuants, stops and an affricate - /l, m, n, b, d, g, dʒ/ - which in English favour longer allophones of their preceding vowels (Gimson and Cruttenden, 1994: 91-3; McMahon, 1994: 62). Also, whereas the vowels of other dialects of English display a range of allophonic vowel durations descending according to environment along a more or less gradual continuum, the SVLR-conditioned Scots vowels show a definite break between the ranges of their SVLR-short and SVLR-long allophones (see especially Aitken, 1981: 134-140). Thus SVLR is manifested as a dual system of vowel-length variation at the phonetic level quite different from that of other varieties of English.

This then resulted in SVLR-governed vowel-length differences between e.g.:

(a) (vowel 2) *tree, speir* 'ask', *grieve* 'foreman', with [iː], and *meet, seed, creep, leek, eel, seen, beef* and *heich* 'high', with [i];
(b) (vowel 3) (mostly merged with vowel 2 or vowel 4);
(c) (vowel 4) *lave* 'remainder' with [eː] and *late* with [e];
(d) (vowel 6) *now* with [uː] and *about* with [u];
(e) (vowel 7) *puir* 'poor' with [øː] and *muin* 'moon' with [ø] (or [iː] and [i], [eː] and [e] or [ɪ], etc);
(f) In addition, vowel 1 ESc /iː/, following its diphthongisation by GVS, yielded SVLR long [aːɪ], [ɑːe] or the like, in e.g. *five*, and SVLR short [ɛi], [əi], [ʌi] or the like, in e.g. *bite, bide*.
On vowel 5, see below.

At some stage, whether originally or later, some dialects have incorporated among the vowels subject to the Rule the modSc diphthongs and the original non-high short vowels, including vowels 1 short, 10 and 13, and vowels 16, 17 and 18 (Aitken, 1981: 134, 139, 142), presumably by lengthening in the SVLR-long environments to conform with the vowel-length patterns now established among the former ESc long vowels. (LAS3 reports this effect only for the monophthongs, vowels 16, 17 and 18, and not for the diphthongs, vowels 10 and 13.) But this tendency has never reached the ESc short high vowels, 15 /ɪ/ and 19 /ʉ/ > modSc /ʌ/.[44]

Thus the dialects which behave in this way have added to an original shortening rule for one set of vowels (the ESc long monophthongs, in what became the SVLR-short environments) a lengthening rule for another set of vowels (the original non-high short vowels and the unmonophthongised diphthongs, in the SVLR-long environments). If, as Lass (1974) has conjectured, the shortening began with the long high monophthongs, conversely, this lengthening affected the short non-high monophthongs without, however, reaching the original high short vowels 15 and 19. This suggests that it may have taken place before the general lowering of the two latter vowels /ɪ/ and /ʉ/ to their present realisations, [ɛ, ë] etc. for /ɪ/ and [ʌ] or the relic [ö] for /ʉ/.

In most modSc dialects north of Forth (and a few south of it), vowel 12 continues fully long in all environments (i.e. not only the SVLR-long ones), contrasting in many dialects, in SVLR-short environments, with vowel 17, either by quantity only, as e.g. *fault* as [fɑːt] and *fat* as [fɑt] or by both quantity and quality, as [fɔːt] and [fat]. Likewise, beyond the area in which vowel 8 has merged with 4 in non-initial SVLR-short environments (cf. Map 2), vowel 8 likewise mostly continues fully long, in many dialects contrasting with vowel 4 solely in quantity: e.g. *bait* and *pain* (vowel 8) with [eː], *gate* and *nane* (vowel 4) with [e]. Vowel 8 does, however, operate the SVLR in the SW.

LAS3 shows many modSc dialects in which vowel 5 has merged with vowel 18 as [o, ɔ] or (in Ork, Sh and N) [ɒ]. So, in SVLR-short environments, SVLR has shortened vowel 5, /ǫː/ or /oː/, in the forerunners of these dialects. In many other dialects, however, to the north and south of sEC and WC, vowel 5 remains separate from vowel 18 in SVLR-short environments. In the SW this distinction is qualitative, vowel 5 as [o], vowel 18 as [ɔ]. Elsewhere, however, the distinction is often solely by quantity, vowel 5 as [oː], vowel 18 as [o], e.g. in *coat* [koːt] vowel 5 versus *cot* [kot] vowel 18: in these dialects vowel 5 has 'opted out' of SVLR, remaining long in the SVLR-short environment, thus avoiding, in these dialects, homonym clash with vowel 18. However, there is still another group of dialects, of north Lnk and north Ayrshire, which have lengthened all SVLR-short vowels except vowel 2, viz. modSc /i(ː)/, and in these of course the contrast just noted is neutralised.[45]

The Rule as stated above may have been its initial form. There are certain concomitant features which may have been added later:

(1) forms with the p.t. inflection /-d/ after a final stem-vowel, e.g. *dee'd* p.t. of *dee* 'to die', normally share the SVLR-long realisation of the morpheme-final uninflected form, so /diːd/ *dee'd* 'died' by analogy with *dee* /diː/ 'to die', is in contrast with SVLR-short /did/ *deed* n. The first record of this feature is by Sylvester Douglas (c1775), who states that *pride* and *deny'd* are non-rhyming, since, though both contain the 'diphthongal sound of *i*... in *pride* that sound is shortened and protracted in *deny'd*' (Kohler, 1966: 36). But in OSc there are many rhymes of pairs of words of this sort, suggesting that this type of long-short contrast did not yet operate, at first no doubt (perhaps in the case of Henryson and Dunbar) because the SVLR-shortening of original long vowels had not yet taken place; later (perhaps in the case of Fowler, Alexander and Ayton) because the unshortened final vowel of e.g. *deny* or *dee* 'die' had not yet been substituted for the regularly shortened vowel in the p.t. forms *deny'd* and *dee'd*:

e.g. *seid* 'seed' : *beid* 'be it' : *dreid* 'dread' (Henr.); *leid* 'lied' : *neid* 'need' : *gallowbreid* 'gallows-bird' : *weid* 'weed, garment' (Dunb.); *denyde* 'denied' p.p. and *espyde* 'espied' p.t., both rhyming with *syde* 'side' (William Fowler c1590); *seed* : *decreed* (Sir William Alexander e17); *pryde* : *spy'de* (Sir Robert Ayton e17, and others);

(2) in stressed penultimate syllables, bimorphemic (inflected or derivational) items share the SVLR-length of the uninflected or underived stem: so *useful* has the SVLR-short in [ˈjïsfɪ] but *using* the SVLR-long in [ˈjeːzɪn], and *leafy* has [i] like *leaf*, but *leaving* has [iː] like *leave*. In monomorphemic items, vowel-length may follow regular SVLR environmental conditions, e.g. in *deevil* 'devil' [ˈdiːvḷ], *music* [ˈmøːzɪk], *needle* [ˈnidḷ], *stupid* [ˈstïpɪt]. But in addition there are a few items of apparently similar structure in open syllables which select long variants before consonants which in

monosyllables would dictate SVLR-short vowels: *feeble* with [iː]; *feline* ['fiːləin], compare *feeling* ['filɪn]; *pylon* ['paˑelɔn], compare *piling* ['pəilɪn]; perhaps by analogy with morpheme-final SVLR-longs in such compounds as *tree-line*, *dye-cloth*. Such items - the initial open syllable in *feline* etc. - we may call 'pseudo-morphemes'. Perhaps these 'pseudo-morpheme-final' items were later additions to the Rule, like the morpheme-final ones in (1).

These addenda to the Rule can be conveniently stated in terms of morphemes: affected vowels are also long when (1) the morpheme, (2) the pseudo-morpheme, in which they occur in itself fulfils the SVLR-long conditions (of ending in the vowel, having a voiced fricative after the vowel, etc.).

From the beginning SVLR appears to have been a *phonetic* rule, operating over a particular set of phonemes in a given dialect and controlling the allophonic systems of these phonemes. From the beginning of SVLR to the present day, the SVLR-short and SVLR-long allophones of most of the affected phonemes in most dialects seem to have maintained virtually uniform quality over the whole allophonic range, while displaying the regular SVLR quantitative distinctions: this is for example the case with vowel 2 [i(ː)] and vowel 4 [e(ː)] virtually everywhere.

Nevertheless there have also from time to time occurred SVLR-conditioned splits at the phonological level, when in a particular dialect or group of dialects the SVLR-short allophone of a certain phoneme has parted finally from its SVLR-long companion. Such splits manifest themselves as such because their limit of incidence lies precisely along the SVLR fault-line, as for example the several S and C splits of vowel 7, with the SVLR-long continuing as [øː] or unrounding to [eː] in e.g. *puir* 'poor' and *yuize* 'use' v.; and the SVLR-short deviating as [ɪ] or [ë] in e.g. *muin* 'moon' and *yuis* 'use' n., the contrast according exactly with the SVLR long-short allophonic distinction.

The most widespread of these splits in its modSc outcomes has been that of the SVLR-short of vowel 1, when this diphthong had opened as far as [ɛːi]. This then shortened in the SVLR-short environment to [ɛi, əi], which has remained ever since; while the SVLR-long has continued the opening process to the [aːɪ] or [ɑːe] which it has eventually reached in many dialects. Still another SVLR-conditioned split has been that of word-initial vowel 4 into /jɪ/ or the like in the SVLR-short environments in C and S, e.g. *yin* 'one', and regular /eː/ SVLR-long (for analogical C and S *yae* 'one' adj., see §22.2.4).

In a relatively small number of words, vowel 4 has shortened to [ɛ] at the [ɛː] stage of its GVS progress to [eː], yielding new, fully established, lexemes which survive as doublets in [ɛ] alongside the regular forms in [e(ː)], e.g.:

modSc /gɛm/, OSc <gemm> 16 (beside modSc /gem/) 'game'; modSc /'gɛlʌk/, OSc <gellok> 1600 'crowbar' (beside OSc and modSc *gavelok* /'gevlok/); modSc /'hɛmɪr/, OSc <hemmer> 16 'hammer' (beside OSc and modSc *haimmer* /'hemɪr/); modSc /ɛnd/, OSc <end> la16 (beside OSc and modSc *aynd* /end/) 'breath'.

It seems possible that these took place in conservative dialects in which vowel 4 lagged at its [ɛː] stage of the GVS when SVLR overtook it.

On the merger of vowel 5 with vowel 18 in the SVLR-short environment, see above. On the merger of vowel 8 with SVLR-long vowel 4 only, in some dialects, see §22.3.

21.2.3 The date of the establishment of SVLR

We know that vowel 1, ESc /iː/, had diphthongised and opened as far as [ɛ(ː)i] when its SVLR-short became detached as vowel 1 short /ɛi/. This does not of itself tell us when the phonetic SVLR was established, except that it was prior to the vowel 1 split at the [ɛ(ː)i] position; but the date of this is at present quite obscure.

Grant and Dixon (1921: §151) assemble the scanty spelling and rhyme evidence tending to suggest that SVLR had been set up prior to 1635. They point to the apparent occasional spellings *pare* 'poor' (1674 Stitchil, Rox) and *shin* 'shoes' (1635, Galston, Ayr) as evidence of the unrounding by these dates of vowel 7. If these are not editorial or scribal errors, they seem to be evidence for an SVLR arrangement already existing in vowel 7. Grant and Dixon (ibid.) cite in support Burns' rhyme of *ane* i.e. /jɪn/ (vowel 15) and *abune* i.e. /ʌ'bɪn/ (vowel 7).[45a] A good deal more evidence of this sort needs to be collected from 17c and 18c sources (Aitken, 1981: 153).

A stronger indication that the Rule is long-established lies in its universal application throughout Scotland and Scots-speaking N. Ireland, albeit it is all but bounded by the English Border (Aitken, 1981: 153-4). Of the186 localities in Scotland and N. Ireland reported on by LAS3, only 9 fail to show some SVLR-governed vowel-length contrasts of the type /i/ in *meet* and *heel*, /iː/ in *freeze*, /e/ in *late* and *pale*, /eː/ in *grave*, and all 186 (including the 9 exceptions) distinguish between SVLR-short and SVLR-long outcomes of vowel 1 as /ɛi/, etc. in *bite*, /aɪ/, etc. in *five*.

In addition to the 9 exceptions, there are 17 further dialects in which the Rule manifests itself in only some of the expected environments: in some dialects, e.g. of Sh, the expected long realisation is reported only for the word-final environment; in other dialects, e.g. Fowlis Wester, Per, it fails in the word-final position only. In some dialects the effect of the Rule is neutralised because certain vowels (often vowel 4) show long realisations in SVLR-short positions; it is not apparent whether these failures of the Rule existed from the outset or are due to subsequent re-lengthening of the vowels in questions. Numerous other vagaries in the precise conditions of adherence to the Rule by the various dialects are detailed in Aitken (1981), and many others may be observed in the word-lists of LAS3.

Even so, some 160 of the dialects of Scotland reported on in LAS3 show total adherence to the Rule in at least three of vowels 1, 2, 6 and 7. Completest adherence to the Rule is found especially in Sh, WC, SW and Uls. Of the phonemic splits along the fault-line set by the Rule, only that of vowel 1 into SVLR-short [ɛi], etc. versus SVLR-long [aːɪ], etc. operates throughout the whole SVLR region (Scotland and N. Ireland). Of the more localised splits mentioned in §21.2.2 (local to Central Scotland and to N. Ireland), the split of vowel 7 may be somewhat more recent, but nevertheless all testify to the continued presence of the Rule. The remarkably wide diffusion of the Rule and its secure entrenchment within Scots speech makes it certain that it has long existed there. And since SVLR is fully and firmly established in the dialects of Sh and of Ork, it seems to follow also that it was in operation before the main colonisation of these islands by Scots-speakers was completed (i.e. by the late 16c), and the same argument applies to the early 17c plantation of Ulster (see also §20.7).

There is also at least one fairly definite indication of a date before about 1560 for the establishment of SVLR. In some Sh dialects certain vowels normally subject to SVLR appear before /d/ with both short and long realisations. Thus [hiḑḑ] *heed* and [niḑḑ] *need* contrast with [miːḑ] *meethe* or *meed* 'landmark' and [liːḑ] *leethe* or *leed* 'will to work'; also [gøḑḑ] *good* and [fløḑḑ] *flood* with [røːḑ] *rood* 'drizzle, chatter' and [bøːḑ] *booth*.[46] The items with the long realisation all derive from earlier forms with the voiced fricative /ð/ as the syllable-closing consonant, one of the SVLR-long environments.

It follows that SVLR was established in Sh before the Sh closure of [ð] to [ḑ]. That this had taken place before the end of the 17c seems probable from John Brand's (1701: 69-70) statement about the parallel case of [θ] and [t̞]: '[Shetlanders] often use to leave out the letter H in their Pronunciation, as if it did not belong in the Word, so *Three* they pronounce as *Tree*, *Thou* as *Tou* or *Tu* &c.' OSc spelling-evidence of the Sh closure of [ð] to [ḑ], merging under /d/, is mostly lacking: see e.g. *Methe* n and v., and *Roth* n. in DOST. (In at least one modern dialect of south Sh, Dunrossness, this change has not yet taken place.[47]) There are nevertheless some spellings of *Outhall* n. 'udal, land tenure', q.v. in DOST (ON *óðal*), which appear to provide a date for Sh /ð/ > /d/. In its earliest occurrences this word is spelled <-th-> in keeping with its etymology, but spellings with <-d->, at first apparently less frequent, are on record from 1567 <owdell>. It follows that SVLR was established in Sh before the completion of the change from [ð] to [d], i.e. before the late 16c.[48]

Diphthongs, particularly ESc /ai/ vowel 8

22 The diphthongs in OSc: some general remarks

Early Scots had four or five diphthongs with a high back vowel position [u], as the target of the glide. With the merger of /iːu/ and /eːu/ from earlier /ɛːu/ under /iːu, juː/ this number was reduced to three. In addition some dialects possessed a lexically rather marginal backward gliding diphthong 14b(ii) ?/ɛǫu/. The MSc outcome was vowels 12 /au/, 13 /ǫu/, 14a /iu, juː/, 14b(ii) /ɛǫu/.[49] With the exception of vowel 12, these maintain to this day their diphthongal character.

Of the diphthongs with a high front vowel position [i] as the target of the glide, vowel 11 /eːi/ (possibly in consequence of GVS raising of its first element) merged with vowel 2 /eː > iː/, and thus disappeared. Vowel 9 /ǫi/ and vowel 10 /ui/ continued as diphthongs to the present day. Vowel 8 /ai/, however, maintains its diphthongal character in only one allophone, the word-final uninflected form (§22.5). Otherwise it has largely become smoothed to a monophthong of the same or lower height than the eventual outcome of post-SVLR vowel 4 [e(ː)], in many dialects merging with the latter in SVLR-long environments or, in many C and S dialects, in all environments.

At first sight it is surprising that the phonemes which have maintained their diphthongal character are the 'narrower' ones, with less protracted vowel glides, restricted to relatively narrow, high vowel space. A functional explanation is not easy to sustain: two of the phonemes in question, vowels 9 and 10 did have low lexical loads to begin with, but the same is not true or is less true of vowels 13 and 14.

Of the two phonemes which have become monophthongs, vowel 12 /au/ did so quite early in the MSc period (see §18.1). It is not clear when vowel 8 /ai/ monophthongised in non-final SVLR-short environments, but seemingly it did so at the latest soon after the onset of SVLR (§21.2.1).

All of these phonemes are adequately treated in the foregoing, except vowel 8, ESc /ai/. To the multi-facetted history in later OSc of this vowel and its neighbouring long vowels the following paragraphs are devoted.

22.1 ESc /ai/ vowel 8 and its relations in OSc with /aː/ vowel 4 and /yː/ vowel 7

The subsequent history of ESc /ai/ vowel 8 and its relations with, in particular, vowel 4, differs greatly amongst its several environments, specifically amongst word-initial, word-medial SVLR-short, word-medial SVLR-long, and word-final. It will be necessary to discuss each of these separately.

22.2 The development of ESc vowels 4 /aː/, 7 /yː/, 8 /ai/ and 15 /ɪ/ in word-initial environments

The following exemplify these vowels in the environments in question (SVLR-short environments first):

(a) (vowel 4) *ane* 'one', *ale, ape; are* 'oar', *ae* 'one', *ave* 'nave';
(b) (vowel 7) *uis* 'use' n., *une* 'oven'; *use* v.;
(c) (vowel 8) *ain* 'own', *ail, aim; air*;
(d) (vowel 15) *inn* 'inn', *ill*.

22.2.1 Preiotation of initial vowels in OSc

(1) Vowel 4: the following occasional spellings are evidence of the development in OSc of variants with a palatal glide onset before initial vowel 4 ESc /#aː/ > MSc /#ɛː/ > late MSc /#eː/:

<ȝane> *ane* 'one' 1527 Prestwick, 1567-8, etc., also <yeane> and <yene> in a la16 or e17c copy of Dunbar's 'In secreit place' (Bawcutt, 2000: 10);[49a] <ȝak> *ake* 'ache' 16c, <ȝaking> 'aching' *c*1535; <ȝaikin> *akin* 'oaken' 1578-9 Elgin; <yeal> *ale* 1691 S; <Yealrig> *Alerig* place-name 1701 S (the two last from Watson, 1923); <ya> *ae* 'one' 1686 S; and the English dramatist Robert Greene (*c*1594) has a 'Scots' pronunciation of **arequhile* 'before-while' as <yearwhayle>.

Whereas in nearly all the OSc examples it appears from the spellings that vowel 4 remains unchanged following the preiotised /j/, in the modern C and S instances the regular outcome of word-initial SVLR-short vowel 4 is vowel 15 preceded by /j/, e.g. <yin> 'one' (see §22.2.2 below). There is also a possible early example of /jɪ/ for /#eː/ in the spelling *yin*, apparently for 'one', on a *c*1577 Monkland, Ayrshire, gravestone (see note 52). The regular SVLR-long outcome is either unchanged vowel 4 e.g. *aiver* 'work-horse', *are* 'oar', or, with preiotation, e.g. *yae* /jeː/ 'one' adj. We shall consider in §22.2.4 whether the modern /jɪ/ outcome derives from OSc /je/ forms.

(2) Vowels 2, 3 and 7, and other front vowels: excluding <ȝerl> 'earl', <ȝerd, ȝeird> varr. of *erde* 'earth', and <ȝirne> 'to curdle', in which the prefixed /j/ apparently already existed in PreSc (for a speculative explanation see s.v. *Y* in SND). OSc instances of preiotation before other initial front monophthongs also exist:

< ʒeild> ? *elde* 'age' (vowel 2) 1513; <ʒet> ? *et*, ? *ete* 'eat' (? vowel 3) 15c; <yer> *ere* 'before' la16; <yells> *ells* 1640, and (vowel 7) <ʒown> *une* 'oven' Wgt 1519.

Whether or no such spellings as <hyech> (high) 16c, <hyechlie> la16, <hyechnes> 1522, point to early instances of /hj-/ for /h-/ is matter for speculation.

(3) ModSc instances with front vowels: sporadic examples with other front vowels occur in modSc over most of Scotland, but chiefly in S: see SND s.v. *yeagle*, *yean* (OE *ēanian*) 'of a ewe: to give birth', *yeast* 'east', *(y)eenoo* 'just now', *yeer* = *ere* 'to plough' NE, *yeerie* = *eerie* Rox, *yerb* 'herb' Angus and S; see also *Y* 2(2) in SND. LAS3 also has /jil/ *eel* in some Cai dialects.

(4) ModSc instances with back vowels: Sh, Ork and N also have examples before back vowels: see e.g. *yokkel*, *yowder* and *yoag* in SND, and /jap/ *ape* in various Ork and N dialects in LAS3.

22.2.2 The modern dialect outcomes of initial vowels 4 and 8

James Elphinston, who hailed from Edinburgh, lists preiotised (possibly representing initial /jɪ/) forms of his time: *ya, yen, yale* or *yel, yabel* or *yebbel, yerth, yeternity,* also *hyame* 'home' (1787: II, 10-11). Note that *ane* 'one' and *airth* 'earth' yield only the <*ye*> ? /jɪ/, form apparently with vowel 15, and that *ale* and *able* yield forms both with this and with maintained vowel 4. Similar variant pairs for word-initial vowel 4 forms in the SVLR-short environment are evidenced in many 18c spellings of other authors (see the various entries in Y- in SND).

/jɪ/ forms are evidenced in such spellings as:

<yin> 'one' C and S, apparently originally WC and SW, from 1761-; <yill> 'ale' Burns 1786, <yind> *aynd* v. 'knock the breath from' Dmf, <yip> *ape* S, and see SND s.v. *Yit, Yix*. Other similarly treated words are *yibble* 'able', *Yid* 'Adam'.

In some of the same modern dialects, words beginning with ESc /haː-/ have similar outcomes, e.g. *hyim* /hjɪm/ *hame* 'home', *hyil* /hjɪl/ *hale* 'whole'.

According to LAS3 (Maps W125, W144, and the word-lists), in Clackmannan and in sEC, WC, SW and S, the most common modern outcome of ESc /#aː(C)(VC)/ is initial /j/ followed by vowel 15 /ɪ/ (in many dialects realised as [ë]). This is regular in *ane* /jɪn/, [jën], usual in *ale* /jɪl/, occasional in *ape* /jɪp/. But some of these dialects have instead forms

Map 2: Preiotation of initial vowel 4 in SVLR-short environments, as in *yin* 'one'

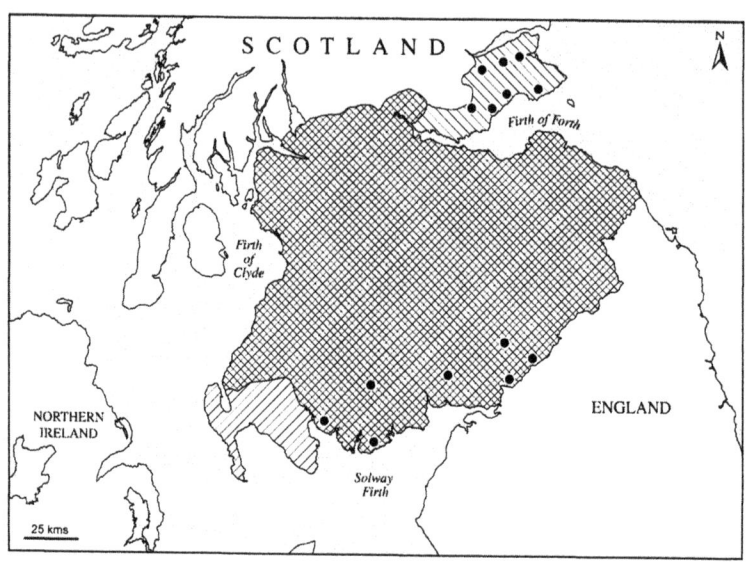

Individual localities in which non-initial vowels 4 and 8 remain unmerged before /l/ and /n/, ●

Area merging non-initial vowels 4 and 8 before /l/ and /n/, e.g. *nane* (none) and *pain* (see §22.3.1)

Area with preiotation of initial vowel 4, e.g. *ane* (one) as *yin* (see §22.2.2)

Editor's note: this map is apparently based on LAS3 maps and lists. Keith Williamson points out to me that the second lexical questionnaire also contained a question about forms of 'one', and that the unpublished responses to this show a more extensive distribution of *yin*, though generally alongside other forms, in Fife and in scattered localities as far north as the Black Isle.

Map 3: Modern distribution of *yae* forms of 'one' adj.

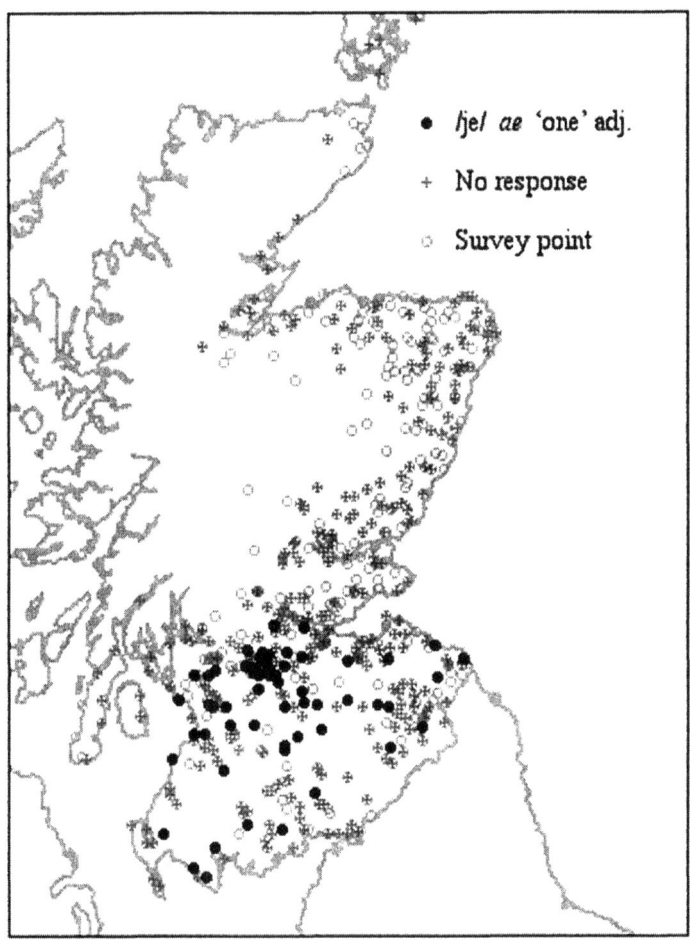

Editor's note: the question from which these data were collected was appended to a question about forms of 'one' (see Map 2). Keith Williamson, who kindly supplied this map, points out that there is a high proportion of non-responses, which are probably to be taken as indicating that the informant did not have a distinct adjectival form. *Yae* forms also occur together with *ya* forms in Cumberland.

presumably borrowed from StE or from more northerly dialects, such as /el, ep/, superseding the /jɪ/ forms, especially of the last two words. A few dialects have /j-/ forms but with other short front vowels: e.g. in Eckford, Rox, *ane* and *ale* have vowel 16 /ɛ/ not 15, thus /jɛn/, etc.; and in a number of localities (Innerwick and Oldhamstocks, East Lothian; Coldstream, Bwk; and Roxburgh) one or more of these items is merged with vowel 7 short, contrasting with vowel 15.

This outcome of word-initial vowel 4 as /jɪ/ is confined to SVLR-short environments and to the dialects of C and S only, plus, in the case of /jɪn/ 'one' at least, N. Ireland. Modern N. English dialects also have forms with initial /j/, as [jan, jɛn], etc.

This of course contrasts with the outcome of ESc /aː/ vowel 4, SVLR-short but non-initial, in e.g. *bane* 'bone', *kale* 'cole', which almost everywhere has [e] or some closely similar vowel, without preiotation, as /ben, kel/, etc.

Distinct from /jɪ/ is the outcome of word-initial vowel 8 ESc /ai/ in the same environments, in e.g. *ain* 'own', *ail, aim*. This is without preiotation everywhere, and in the more conservative dialects, where later merger with vowel 4 has not yet taken place, its treatment is the same as that of non-initial vowel 8 in pre-consonantal position, as described below, that is, it continues as a fully long vowel /eː/ or /eːə/, often of a lower quality than vowel 4, contrasting with SVLR-short vowel 4: thus /eːn/ *ain* 'own', cf. /jɪn/ or /en/ *ane* 'one'. Even within the area in which non-initial vowels 4 and 8 have now merged (see Map 2), in the initial position they are distinguished over most of the area by virtue of vowel 4's initial /jɪ/, against vowel 8's /e(ː)/ without preiotation.[50]

Over the same C and S area (see Map 3),[51] SVLR-long word-initial vowel 4 appears today as /jeː/ in *yae* 'one' adj. (apparently since 1686, see §22.2.1). There is also an instance of preiotised SVLR-long vowel 4 in *yave* Rox (Watson, 1923) as an apparent relic of MSc preiotation beside *eave, ave* Rox 1825 (Jamieson), Argyll e20, 'nave of a wheel', and note <yearwhayle> c1594 (see above); but evidence of initial /j-/ forms seems to be lacking for any other SVLR-long initial vowel 4 word, such as *aiver* 'cart-horse' or *are* 'oar'. The northern boundaries of vowel 4 SVLR-short /jɪ/ and SVLR-long *yae* are to all intents and purposes identical. /j/-prefixed forms in the word *yae* 'one' are common and widespread also in N. English dialects as [jaː, jeː].

North of the area we have been considering initial vowel 4 in *ane*, etc. or *ae*, etc. has everywhere the regular vowel 4 outcome, almost always without preiotation, viz.:

(a) SVLR-short /e/ or (in the N, before /n/, /m/ or /l/) /i/, e.g.: *ane, ale*, etc. or (in the N) *een, eel*, etc.; note, however, *yeel* 'ale' in Ork;

(b) SVLR-long /eː/, in e.g.: *age, aiver* 'work-horse', *are* 'oar', *are* 'early', with the same vowel as e.g. *mare* 'more', *grave, yare* 'fish-trap' (OE *gear*).

22.2.3 The modern dialect outcomes of initial /yː/ vowel 7

Throughout C and S, preiotised forms of word-initial vowel 7 ESc /yː/, MSc /ø/, and unrounded derivatives, are regular, e.g. *use* v. as /jøːz/ or /jeːz/; *use* n. as /jøs/ or /jɪs/; *used* as /jøːzd/, /jeːzd/, /jøst/ or /jɪst/. In part of this area, including much of the S and SW, vowel 7 also remains distinct in all SVLR-short environments (i.e. not only word-initially) mostly as [ø], [ë] or [ɪ], i.e. with a vowel usually of closer quality than vowel 15, e.g. *muin* 'moon', *guid* 'good', *fuil* 'fool', *tuip* 'tup', *yuiss* 'use' n. But north of this, in WC and part of sEC, vowel 7 has unrounded and merged with vowel 15, so that *muin* 'moon', etc. all share the same vowel as e.g. *inn, bid, fill, lip*, i.e. /ɪ/, mostly realised as [ë], as also of course does the preiotised item *yuiss* 'use' n. /jɪs/, rhyming with e.g. *miss*. Note that in this case vowel 7 merges with vowel 15 throughout vowel 7's lexical inventory (i.e. in all SVLR-short environments), not solely, like vowel 4, in the vowel-initial /jɪ/ items.

Further north preiotised forms of vowel 7, in e.g. *yuise* 'use' v. and *yuiss* 'use' n., are regular in nEC. In Angus they are mostly unmerged as /ø(ː)/, thus /jøːz/, /jøs/, etc.; in Fife they are unrounded and merged, mostly with vowel 4 (not vowel 15), as /e(ː)/, thus /jeːz/, /jes/. Still further north, preiotised forms are sporadic, merged in N with vowel 2, as /jiːz/, /jis/, alongside unpreiotised forms, e.g. in Sh /iːz/, /is/.

22.2.4 How did /jɪ/ for ESc initial vowel 4 /#aː/ come about?[52]

It would seem intrinsically likely that the modern dialectal /jɪ/ outcome of initial vowel 4 is derived from the older Scots preiotised /je/ forms, evidenced for the 16c (§22.2.1(1)). Since /jɪ/ occurs only on SVLR-short environments, the vowel would be seen as a shortened variant of vowel 4, with its quality contextually modified following the /j/, later merging with vowel 15 (or occasionally vowel 7, see below). This theory would have the benefit of explaining why vowel 8 does not also show initial /jɪ/: it was not affected by preiotation in OSc, perhaps still being a diphthong. Possibly the OSc development affected only the half-close long front vowels, vowels 4 and 7, whereas vowel 8 if already a monophthong was a half-open vowel.

This theory must then account for the occurrence of diphthongal realisations of vowel 4, attested by Murray (1873) and surviving in a small number of localities in SE Dmf (see below). This diphthong would be seen as an intruder from N. England, where it still exists, spreading into Scotland and superseding original /e(ː)/ in the 17c or 18c, in the S (and perhaps even

137

part of the C area, cf. the argument from *wean* below), where preiotised vowel 4 was already established by a different derivation.

However, most of the evidence points in the direction of the explanation advanced by Murray (1873: 105) and followed by Zai (1942: §97), Kohler (1967) and Mohr (1990). Murray believed that S /jɪ/ arose out of the Teviotdale realisation of vowel 4, which in his time was a diphthong [ɪə], now superseded by the more widespread Sc outcome of this vowel, namely the monophthong [e] (Zai,1942: §92 f.). In initial position, [ɪə] shifted its stress to yield [jɪ]. Kohler (1967), followed by Mohr (1990), added the corollary that the area occupied by the [ɪə] realisation of vowel 4 had earlier been much more extensive than in Murray's time, but had been receding in the face of C [e], as it has since continued to do. The area occupied by /jɪ/ in *yin = ane* 'one', etc., would thus seem to mark out the former extent of the [ɪə] area. The latter of course includes the northern counties of England, where [ɪə], [ɪa] and similar realisations of vowel 4 also occur (Wakelin, 1972: 89), as well as /jɪn/ 'one' and /jɪl/ 'ale'.

In support of a former presence of the diphthong in C, Kohler suggests, followed by Mohr, that it explains the history of *wean* 'child', now C /wen/, formerly N and nEC <we'an> 18-19, OSc <wyne> e17. Originally, it is suggested, this was *wee ane* /'wi'en/ 'little one', either [*'wiː'en] or [*'wi'ɪən], which contracted to [*wiən], and was captured by vowel 4, at that time realised as [ɪə], followed by its subsequent replacement by [e], yielding the present-day C /wen/. Since the word *wean* is not found in the S area, it cannot, it is suggested, have originated there. It follows that the [ɪə] type must at one time have flourished in at least part of the C area where *wean* is now found.

A further point that can be adduced in favour of Murray's theory is the fact that *yape* (< OE *ʒeāp*) yields only /jep/, with the regular *non-initial* outcome of vowel 4, never /jɪ/, as initial vowel 4 does. This suggests that /jɪ/ indeed arose directly from word-initial vowel 4, rather than developing from earlier /je/.

Also telling in favour of the Murray theory is the fact that the northern boundary of the /jɪ/ initial SVLR-short outcome of vowel 4 appears to coincide with the northern boundary of the C area in which vowel 3 merged with vowel 2 as the close front vowel /i(ː)/, thus leaving phonetic space for vowel 4 to be raised above its regular [e(ː)] position, leading to the diphthongisation, which, it is suggested, preceded the /jɪ/ outcome (see e.g. LAS3: Maps W2, 21, 22, 64, 123, 142, 158-60.).[53]

Finally, there is the evidence of surviving diphthongal realisations in three dialects of SE Dmf, namely Westerkirk, Canonbie and Gretna Green (and also in dialects of N. England and in the accent of Belfast). This is the outcome of SVLR-short vowel 4, and is a long diphthong, in the realisation of Westerkirk [iːjɪ].[54] In the SVLR-long environments the outcome is a long monophthong.[55] In the SVLR-short word-initial position (LAS3 *one* read *ane,* and *ale*), the outcome in all three dialects is /jɪ/, here realised as [jë] or [je]. In the neighbouring dialect of Creca, the SVLR-short and long outcomes of vowel 4 are the same, namely [ɪː].[56]

How does the Murray theory account for the fact that *yae* 'one' adj. has the same geographical extent in modern Sc as /jɪ/ forms (Map 3)? If *yae* arose by preiotation in OSc (§22.2.1), this item might have been reinforced by its cognate *yin,* spreading into the *yin* area. No other /jeː/ form would have been thus affected (and indeed the only other survival is the isolated Rox occurrence of *yave* (§22.2.2)).

The suggested sequence of events is as follows:

(1) vowel 3 merged with vowel 2 as /i(ː)/;

(2) vowel 4 was raised as far as [e(ː), ẹː] or [ɪː];

(3) SVLR now occurred. In dialects which had [e(ː)] or [ẹː] the effect of SVLR was normal, and included vowel 4 (and also most probably, as in the modern SW dialects, vowel 8);

(4) in dialects in which vowel 4 had reached [ɪː], this vowel did not undergo SVLR. Apparently, the effect was either, as in Creca, to leave vowel 4 unacted upon (so that it remained a long monophthong in all environments), or, as in Westerkirk, Canonbie and Gretna Green, to split it between:

(a) a long close monophthong, [iː] or something similar in the SVLR-long environments (merged in these environments with vowel 2+3);
(b) in the SVLR-short environments, a high (long) diphthong of the /ɪə/ type such as [iːʲ¹].

If vowel 4 was tending to be raised further, we could explain the diphthonging as a means of avoiding homonymic clash with vowel 2+3. But why is this outcome confined to the SVLR-short environments? Perhaps originally it was not so confined, but the entire phoneme diphthongised. The split was then brought about by partial merger with vowel 2+3: when this had undergone SVLR, merger between vowel 4 and vowel 2+3 would be possible only in the SVLR-long environments, where vowel 2+3 remained long, but in the SVLR-short environments, merger was not possible. It would seem that this applied over part of the C and S region considerably more extensive than the present relic area in SE Dmf; even in Murray's time (mid 19c), it extended as far as his Teviotdale dialect, at least;

(5) in the word-initial position, the vowel 4 diphthong, in the dialects which had this, then became /jɪ/, either by shift of diphthongal stress, or, perhaps more probably, by absorption of its first element by preceding vowels, for example in the word *the*. (The most likely explanation of the occurrence of word-initial /jɪ/ forms in Creca (see above), which does not have the diphthongal outcome of vowel 4, is borrowing from neighbouring dialects.) The /jɪ/ forms then diffused as far north as the Forth;

(6) outside the area in which the diphthongal form of vowel 4 arose, vowel 4 and vowel 8, each having undergone SVLR, now merged as [e(:)] or the like, and this spread through the C and S area between the Tay and Galloway, but did not reach some localities in Fife or the SW where, for example in Wgt, vowel 4 remains as [ẹ] and vowel 8 as [ẹ:]:

(7) this outcome of vowel 4 replaced the diphthongal forms, except in the relic area of Dmf discussed above. But this replacement was confined to the non-initial forms which consisted of a single segment, and not to the consonant + vowel sequence /jɪ/.

In either theory, the development of preiotised vowel 7 to /jɪ/ has to be seen as an independent and coincidental development. /ɪ/ arises as a local outcome of vowel 7 in all SVLR-short environments, not only following /j/, suggesting that /jɪ/ arose out of regular OSc preiotised vowel 7 by unrounding, /jø/ > /jɪ/. In many dialects, unrounded SVLR-short vowel 7 has merged with vowel 15, but where they are separate, initial vowel 4 normally merges with vowel 15, except in the localities noted in §22.2.2, where the merger is instead with vowel 7.

22.3 The development of vowel 8, ESc /ai/, in non-initial, non-final environments

22.3.1 Short environments: the position in the modern dialects

As we saw above, in many dialects of modSc vowel 4 and vowel 8 remain distinct in SVLR-short environments in the word-initial position, either by virtue of the initial /j/, exclusive to vowel 4, as /jɪn/, etc., or by virtue of the contrast between the long vowel representing vowel 8, [e:] or [e:ə], and the SVLR-shortened [e] representing vowel 4. In non-initial, non-final SVLR-short positions, likewise, vowels 4 and 8 remain unmerged also in two major regions - though, it is true, many individual dialects have carried out some lexical re-selection or lexical interchange between the two historical phonemes, as a result of 'dialect mixing' or of interference from StE.

The two regions in which vowels 4 and 8 generally remain separate are (a) the entire region north of Fife and (b) the extreme SW. There are also rare individual dialects of sEC and S where they remain separate in single environments (see Map 2).

Typically, from Fife northwards, vowels 4 and 8 are quantitatively, not qualitatively, distinguished, vowel 4 having SVLR-short [e] against vowel 8's fully long [eː]; while, in Cai, vowel 4 is mostly merged with vowel 3 as /ɛi/. In some dialects within these regions a quantitative distinction is the situation in all of the SVLR-short environments, albeit usually with some lexical re-selection, e.g. Newbyth, Abd. In many other dialects merger has taken place in some of the candidate environments but not in others, e.g. in Rackwick, Hoy, Ork, vowels 4 and 8 have merged, as SVLR-short vowel 4, before /d, p/, but not e.g. before /t, l, n/, where the length contrast described above obtains; in Leuchars, Fife, vowels 4 and 8 have merged, as SVLR-short vowel 4, before /l, m, n/, but before /t, d/ the regular outcome, vowel 4 having [e], vowel 8 [eː], obtains. Traces of the same contrast are also found, albeit rarely, further south: in Coldstream, Bwk, before /l/; in Ancrum, Rox, before /n/. In other dialects of Fife, however, as well as in a minority of the dialects of nEC, Stlg, N. Lnk, and E. Rox, 4 as well as 8 has full length; mostly, these two have merged (thus as [eː], the regular vowel 8 outcome), but in a few dialects, they show, in a few environments, distinct qualities, both long: thus Cowdenbeath before /l/, Newhaven before /m/.

But in the extreme SW, in Wgt and in individual localities in Kcb, Dmf and S. Rox (see Map 2), the distinction is one of quality, vowel 4 either having a closer realisation [ẹ] than the opener [ę] for vowel 8; or (in SE Dmf and Newcastleton, Rox) a diphthong with a closer starting position (see §22.2.4) than the corresponding vowel 8 diphthong, e.g. [ẹːⁱ] as against [ęːᵊ]. The quantities of both vowels in this region are usually short, in SVLR-short environments, except in the localities with diphthongal realisations, and in Balmaclellan, Kcb, where these vowels similarly differ in quality, but both have long quantity.

Between the two regions of non-merger lies a large area, viz. sEC, S, WC and part of SW, in which (with the rare exceptions noted above) vowels 4 and 8 have merged before /l, n/ and in other SVLR-short environments mostly as [e], i.e. as SVLR-short vowel 4, but, as mentioned above, in several clusters of localities as [eː], i.e. as vowel 8.

22.3.2 When did the merger of vowels 4 and 8 begin?

Did this merger begin in the OSc period? A much more definitive answer may be possible once a fairly exhaustive and detailed survey of the 'rhyming sets' of the OSc poets has been carried out. Meantime I set out the scanty evidence known to me.

As I discuss at §1.1, OSc possessed a large number of sets of synonymous doublets or 'morphemic variants' of cognate etymology, constituting a substantial minority of the items in the dictionary. A significant body of these were doublets of vowel 4 and vowel 8, as set out below. The overwhelming majority of the OSc rhymes apparently showing vowel 4 rhyming with vowel 8 involve members of these pairs of doublets. These rhymes therefore tell us nothing of any ongoing mergers of vowels 4 and 8.[57] The following present doublets in /aː/ and /ai/ in ESc:

(1) certain word-pairs of separate though cognate derivation: ESc /aˈgaːn/ (OE *ongēan*) and /aˈgain/ (OE *ongegn*); *sla(y)* v. with original pres.t. from ONhb *slā(n)*, ON *slá* > ESc /slaː/, and original p.p. from OE *slægen*, ON *sleginn* > ESc /slain/, with reciprocal interchange of vowels, yielding doublets of both parts of the verb; /θaim/ (ON *þeim*) and /θaːm/ (OE *þām*) 'them'; but none of the evidence as yet seen by me makes it necessary to postulate doublets in */ai/ for *hale* 'whole' ESc /haːl/ (OE *hāl*) or *thare* 'there' ESc /θaːr/ (OE *þār*) or in */aː/ for *thair* 'their' ESc /θair/ (ON *þeirra*). On OSc *thai* 'they' and *may* v. see §22.4 below;

(2) p.t. and p.p. forms of weak verbs which had acquired doublet pres.t. forms, such as *lay, say, pay, pray* (see §22.4 below) naturally also display doublets;

(3) forms arising out of the OE and ON sequences -*ǣg(e)*, -*ĕg(e)* before a liquid or nasal, in e.g. *hæg(e)l* 'hail', *fæg(e)n* 'fain', *fæg(e)r* 'fair', *seg(e)l* 'sail', *regn* 'rain', *leg(e)r* 'lying place'. In the OE contracted forms of these sequences, *hægl* etc., the glide *g* /j/, falling within the same closed syllable as the preceding vowel, readily vocalised to yield the diphthong /ai/ or /ei/ > /ai/, vowel 8 (§6.1.1), thus: OE *hægl* > /hajl/ > /hail/. For the uncontracted forms, which eventually yielded ESc vowel 4 /aː/, we must suppose that the ǣg- and ĕg- sequences first merged to yield /ai-/, just as in the contracted forms. Thereafter the [i] element of the diphthong was absorbed by the inflectional vowel and the [a] lengthened in compensation, thus OE *hægel* > /ˈhajɪl/ > /haiɪl/ > /haːɪl/, which with deletion of the inflectional vowel in hiatus became 14c /haːl/.

Consequently, all the words already instanced had ESc doublets in /-ail/ and /-aːl/, /-ain/ and /-aːn/ or /-air/ and /-aːr/, and similarly *sail*, *main* 'strength', *sain* 'bless', and possibly *hain* 'protect' (ON *hegna*). The vowel 4 forms of *quak* modSc /kwek/ (beside *quyok* /ˈkwɛiʌk/) 'heifer', and /kwet/ *quiet* probably developed in the same way (*pace* Kohler, 1967: 38);

(4) forms of /a/ + /ʎ/ or /ɲ/ (§§8.2.1 and 8.2.2) arising by Treatment I (yielding PreSc /ai/) and Treatment II (yielding PreSc /a/ > /aː/ by OSL) interchanged their vowels. Thus e.g. /fail/ (Treatment I) and /faljɪ > faːljɪ/ (Treatment II) yielded in addition /faːl/ and /failjɪ/;

(5) some words have doublet forms of F and L derivation, e.g. *certain* and *certane*, *soverain* and *soverane*, and, apparently by parallel formation, *cheftain* and *cheftane*, *hautain* and *hautane*.

22.3.3 Vowel 4 and vowel 8 unmerged in earlier OSc, in environments subsequently short

Throughout OSc verse there are very numerous rhymes of individual members of these several sets of doublets both with other doublet items and with invariable vowel 4 or vowel 8 items: thus Barbour rhymes *agane* both with *tane* p.p. 'taken' vowel 4 and with *pane* 'pain' vowel 8; in *Troy-bk*, *certain* rhymes both ways; *said* p.t., p.p., rhymes both with *braid* 'a quick movement' (OE *gebregd*) vowel 8 in *Seven.S.*, and with *maid* 'made' vowel 4 in *Bk. Chess*, etc. etc.

But once these doublets are excluded, the number of rhymes between vowels 4 and 8 in SVLR-short environments is, so far as my own researches have gone, exiguous. Before /l/, qualifying rhyme-words in invariable vowel 8 are all but limited to *vail* 'veil' and *wail*, and I have no rhymes of these to hand. Before /n/ at least some poets treat vowels 4 and 8 as distinct. In Dunbar's *In Secret Place*, he has 18 rhymes for *ane* 'one' or *gane* 'face', all with vowel 4 (*nane* 'none', *gane* 'gone', *grane* 'groan', etc.); while in *All Erdly Joy*, he has 20 rhymes for *pane*, spelled *-ane*, but all with vowel 8 (*plain, pain, again, grain* 'seed', *train* 'deceit', *rain*, etc.). Similarly, Holland's *Howlat* has many sets of three or four rhymes in which vowels 4 and 8 are rhymed separately.

Henryson, in his *Fables*, keeps separate historic /ai/ vowel 8 and /aː/ vowel 4 before /n/, with no recourse to doublet alternatives, rhyming, for instance, vowel 8 in *mane* 'main, strength', *agane* 'again', *pane* 'pain' (2890 f.) on the one hand, and vowel 4 in *mane* 'complaint', *nane* 'none' (1529 f.) on the other, and at one locus (2743 f.) he rhymes *lane* 'loan' : *tane* p.p. 'taken' : *gane* 'gone' against *fane* 'fain' : *agane* 'again'. And, citing many instances, DOST notes that *layne* 'to conceal' (ON *leyna*) rhymes only with vowel 8. Since vowel 8 largely shares the same spelling with vowel 4, especially <-ane>, these clear instances of the separation of 4 and 8 in rhyme can hardly be due merely to poetic tradition.

Against these strong indications of the separation in rhyme of vowel 8 from vowel 4, there are some counter-examples. At *Howlat* 211 f. the adj. *plain* rhymes with *tane* p.p. 'taken', *ane* 'one' and *ran* 'rigmarole'; and Dunbar (6/62 f.) has *trayne* 'deceit' vowel 8 and *grayne* 'seed' or 'branch' (both of these vowel 8) in rhyme with vowel 4 in *stane* 'stone', *suffragane*, *meridiane*, as well as the potential doublet *soverayne*. *Clariodus* rhymes *alleane* vowel 4 with *plane* 'plain' vowel 8. A possible explanation of these exceptions seems to be that the two sounds remained separate, but at the time were phonetically and apperceptionally similar in their realisations, vowel 4 as [æː] or [ɛː], vowel 8 as [ai] or [æi], and that the rhymes in the preceding paragraph were imperfect but approximate.

The evidence I have before me for other SVLR-short environments is much too scanty for any definite conclusions. At *Fab.* 741 f. Henryson rhymes *bait* (ON *beit, beita*) : *lait* 'to seek' (ON *leita*) : *gait* pl. 'goats' (ON *geitr*), all vowel 8, as if this was a separate item in this environment in his system, as it seems to be still in some modern Fife dialects (though the picture is somewhat confused by lexical re-selection), e.g. Auchtermuchty, Pitscottie, Kilconquhar. Rhymes of *waith* 'hunting' (ON *veiðr*) with *skaith* 'harm' (ON *skaðe*) (Henr.) and of *graitht* (for *graid* contracted from *graithid*) 'equipped' (ON *greiða*) with *mad* 'made' (*Leg.S.*) perhaps have /aː/ from /ai/ before fricatives (§12.3). Douglas rhymes *saim* 'grease' (OF *saïm*) vowel 8 with *hame* 'home' vowel 4, while Alexander Scott rhymes *maid* 'maiden' vowel 8 with *undegraid* vowel 4, both apparently 'mixed rhymes'. Perhaps a more exhaustive study of the rhymes than I have carried out will enhance this scanty number of 'mixed rhymes'. Even so, in view of the likely chronology set out below, the explanation that they are imperfect rhymes must seem the most tenable.

22.3.4 Vowels 4 and 8 in non-final long environments

(i) Before /r/: the modern dialects

In most modSc dialects vowels 4 and 8 have merged before /r/, mostly as [eː], as they have in other SVLR-long environments. There are also a few dialects without this merger, in Sh, Angus, Per and elsewhere. In these the vowel 8 outcome before /r/ typically has an opener monophthong [ẹː] or [ɛː] than that of vowel 4. In SW dialects, including all of Wgt, 4 and 8 *have* merged, but under the local realisation of vowel 8 [ẹː] in other environments, not that typical of vowel 4 - the same realisation as that of unmerged vowel 8 of (iii) below, and in the unmerged SVLR-short environments (§22.3.1 and Map 2). Here in this environment, the [ẹː] slot is occupied by merged vowels (3+4).

(ii) Before /r/: the OSc rhymes

Some earlier OSc poets, including Barbour and Henryson and the authors of the *Seven S.* and *Bk-Chess*, seem to have kept ESc /aː/ vowel 4 separate in rhyme from /ai/ vowel 8 before /r/. Others, however, rhyme them freely. Thus e.g. at *Howlat* 15 f. we have *bair* p.t. 'bore' vowel 4 : *levar* 'rather' (with promoted stress on the ending, thus vowel 17 lengthened) : *fair* (OE *fæger*) with vowel 4 and vowel 8 doublets : *pair* vowel 8; and five more sets of 'mixed rhymes' of this type. *Wall.* has rhymes of *evirmar* '-more' vowel 4 : *pair* 'impair' vowel 8; *ayr* 'heir' vowel 8 : *bar* 'bore' vowel 4; and other such rhymes (Buss, 1886: 16). Dunbar, Douglas, Lyndsay, Alex. Scott, the author of *Clariodus*, and Alex. Montgomerie are among other poets practising these mixed rhymes. It seems then that vowel 4 (possibly a lowered allophone) and vowel 8 merged before /r/, beginning in the early to mid 15c, apparently by smoothing of the diphthong of vowel 8. This must have occurred about the same time as vowel 2 ESc /eː/ and vowel 3 ESc /ɛː/ merged before /r/ (§20.8.3).

(iii) In non-final SVLR-long environments other than before /r/

Before /v/, /ð/ and /z/, most or all of the words which would otherwise have yielded vowel 8, ESc /ai/, had already had their diphthongs smoothed to vowel 4 /aː/, as described at §12.3. In the modern dialects, accordingly, the LAS3 test-words in this case, *praise* and *raise*, widely share the outcome of vowel 4, as /eː/. In some SW dialects, however (§22.3.1), these words appear with the local realisation of vowel 8, in most cases [ę(ː)], accompanied by one or more words with historical vowel 4, examples of the not-infrequent phenomenon of lexical misplacement (§19), but on the whole distinct from vowel 4, which in most cases is [ęː], e.g. *blaze*, *clothes*. It appears that the PreSc smoothing in these environments did not extend to these SW dialects.

22.3.5 Summary of developments of ESc /ai/ vowel 8 in non-final environments

At some point diphthongal vowel 8 in non-final position, where it had not yet undergone smoothing as in §12.3 and (ii) above, was smoothed to modSc /eː/, less often /eːə/, or, in many of the dialects in which it has merged with vowel 4, /e(ː)/. There seem to be no clear clues as to when vowel 8 became a monophthong before a tautosyllabic consonant. The strongest indication perhaps is that the monophthongal outcome prevails throughout the entire Scots-speaking area, as [ɛː] or [e(ː)] or some similar vowel, including Ork and Sh (cf. §22.3.4(iii)).

The quality of the smoothed vowel 8 is in nearly all dialects close to or identical with that of vowel 4. In many conservative dialects the distinction between the two is that of quantity only, vowel 4, being subject to SVLR, having undergone shortening to [e] in the SVLR-short environments; while vowel 8, not subject to SVLR, remains long in all environments. It seems to follow from this that vowel 4 had already undergone SVLR-shortening before vowel 8 became smoothed from a diphthong to a monophthong, or the two, being of very similar quality, would have merged as [eː] and shown identical outcomes in the same environments. Thus it seems that the smoothing of vowel 8 to a long monophthong, probably [eː], in all of its non-final environments, came about later than the establishment of SVLR in these dialects.

This chronology accounts well enough for those dialects in which merger of vowel 8 (invariably long) with SVLR-short vowel 4 has not taken place. However, in many SW dialects, vowel 8 has remained unmerged, as the result of maintaining a lower height than vowel 4, but nevertheless operates SVLR. Whether this was due to early monophthongisation, with vowel 8 shadowing vowel 4 through the GVS at a lower height, as conjectured for vowel 8a, does not seem ascertainable.[58]

We may then assume that the merging of smoothed vowel 8 with vowel 4 in SVLR-short environments ensued thereafter in many C and S dialects, by adoption of SVLR by vowel 8. Since SVLR shortening spread from long high to long non-high vowels, vowel 8 undergoes SVLR only after vowel 4 and only in dialects in which vowel 4 has SVLR.[59] In some Tayside dialects, SVLR has not reached the non-high vowels, including vowel 4, which has accordingly merged, as a uniformly long vowel, with vowel 8.

The dialectological evidence (see §22.3.1 and Map 2) suggests that the more usual merger of SVLR-subject vowels 4 and 8 is an on-going change, which has been spreading outwards since its beginning, apparently in some C dialect, some time after the establishment of SVLR. It has not reached some SW dialects in which vowels 4 and 8 are nevertheless both subject to SVLR.

A possible chronological order (but see note 58) for the events so far covered in §22 might then be:

(1) smoothing of vowel 8 /ai/ to merge with vowel 4 /aː/ before fricatives (§12.3);
(2) merger of vowel 8 before /r/ with vowel 4, possibly as [aː > æː] (§22.3.4);
(3) establishment of SVLR (§21);
(4) shortening of vowel 4 to [e] in the SVLR-short environments (followed by raising and preiotation in initial position (§22.2));
(5) smoothing of non-final vowel 8 to [eː] or [ẹː], in many dialects merging with SVLR-long vowel 4 [eː], but not with SVLR-short vowel 4 [e];
(6) in some dialects, shortening of vowel 8 to [ẹ] in the SVLR-short environments;
(7) beginning of the spread of the merger of SVLR-short vowel 4 with SVLR-short vowel 8, centred in the C and S dialects (§22.3.1 and Map2).

22.4 The development of ESc /ai/ vowel 8 in final position

There are three different outcomes of vowel 8 in final position (in what follows * denotes items included in LAS3):

(1) a diphthong, often [ɛi], [ëi] or, in WC, [əi]. In many, but not all, modSc dialects, this shares the quality of vowel 1 short in e.g. *bite, bide*, and of vowel 10 in e.g. *doit, join, oil, poison*. This must have arisen by a diaphonemic split from the other allophones of vowel 8 at the [ɛi] stage in the closing of this phoneme from its original open diphthong [ai] to its eventual outcome as a long monophthong [eː]. This applies for example to *aye** 'always', *fey* 'doomed to die', *gey** 'gay, very', *hay**, *key** (from OE uninflected *cǣg*, see §§6.1.1, 6.3.2);

(2) early doublets in a diphthong as in (1) above and vowel 4 /eː/. In the case of two of these words, both of OF origin, *pay* and according to Murray (1873: 77) *pray*, these doublet outcomes arose quite early in PreSc: OF *pajier* and *prejier* > respectively *paijer* and *preijer* > PreSc /ˈpaijə(n)/ and /ˈpraijə(n)/, yielding dual results when the sequence /-aij-/ was simplified, either /ai/ when the /j/ was absorbed or, when the /i/ was absorbed, /ˈp(r)aːjə(n)/, with the vowel lengthened either by OSL or by compensatory lengthening; followed in both cases by eventual loss of the unstressed syllable and the /j/, /ˈp(r)aː.jə(n)/ > /ˈp(r)aː.jə/ > /ˈp(r)aːj/ > /ˈp(r)aː/, much as in the case of PreSc /eːjə/ *eye* (§6.3.2). The other two words of this group are: *thay* pron., with doublet outcomes from /θai/ < ON *þeir* and /θaː/ < OE *þā* 'those' pl. demonstrative, with which the former was confused; and *may* /mai/ < OE *mæg* and its doublet /maː/ < ON *má*;

(3) doublets with a diphthong as in (1) above and a monophthong, vowel 8b, merged in most modSc dialects with ESc /aː/ > /eː/. But this merger with vowel 4 was evidently not always the case. In some dialects of Angus and its neighbouring counties and in a group of dialects extending from south Dmf along the Border with England then west to Wgt, the outcome is a (mostly long) monophthong distinct from the outcome of vowel 4, having an opener realisation, as [ẹː] or [ɛː], than that of regular vowel 4 [eː] in the same and other dialects. A monophthong, whether merged with vowel 4 or not, is:

(a) all but regular in *day*, Tay*, lay* v., and possibly *play* v.;
(b) sporadic in *play*, May*, stay**, and *way**.

The failure of the monophthong to merge with vowel 4 is also most regular in (a) *day*, etc. It seems that we are witnessing the latter stages of a process of lexical diffusion whereby vowel 4 /eː/ is superseding a more original monophthong now represented in certain relic areas by [ẹː] or [ɛː], with (a) *day*, etc. the most stubborn of the relic forms. From this it would follow that the monophthong which first arose by smoothing of the PreSc /ai/ diphthong had an opener and/or backer quality than that of vowel 4 at that time;

(4) my collections as yet have not revealed to which group to assign the set of words including *cuntray* and *journay* (§14.8(5)), but their occasional, or for some words frequent, spelling with <-a#> suggests group (3).

The opener and/or backer quality of this new monophthong would naturally follow if, as seems likely, it first arose by lengthening of the first element of its diphthongal source /ai/, and if that was by then of opener and/or backer quality than vowel 4 /aː > ɛː/. This would naturally be the case if vowel 4 had by then already begun its GVS fronting and raising process. It follows that this monophthonging took place after the beginning of the GVS of vowel 4. Thereafter, we may assume, the new monophthong shadowed vowel 4's raising process at a somewhat lower vowel height, thus itself participating, as an additional vowel component, in GVS. Soon after its creation, this began merging with vowel 4, but the merged outcome has not yet reached the relic dialects specified above.

Figure 19: Vowels 4 and 8 word-final

examples	vowel number	PreSc	ESc	MSc	modSc
hay	8a	ai ———	ai ———	ɛi** ———	ɛi (əi, ʌi)
day, way, away	8b	ai ———	ɑː* ———	e̞ː ———	e̞ː
pay, may	8/4	aː ———	aː ———	ɛː ———	eː
ga 'go'	4			labialised***	
draw	12	au ———	au — ɑː — ɑː ———	ɑː / ɔː	

* Opener and/or backer than vowel 4.
** Diphthong-closing arrested at this point by phonemic identification with the new SVLR-short vowel 1.
*** As in §20.9, e.g. *away*.

Note: see also note 65.

The mechanism of the monophthongisation in this group of words may be conjectured (partly following Kohler, 1967: 36-9) as follows. A distinguishing feature of the words in question was that all occurred in inflected forms, albeit only infrequently in the case of some items. In addition to the more obvious cases of *day, say,* etc., which regularly and frequently occurred in inflected forms, the noun *clay* had in OSc a derived verb 'to smear with clay'; *May* appears in *Mayis month, Mayes* pl. and *Maying* vbl. n. 'May festivities'; even *Tay* has an attested inflected form in the folksong *Tayis bank*; for *way* and *away* Kohler (1967: 40) points to the later Sc phrase *gang your ways* or *gang your wa's*, the resultant monophthong of which, he suggests, was imported into *away*, whence also *awaw*. The modSc forms *waw* 'way' and *awaw* 'away' and OSc *maw*, rare variant of *may* v., arise out of vowel 4 forms treated in labial environments as described in §20.9. In these inflected forms, such as [ˈdaɪɪz], pl. of *day*, the [i] element of the diphthong was absorbed by the inflectional vowel and the [a] lengthened in compensation, yielding [ˈdaːɪz], which, with deletion of the inflectional vowel in hiatus > 14c [daːz] (as for *hail* etc., §22.3.2(3)). From Barbour on there are numerous rhymes proving the contraction of inflectional /-ɪz/ in such cases, after vowels 4 and 8, thus *was : mais* 'makes' (Barb. 2, 471 f.), *gais* 'goes' : *wais* 'was' (ibid. 5, 283 f.), *rais* p.t. 'rose' : *gays* 'goes' (ibid. 7, 342 f.), and similar rhymes between *was* and *cas* 'case' (Doug.); also *Thomas : assayis* and *Thomas : sayis* (Barb.); among many similar rhymes in later poets are *sayis : pais* 'weight' (Henr.), and *prais* v. 'praise' : *dais* 'days' (Dunb.).

The list of rhyme examples that I am aware of is hugely inadequate for anything approaching a complete account of the behaviour in OSc of the forms of vowel 8 word-finally. But it appears that some (perhaps only the earlier) 15c and 16c poets keep separate in rhyme vowel 4 final from any vowel 8 final, including our group (3). Barbour has no rhymes of vowel 4 with any vowel 8, except one of *thai* 'those' (see above) with *way* and one of *þai* 'those' or 'they' with *alsua*; and there is a rhyme, almost certainly scribal rather than authorial, of *way* with *ga* in the la15 Cambridge MS of Barbour. On the other hand Barbour rhymes vowel 4 *against* vowel 8 group (3), thus *alsua : ma* 'more' against *say : day* (2, 493 f.), and *sla : our-ta* against *yai* 'they' : *day* against *ma* 'more' : *to ga* (17, 99 f.) Wyntoun is said never to rhyme vowels 4 and 8 (Buss, 1886:15; no environments specified), and *Wall.* to do so no more than Barbour. *Seven S.* keeps final vowels 4 and 8 well separated, rhyming vowel 4 e.g. *ga* 'go', *ma* 'more', *sa* 'so', *stra* 'straw', *wa* 'woe' and *sla* 'slay', as one rhyming set, and, quite separately, 26 rhymes of members of vowel 8 group (3) with other words from the same group, and 12 rhymes of vowel 8 groups (1) or (2) with another vowel 8 item of the same or another group, e.g. *ay* 'always' : *may* v.; *ay* 'always' : *may* 'girl'; *may* v. : *away*. *Bk. Chess*[60] likewise rhymes vowel 4 only with itself and with *sla* v. and *pa* v. 'pay', both of which had doublets in vowels 4 and 8 (see above); it has three vowel 8 rhymes, one of group (3) only, *daye* : *laye*, two including the group (1) word *aye* 'always'.

Other poets, however, do rhyme vowel 4 and vowel 8 group (3), among them Henryson and Lyndsay; Henryson with e.g. *fray* 'from' : *day* : *say* and *tay* 'toe' : *day* : *gay* 'go'.[61] So vowel 8 group (3) is separate from vowel 4 in some earlier poets, but rhymes with vowel 4 in other (probably later) poets, smoothed vowel 8 having presumably merged with vowel 4.

Short vowels

23 The subsequent history of vowel 19, OSc /u̯/

According to LAS3, in the region between the Tay and the Kcb Fleet and in N. Ireland, vowel 19, OSc /u̯/, is now virtually universally realised, in all environments, as [ʌ], in some dialects fronted to [ӓ]. North of Tay [ʌ] is predominant also, except in Cai, Ork and most of all Sh, in which more rounded and/or centred realisations, [ɔ] or [ө], are more common than [ʌ]. In the SW less lowered and/or more rounded sounds [ʏ, ö, ө], are regular. We may suppose that in these peripheral and conservative dialects the realisations are less far removed from, or even close to, those formerly prevalent in OSc.

The wide regional distribution of the (apparently innovative) [ʌ] realisation suggests that lowering and unrounding has been proceeding for some time. In the 18c it appears that lexical diffusion through the several allophonic subsets of the phoneme was still incomplete. Writing *c*1779, Sylvester Douglas, of NE origin, distinguishes two realisations of vowel 19, one 'a sort of smothered vocal sound, as in Tully, scull, rut', the other 'which approaches nearer' [what is clearly our vowel 6 /u(:)/] 'in such words as punt, hulk, rump, dub, mud' (Jones, 1991: 139). Also in 1779, in a parody (*The Contrast*, in Jones, 1995: 248-9) of old-fashioned Scottish English of the time, in a near-phonemic invented orthography, one (? pseudonymous) 'Aulaxaunder Scoat' similarly distinguishes in his orthography between <u> ? /ʌ/ in *enstruck* 'instruct', *nurter* 'nurture', *uz* 'us', etc., and <oo> ? /u/ in *oonlas* 'unless', *auboov* 'above', *boot* 'but', etc. It appears that the unrounding had not yet been carried through in labial or pre-nasal environments.[62]

It seems possible that the change may have begun some time in the late 17c from a rounded, half-close to close realisation (in the [u̯, o̞] area), which existed in OSc, to the now prevalent unrounded half-open realisation [ʌ]. This was at first retarded by the influence of an adjacent labial consonant or a following /n/, but has now been completed in all allophones in many dialects, e.g. of C and S. What initiated the change is open to speculation. Noteworthy, however, is the close coincidence of the Sc outcome with that of StE of the south Midlands and South of England. Influence of the standard dialect on the vernacular dialects in matters of vocabulary and selectional phonology (*home* replacing *hame*, and so on) is manifest and has been observed and recorded, whereas influence from the standard on the vernacular in matters of phonetic realisation has been little regarded. Nevertheless, such influence clearly operates also.[63] Thus we may conjecture that we have here a sound-change, OSc /ʉ/ > modSc /ʌ/, by way of [o], [ö] and/or [ɤ], a trend adopted by late 17c vernacular dialect speakers from their betters who were then given to frequenting the English court. We may also speculate that in the development of OSc /ui/ vowel 10 to modSc /ʌi/, the first element was at some date equated with OSc /ʉ/ vowel 19 and thereafter followed its progress to /ʌ/.

Editor's note: AJA's treatment of the short vowels is probably to be regarded as unfinished. He makes no mention, for instance, of the dialectal backing and rounding of vowel 17 before /nd/ and /r/ to merge with vowel 12 (Johnston's 'HAND-darkening' (1997a, 1997b: 484)) or the backing of Vowel 15 to merge with vowel 19 after /w, ʍ/, as in *whistle*, and, less generally, before /l/, as in *hill* (Johnston, 1997a, 1997b: 468) (but cf. §14.16(5)). For references to remarks *passim* on the short vowels, see Index II.

24 Recapitulation: ESc to modSc in outline
Figure 20a: *The later development of the ESc vowel-systems*[64]

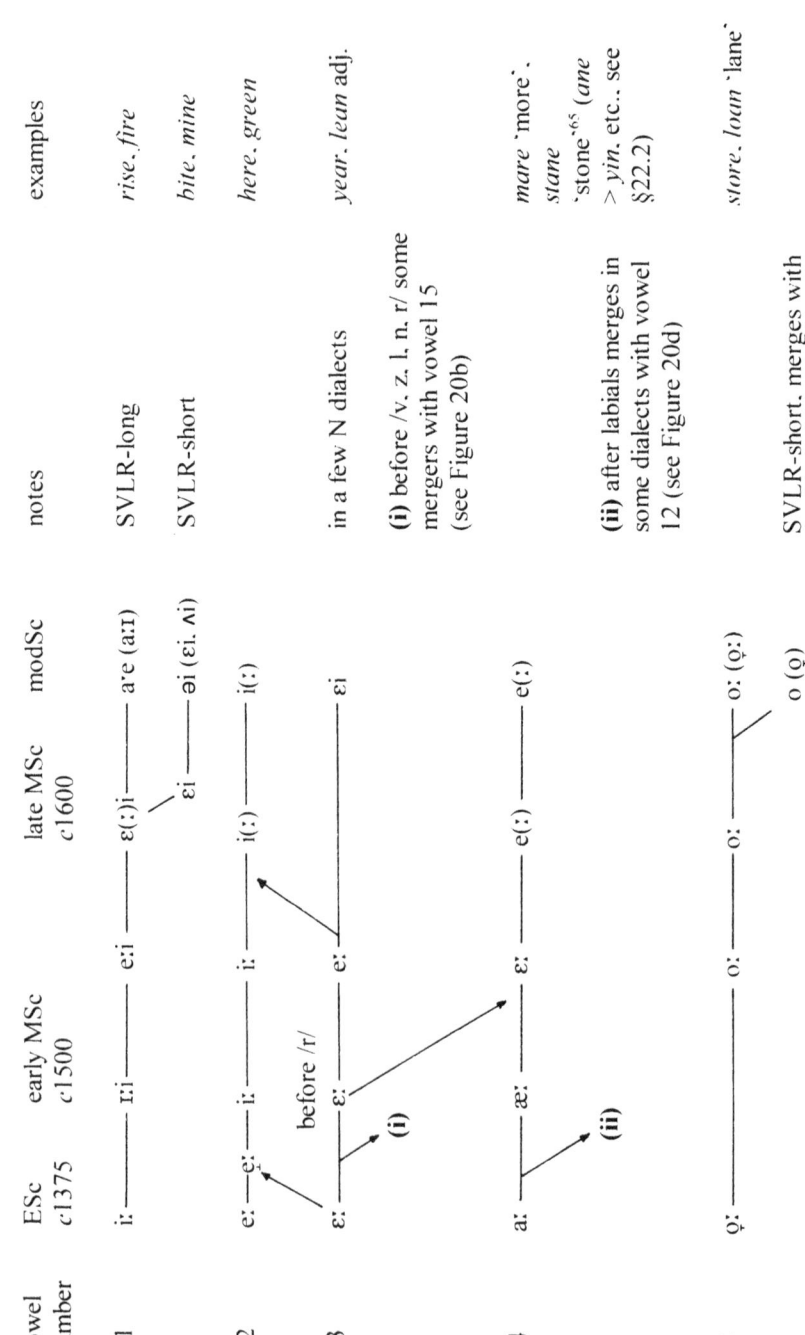

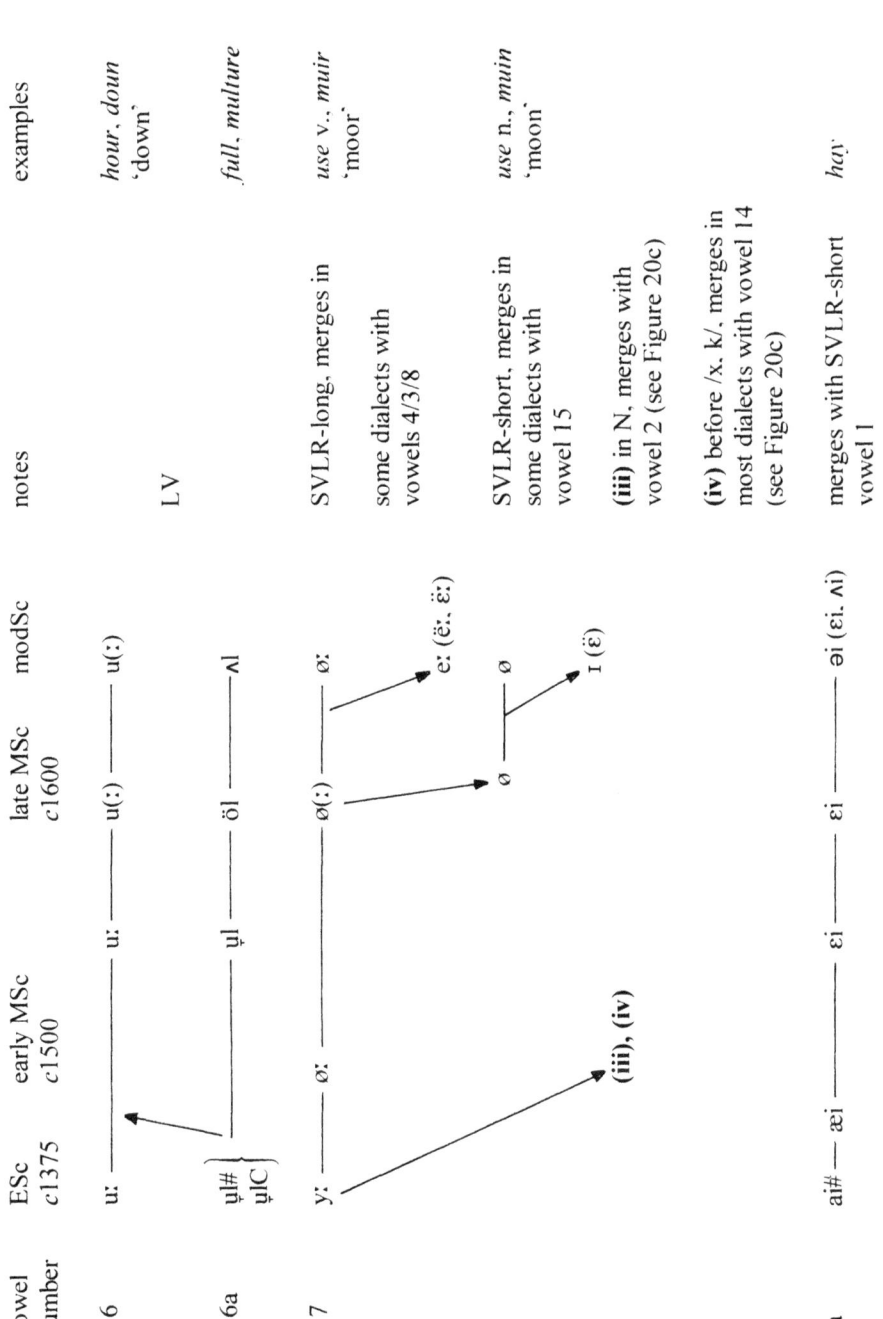

THE OLDER SCOTS VOWELS

vowel number	ESc c1375	early MSc c1500	late MSc c1600	modSc	notes	examples
8	ai ——	æi ——	ɛi ——	ei ——	ɛ:ə e(:)	merges in most dialects with vowel 4	pain
		(v)			(v) merges before /v, ð, z, r/ with vowel 4 (see note 65) in most dialects	raise, pair
8b	?ɑ̈:#, ?ɑ:# — a: ——	ɛ: ——	ẹ̈: ——	ẹ̈:	undergoes GVS	day
9	o̧i ——	o̧i ——	o̧i ——	ɔi		noise, void
10	ui ——	ü̧i ——	ö̧i ——	əi (ɛi, ʌi)	merges with SVLR-short vowel 1	point, join, doit 'the coin'
11	ei — e:				merges with vowel 2	hey 'high', drey 'endure'
12	au —— a̧: ——	ɑ: (a:) ——	ɑ: (a:) ——	ɑ: (a:) ɔ:		hawk, faut 'fault'
12a	al# ——	al ——	al ——	al	LV remains in some dialects	balk 'beam', salt,

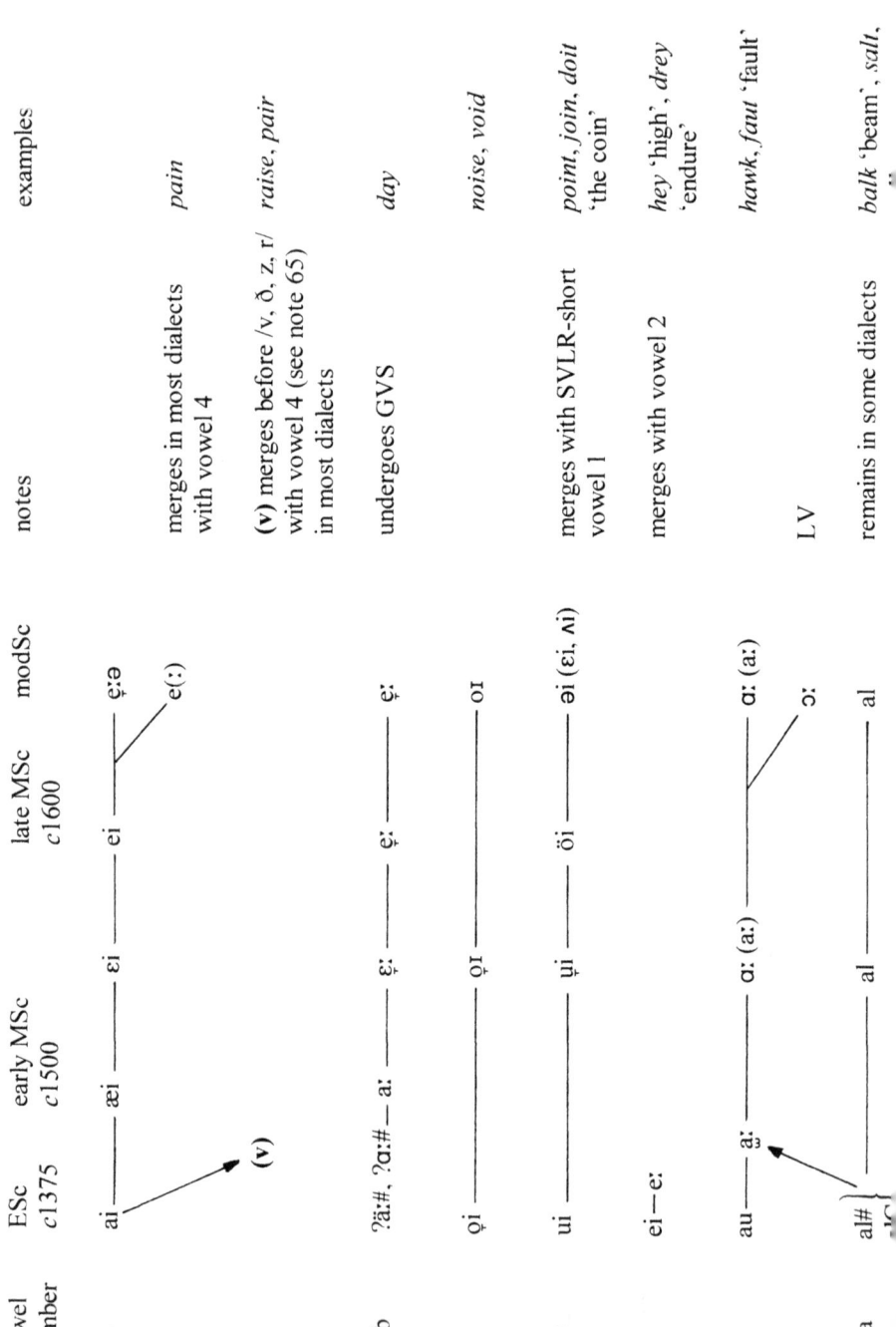

VOWEL PHONOLOGY FROM 1375

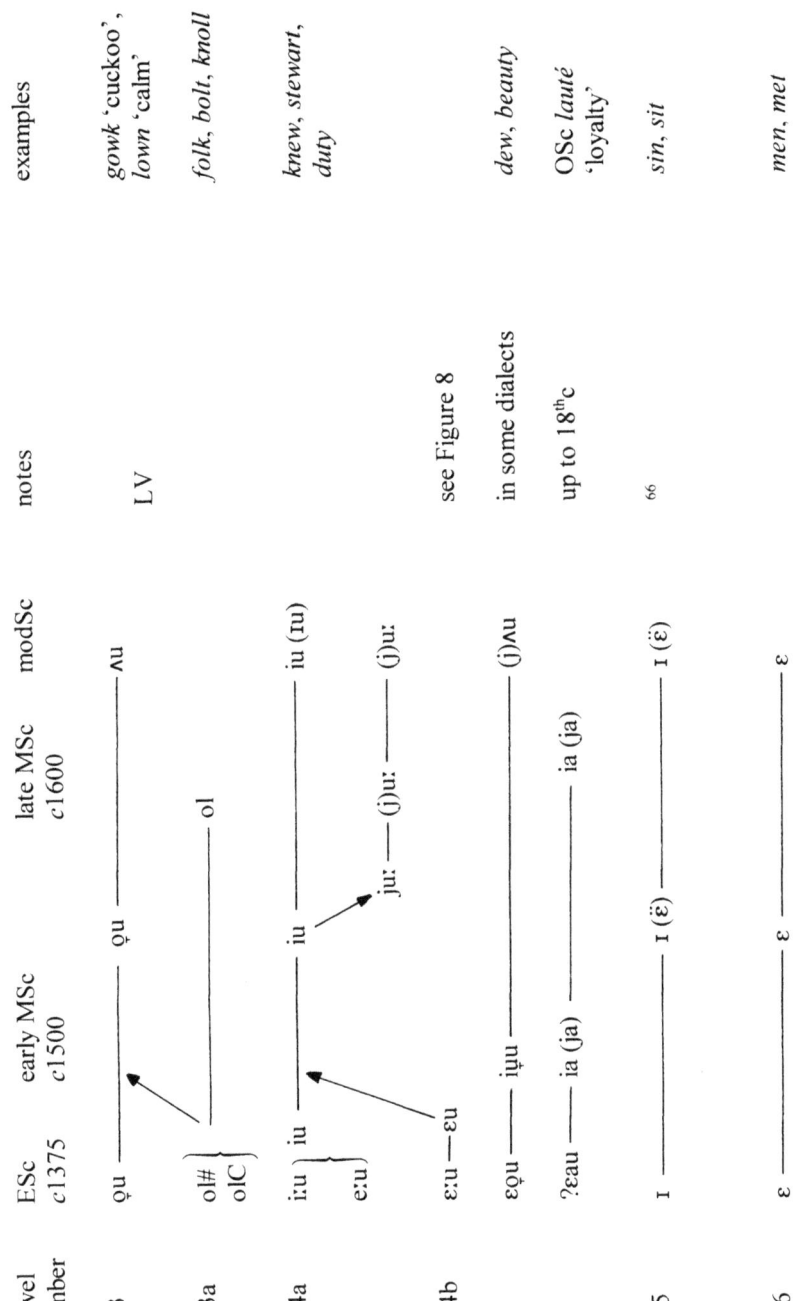

vowel number	ESc c1375	early MSc c1500	late MSc c1600	modSc	notes	examples
13	ǫu ────	ǫu ────	ǫu ────	ʌu	LV	*gowk* 'cuckoo', *lown* 'calm'
13a	ol# / olC {		ol			*folk, bolt, knoll*
14a	iːu / eːu {	iu	iu ─── juː ─── (j)uː	iu (ɪu)		*knew, stewart, duty*
14b	ɛːu─ɛːu	iʉ̧	nʉ̧ ─── (j)ʉː	(j)ʌu	see Figure 8	*dew, beauty*
	ɛǫu				in some dialects	
	ʔɛu ── ia (ja)	ia (ja)	ia (ja)		up to 18th c	OSc *lauté* 'loyalty'
15	ɪ ────	ɪ (ë) ────	ɪ (ë) ────	ɪ (ë)	66	*sin, sit*
16	ɛ ────	ɛ ────	ɛ ────	ɛ		*men, met*

155

THE OLDER SCOTS VOWELS

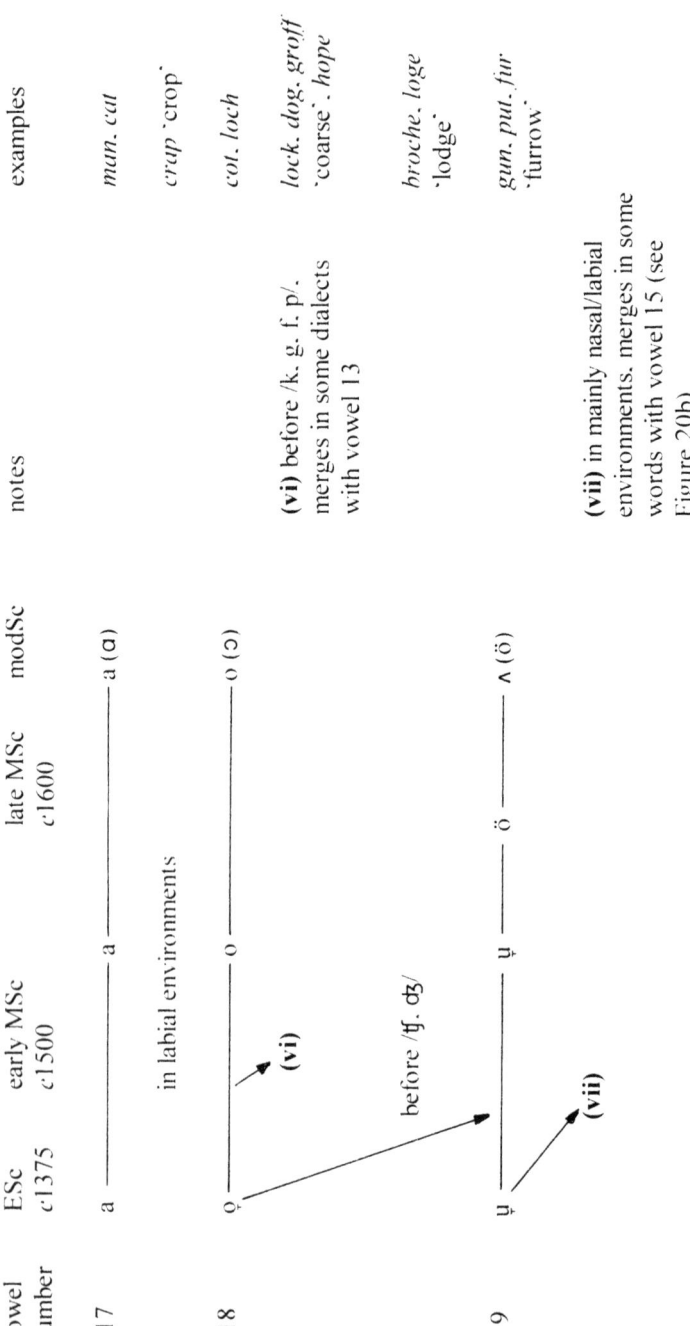

vowel number	ESc c1375	early MSc c1500	late MSc c1600	modSc	notes	examples
17	a	——— a ———		a (ɑ)		*mam, cat*
		in labial environments				*crap* 'crop'
						cot, loch
18	ǫ	——— o ———————		ɔ (o)	(**vi**) before /k, g, f, p/, merges in some dialects with vowel 13	*lock, dog, groff* 'coarse', *hope*
		(**vi**)				
		before /tʃ, dʒ/				*broche, loge* 'lodge'
19	ų	——— ų ——— ö ———		ʌ (ö)	(**vii**) in mainly nasal/labial environments, merges in some words with vowel 15 (see Figure 20b)	*gun, put, fur* 'furrow'
		(**vii**)				

General notes: LV = l-vocalisation (§17).
SVLR = Scottish Vowel-Length Rule (§21.2).
GVS = Great Vowel Shift (§20)

Brackets enclose variant realisations.

VOWEL PHONOLOGY FROM 1375

Figure 20b: Mergers with vowel 15 /ɪ/

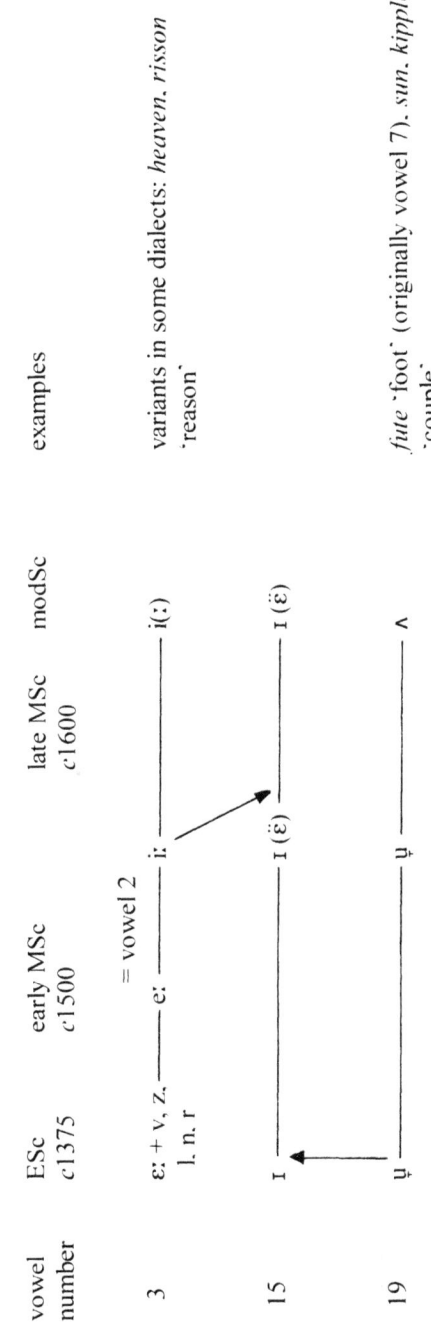

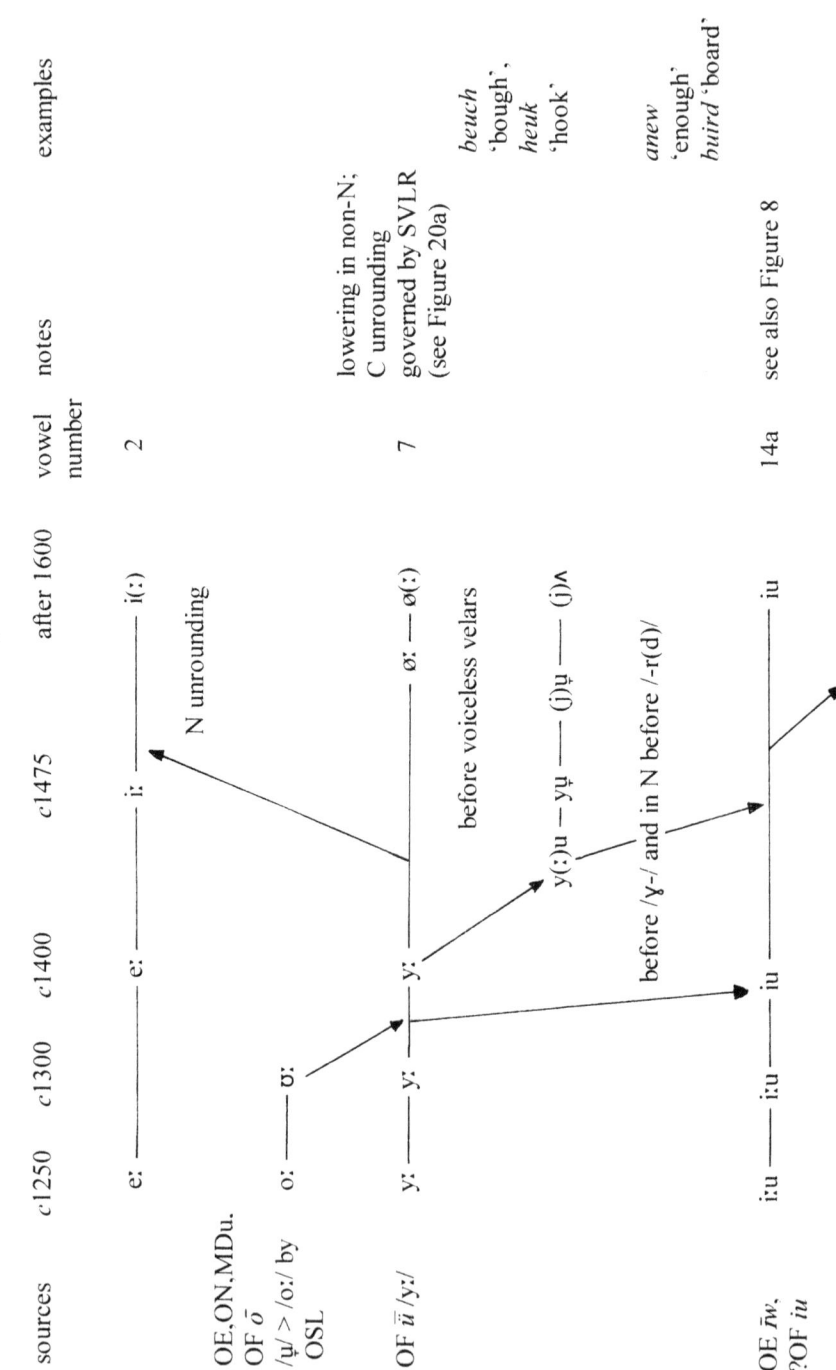

Figure 20c: Fronting of PreSc /oː/ vowel 7 and associated developments

VOWEL PHONOLOGY FROM 1375

Note to Figure 20c: The merger in N of vowel 7 with vowel 2 took place directly with 2, not by the intermediacy of vowel 3. This is evident because in some localities (chiefly along the Moray Firth) that show this outcome, vowel 3 has not reached vowel 2, but remains at vowel 4, as [e] or, in Avoch, [ɛi], the realisation there of vowel 4.

Figure 20d: Merger of vowel 4 in labial environments with vowel 12

vowel number	ESc c1375	early MSc c1450	early MSc c1500	late MSc c1600	modSc	modern dialect distribution	examples
4a	aː	aː	æː	ɛː	e(ː)	sEC, S, SW	wake, water, wha 'who', twa 'two', labour
12	au			ɑː (aːː)	ɑː (aːː) ɔː	SW, WC, nEC, N	

159

THE OLDER SCOTS VOWELS

Figure 21: Vowel systems of Scots: a rough historical outline

Vowel number	Early Scots (to 1450)	Middle Scots (to 1700)	Modern Scots	Principal Older Scots graphemes
1	iː ————	ei ———⟨	əi aˑe	iCe, yCe, y; yi, ay; y#
2	eː ————	iː ————	i	e, eCe, eC-; ei, ey, ea; e(e)#,
3	ɛː ⤴ or			ey#, ie#
4	aː ⤵ ————	eː ————	e	a, aCe, aC-; ai, ay, e, ea; a#, ay#, ae#
5	ǫː ————	ǫː ————	o	oCe, oC-, o; oi, oy; o#, oo#
6	uː ———— ⤴	u ————	u	ou, ow; (ul); ow#
6a	ul			ul(l), (w)ol; ull#
7	yː ————	ɵː ————	ø or ———— i or ———— e or ⟨ e ɪ	oCe, oC-, oi, oy, o(me), o(ne), (w)o, uCe, uC-, wCe, wC-; ui, uy, wi, wy, ou, ow, oo; o#, oe#, oo#, ou#, ow#, u(e)#, w#

160

VOWEL PHONOLOGY FROM 1375

Vowel number	Early Scots (to 1450)	Middle Scots (to 1700)	Modern Scots	Principal Older Scots graphemes
8	ai — εi —	ɛ̈ː, eə / or \ e		ai, ay, aCe, aC-, ae, ei, ey; e, ea
8a	ai# — εi# — əi#			ay#, ey#
9	o̜i — o̜ɪ — oe			oi, oy
10	ui — ui — əi			oi, oy; ui, uy, wi, wy, i, y, iy
11	ei# — eː# — iː# — i#			ey#, e#, ee#; ie#
12	au — ɑː — ɑ / or \ ɔ			au, aw; (al): aw#, a#
12a	al			al, all, aul; au, aw, a: aw#, a#
13	o̜u — o̜u — ʌu			ou, ow; (ol): ow#
13a	o̜l			ol, oul: oll#
14a, 14b(i)	iu — iu — iu / or (j)u			eu, ew, uCe: ew#, ue#
14b(ii)	εo̜u — iṷu — (j)ʌu			eu, ew; ou, ow: ew#, ow#

THE OLDER SCOTS VOWELS

Vowel number	Early Scots (to 1450)	Middle Scots (to 1700)	Modern Scots	Principal Older Scots graphemes
15	I ————	I ————	I	i, y
16	ɛ ————	ɛ ————	ɛ	e
17	a ————	a ————	a	a
18	o̞ ————	o̞ ————	o or ɔ	o
19	u̞ ————	u̞ ————	ʌ	u, o(m), o(n), w(o); ou

Note: In the lists of graphemes, the semi-colons divide spellings dominant in ESc from those which become common only in Middle Scots; the colon precedes word-final spellings.

NOTES

1. This account draws not only from my own previous work, published and unpublished, but on that of many other scholars and works of scholarship. Among the latter it will be obvious that I have leaned especially heavily on *A Dictionary of the Older Scottish Tongue* (DOST) and *The Linguistic Atlas of Scotland, Scots Section*, vol.3 (LAS3). Among other scholars I am conscious of borrowing most heavily from the work of Caroline Macafee, Catherine van Buuren and Volker Mohr.

2. *Editor's note*: in a draft note to Figure 8, AJA mentioned that Murray (1873: 117) heard the realisation in Southern Scots as [øu]. Zai (1942: §§162-64) interpreted this as indicating that /iːu/ (< /iːu/ and /eːu/) and /ɛu/ were levelled under the /yːu/ which arose from the diphthongisation of OF $\bar{u}$ pre-pausal and pre-vocalic. AJA considered that 'for several reasons Zai's argument seems flawed' and he notes that 'a scenario to account for this outcome could be conjectured', but unfortunately he does not give his own interpretation.

3. Earlier spellings of this type cited in DOST, s.vv. e.g. *Cukstule* and *Furd(e)*, are apparently often from later copies. Unfortunately the abundant information on early forms in the early volumes of DOST and in Craigie (1925), loses much of its value because of a failure to indicate the contemporaneity or otherwise of the sources cited. We badly need a full investigation of the vernacular matter in the early (pre-literary) Scots records, that will, *inter alia*, take account of the originality or otherwise of the documents. But the forms cited above are apparently contemporary with the dates given.

4. ESc and early MSc also rhyme vowel 7 (from both native $\bar{o}$ and OF $\bar{u}$) + /r/ with vowel 6 /uː/, e.g. *cure* : *sawure* (*Leg. S.*), *bur* (analogous p.t. of *bere* 'bear' v.) : *apparitur* (Henr.); perhaps vowel 7 had a retracted allophone before /r/, or was in some dialects captured by Vowel 6 in this environment (cf. modern dialects with a Vowel 7 = 6 merger, below).

Editor's note: AJA had begun to search through DOST for examples of vowel 6 spellings and rhymes for vowel 7 items, and had reached the end of F. His rough notes list the following:

> *aventour, endour, combure* (late), <coniour> *conjure* (once only, *Leg. S.*), <dour> *dure* 'door' (1525 Gau), <dour be dure> (1555 Peebles), <endowre> *endure* (Wynt., 1431 Ayr, *Wall.*), <figour>

figure (Wynt. onwards), <flowk> *fluke*, reverse spelling ? <flure> *flour, foule* : *stule* (*Leg. S.*), *fowl* : *schule* (*Leg. S.*), <four> *fure* v. (not cited except in headnote), <Fowresday> *Furisday*, <fowt> *fute* (*Leg. S.*).

5. *Editor's note*: this is in contrast to Aitken (1977: 6), where he chooses /yː/ for the NE but otherwise /øː/ 'in view of (*a*) its earlier ME starting point (as a half-close (back) vowel) and (*b*) its modern reflexes ... .' However, there is one position that would have argued in favour of a closer realisation but which he no longer accepted: 'the early shortening (earlier than that of the Vowel-length Rule) of vowel 7 to yield vowel 15 in *fit* 'foot', *sit* 'soot', *nit* 'nut', *pit* 'put', *wid* 'wood', *ither* 'other', *brither* and *mither* and other words' (1977: 10). Instead he now derives vowel 15 in these words from vowel 19 forms (see §16.1).

6. Were these realised, as by many speakers today, with lip-protrusion, which would naturally tend to cause 'over-rounding' and raising?

7. Except for Chepman and Myllar's black letter prints (*c*1507-8), and Myllar's separate 'Twelfth Tract' (? 1505), for both of which a special *ʒ* letter was cut.

8. These spellings are of course ambiguous and might equally represent ESc /aː/ vowel 4.

9. But the early frequency of forms in <ai, ay> suggests contamination from Treatment I.

10. *Editor's note*: cf. *wyme* for *wame* 'belly', etc. (see LAS3: Maps W2, W25, W95; Macafee, 1989: Map 4).

11. With the doubtful exceptions of OF *benigne* fem., *maligne* fem.

12. Apparently from an OF doublet in *i* of the regular form in *e*, the latter represented in OSc as <regn(e), reign(e), rengne> and rarely <renye> 1601.

13. These forms may be derived from vowel 4 + /n/ in the manner described by Macafee (1989: 433) for NE /aːn/ > modSc /in/ (see §9.3(1) below).

Editor's note: for the reader's convenience, I quote from the relevant section (with minor corrections to the table):

> If [the merger is of Vowel 4 with Vowel 3], then Vowel 4 cannot reach /i/ except in those dialects where Vowel 3 also does. This is confirmed by LAS vol III ... ... It is attractive to speculate that this might be a very

NOTES

early [Early Scots] merger. ... Unfortunately the spelling evidence does not support such an early sound change. ... However, there is other internal evidence for an early merger of Vowel 4 with Vowel 3 in certain environments. A number of words, with both Vowel 3 and Vowel 4 originally, have /əi/ in modern North-eastern Scots ... there is usually a labial element, e.g. *wame, weaver, quine*. ... In Aitken's reconstruction, Vowels 1 and 3 pass phonetically close to each other, Vowel 3 having reached /e/. That the merger with Vowel 1 should be at this point ... is confirmed by the modern distribution ... The distribution of /əi/ forms is regardless of the outcome of Vowel 3. ... This merger is surely of some antiquity, since those words originally with Vowel 4 have a considerable phonetic distance to cover. ... ...

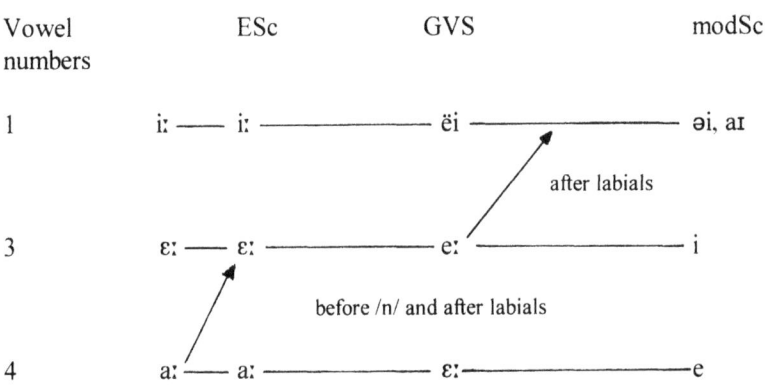

14. But there is no certain evidence of a surviving /a/ in *chamber* (cf. Bliss. 1969: §34).

15. Not, apparently, in the case of OSc *chamber*: see §9.1(3) above.

16. *Editor's note*: if the /ʌuld/ forms were found only in Uls and adjacent areas of the West of Scotland, we would probably have no hesitation in seeing these as Northern Hiberno-English forms (of English West Midlands origin). Although their peripheral distribution tends to suggest antiquity, they are not attested early, nor are they necessary stages in the reconstruction of the surviving forms. The argument for their antiquity in Scots is almost entirely geographical, with little support from spelling evidence. I tend to agree with Johnston (1997b: 489) that there must be *some* influence in Ulster from dialects of England, via Hiberno-English, even if only reinforcement, and probably therefore also in the West of Scotland (Macafee, forthcoming b).

17. Not according to - presumably prior to - SVLR, which favours maintenance of length in these environments.

18. Kohler's argument (1967: 49) that the rhymes of *consave* etc. with the vowel 4 monophthong are due to monophthongal stems of the OF etymons will of course not work, since the OF vowel in the latter is *e*, which would have yielded vowel 3, not 4.

18a. *Editor's note*: however, Bawcutt (1998: 14-15) is sceptical of such a use of final *-e* by Dunbar or his contemporaries, and in her 1998 edition of Dunbar does not follow earlier editors in their emendations to introduce *ë*. A wide range of metrical licences were permitted (see Macafee and †Aitken, 2002: §9.1.2), but even when these are taken into account, there are many MSc works where a five-stress line seems to be varied from time to time with a four-stress one (Bawcutt, 1998: 15), perhaps suggesting a lingering influence of the older metrical tradition (McClure, forthcoming).

19. Following the commonest spelling, this is here assumed to be of [ɪ] rather than [ə] quality.

20. As previous note.

21. So far the nearest approach to an exhaustive listing of the sources with full etymological details is Glenn (1987: 26-73).

22. *Leme* 'gleam' (OE *lēoma*) rhymes, e.g. in Dunb. *Golden Targe*, with indubitable vowel 3 words, including its near synonyms, *beme* and *gleme*, to which presumably its vocalism was conformed, at least for rhyme purposes.

23. *Were* n. 'doubt, perplexity' always rhymes with vowel 2, whereas *were* 'war' rhymes with vowel 3, so it is unlikely that they are cognate, as suggested in e.g. OED.

24. *Fere* n. 'fear' (OE $\bar{æ}^1$) had vowel 3 (see e.g. the rhyme with *wer* 'war', *Wall.* 9, 265 f.).

25. For the shortening of the vowel in *broche*, *loge*, *motioun* and *sojourn*, see §§14.19, 16.2.

26. Also OSc *distroy*, but the spellings <dystrwyand> 15, <dystrwyt> *c*1517, most probably represent a variant from OF *üi* < Rom. **dēstrūgĕre*, which also exists in ME (Jordan and Crook, 1974: §237 Remark), in OSc possibly with vowel 7.

NOTES

27. The date of the sound change represented by (6) is problematic. The form <waut> 'welt' indicates a date before l-vocalisation. If so, the failure of *twal* 'twelve' to show similar l-vocalisation must be explained as avoidance of homonymic clash with *twa* 'two'.

27a. *Editor's note*: The reading *contreit* is found only in the *Bann. MS* (Priscilla Bawcutt, personal communication).

28. *Editor's note*: in contrast to AJA's earlier (1977) acceptance of this theory (see note 5).

29. *Editor's note*: it is attractive to see NE forms such as *bljaave* for *blaw* 'blow' as survivors of vowel 14b(iii), the merger of these vowel 12 items having been with vowel 14b(iii) rather than *vice versa*.

30. An apparent exception to this is *dowie* 'sad' la16, apparently from *dolly* la15, itself? < OF *dol* 'sorrow'.

31. The 'mute' <l> in the spellings of the place-names *Kirkcaldy*, *Culross*, *Tillicoultry* on the other hand results directly from the operation of l-vocalisation on the older forms of these names, in which the /l/ was original.

32. The apparent reverse spellings <wauld, wald> 'woad' in one section of the Bute MS (*a*1424), now in the National Library of Scotland, beside <wad, wade, waid> elsewhere in the same MS, would suggest a much earlier date for this change, and consequently for the l-vocalisation of /al/ and the beginning of the shift of ESc /a:/ vowel 4 by GVS, than the rest of the evidence supports. But it is also possible that <wauld, wald> are patterned on spellings of the set <wald, wauld, wad> 'would', p.t. of *will* v., in which the loss of /l/ is most likely due to lack of stress in weak forms.

33. *Editor's note*: Aitken (1997b) notes:

> LAS is far from being a complete report of the Linguistic Survey of Scotland, Scots Section's findings. *Inter alia*, not all of the localities surveyed are reported: e.g. in southern Scotland, Stewarton, Glencairn, Selkirk, Flemington, Ayton and Glasserton have all been omitted from the published volume. For this, as for other apparent inconsistencies mentioned below, no explanation is given in the published volume.

On the correspondence between the fieldworkers' books and the published findings, he points out (ibid.) that 'a partial check on the LAS3 in this matter is accessible in the theses of Kohler (1964) and Vaiana (1972).'

On the non-transcription of length in the first element of SVLR-long vowel 1 (see below), he remarks:

> Indeed, I have heard two of LSS's chief fieldworkers, Trevor Hill and Jim Mather, agree that vowel 1's two outcomes were respectively a slow and a fast diphthong - a slow diphthong = one with a long first element. (*ibid*)

34. *Editor's note*: see §22.4 for the suggestion that monophthongised vowel 8 also participated in GVS.

35. So it must have remained a separate phoneme here until after the unrounding of vowel 7, of which there are no indications before the 17c at earliest.

36. It will be noticed that *slate* is a stray from the vowel 4 +8 set into vowel 3 set, and *wheat* is perhaps a similar stray from the vowel 3 +7 set to vowel 2 (also in a few other East Fife dialects). Cases of 'lexical misplacement' or 'lexical mis-allocation' such as this are endemic among LAS3's word-lists. The explanation appears to be that these are borrowings from StE or from some other dialect in which the phonemic-lexical correspondences differ from those of the borrowing dialect, for example by having only one phoneme with the conflated set of lexemes appropriated to it where the borrowing dialect has two phonemes, each therefore having a more limited set of lexemes attached to it. When a borrowing is made the speaker making the borrowing can therefore easily make the 'wrong' choice between the two alternative phonemes in his own system to which to allocate the borrowed lexeme. When it is otherwise clear which historical vowel a set of words represents, e.g. by the quality [i] in the case of vowel 2, or by containing a preponderance of examples of a particular origin (cf. §14), I have followed these indications, and ignored what appear to be 'lexical misplacements'.

Editor's note: Johnson (1997b: 451; 2000) follows the same method of identifying what he calls 'majority forms'.

In an earlier draft, AJA mentioned that a special study, not attempted here, would be needed to determine whether the apparent deviation from the normal course of vowel 3 that led to the diphthong (unmerged or merged with vowel 8) happened in the course of GVS (with vowel 3 diphthonging rather than raising as elsewhere in Scotland), or at some later date.

37. *Editor's note*: on /e/ for vowel 3 in Wgt and Uls, see Milroy (1982) and Macafee (forthcoming b).

NOTES

37a. *Editor's note*: and apparently in *na* 'no, nay' (see DOST s.v. *na* adv.³); and perhaps also in modSc *yaup* alongside *yape*.

38. *Editor's note*: the geographical distribution of this merger does not really coincide with Southern Scots (see LAS3: Maps S23, S24, S26, S28-33: nil values for polyphoneme A). There is some spelling evidence in the *Peebles Burgh Records* of the 1560's for the merger: <sailfand> (= *saufand* 'saving') 28 October 1564, and *bailk* 'back' 20 August 1564, seem to combine the Vowel 4, hence vowel 17, spelling <ai> with vowel 12's <al>. From 25 April 1571 on, there are vowel 12 spellings of vowel 17, e.g. *wauch(ing)* 'watch(ing)', and *lawdis* 'lads' 7 February 1572.

Meurman-Solin (1999) has also suggested that the use of short vowel spellings for long vowels, for which she has examples from as early as the 1540's, indicates SVLR-shortening. However, as she also points out, a number of her examples are in the pre-/r/ environment.

39. See e.g. the DOST entries for *Hukstar, Hunter, Hurt, Hussy, Lukkie, Lum, Lump, Lung, Lunt, Muk, Mukill, Nun*.

40. See e.g. the DOST entries for *Mouth* n. (<muth(t), mwth(t)>), *Outhall* n. (<uthale, udall, etc.>), *Outit* ppl. adj. (<utted>), *Outland* n. (<utlan, -len>), *Outlandis* adj. (ut-, wtlandis>), *Outlaw* n. (<wt(e)law> la15).

41. Including one (vowel 1) which early in OSc became a diphthong, but excluding two diphthongs (vowel 8 /ai/ and vowel 12 /au/) which in the course of OSc became monophthongs.

Editor's note: in a manuscript note, AJA suggested that the opting out of vowels 8 and 12 was not owing to their diphthongal character, but rather to the pattern of diffusion of the SVLR, from the highest to the lowest vowel-height, thus leaving vowels 8 and 12, and also 5, as exceptions in many dialects. This has implications for the reconstruction of the date of smoothing of vowel 8 (§22.3.5; see note 58).

42. *Editor's note*: Aitken (1995/6: 22) points out that it was Murray (1873) who 'first observed and formulated' the Scottish Vowel-Length Rule. However, it was AJA who brought it to the attention of modern scholarship, and fully explored its ramifications and implications. In recognition of this, many scholars have taken up the alternative name, Aitken's Law, and the Rule is listed as such by Collinge (1985) in his *The Laws of Indo-European*. AJA himself referred to the Scottish Vowel-Length Rule. He explains the origin of 'Aitken's Law' in Aitken (1981: 156, note 1):

The name 'Aitken's Law', which was taken up and promulgated by Mary Taylor and Roger Lass in their contributions to the 1973 Edinburgh Conference on Historical Linguistics, was first coined jokingly by David Murison. This was in gentle mockery of the fuss I used to make about the phenomenon in a seminar-course on Scots phonology I conducted some time in the 1960's.

Scobbie, Hewlett and Turk (1999) reanalyse the available instrumental data from various studies of vowel-length and show convincingly that there is a distinctive SVLR. However, only three vowels - /i, u, ai/ - are governed by the SVLR in these data, mainly from native ScStE speakers. As Aitken (1997b) pointed out, there is a need for instrumental studies of conservative rural speakers. Scobbie *et al.* are presently engaged on research on the SVLR.

43. For some other environments which less regularly offer long variants, see Aitken (1981: 135, §5).

Editor's note: AJA also suggested (1997b) that the fairly common Eastern realisation, from Shetland southwards, of vowel 16 as long [ɛː] is motivated by the avoidance of merger with vowel 15 as [ë].

44. *Editor's note*: AJA's earlier draft read:

> perhaps because the realisations of these were of less duration than those of any other vowels when SVLR was set up, further shortening thus being impossible.

This is compatible with the recent work of Scobbie, Hewlett and Turk (1999).

Evidence for the lowering of /ɪ/ is provided by <e> spellings from at least 1456 (Aitken, 1971: 202), which seems rather early for the interpretation offered in the next paragraph.

45. *Editor's note*: cf. Johnston's '(Glasgow) drawl' (1997b: 461, 480).

45a. *Editor's note*: in some LAS3 localities (see §22.2.2), vowel 7 short and preiotised vowel 4 (as in *yin*) go together and are distinct from vowel 15, in at least some environments.

46. *Editor's note*: at this point, AJA referred the reader for further details to Aitken (1981:141). For the reader's convenience, the relevant sentences are quoted below:

Some seeming vowel-length irregularities ... occur in some Shetland dialects. In these dialects SVLR vowels before /d/ appear with both long and short realizations: as, [hiḓḁ̇] *heed*, [niḓḁ̇] *need*, etc., but [miːḑ] *meethe* or *meed* 'landmark', [liːḑ] *leethe* or *leed* 'will to work', and [gøḓḁ̇] *good*, [fløḓḁ̇] *flood*, but [røːḑ] *rööd* 'drizzle, chatter', [bøːḑ] *booth*. These results, which must have been anticipated by J. C. Catford and his collaborators in compiling the L.S.S phonological questionnaire, are easily explained as consequences of the SVLR. The dialect just cited, which is typical of others, was that of Fetlar in the north-east of Shetland. That of Burra in the south-west, gives similar results. .... A statement by George Low suggests that the parallel change of /θ/ to /t/ had taken place in Orkney by 1773 and Shetland by 1836 (see S.N.D. s.v. T, 9 (1) (v)). .... The occurrence of these long vowel realizations before /d/ in Fetlar and Burra is predictable only if one knows the etymologies of the words in question. Consequently, according to strict structural phonemics, these dialects display certain additional long vowel phonemes which occur only before /d/.

47. *Editor's note*: at this point, AJA again referred the reader to Aitken (1981:141):

The dialect of Dunrossness in the extreme south has, however, [hiḑ] *heed*, [niḑ] *need* but [miːd̥] *meethe* and [liːd̥] *leethe*, [gǫd̥] *good* and [flǫd̥] *flood*, but [rǫːd̥] *rood* and [bǫːd̥] *booth*.

He also notes (ibid., note 9) that the merger of /ð/ with /d/ is only partial:

Since e.g. *breathe*, *bathe* and *smooth* appear as [breːd̥], [beːd̥] and smuːd̥] or (Dunrossness) [smœːθ] (the last also retaining a long realization as a relic of earlier /ð/ in this word) in all three of the Shetland dialects cited.

48. *Editor's note*: AJA was concerned to identify the earliest concrete evidence of the operation of the SVLR. His earlier suggestion that it was incipient by the 15c (1977: 9) depends on the line of argument from the participation or not of diphthongs (see note 41). He occasionally suggests that it could be responsible for earlier developments, for instance *lippie* (1542) (§5.3) (but not the 15th century shortening of vowel 4 before n-mouillé and l-mouillé, §8.3, although he toyed with the idea of an ESc split of vowel 4 - see note 65). In his 1981 treatment, he set the earliest limit as the GVS:

had the Rule been in full operation at the time of the Great Vowel Shift (15th century) a merger of Vowel 4 (Early Scots /aː/, Middle Scots /eː/)

where shortened by the Rule in the short environments, with vowel 16 (Early Scots /ɛ/), might well have been expected. (1981: 154)

Contrary to his earlier statement (*ibid*) that there were no such mergers, he points out here (§21.2.2) that there are a few isolated lexical items with vowel 16 by shortening of vowel 4, from the 16c on. However, he continued in his more detailed (1997b) treatment to take the view that the GVS represented the *terminus post quem* for the establishment of the SVLR:

> With one exception [vowel 1], we don't get shorts or longs of a given SVLR-subject vowel in a given dialect at widely different vowel-heights, so there has been no change in vowel height since the GVS.

Gburek (1986) suggested that an incipient SVLR was involved in pre-GVS changes in strong verb paradigms, and Mohr (2000) has similar arguments based on different evidence. AJA did not rule out the possibility of allophonic shortening at an early date, particularly in the Central dialects where the Rule apparently originated, but:

> Whether or no this tendency to shortening existed prior to the Great Vowel Shift, it could only manifest itself fully after G.V.S. had brought about the changes of vowel quality which made the former oppositions by quantity functionally redundant. (1981: 154)

Presumably, this is compatible with occasional captures by short vowels of shortened (? half-long) allophones of their long equivalents.

49. *Editor's note*: see also §6.5.2 for a possible /ɛau/ vowel 14b(iii), with a small base of lexical variants, which do not survive beyond the 18c (but see note 29).

49a. *Editor's note*: Bawcutt (2000: 10) cites Aitken's earlier view, that these spellings (understood as evidence for the modern form of the sound-change) are 'associated with south or central Scotland'.

50. Exceptionally, in the heart of the area of merger, Newhaven, Midlothian, keeps vowel 8 separate from any other in *aim*, *maim*, though not in any of the other SVLR-short environments (except of course the word-initial as in /jɪn/ 'one').

51. *Editor's note*: this information does not come from the published materials of the Linguistic Survey of Scotland. Map 3 shows the relevant data.

52. *Editor's note*: it appears that AJA originally intended to argue that /jɪ/ derived from preiotised OSc /je/, as seems intrinsically likely, in SVLR-short environments, the evidence of *yape* notwithstanding. In the revised version, he comes down in favour of the widely accepted explanation offered by Murray. However, the incomplete revision bears the marks of having been written towards the opposite conclusion, and the twists and turns of the argument are difficult to follow. I have accordingly rewritten this section. I have also cut out some material elsewhere in the book that depends on the rejected line of argument. When he saw /jɪ/ as being derived from /je/, AJA had intended to use the evidence of the Monkland, Ayr, gravestone (§22.2.1) as evidence not only for the dating of this change, but for the dating of the SVLR, since the change would have been from a long vowel (vowel 4) to one invariably short (vowel 15), producing another SVLR-conditioned phonemic split. The inscription is quoted in full in Aitken (1971: 208, note 40):

> Heir lys yin vary honrible mon David Blair of Adamtoun spouse to Marget Hamiltoun quo decesit Sep. 1577 (quoted in Kirkwood Hewat, *A Little Scottish World*, Ayr, 1908, *p* 84).

Much of the evidence for preiotation, as AJA noted in an earlier draft, had previously been overlooked.

53. An apparent parallel to the development of /jɪn/ by spontaneous preiotation is the development of the cognate *wan* /wan/ (1642). This is more plausibly derived directly from PreSc *ane* /aːn/ than by borrowing of modEng *one* /wʌn/, especially as the form /wan/ is well-established in several Scots dialects. This form seems to have arisen by the development of a labial on-glide to PreSc /#aːn/, perhaps realised as a nasalised [ãːn] > [waːn], treated as in §18, yielding MSc /wɑːn/, shortened by SVLR to [wɑn] /wan/. PreSc /waːt/ 'wet' < ON *vát-r* has a similar development to MSc /wat/ *wat* beside *wate, wait*. In the modern dialects the /wan/ form, variably realised according to dialect as [æ, a, aː, ɑ, ɑː] is common north of Moray, in some Fife localities, in Glasgow and in Uls, but in all remaining areas only /in/ (NE), /en/ (nEC) and /jɪn/ (C and S) are found, which indeed also occur as alternatives in the /wan/ areas. This locally peripheral distribution suggests that the pre-labialised form is ancient and, indeed, if the above theory is correct, it must pre-date the events related in §18.

Editor's note: *wan* presents the same problems as *ould*, etc. It is the usual form in Ulster, both in Hiberno-English and in Uls Scots, and if found in Uls alone, or in Uls and the West of Scotland (SND also has it in Wgt), would be interpretable as a loan from this direction. In this case, however, both the East Coast distribution and the early Lowland Scots citations (17th century and possibly even earlier, see DOST s.v. *Wan* num.) speak against this interpretation (Macafee, forthcoming b).

54. *Editors' note*: as AJA points out in §22.3, Newcastleton, Rox also has a diphthongal realisation of vowel 4. The starting position here is [ẹ]. *Ale* and *one* have /jɪ/.

55. In Gretna Green this is [ɪ], with which vowel 2+3 has merged, while in Westerkirk and Canonbie SVLR-long vowel 4 has merged with vowel 2+3 as [iː].

56. There are mergers with this in the SVLR-long environments only of vowel 2+3 and also, in two long environments, vowel 7. Note that the other SVLR-subject vowels, e.g. vowels 2+3, 6 and 7, operate SVLR more or less normally in these four dialects.

57. In some cases, we can spot the stylistic preferences of individual poets for one or other member of a pair: thus Barbour strongly favoured the monophthongal (vowel 4) representative of *slane* p.p. 'slain' (in 24 rhymes) against only a few instances of the diphthongal *slayn* (vowel 8), whereas the author of *Leg. S.* strongly preferred the latter (Buss, 1886).

58. *Editor's note*: these differences between dialects could be explained in terms of rule-ordering, with the two changes, SVLR-shortening of vowel 4 and smoothing of vowel 8, overlapping in time as far as their diffusion is concerned. Some dialects received one change first, some the other, with consequent effects on the possibility of merger between vowel 4 and vowel 8 in short environments. On this interpretation, vowel 8 could have smoothed even before the GVS, as AJA also suggests in his 1997b paper, where pre-consonantal vowel 8 is reconstructed as follows (in a table entitled 'A selection of Scots vowels: the Older Scots long vowels'):

vowel no.	ESc	early MSc	late MSc	mod Sc	examples
8	ai ———	?ɛɪ, ?æː ———	ẹː ———	ẹː or eː	*bait, maid, aim, ail, own, pain, pair, graith*

Non-initial, non-final vowel 8 would then go through the GVS more or less as shown for vowel 8b (vowel 8 in final position) in Figure 17. (The difference between [æː] and [ẹː], as shown there, is probably immaterial.)

NOTES

59. *Editor's note*: on the assumption that this represents his final view (cf. note 41), I have not included in the text the following draft paragraph apropos of the date of smoothing of vowel 8:

> It is tempting to argue that in the dialects in which vowel 8 opts out of SVLR it did not fulfil the apparent SVLR conditions (it was not yet a monophthong or, as seems to have been the case with vowel 1, a diphthong with a long first element); but that in the dialects in which it does conform to SVLR (those in which it is merged with vowel 4 and the SW), it may already have been smoothed to a long monophthong.

60. These data, like other rhyme-data from the same sources, are taken from the complete rhyme-lists of *Seven S.* and *Bk. Chess* presented to me by Dr. C. C. van Buuren-Veenenbos.

Editor's note: with the kind permission of Dr. van Buuren, these papers are deposited with AJA's papers in the University of Edinburgh.

61. Henryson also has some exclusively vowel 8 rhymes, e.g. *effray* : *play* (? group (3)) and *array* : *gay* (group (1)).

62. *Editor's note*: at first sight, this is a surprising suggestion. Nevertheless, the combined evidence of Sylvester Douglas, who hailed from Abd, and *The Contrast*, written in 'Cleidbaunk ' (not the present burgh, which did not then exist; possibly a farm in the Upper Clyde valley - I owe this information to Iseabail Macleod and Ian Fraser) argues that the rounded realisation was widespread alongside the unrounded one in educated speech in the 18th century. This is unexpected, given the widespread modSc distribution of [ʌ], even in the most conservative dialects of Uls Scots, and in contact with Hiberno-English (which has a rounded realisation) (Macafee, forthcoming b). If we wanted to argue that the vernacular Scots of the commonality already had an unrounded realisation, we would have to find some explanation for the difference. There are some hints that sociolinguistic differences existed between the Scots of the gentry and that of the commonality (see for instance Tulloch, 1980: 172), but we do not know what these might have been, whether they tended to conservatism, and whether they were carried over into ScStE. It seems unlikely that anglicising Scots could have mistaken their target and adopted a rounded Northern English rather than an unrounded RP realisation in some words. However, it is entirely likely, given the many hyperadaptive forms in 18c ScStE (Macafee, forthcoming a), that they could have been confused by the split in RP between a rounded vowel - mainly in post-labial environments - (e.g. *put*) and an unrounded one (e.g. *but*).

63. *Editor's note*: possible candidates (discussed in Macafee, forthcoming c) include the unrounding of vowel 7, and particularly the identification of the unrounded vowel in SVLR-short environments, e.g. *mune* 'moon', with Vowel 15 /ɪ/; the rounding of vowel 12 from [ɑ] to [ɔ]; and the lowered realisation of vowel 1 long, as in *five*, etc.

64. *Editor's note*: AJA had attempted to draw Figures 20a-d and 21 as a single table, but following Aitken (1977) I have divided the material into a rough historical outline (with spellings) and a more detailed historical outline. Figure 21 is based on the version in Aitken ([1996]).

65. *Editor's note*: AJA's draft of this figure (below) included the suggestion, not discussed in the text, that vowel 4 began to raise earlier in SVLR-long environments, and that the merger of vowel 8 with vowel 4 before voiced fricatives and /r/ was with this raised allophone of vowel 4. It is difficult to think of any way of testing this hypothesis, and it seems unlikely, since there are no captures of this raised vowel 4 by vowel 3 (in contrast to the Northern raising of vowel 4 before /n/ and after labials (see note 13).

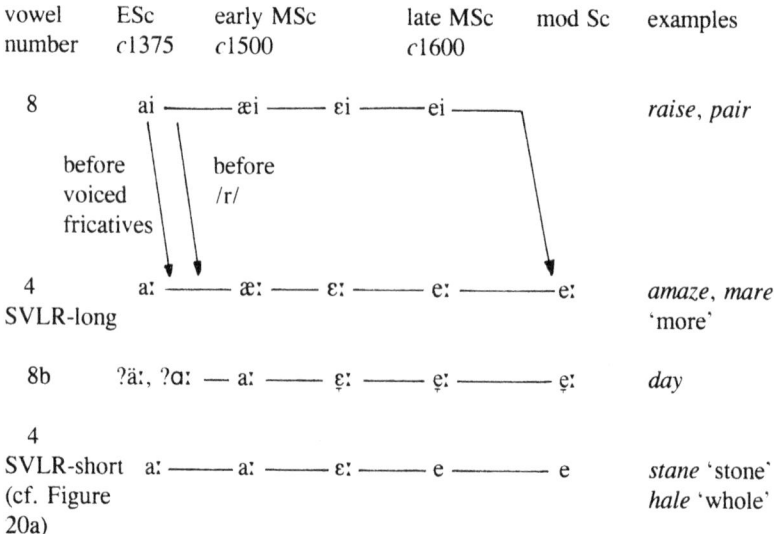

WRITINGS CONSULTED

See 'Conventions and abbreviations' for references to OSc authors and abbreviated titles. For some additional works on OSc phonology, see the notes to Aitken (1991).

Abercrombie, D. (1979) 'The accents of Standard English in Scotland' in A. J. Aitken and T. McArthur eds., *Languages of Scotland*, Edinburgh: Chambers, 68-84.

Ackermann, A. (1897) *Die Sprache der ältesten schottischen Urkunden*, University of Göttingen Dissertation.

Aitken, A. J. (1971) 'Variation and variety in written Middle Scots' in A. J. Aitken *et al.* eds., *Edinburgh Studies in English and Scots*, London: Longman, 177-209. Summarised and revised in Macafee and †Aitken (2002), lxx-lxxv.

Aitken, A. J. (1977) 'How to pronounce Older Scots' in A. J. Aitken *et al.* eds., *Bards and Makars*, Glasgow: University of Glasgow Press, 1-21.

Aitken, A. J. (1979) 'Scottish speech: a historical view with special reference to the Standard English of Scotland' in A. J. Aitken and T. McArthur eds., *Languages of Scotland*, Edinburgh: Chambers, 85-118.

Aitken, A. J. (1981) 'The Scottish Vowel-Length Rule' in M. Benskin and M. L. Samuels eds., *So Meny People Longages and Tonges: Philological Essays in Scots and Mediaeval English presented to Angus McIntosh*, Edinburgh: Middle English Dialect Project, 131-57.

Aitken, A. J. (1983) 'The language of Older Scots poetry' in J. D. McClure ed., *Scotland and the Lowland Tongue: Studies in the Language and Literature of Lowland Scotland in Honour of David D. Murison*, Aberdeen: Aberdeen University Press, 18-49. Summarised in Macafee and †Aitken (2002), cxxxiii-cxli.

Aitken, A. J. (1991) 'Progress in Older Scots philology', *Studies in Scottish Literature* 26, 19-37.

Aitken, A. J. ([1996]) *The Pronunciation of Older Scots: Notes and Tables to accompany the audio cassette (SSC 122) 'How to Pronounce Older Scots'* Glasgow: Scotsoun.

Aitken, A. J. (1995/6) 'James Murray: master of Scots', *Review of Scottish Culture* 9, 14-34.

Aitken, A. J. (1997a) 'The pioneers of anglicised speech in Scotland: a second look', *Scottish Language* 16, 1-36.

Aitken, A. J. (1997b) 'New evidence on the Great Vowel Shift and the Scottish Vowel-Length Rule in Older Scots', unpublished paper given to the Fifth International Conference on the Languages of Scotland and Ulster, University of Aberdeen, 1-5 August 1997.

Anderson, J. M. and C. Jones eds. (1974) *Historical Linguistics: Proceedings of the First International Conference on Historical Linguistics*, vol. 2, Amsterdam: North-Holland.

Baildon, H. B. (1899) *On the Rimes in the Authentic Poems of William Dunbar*, Edinburgh: Neill.

Bawcutt, P. ed. (1998) *The Poems of William Dunbar* 2 vols., Glasgow: The Association for Scottish Literary Studies.

Bawcutt, P. (2000) 'New texts of William Dunbar, Alexander Scott and other Scottish poets', *Scottish Studies Review* 1, 9-25.

Bennett, J. A. W. and G. V. Smithers eds. (1968) *Early Middle English Verse and Prose*, 2nd edn., Oxford: Clarendon Press.

Benskin, M. (1982) 'The letters <þ> and <y> in later Middle English, and some related matters', *Journal of the Society of Archivists* 7, 13-30.

Bliss, A. J. (1948/9) 'Three Middle English studies', *English and Germanic Studies* 2, 40-54.

Bliss, A. J. (1952,3) 'Vowel quantity in Middle English borrowings from Anglo-Norman', *Archivum Linguisticum* 4, 121-47, and 5, 22-47, reprinted in Lass ed. (1969), 164-207.

Bliss, A. J. (1955) 'Quantity in Old French and Middle English', *Archivum Linguisticum* 7, 71-86.

[Brand, J.] (1701) *A Brief Description of Orkney, Zetland, Pightland-Firth & Caithness*, Edinburgh.

Buss, P. (1886) *Sind die von Horstmann herausgegebenen schottischen Legenden ein Werk Barbere's?* Göttingen: Halle. Also *Anglia* 9 (1886), 493-514.

Catford, J. C. (1957a) 'The Linguistic Survey of Scotland', *Orbis* 6, 105-21.

Catford, J. C. (1957b) 'Vowel-systems of Scots dialects', *Transactions of the Philological Society*, 107-17.

Catford, J. C. (1957c) 'Shetland dialect', *Shetland Folk Book* 3, 71-5.

Collinge, N. E. (1985) *The Laws of Indo-European*, Amsterdam and Philadelphia: Benjamins.

The Concise Scots Dictionary (1985), ed-in-chief M. Robinson, Aberdeen: Aberdeen University Press.

Craigie, J. (1939) 'Fowler's language' in H. Meikle *et al.*, eds. *The Works of William Fowler*, vol. 3, S.T.S., 3rd Series, 13, li-lxxix.

Craigie, J. ed.(1941) *Thomas Hudson's Historie of Judith*, S.T.S., 3rd Series, 14.

Craigie, J. ed. (1950) *The Basilikon Doron of King James VI*, vol.2, S.T.S., 3rd Series, 18.

Craigie, W. A. (1925) 'The earliest records of the Scottish tongue', *Scottish Historical Review* 22, 61-7.

Craigie, W. A. (1935) 'Older Scottish and English: a study in contrasts', *Transactions of the Philological Society*, 1-15.

Crystal, D. (1989) *A Dictionary of Linguistics and Phonetics* 2nd edn., Oxford: Blackwell.

Curtis, F. J. (1894) *An Investigation of the Rimes and Phonology of the Middle-Scotch Romance Clariodus*, Halle. Also *Anglia* 16 (1894), 387-450; 17 (1895), 1-68.

A Dictionary of the Older Scottish Tongue (1931-2002), 12 vols., various publishers, currently Oxford University Press.

Dieth, E. (1932) *A Grammar of the Buchan Dialect*, Cambridge: Heffer.

Dietz, K. (1981) 'ME *oi* heimischer provenienz' in P. Kunsmann and O. Kuhn eds., *Weltsprache Englisch in Forschung und Lehre: Festschrift für Kurt Wachtler*, Berlin: Schmidt.

Dobson, E. J. (1968) *English Pronunciation, 1500-1700*, 2nd edn., 2 vols., Oxford: Clarendon Press.

Eckhardt, E. (1910-11) *Die Dialekt- und Ausländertypen des älteren englischen Dramas*, 2 vols., Louvain: Uystpruyst. Especially 'Die schottische Mundart in den einzelnen Dramen', vol.1, 91 f.

Ellis, A. J. (1889) *On Early English Pronunciation*, Part V: *Existing Dialectal, as compared with West Saxon Pronunciation*, London: Trübner.

Elphinston, J. (1786-7) *Propriety Ascertained in her Picture; or, Inglish Speech and Spelling Rendered Mutual Guides, Secure Alike from Distant, and from Domestic, Error*, London: Walter.

The English Dialect Dictionary (1898-1905), ed. J. Wright, 6 vols., Oxford: Oxford University Press.

Erasmus, D. (1528) *Collected Works* 26, ed. J. K. Sowards, Toronto: University of Toronto Press (1985); *Opera Omnia* 1-4, Amsterdam: North-Holland (1973).

Fox, D. ed. (1981) *The Poems of Robert Henryson*, Oxford: Oxford University Press; Appendix: 'Henryson's rhymes', 492-4.

Gburek, H. (1986) 'Changes in the structure of the English verb system: evidence from Scots' in Strauss and Drescher eds., 115-23.

Gimson, A. C. (1972), revised by A. Cruttenden (1994) *An Introduction to the Pronunciation of English*, London: Arnold.

Girvan, R. ed. (1939) *Ratis Raving and Other Early Scots Poems on Morals*, S.T.S., 3rd series, 11.

Glenn, J. A. (1987) 'A New Edition of Sir Gilbert Haye's *Buke of the Ordre of Knychthede*', University of Notre Dame, Indiana, Ph.D.

WRITINGS CONSULTED

Grant, W. and J. M. Dixon (1921) *Manual of Modern Scots*, Cambridge: Cambridge University Press.

Gregg, R. (1985) *The Scotch-Irish Dialect Boundaries in the Province of Ulster*, Port Credit, Ontario: Canadian Federation for the Humanities.

Harris, J. (1984) 'English in the north of Ireland' in P. Trudgill ed., *Language in the British Isles*, Cambridge: Cambridge University Press, 115-34.

Harris, J. (1985) *Phonological Variation and Change: Studies in Hiberno-English*, Cambridge: Cambridge University Press.

Heuser, W. (1896,7) 'Offenes und geschlossenes *ee* im Schottischen und Nordenglischen', *Anglia* 18, 114-28, and 19, 319-47.

Heuser, W. (1897a) 'Die Dehnung -*ēnd*', *Anglia* 19, 398-405; Part B 'Die Dehnung vor -*nd* im Mittelschottischen'.

Heuser, W. (1897b) 'Die Lautveraenderung von $\bar{a}$, $\bar{e}$, $\bar{i}$ im Mittelschottischen', *Anglia* 19, 405-8.

Heuser, W. (1897c) 'Der Ursprung des Unorganischen *i* in der Mittelschottischen Schreibung', *Anglia* 19, 409-12.

Hill, T. (1963) 'Phonemic and prosodic analysis in linguistic geography', *Orbis* 12, 449-55.

Hume, Alexander (c1616, 1865) *Of the Orthographie and Congruitie of the Britan Tongue* ... , ed. H. B. Wheatley, E.E.T.S., Original Series, 5.

Johnston, P. A. (1979) 'A Synchronic and Historical View of Border Area Bimoric Vowel Systems', University of Edinburgh PhD.

Johnston, P. A. (1997a) 'Older Scots phonology and its regional variation' in Jones ed., 47-111.

Johnston, P. A. (1997b) 'Regional variation' in Jones ed., 433-513.

Johnston, P. A. (2000) 'Taming Volume III of the *Linguistic Atlas of Scotland*', *Scottish Language* 19, 45-65.

Jones, C. ed. (1991) *A Treatise on the Provincial Dialect of Scotland by Sylvester Douglas*, Edinburgh: Edinburgh University Press.

Jones, C. (1993) 'Scottish Standard English in the late eighteenth century', *Transactions of the Philological Society*, 95-131. Also contains *The Contrast* (1779), 125-6.

Jones, C. (1995) *A Language Suppressed: The Pronunciation of the Scots Language in the 18th Century*, Edinburgh: Donald. Also contains *The Contrast* (1779), 248-9.

Jones, C. ed. (1997) *The Edinburgh History of the Scots Language*, Edinburgh: Edinburgh University Press.

Jordan, R. (1934), translated and revised by E. J. Crook (1974) *Handbook of Middle English Grammar: Phonology*, The Hague: Mouton.

Kelley, F. M. (1957*)* 'The Origin of the Use of I as a Sign of Length in Middle Scots', University of Columbia PhD.

Kniezsa, V. (1981) 'Some problems of early Scots', *Annales Universitatis Scientiorum Budapestinensis, Sectio Linguistica*, 12, 207-13.

Kniezsa, V. (1983a) 'The problem of the merger of Middle English /aː/ - /ai/ in Northern English' in M. Davenport *et al.* eds., *International Conference on English Historical Linguistics (2nd: 1981: Odense Universitet), Current Topics in Historical Linguistics*, Odense: Odense University Press, 95-102.

Kniezsa, V. (1983b) '<ai> and <a> in Medieval Northern English manuscripts', *Folia Linguistica Historica*, 4, 45-53.

Kniezsa, V. (1986) 'What happened to Old French *ai* in Britain?' in Strauss and Drescher eds, 103-13.

Kniezsa, V. (1989) 'The sources of the <i> digraphs: the place-name evidence' in McClure and Spiller eds., 442-50.

Kniezsa, V. (1991) '"Scotica Pronunciatione": sixteenth- and seventeenth-century English authors on Scots', *Scottish Language* 10, 1-8.

Kohler, K. J. (1964) 'Aspects of the History of English Pronunciation in Scotland', University of Edinburgh PhD.

Kohler, K. J. (1966) 'A late eighteenth century comparison of the "provincial dialect of Scotland" and the "pure dialect"', *Linguistics* 23, 30-68.

Kohler, K. J. (1967) 'Aspects of Middle Scots phonemics and graphemics: the phonological implications of the sign <i>', *Transactions of the Philological Society*, 32-61.

Kristensson, G. (1967) *A Survey of Middle English Dialects 1290-1350*, Vol. I: *The Six Northern Counties and Lincolnshire*, Lund: Gleerup.

Kuipers, C. H. ed. (1964) *Quintin Kennedy (1520-1564); Two Eucharistic Tracts*, Nijmegen: University of Nijmegen.

A Linguistic Atlas of Late Mediaeval English (1986), eds. A. McIntosh, M. L. Samuels and M. Benskin, 4 vols., Aberdeen: Aberdeen University Press.

The Linguistic Atlas of Scotland, Scots Section, Vol. III: *Phonology* (1986), eds. J. Y. Mather and H.-H. Speitel, London: Croom Helm.

Lass, R. ed. (1969) *Approaches to English Historical Linguistics*, New York: Holt, Rinehart and Winston.

Lass, R. (1974) 'Linguistic orthogenesis? Scots vowel quantity and the English length conspiracy' in Anderson and Jones eds., 311-43.

Lass, R. (1976) *English Phonology and Phonological Theory*, Cambridge: Cambridge University Press.

Lass, R. (1992) 'Phonology and morphology' in N. Blake ed., *The Cambridge History of the English Language*, Vol. II: *1066-1476*, Cambridge: Cambridge University Press, 23-155.

Luick, K. (1896) *Untersuchungen zur englischen Lautgeschichte*, Strasbourg: Trübner.

Luick, K. (1903) *Studien zur englischen Lautgeschichte* Wien and Leipzig: Braumüller.

Luick, K. (1940, 1964) *Historische Grammatik der englischen Sprache*, 2 vols., Leipzig, 1940; Cambridge, Mass., 1964.

Macafee, C. (1989) 'Middle Scots dialects - extrapolating backwards' in McClure and Spiller eds., 429-41.

Macafee, C. (forthcoming a) 'Scots and Scottish Standard English' in R. Hickey ed., *The Legacy of Colonial English: A Study of Transported Dialects*, Cambridge: Cambridge University Press.

Macafee, C. (forthcoming b) 'Lowland sources of Ulster Scots: Gregg and *The Linguistic Atlas of Scotland* (volume 3) compared' in M. Montgomery and A. Smyth eds., *The Academic Study of Ulster Scots: Essays for and by Robert Gregg* (provisional title).

Macafee, C. (forthcoming c) 'The impact of anglicisation on the phonology of Scots: a keethin sicht' in K. Lenz and R. Möhlig eds. *Of Dyuersitie & Chaunge of Langage: Essays Presented to Manfred Görlach on the Occasion of his 65th Birthday* Heidelberg: Winter, 240-56.

Macafee, C. and †A. J. Aitken (2002) 'A History of Scots to 1700', in DOST, vol. XII.

Macafee, C. and C. Ó Baoill (1997) 'Why Scots is not a Celtic English' in H. L. C. Tristram ed., *The Celtic Englishes*, Heidelberg: Winter, 245-86.

McClure, J. D. (1977) 'Vowel duration in a Scottish accent', *Journal of the International Phonetic Association* 7, 10-16.

McClure, J. D. (1994) 'English in Scotland' in R. Burchfield ed., *Cambridge History of the English Language*, Vol. V: *English in Britain and Overseas: Origins and Development*, Cambridge: Cambridge University Press, 23-93.

McClure, J. D. (forthcoming) 'Blind Harry's metrics' in S. Mapstone ed., *Proceedings of the 8th International Conference on Scottish Language and Literature 1996*.

McClure, J. D. and M. R. G. Spiller eds. (1989) *Bryght Lanternis: Essays on the Language and Literature of Medieval and Renaissance Scotland*, Aberdeen: Aberdeen University Press.

MacDiarmid, M. P. ed. (1973) *The Kingis Quair of James Stewart*, London: Heinemann.

McKenna, G. E. (1989) 'Vowel Duration in the Standard English of Scotland', University of Edinburgh MLitt.

McMahon, A. M. S. (1990) 'Constraining Lexical Phonology: Evidence from English Vowels', University of Edinburgh PhD.

McMahon, A. M. S. (1991) 'Lexical phonology and sound change: the case of the Scottish Vowel Length Rule', *Journal of Linguistics* 27, 29-53.

McMahon, A. M. S. (1992) 'Lexical phonology and diachrony' in Rissanen *et al.* eds., 167-90.

McMahon, A. M. S. (1994) *Understanding Language Change*, Cambridge: Cambridge University Press.

MacRae, G. D. (1975) 'An Edition of Nine Early Scots Texts, 1379-1402', University of Edinburgh Undergraduate Dissertation.

Mather, J. Y. (1978) 'The dialect of Caithness', *Scottish Literary Journal*, Supplement 6, 1-16.

Mather, J. Y. (1980) 'The dialect of the eastern borders', *Scottish Literary Journal*, Supplement 12, 30-42.

Meurman-Solin, A. (1999) 'Letters as a source of data for reconstructing Early Spoken Scots' in I. Taavitsainen *et al.* eds., *Writing in Nonstandard English* Amsterdam and Philadelphia: Benjamins, 305-22.

Meurman-Solin, A. (2001) 'Women as informants in the reconstruction of geographically and socioculturally conditioned language variation and change in 16th and 17th century Scots', *Scottish Language* 20, 20-46.

Middle English Dictionary (1952-2001), eds. H. Kurath and S. M. Kuhn, 12 vols. plus Plan and Bibliography, Ann Arbor, Michigan: University of Michigan Press.

Milroy, J. (1982) 'Some connections between Galloway and Ulster speech', *Scottish Language* 1, 23-29.

Minkova, D. (1982) 'The environment for Open Syllable Lengthening in Middle English', *Folia Linguistica Historica* 3, 29-58.

Minkova, D. (1991) *The History of Final Vowels in English: The Sound of Muting*, Berlin: Mouton de Gruyter.

Minkova, D. and R. Stockwell (1992) 'Homorganic clusters as moric busters in the history of English: the case of *-ld, -nd, -mb*' in Rissanen *et al.* eds., 191-206.

Mohr, V. (1990) 'ESc /aː/ and ESc /ai/ reconsidered', Anglistisches Seminar der Universität Heidelberg Dissertation.

Mohr, V. (2000) 'Verb morphology, Aitken's Law and Old Norse: evidence from Southern Scots', paper given to the conference, Dialect 2000: Language Links, The Queen's University of Belfast, 9-16 August 2000.

Morsbach, L. (1896) *Mittelenglische Grammatik*, Halle: Niemeyer.

Müller, P. (1908) *Die Sprache der Aberdeener Urkunden des 16 Jahrhunderts*, Friedrich-Wilhelms-Universität, Berlin, Dissertation.

Murray, J. A. H. (1873) *The Dialect of the Southern Counties of Scotland*, London: Asher. Originally published in *Transactions of the Philological Society* (1870-72).

Orton, H. (1929) 'The medial development of ME. $ō_1$ (tense), Fr. $ü$ (= [ȳ]) and ME. *eu* (OE. *ēow*) in the dialects of the North of England', *Englische Studien* 63. 229-51.

The Oxford English Dictionary (1989), 2nd edn., Oxford: Oxford University Press.

Pődör, D. (1995/6) 'The phonology of Scottish Gaelic loanwords in Lowland Scots', *Scottish Language* 14/15, 174-89.

Pope, M. K. (1934) *From Latin to Modern French with Especial Consideration of Anglo-Norman: Phonology and Morphology*, Manchester: Manchester University Press.

Prins, A. A. (1972) *A History of English Phonemes*, Leiden: Leiden University Press.

Rissanen, M., *et al.* eds. (1992) *History of Englishes: New Methods and Interpretations in Historical Linguistics*, Berlin: Mouton de Gruyter.

Samuels, M. L. (1985, 1989) 'The Great Scandinavian Belt' in R. Eaton *et al.* eds., *Current Issues in Linguistic Theory* 41 (1985) 269-81; reprinted in A. McIntosh, *et al.* eds., *Middle English Dialectology*, Aberdeen: Aberdeen University Press (1989), 106-15.

Scobbie, J. M., N. Hewlett and A. Turk (1999) 'Standard English in Edinburgh and Glasgow: the Scottish Vowel Length Rule revealed' in P. Foulkes and G. J. Docherty eds., *Urban Voices. Accent Studies in the British Isles*, London: Arnold, 230-45.

The Scottish National Dictionary (1931-1976), 10 vols., eds. W. Grant and D. D. Murison, Edinburgh: The Scottish National Dictionary Association.

Sheppard, E. A. (1936) 'Studies in the Language of Bellenden's Boece', University of London PhD.

Slater, J. (1952) 'An Edition of Early Scots Texts from the Beginnings to 1410', 2 vols.,University of Edinburgh PhD.

Smith, G. G. (1902) *Specimens of Middle Scots* Edinburgh and London: Blackwood and Sons.

Smith, Sir Thomas (1568) *De Recta et emendata Linguae Anglicae Scriptione Dialogus*, in B. Danielsson ed., *Sir Thomas Smith, Literary and Linguistic Works*, vol. 3, 1983, Stockholm Studies in English 56, Stockholm: Almquist & Wiksell.

Speitel, H.-H. (1969) 'An early specimen of Edinburgh speech', *Work in Progress*, Department of Phonetics and Linguistics, University of Edinburgh, 3, 26-36.

Stockwell, R. P. (1961) 'The Middle English "long close" and "long open" mid vowels', *Texas Studies in Literature and Language* 2, 529-38; reprinted in Lass ed.(1969), 154-63.

Strauss, D. and H. Drescher eds. (1986) *Scottish Language and Literature, Medieval and Renaissance. Fourth International Conference 1984 - Proceedings*, Frankfurt: Lang.

Tulloch, G. (1980) *The Language of Walter Scott*, London: Deutsch.

Vaiana, M. (1972) 'A Study in the Dialect of the Southern Counties of Scotland', University of Indiana PhD.

Vaiana-Taylor, M. (1974) 'The great Southern Scots conspiracy: patterns in the development of Northern English' in Anderson and Jones eds., 403-26.

van Buuren, C. C. ed. (1982) *The Buke of the Sevyne Sagis*, Leiden: Leiden University Press.

van Buuren, C. C. ed. (1997) *The Buke of the Chess*, S. T. S, 4th Series, 27.

Watson, G. (1923) *The Roxburghshire Word-Book*, Cambridge: Cambridge University Press.

Wakelin, M. (1972) *English Dialects. An Introduction*, London: Athlone.

Wells, J. C. (1982) *Accents of English* 3 vols., Cambridge: Cambridge University Press.

Wettstein, P. (1942) *The Phonology of a Berwickshire Dialect*, University of Zürich PhD.

Williams, O. T. (1907-10) 'The development of *ai* and *ei* in Middle Scotch', *Transactions of the Philological Society*, Supplement, 285-87.

Williams, O. T. (1911-16) 'On O.E. *a*, *ā* and *æ* in the rimes of Barbour's *Brus* and in Modern Scotch dialects', *Transactions of the Philological Society*, 7-26.

Wright, J. (1905) *The English Dialect Grammar*, Oxford: Frowde. Also in *The English Dialect Dictionary*, vol.VI.

Wright, J., and E. M. Wright (1928) *An Elementary Middle English Grammar*, Oxford: Oxford University Press.

Zai, R. (1942) *The Phonology of the Morebattle Dialect*, Lucerne.

GLOSSARY OF LINGUISTIC TERMS

allophone - one of a number of variant phonetic realisations conditioned by phonetic environment

bimoric - consisting of two units of time, e.g. a long as opposed to a short vowel

bimorphemic - consisting of two morphemes (as distinct from syllables), e.g. a root plus a derivational or inflectional suffix

breaking - diphthongisation

continuant - a sound produced without complete closure of the vocal tract, thus vowels, approximants (glides), fricatives, nasals, liquids, some realisations of /r/

countertonic - with reference to French, the syllable or vowel carrying secondary stress

covered - of a vowel, checked, followed by (a) consonant(s) to produce a closed syllable

degemination - shortening of a long consonant

diaphone - one of a number of variant phonetic realisations differing between dialects

epenthesis - the insertion of a sound within a word

falling - applied to a diphthong/triphthong where the first element receives the greater prominence (the more typical case)

hiatus - a phonetic environment where two vowels belonging to different syllables are contiguous (e.g. *create*), hence *hiatical*

labialised - having lip-rounding as a secondary articulation, also applied to unrounded vowels with a slight degree of lip-rounding

lenis - produced with a less forceful articulation (typically the voiced as opposed to the voiceless consonants)

lexeme - a lexical unit (as listed in a dictionary), typically a stem to which various inflectional endings may be added

lexical diffusion - the spread of a sound-change through the lexicon, often leaving a small residue of unaffected words, especially, but not solely, in dialects distant from the origin of the change

lexical distribution/incidence/selection - the range of words taking a particular phoneme, often differing between two dialects even when the same phonemes occur in both

lexical inventory - the words taking a particular phoneme in a given dialect

monomoric - consisting of one unit of time, e.g. a short as opposed to a long vowel

monomorphemic - consisting of one morpheme (as distinct from one syllable), i.e. a root without derivational or inflectional affixes

obstruent - a consonant sound (voiced or voiceless) where there is constriction of the airflow, thus plosives, fricatives, affricates

opening - a process of sound-change where the degree of closure between the tongue and the roof of the mouth decreases, applied to the lowering of a vowel, and also for instance to the change from a fricative to an approximant

peripheral - of a vowel, produced with the highest point of the tongue in the outer part of the space within which vowels can be produced (typical of vowels of stressed, including secondarily stressed, syllables); of a dialect, geographically distant from the centre(s) of linguistic innovation

preiotation - the development of a /j/ glide before an initial vowel (term borrowed from the linguistics of the Slavonic languages); also used when the vowel is preceded by /h/

rising - applied to a diphthong/triphthong where the final element receives the greater prominence, or to a combination of an approximant (/j, w/) plus monophthong or diphthong

rule-ordering - the sequence of application of the rules that derive phonological output from underlying representations, viewed as recapitulating the chronological sequence in which the rules reached the dialect in question

schwa - the vowel represented in IPA by 'ə'

secondary articulation - in a sound with two points of articulation (e.g. one involving the tongue, the other the lips), the point of articulation with the lesser restriction of the airstream

smoothing - monophthongisation

sonorant - a voiced sound with a relatively free airflow, thus vowels, approximants, nasals, liquids, some realisations of /r/

syncope - dropping of a vowel, resulting in the loss of a syllable

tautosyllabic - in the same syllable

tonic - with reference to French, the syllable or vowel carrying primary stress

trimoric - consisting of three units of time (typically a diphthong with a long first element)

velarisation - having the back of the tongue raised towards the velum, as a secondary articulation

vocalisation - a sound-change whereby a consonant (usually a sonorant, but sometimes a continuant) opens in articulation to become a vowel

yod - the consonant represented in IPA by 'j'

yod-absorption - the loss of /j/ by its being reduced to a glide off the previous sound

yod-deletion - the loss of /j/ by its articulation becoming indistinct

INDEX I: SOURCE VOWELS (OE, ON, OF)

The table below can be used in conjunction with Index II to locate relevant sections in the text.

Source	Developments, with examples	ESc vowel
OE ī, ȳ	OE shortenings, e.g. *fīfte* > *fift*, *cicen-* > *chikkin*	15
	before *w*, e.g. *spīwan* > *spew*	14a
	irregularly, e.g. *wīr* > *were* 'wire'	3
	otherwise, e.g. *bite, fire, drȳge* > *dry*	1
OE ē, incl. Anglian ē = WS ēa and WS ǣ¹ (but see below)	OE shortenings, e.g. *grēttra* > *gretter* 'greater', *hēhþu* > *hecht* 'height', *cēpte* > *kept* p.t. hence *kep* 'keep', *blētsian* > *bles*	16
	irregularly, e.g. *gēotan* > *ʒett* 'pour' var. of *ʒete*	16
	before final *g* /j/, e.g. *hēg* > *hay*, *cǣg* > *kay* 'key'	8
	before *g* /j/ + V, e.g. *drēogan* > *dre* 'endure', *ēage* > *e* 'eye', *cǣg-* > *key*; including *g* for *h* in inflected forms e.g. *hēag-* > *he* 'high'	11
	otherwise, e.g. *hēr* > *here* 'here', *hēran* > *here* 'hear', *scēp* > *schepe*	2
OE ēo	var. rising diphthong *eō*, see *ō*	
	before *w*, e.g. *trēowþ* > *treuth* 'truth' *nēowe* > *new*	14a
	otherwise as ē, e.g. *dēop* > *depe*, *sēoc* > *seik* 'sick', *cēosan* > *chese* 'choose'	2
OE ǣ¹	normally = Anglian ē	
	exceptionally, e.g. *brǣþ* > *brethe*	3

THE OLDER SCOTS VOWELS

OE ǣ²	OE shortenings, e.g. brǣmblas > *brammill 'bramble'	17
	word-final, e.g. sǣ > se 'sea'	2
	inconsistently before d, n, l, r, e.g. clǣne > clene	2
	before w, e.g. slǣwþ > sleuth 'sloth'	14b(i) 14b(ii)
	before g /j/ e.g. clǣg > clay	8
	otherwise, e.g. hlǣne > lene, ǣr > ere 'before'	3
OE ēa	var. rising diphthong eā, see ā	
	exceptionally, e.g. lēaf > leve 'permission'	2
	grēat > grete (alongside metathesised forms with shortened vowel)	3
	before w, e.g. dēaw > dew, scēawian > schew 'show'	14b(i) 14b(ii)
	otherwise, e.g. dēad > dede 'dead'	3
OE ā	OE shortenings, e.g. hlāfmæsse > lammes 'Lammas'	17
	before w, e.g. cnāwan > knaw 'know', sceāwian > schaw 'show'; includes g /ɣ/ > w/, e.g. āgen > awn 'own' v.	12
	before h /x/, including h for final g /ɣ/, e.g. daich 'dough'; dial. deuch	4 14b(i)
	otherwise, e.g. stān > stane "stone'	4
OE ū	OE shortenings, e.g. hūsbonda > husband, sūðerne > sutheron	19
	irregularly, e.g. clūd > clud var. of cloud	19
	before h /x/, var. shortening, e.g. ruch var. of rouch 'rough'	19
	with vocalisation of v, e.g. dūfa > dow 'dove'	6

INDEX I: SOURCE VOWELS

	otherwise, e.g. *mūþ* > *mouth*, *trūwian* > *trow* 'believe', *būgan* > *bow* 'bend' v.	6
OE *ō*	OE shortenings, e.g. *ōhsta* > *oxter* 'armpit', *þōht* > *thocht*	18
	before *w*, e.g. *grōwan* > *grow*, *treōwþ* > *trowth* 'truth'	13
	before *g* /ɣ/ + V, e.g. *bōgas* > *bewis* 'boughs' pl.; including *g* for *h* in inflected forms e.g. *clōg-* > *clewis* 'ravines' pl.	14a
	otherwise, e.g. *gōd* > *gude* 'good', *ceōsan* > *chuse* 'choose', *hōh* > *heuch* 'hough', *bōg* > *beuch* 'bough'	7
OE *i, y*	HOCL, e.g. *wilde* > *wild*, *cynde* > *kind*	1
	ic > *I*	1
	before *w*, e.g. *siwan* > *sew*	14a
	before *g* /j/, e.g. *stigel* > *stile*, *-ig* > *-y* as in *haly* 'holy'	1
	belated HOCL, e.g. *cild* > *chelde* 'child'	2
	inconsistently before *l, n, d, sc* /ʃ/, e.g. *glida* > *gled* 'kite, the bird'	16
	otherwise, e.g. *biddan* > *bid*, *hyll* > *hill*; including failure of HOCL, e.g. *blind*	15
OE *e, eo*	HOCL, e.g. *eldu* > *eild* 'old age'	2
	final in monosyllables, e.g. *he*	2
	wel > *wele* 'well' adv.	2
	var. before *h* /x/ + *t*, e.g. *feohtan* > *ficht* var. of *fecht* 'fight'	15
	before final *g* /j/, e.g. *weg* > *way*; before *g* /j/ + C, e.g. *regn* > *rain*	8
	before *g* /j/ + V, e.g. *swegan* > *swey*; var. *swe* 'sway'	8 11

THE OLDER SCOTS VOWELS

	otherwise, e.g. *bedd* > *bed*; including failure of HOCL, e.g. *mend*	1
OE æ	var. before alveolars, e.g. *glæs* > *gles* var. of *glas*	16
	before *h* /x/, e.g. *hlæhhan* > *lauch* 'laugh'	12
	before *g* /j/, e.g. *dæg* > *day*, *hægl* > *hail*	8
	otherwise, e.g. *græf* > *graf* 'grave' n.	17
OE *ea*	*beard* > *berde*	3
	before *h* /x/, e.g. *eahta* > *aucht* 'eight'	12
	before alveolars, e.g. *ears* > *erse*	16
	otherwise, e.g. *eall* > *all*	17
OE *a*, incl. Anglian *ald* = WS *eald*	HOCL, e.g. *camb* > *kame* 'comb', *-ald* as in *cald* 'cold', etc.	4
	before *w*, e.g. *clawu* > *claw*; including /ɣ/ > /w/, e.g. *lagu* > *law* 'law'	12
	otherwise, e.g. *catt* > *cat*; including failure of HOCL, e.g. *band*	17
OE *o*	HOCL, e.g. *bord* > *buird* 'board'	7
	dial. before *h* /x/, e.g. *dohtor* > *douchter* 'daughter'	13
	before *g* /ɣ/ > /w/ + V or syllabic C, e.g. *boga* > *bow* 'the weapon', *logn* 'calm';	13
	after *w* in *geswogen* > *swoun* 'swoon'	6
	otherwise, e.g. *dohtor* > *dochter* 'daughter', *loc* > *lok*; including failure of HOCL, e.g. *gold*	18
OE *u*	HOCL, e.g. *bunden* > *bound* p.p.	6
	before *w*, including *g* /ɣ/ > /w/, e.g. *fugol* > *foul* 'bird'	6
	after *w*, e.g. *wucu* > *(w)ouk* 'week'	6
	otherwise, e.g. *cuman* > *cum* 'come'; including var. failure of HOCL, e.g. *bunden* > *bund*	19

INDEX I: SOURCE VOWELS

ON *í, ý*	as OE *ī, ȳ*, e.g *knífr* > *knife*	1
ON *é*	as OE *ē*, e.g. *sér* > *sere* 'separate'	2
ON *ǽ*	e.g. *sǽma* > *seme* 'seem'	2
ON *ǽ*	as OE *ǣ*, e.g. *sǽti* > *sete* 'seat'	3
ON *á*	as OE *ā*, e.g. *báðir* > *bathe* 'both'	4
ON *ú*	as OE *ū*, e.g. *drúpa* > *droup* 'droop'	6
ON *ó*	as OE *ō*, e.g. *lófe* > *lufe* 'palm of the hand'; Norn *óðal* > *outhall* 'udal'	7 6
ON *i, y*	as OE, e.g. *kirkja* > *kirk*, *byggja* > *big* 'build'	15
ON *e*	as OE, e.g. *klegge* > *cleg* 'horsefly'	16
ON *a*	as OE, e.g. *kasta* > *cast*; *mav-* > *maw* 'gull', *maðkr* > *mauch* 'maggot'	17 12
ON *o*	as OE, e.g. *toft* 'homestead'	18
ON *u*	as OE, e.g. *buski* > *bus* 'bush'	19
ON *ei, ey*	e.g. *þeir* > *thai* 'they', *leyna* > *lain* 'conceal'	8
ON *au*	e.g. *gaukr* > *gowk* 'cuckoo'; *haukr* > *hawk*	13 12
OF *ī*	e.g. *pris* > *prise* 'price'	1
OF *-y*	e.g. *mercy*	1
AN *ō̄* = OF *ue*	*boef* > *befe*, root-stressed forms of *mover*, *prover* > *meve* 'move', *preve* 'prove'	2
AN *ē*, incl. = OF *ie*	e.g. *pece* 'piece', *frere* 'friar'	2
OF *-é*	e.g. *cite* 'city'	2
OF *-ée*	e.g. *cuntre*; var. *cuntray*	2 8
Latin *ē*	e.g. *redeme*	2

THE OLDER SCOTS VOWELS

OF ẹ̄ from Latin ē	e.g. *remede* 'remedy'	3
AN ẹ̄ = OF *ai* and countertonic *ei*	e.g. *pese* 'peace', *fede* 'feud'; exceptionally, e.g. *praise, laisere* 'leisure'	3 8
OF ā	e.g. *estate*	4
AN ã	e.g. *aunt, branche, change, danger*	17 12 ?4
OF ǭ	e.g. *estore > store, glore* 'glory'	5
OF ū	e.g. *flour* 'flower', *prisoun* 'prison'	6
OF ō	e.g. *povre > pure* 'poor', *mover > muve, prover > pruve*	7
OF ǖ incl. AN ǖ = OF *üi*	final, e.g. *valew* 'value'; var. (? sociolectal) *valow*	14a 6
	in hiatus, e.g. *cruel*	14a
	dur > dour	6
	var. in *juge, justice*	19
	otherwise, e.g. *use, fruit, duc > duke*	7
OF *i*	before /ʎ/ borrowed as /l/, /ɲ/ borrowed as /n/, e.g. *famyle* 'family', *desyne* 'design'	1
	otherwise, e.g. *riche, ligne* 'lineage'	15
OF *e*	before /ʎ/ borrowed as /l/, /ɲ/ borrowed as /n/, e.g. *feign*	8
	breme 'bream', *preche* 'preach'	3
	before *r* + C, e.g. *perce* 'pierce'	2
	otherwise, e.g. *serve, det* 'debt', *menʒee* 'company'	16

INDEX I: SOURCE VOWELS

OF *a*	before /ʎ/ borrowed as /l/, /ɲ/ borrowed as /n/, e.g. *fail*	8
	otherwise, e.g. *fasch* 'vex', *falʒe* 'fail'	17
OF *-al*	e.g. *bestiale*	17 / 4
OF *o*	before final C, e.g. *los* 'praise' n.	5
	before *st*, e.g. *host* 'army'	5
	otherwise, e.g. *joly*	18
OF *u̥*	before /ʎ/ borrowed as /l/, /ɲ/ borrowed as /n/, e.g. *boil, oyll*	10
	tonic in closed syllables, e.g. *trubill, numir*; var. *trouble, noumer*	19 / 6
	otherwise, e.g. *buket, cunʒe* 'coin', *ulʒe* 'oil'	19
AN *ai* incl. = OF *ei*	e.g. *faith, verray* 'true'	8
OF *o̥i*	e.g. *joy, noise, voice*	9
	var. e.g. *voice*	10
AN *ui* = OF *o̥i*	e.g. *point*	10
OF *au*	e.g. *faut* 'fault', *sauf* 'safe'	12
	Lowrence	13
OF *ou*	e.g. *couper* > *cowp* 'overturn', *poulenet* > *powny* 'pony'	13
OF *e̥u, iu*, AN *iw*	e.g. *bleu* > *blew* ' blue', *griu* > *grew* 'Greek', *pursiwer* > *persew*	14a
OF *eau*	e.g. *lewtee* ' loyalty'; var. (?sociolectal) *laute*	14b(i) 14b(ii) 14b(iii)

INDEX II: SOUND-CHANGES

The numbers in bold are the vowel numbers.

1: *Sources* 14.1; (HOCL) 3.1, 3.1.1; 6.1.2, 6.3.1, 8.2.1, 15. *Unconditioned* (GVS) 20.1, 20.6, 20.7. *Realisation* 20.1, 21.
2: *Sources* 14.2; (HOCL) 3.1, 3.1.1; (OSL) 4.2.1; (late HOCL) 5.1; 6.2.1, 8.3,15. *Unconditioned* (GVS) 20.1, 20.2, 20.4, 20.6. *Conditioned* (dial. /i:v/) 6.4.0; (preiotation) 22.2.1. *Realisation* 21.
3: *Sources* 14.3; (HOCL in *beird*) 3.1.1; (OSL) 4.1, 8.3. *Unconditioned* (merger 2) 20.8.1, 20.8.3, 22.2.4; (dial. merger 4) 20.8.1, 20.8.3; (dial. merger 7) 20.8.1; (dial. merger 8) 20.8.1. *Conditioned* (> 1 / tʃ, (st)r - ndʒ) 8.4, 9.3, (also *gryte*) 14.1(12), (conversely) 14.3(10); (> 15 / - v, z + syllabic C) 16.5; (preiotation) 22.2.1. *Realisation* 20.8.1.
4: *Sources* 14.4; (HOCL) 3.1, 3.1.1; 3.2; (OSL) 4.1, 8.3; 6.2.1, 9.1, 9.2, 22.3.2. *Unconditioned* (GVS) 20.1-7, 22.2.4; (dial. merger 16) 20.1. *Conditioned* (dial. > 3 / - n) 8.4, 9.2, n.13; (dial. > ?3 > 1 in mainly labial environments) 8.3; (> 3 / tʃ, r - n + affricate) 9.3; (captured by 16) 8.3, 20.1, 21.2.2; (> 8 / - nasal + affricate) 9.2; (> ?(/j/) + 12, ?14b(iii) / - k, v, rC)) 16.6, n.29; (except dial. > 12 in labial environments) 20.9, n.37a; (preiotation: /j/ + 4) 22.2.1; (preiotation: /j/ + 15) 22.2.1, 22.2.2, 22.2.4; (dial. > 8 / - r) 22.3.4. *Realisation* 22.2.4, 22.3.1, 22.3.3.
5: *Sources* 14.5, 3.2; (OSL) 4.1. *Unconditioned* (GVS) 7.1. *Conditioned* (> 19 / - tʃ, dʒ) 16.2; (variably > 13 / - k#, g#, p#, f#) 16.4; (SVLR, merger with 18) 21. *Realisation* 14.20, 20.1, 21.1, 21.2.2.
6: *Sources* 14.6; (HOCL) 3.1, 3.1.1; 6.2.1, 6.4.3, 6.5.1, 8.3. *Realisation* 20.1; (SVLR) 21.
7: *Sources* 14.7; (HOCL) 3.1, 3.1.1; (OSL) 4.2.2, 8.3; 7.1, 7.2.1. *Unconditioned* (fronting) 6.5.1(iii), 7.1; (and GVS) 7.1. *Conditioned* (> 6 / - r) n.4; (> 6 / labial -) 14.6(10); (dial. > 14a / - r(d)) 6.5.1(ii), 7.3; (dial. > 14a / - k, x) 6.5.1(ii), 7.2.1; (dial. > (/j/) + 19 / - k, x) 7.2.1; (> 19 > 15 in mainly nasal, labial environments) 16.1; (preiotation) 22.2.1, 22.2.3, 22.2.4); (SVLR) 7.1, 20.7, 21; (unrounding) 7.1, 20.7; (dial. merger 4) 7.1; (dial. merger 2) 7.1, 8.3; (dial. merger 6) 7.1; (dial. split and merger 4, 15) 7.1.
8: *Sources* 14.8, 6.1.1, 6.3.2, 8.2.1, 8.3, 22.3.2. *Unconditioned* (except dial. non-final > 4) 20.4, 20.7, 22.2.4, 22.3, (GVS) n.58; (SVLR) 21.2.2. *Conditioned* (? > 1 / - ʎ) 8.3; (early, except dial. > 4 / - front fricatives) 12.3; (> 16 / - n + affricate, t) 9.2; (final 8a > 1) 22.4; (final > 4) 22.4; (final 8b) 22.4, Fig. 17. *Realisation* 21.2.2, 22.2.2, 22.3.1, 22.3.3.
9: *Sources* 14.9. *Conditioned* (> 5 / - s, z, ?d, also *jo*) 12.4, 14.5(4).

199

10: *Sources* 14.10, 8.2.1. *Unconditioned* (> 1) Figs. 20, 21; *Realisation* (SVLR) 21.2.2; 23.
11: *Sources* 14.11, 6.0, 6.3.2. *Unconditioned* (merger 2) 6.3.2.
12: *Sources* 14.12, 6.0, 6.2, 6.2.2, 6.4.1, 9, 9.1; (17 + ld) 10. *Unconditioned* (smoothing) 18. *Conditioned* (dial. /ɑːv/) 6.4.0, n.29; (> 4 / - labials, affricates) 9.2, 12.1. *Realisation* 14.20, 18, 21.2.2; (SVLR, dial. merger 17) 21.1, n.38.
13: *Sources* 14.13, 6.0; (dial.) 6.2.2; 6.4.2; (17 + ld) 10. *Realisation* (SVLR) 21.2.2.
14a: *Sources* 6.0, 6.5.1, 7.2.2. *Unconditioned* (except dial. > (/j/) + 6) 6.5.1, 7.2.2, 6.5.3; (dial. merger 14b(i)) 6.5.3. *Conditioned* (early yod-absorption) 6.5.3. *Realisation* n.2.
14b(i): *Sources* 6.0; (dial.) 6.2.1, 6.5.2. *Unconditioned* (merger 14a) 6.5.2, 6.5.3; *Realisation* 14.13.
14b(ii): *Sources* 6.0, 6.5.2. *Unconditioned* (> (/j/) + 13) 6.5.2, 14.13(7).
14b(iii): *Sources* 6.5.2. *Unconditioned* (> (/j/) + 12) 6.5.2.
15: *Sources* 14.15, 3.1; (shortening of 2) 5.3; 6.2, 6.2.1, 8.3, 15. *Unconditioned* (SVL) 3.3. *Conditioned* (variably > 19 in labial environments before unstressed syllable) 8.3, 14.19(9); (variably > 16 / - n, l) 14.16(5); (> 19 / - labio-velars, dial. / - l) 23. *Realisation* 14.15, n.43.
16: *Sources* 14.16; 3.1; (shortening of 2, 3) 5.2; 6.2, 6.2.1, 8.3. *Unconditioned* (SVL) 3.3; (SVLR) 21.2.2. *Conditioned* (> 15 / - ŋg, ŋ(g)C, nC) 8.3, 14.15(9); (variably > 17 / - r) 11.2, 14.17(5); (variably > 15 / - alveolars, palatals) 14.15(8); (variably > 17 / - k#) 14.17(3); (variably > 17 / w -) 14.17(6), n.27. *Realisation* 14.16, n.43.
17: *Sources* 14.17; (shortening of 4) 5.2; 6.2.1, 8.3, 9.1, 9.2. *Conditioned* (variably > 4 / - rC) 11.1; (+ l > 12) 17, n.27; (variably > 16 / tʃ -) 14.16(4); (variably > 18 / labial - l, labial) 14.18(6); (> 18 / - n in *mony*, etc.) 14.18(7); (dial. > 12 / - nd, r) 23; . *Realisation* 21.2.2.
18: *Sources* 14.18, 3.1, 6.2.1, 16.2. *Unconditioned* (SVL) 3.3; (SVLR) 21.2.2; (dial. merger 5) 21.1. *Conditioned* (+ l > 13) 17; (variably > 17 in labial environments) 16.3; (> 5 / - rC) 14.5(3). *Realisation* 14.20, 21.2.2.
19: *Sources* 14.19; 3.1; (shortening of 7) 5.3; 6.2.1, 8.3. *Unconditioned* (SVL) 3.3. *Conditioned* (+ l > 6) 17; (> 15 in mainly nasal/labial environments) 8.3, 16.1. *Realisation* 3.3, 21.1, 23, n.62.

INDEX III: SELECTED SCOTS WORDS

A selection of items, including some suffixes, is indexed below. For the most part, words that are predictable and phonologically invariable, and whose spellings are unambiguous (often mentioned in the text only to illustrate the vowel numbers), are omitted, thus the unconditioned reflexes of most of the short vowels and some of the long vowels and diphthongs. For the items listed, the index can be used as a guide to stressed vowel pronunciation, in conjunction with Figures 20 and 21. Variant pronunciations (persisting or coming into existence in the period between OSL and 1700) are gathered together below, with minimal cross-reference. Space does not allow the listing of orthographic forms: instead the vowel numbers are used. A large number of rare spelling variants are cited in the text, sometimes (especially in the early letters of the alphabet) additional to DOST. Spellings listed in DOST are preferred in this index. These are not necessarily DOST headwords: the cross-references and variant lists in the dictionary should be consulted if necessary. The label 'modSc' is used when there is no clear evidence for the form in OSc, although it may well have existed then. Such modSc forms are often dialectal. Where the text is inexplicit about the more usual forms, the entries below have been augmented by reference to DOST and to AJA's pronunciation entries in CSD. However, the lists of forms below are not intended to be exhaustive.

The vowel numbers are given (bold, in brackets) for the stressed vowel unless otherwise indicated. If necessary, the stress placement is indicated by '[1st]' (= 1st syllable), etc. Sound-changes taking place during the OSc period are indicated by '>'.

abais 'dismay' (? early **8 > 4**) 12.3.
-able (**4**) 14.4(2).
able (**4**) 14.4(2); (modSc /j/ + **4, 4 >** /j/ + **15**) 22.2.2.
abound (**6**) 14.6(5); (**19**) 14.19(4).
abune, abuve (**7**) 4.2.2; (**7 > 15**) 21.2.3.
adewe 'adieu' (**14a**) 7.2.2
advertise [final] (**1, 2**) 15.
ae 'one' (**4**) 22.4, 22.2.1; (/j/ + **4**) 21.2.2, 22.2.1, 22.2.2, 22.2.4.
afald 'one-fold' [1st] (**4, 4 > 12**) 20.9.
aff see *off*.

affere 'bearing' (**3**) 14.3(9).
aft see *oft*.
again (**8**) 20.7, 22.3.2, 22.3.3; (**4**) 22.3.2, 22.3.3.
ain see *awin*.
-ain (**8**) 22.3.2.
air 'heir' (**8**) 14.8(3); (**8 > 4**) 22.3.4.
airth, yerth 'earth' (**4,** mod Sc **4 >** /j/ + **15**) 22.2.2 (*anglice* - see also *erd*) .
aither 'either' (**8**) 6.1.1, 12.3; (early **8 > 4**) 12.3.
aiver 'cart-horse' (**4**) 4.1, 22.2.1, 22.2.2.
ake 'ache' (**4,** /j/ + **4**) 22.2.1.
akin 'oaken' (**4,** /j/ + **4**) 22.2.1.

201

ald 'old' (**4**?) 10; (**4** > **12**) 6.0, 10, 14.12(2); (**4** > **13**) 10, 14.13(5).
-al, -ale (**4**) 14.4(8); (**17**) 14.4(8), 17.
ale (**4**) 20.4, 22.2.1; (/**j**/ + **4**) 22.2.1, 22.2.2; (modSc **4** > /**j**/ + **15**) 22.2.2, 22.2.4; (modSc **2**, /**j**/ + **2**) 22.2.2.
Alerig (**4**, /**j**/ + **4**) 22.2.1.
all (**17**, **17** + /**l**/ > **12a**) 17, 18, 20.9.
allya 'ally' [2ⁿᵈ] (**2**) 14.2(18); (**8**) 14.8(5).
almeral 'admiral' (**17**, **17** + /**l**/ > **12a**) 17.
almous 'alms' (**17**, **17** + /**l**/ > **12a**) 17.
amble (**17**, **12**) 9.1 (DOST s.v. *Ambland*).
ancester (**17**) 9.1; (**12**).
ane (**4**) 20.6, 20.7, 22.3.3; (**4** > **?3** > **2**) 9.3, 22.2.2; (/**j**/ + **4**) 21.2.3, 22.2.1; (**4** > /**j**/ + **15**) 21.2.3, 22.2.1, 22.2.2, 22.2.4; (modSc **2**) 22.2.2; *wan* (**17**) n.53.
-ane (**4**) 22.3.2.
anew see *ineuch*.
angel (**4**) 9.2.
ansenʒe 'ensign' (**3**, **16**) 8.3.
ant 'aunt' (**17**, **12**, ?**4**) 9.1.
ape (**4**) 22.2; (modSc **4** > /**j**/ + **15**) 22.2.2; modSc *yap* 22.2.1.
(*apill*) *oranʒe* 'orange' [2ⁿᵈ] (**17**, **16**, **16** > **3**) 8.4.
apparitour [final] 'court officer' (**6**) n.4.
appele 'appeal' (**3**) 14.3(1).
appere (**2**) 14.2(10).
approche (**5**) 14.5(1).
apron (**4**, **4** > **12**) 20.9.
archer (**17**, **17** > **4**) 11.1.

arequhile 'erewhile' [1ˢᵗ] (**4**, /**j**/ + **4**) 22.2.1; (**17**) 11.1. [2ⁿᵈ] (**1**) 20.7.
argh 'timid' (**17**, **17** > **4**, **4** > **16**) 11.1.
argu [2ⁿᵈ] (**14a**, **6**) 6.5.1.
arm (**17**, **17** > **4**, modSc **4** > **16**) 11.1.
armie (**17**, **17** > **4**, **4** > **16**) 11.1.
arrow [2ⁿᵈ] (**13**) 6.4.2.
assailʒe 'assail' 8.1; (**4**, **17**, **4** > **16**) 8.3.
assignee [final] (**2**) 14.2(18); (**8**) 14.8(5).
assise [2ⁿᵈ] (**1**, **2**) 15.
-atioun (**4**) 14.4(2).
atis 'oats' (**4**); modSc (**4** > /**j**/ + **15**) 22.2.2.
attire (**1**, **2**) 15.
aucht 'eight' (**12**) 3, 6.0, 6.2, Fig.13.
aucht p.t. 'owed' (**12**) 6.2.
augury [final] (**1**) 14.1(10).
auld see *ald*.
avance 'promote' (**17**) 9.1; (**12**).
ave 'nave of a wheel' (**4**) 22.2; (/**j**/ + **4**) 22.2.2, 22.2.4.
aw 'owe, own' (**12**) 3.
awake, awalk (**4**, **4** > **12**) 20.9.
away (**8**, ?**8b** > **4**, **4** > **12**) 22.4.
awin adj. 'own' (**12**) 6.4.1, 14.12(1); modSc *ain* (**8**) 9.2, 14.8(2), 22.2.2.
ax (**17**, **4**, **4** > **16**); modSc (**4** > /**j**/ + **15**) 22.2.2.
-ay '-ey' (**8**) 14.8(5).
ay 'always' (**8**) 14.8(2), 22.4; (**8a** > **1**) 22.4.
aynd 'breath, knock the breath from' (**4**) 3.1.1, 14.4(3); (**4** > **16**) 21.2.2; modSc *yind* (**4** > /**j**/ + **15**) 22.2.2.
bahuvis 'coffers' (**4**, **4** > **12**) 20.9.

bailȝe 8.4; (**17**) 8.3; (**4**) 8.3; (**4 > 16**) 8.3; (**8**) 8.2.1; (modSc **?8 > 1, ?4 > 1**) 8.3.
bailȝery (**17, 4**) 8.3.
baird 'bard' (**4**) 3.1.1, 11.1.
bairn (**4**) 4.1, 11.1; (**3**) 4.1; (**?4 > 16**) 11.1.
bait '(stop for) feed' (**8**) 12.3, 14.8(2), 21.2.2, 22.3.3.
balk (**17, 17 + /l/ > 12a**) 17.
bane (**4**) 20.2, 20.4; (**4 > ?3 > 2**) 9.3.
baptime [2ⁿᵈ] (**1, 2**) 15.
baptise [2ⁿᵈ] (**1, 2**) 15.
barge (**17, 17 > 4**) 11.1.
baudkin 'embroidered cloth' (**12**) 18.
baum 'balm' (**12**) 14.12(4).
befe (**2**) 14.2(12), 21.2.2.
before (**5**) 3.2, 14.5(1).
behind (**15**) 3.1.1.
beid 'be it' (**2**) 21.2.2.
beild 'build' (**2, 15**) 5.1.
beisand 'bezant' (**3**) 4.1.
bekin 'beacon' (**2**) 14.2(6).
bellys 'bellows' [2ⁿᵈ] (**1**) 6.3.1.
beme (**3**) 14.3(2).
ben 'inwards' (**16**) 14.16(5).
bene 'bean' (**2, 3**) 14.2(20), 14.3, 20.8.2.
bene p.p. 'been' (**2**) 14.3, 20.8.2.
benigne (**15**) 8.3.
berar 'bearer' (**3 > 2**) 20.6.
berde 'beard' (**3**) 3.1.1, 14.3(3).
bere 'bear, carry' (**3 > 2**) 20.8.3.
bern 'barn' (**16, 16 > 17**) 11.2.
bery 'bury' [2ⁿᵈ] (**1**) 6.3.1.
beste 'beast' (**3**) 14.3(1), 20.8.2.
besy see *bisy*.
bete 'beat' (**3**) 14.3(2).

bete 'beet, the vegetable' (**2**) 14.2(1).
beuch 'bough' (**7 > /j/ + 19**) Fig.13; (**7 > 14a**) 1.1, 6.2, 7.2.1; pl. *bewis* (**14a**) 1.1, 7.2.2.
beuk see *buke*.
bewté [1ˢᵗ] (**14b(i), 14b(ii), 14b(iii)**) 6.5.2, Fig.13. [2ⁿᵈ] (**2**) 14.2(17).
bind (**15**) 3.1.1, 14.15(3).
bisy 'busy' (**15, 2**) 4.2.1, Fig.13; *bussie* (*anglice* **19**) 14.19 (9).
blaw 'blow' (**12**) 6.4.0; (modSc /j/ + **12**) 6.4.0, 16.6.
blese 'blaze' (**3**) 14.3(4).
blether 'bladder, talk foolishly' (**16**) 14.16(3).
blew 'blue' (**14a**) 6.5.1, 6.5.3, Fig.13.
blew p.t. (**14a**) 6.5.1.
blind (**15**) 3.1.1.
blis 'bless' (**15**) 14.15(8).
bluid 'bluid' (**7**) 5.3, 14.7(1).
boil (**10**) 8.2.1, 14.10(2); *builȝe* (**7**).
bollyn 'swollen' (**18**) 17; *boldin, bowdin* (**18 + /l/ > 13a**) 17.
bolt (**18 + /l/ > 13a**) 17.
bonnet (**18**) 14.18(3); (**18 > 17**) 16.3.
borch 'pledge' (**18**) 6.2.1.
born (**18?, 5?**) 14.5(3).
bost 'boast' (**5**) 14.5(2).
bouk 'carcass' (**6**) 17.
bound p.p. (**6**) 3.1.1; *bund(in)* (**19**) 3.1.1.
bow 'the weapon' (**13**) 6.0, 6.4.2, Fig.7, 14.13(2).
bow 'ox-bow' (**13**) 17.
bow v. 'bend' (**6**) 6.4.3, Fig.7, 6.5.3, 14.6(3).
boy (**9**) 14.9(3).
braid 'a quick movement' (**8**)

22.3.3.
brainge v. 'dash' (**4**?) 9.2;
modSc *breenge* (**4** > **3**?) 9.3.
brak see *brek*.
branch (**12**, **4**, **4** > **8**, **8** > **16**) 9.2.
brase 'brass' (**4**) 12.3; (**16**) 14.16(3).
brave (**4**, **4** > **12**) 20.9.
braw (**4** > **12**) 20.9.
brede 'breadth' (**2**) 14.2(19).
brede 'bread' (**3**) 5.2, 14.3(2); (**3** > **4**) 20.8.3.
breird 'first shoots' (**2**) 3.1.1, 11.2; *braird* (?**16** > **17** > **4**) 11.2.
breist 'breast' (**2**) 20.8.2.
brek 'break' (**16**) 4.1, 5.2, 14.17(3); (**17**) 14.17(3); (**3**) 4.1, 5.2.
breme 'bream' (**3**) 14.3(7).
bress see *brase*.
brethe 'breath' (**3**) 5.2, 14.3(5).
brew (**14a**) 6.5.1; *brow-* (**14** > (/j/) + **6**) 6.5.3.
bro 'broth' (**7**) 7.1, 14.7(7).
broche 'brooch' (**5**) 14.5(1); (**5** > **19**) 14.19(8), 16.2.
brother (**7**, **19**, modSc **19** > **15**) 16.1.
bruit 'noise' (**7**) 14.7(10).
brulʒe 'broil' (**19**) 8.2.1.
bucht 'sheep fold' (**19**) 6.2.1.
buird 'board' (**7**) 3.1.1, 14.7(6); (**7** > **14a**) 7.1, 7.3, Fig.8; (**14** > (/j/) + **6**) 7.3; *brod* (**18**) 3.1.1.
buist 'box' (**7**) 16.1.
buke (**7**) 7.2.1, 14.7(1); *beuk* (**7** > **14a**) 7.2.1.
bukkil 'buckle' (**19, 6**) 14.19(4).
bull 'the animal' (**19**, ?**19** + /l/ > **6a**) 17; *bule* (**7**) 17.
bull, bow 'papal bull' (**19, 19** +

/l/ > **6a**) 17.
bullet (**19**) 4.2.2, 16.1, 17; (**19** > **15**) 16.1.
bur p.t. 'bore' (**6, 7**) n.4.
burch 'burgh' (**19**) 1.1, 6.2.1, 14.19(1), 14.20; pl. *burrowis* [1ˢᵗ] (**19**) 1.1, 14.20; [2ⁿᵈ] (**13**) 6.4.2.
bus 'bush' (**19**) 14.19(1).
but 'outside' (**19**) 14.19(3).
buth 'booth' (**7**) 7.1, 21.2.3.
caird 'tinker' (**4**) 3.1.1, 11.1.
cairn (**4**) 3.1.1, 11.1; modSc (/j/ + **12**) 16.6.
cairt 'card' (**17**); (**17** > **4**) 14.4(6).
cairt 'cart' see *cart*.
cald 'cold' (**4, 4** > **12, 4** > **13**) 10.
calf (**17, 17** + /l/ > **12a**) 17.
calk 'chalk' (**17, 17** + /l/ > **12a**) 17.
call (**17, 17** + /l/ > **12a**) 17.
calve (**17, 17** + /l/ > **12a**) 17.
canaille 'mob' 8.4; (**4**, modSc **17**) 8.3.
cap 'cup' see *cop*.
capercailzie 8.1.
car 'left(-hand)' (**17**) 11.1.
carl (**17**) 4.1; (**4**) 4.1, 11.1; (**4** > **16**?) 11.1.
carp v. 'talk' (**17, 17** > **4**) 11.1.
cart (**17**) 11.1; (**17** > **4**) 11.1, Fig.13; *kert* (**4** > **16**) 11.1.
caus (**12**) 6.0, 14.12(4).
causay 'causeway' [1ˢᵗ] (**12**) 14.12(4), 17. [2ⁿᵈ] (**8**) 14.8(5).
cautele 'cunning' [2ⁿᵈ] (**2**) 14.2(10).
cautioun (**12**) 12.1, 14.12(4); (**12** > **4**) 12.1, Fig.13.
cercle (**16**) 11.2; *circle* (**15**) 11.2.
certane [1ˢᵗ] (**16, 16** > **17**) 11.2. [2ⁿᵈ] (**4, 8**) 22.3.2, 22.3.3.

INDEX III: SCOTS WORDS

cese 'cease' (**3**) 14.3(1).
cha- see *che-*.
chafer 'warming dish' (**12, 12 > 4**) 12.1.
chain see *chenȝe*.
chaipel 'chapel' (**4**) 4.1.
chance (**17, 12**) 9.1.
change (**12**) 9.2; (**4**) 9.2, Fig.13; (**4 > ?3 >2**) 9.3; (**3 > 1**) 9.3, 14.1(12); (**4 > 8, 8 > 16**) 9.2.
chastise [1ˢᵗ] (**17, 4**) 4.1. [2ⁿᵈ] (**1, 2**) 15.
chaumer 'chamber' (**12**) 9.1, 14.12(5), 17.
cheenie 'china' (modSc **2**) 15.
chefe 'chief' (**2**) 14.2(11).
cheftane [2ⁿᵈ] (**8**) 22.3.2; (**4**) 20.4, 22.3.2.
chelder 'chalder' (**17, 16**) 14.16(4).
chelice 'chalice' (**17, 16**) 14.16(4).
chennon 'canon' (**17, 16**) 14.16(4).
chenȝe 'chain' 8.1, 8.4; (**16**) 8.2.2; (**16 > 15**) 8.3; (**17**) 8.4; (**3, 3 > 1**) 8.4, 9.3.
cheplane 'chaplain' (**17, 16**) 14.16(4).
chepman 'chapman' (**17, 16**) 14.16(4).
cheppil 'chapel' (**17, 16**) 14.16(4).
cheptour 'chapter' (**17, 16**) 14.16(4).
chere 'chair' (**3**) 14.3(9).
chere 'cheer' (**2**) 14.2(11).
chese see *chuse*.
cheritee 'charity' (**17, 16**) 14.16(4).
chevalry [final] (**1**) 14.1(10).
chikkin (**15, 2**) 4.2.1.

child (**1**) 3.1, 3.1.1, 5.1, 14.1(2), 20.6; (**2**) 14.2(16).
chinȝie see *chenȝie*.
chock 'choke' (**5, 18**) 16.4; (modSc **18 > 13**) cf. next.
chokis 'quinsy', 'jougs, the instrument of punishment' (**18, 18 > 13**) 16.4. See also *chock, jogis*.
chose 'choice' (**9**) 12.4; (**9 > 5**) 12.4, 14.5(4).
chow 'chew' (**13**) 6.4.2.
chuse 'choose' (**7**) 14.2(5), 14.7(4); *chese* (**2**) 14.2.
chymmer 'chimera' (**15, 2**) 4.2.1.
cipher (**1, 2**) 15.
cite (**1, 2**) 15.
cité 'city' [1ˢᵗ] (**15**) 4.2.1; (**2**) 4.2.1, 14.2(15). [2ⁿᵈ] (**2**) 14.2(17).
citeyane 'citizen' (**15, 2**) 4.2.1.
civill (**15, 2**) 4.2.1.
claw (**12**) 6.0, 6.4.0, 6.4.1, Fig.13.
clay n. (**8**) 6.1.1, Fig.13; (**8a**). v. (**8b > 4**?) 22.4.
clene 'clean' (**2**) 14.2(19).
clepe 'call' (**15, 2**) 4.2.1.
clere 'clear' (**2**) 14.2(10).
clethe 'clothe' (**3**) 14.3(4).
cleuch 'a ravine' (**7 > 14a**) 7.2.1; pl. *clewis* (**14a**) 7.2.2.
clim 'climb' (**15**) 3.1.1.
cloke (**18**) 4.1, 14.18(4); (**5**) 4.1, 14.5(1).
close adj., n. (**5**) 14.5(2).
closter 'cloister' (**9 > 5**?) 14.5(4).
clout (**6**) 14.6(1).
clow 'clue of yarn' (**14a > (/j/) + 6**) 6.5.3.
clud 'cloud' (**6**); (**19**) 14.19(3).
cole 'coal' (**18**) 4.1, 17; (**5**) 4.1.
colpindach 'young cow' (**18 + /l/**

205

> **13a**) 17.
command (**17, 12**) 9.1.
complene (**3**) 14.3, 20.8.2.
complete (**2**) 14.2(10), 15.
concele (**3**) 14.3(6).
condign (**15**) 8.3.
condyte 'conduct' (**1, 2**) 15.
confuse (**7**) 14.7(9).
confusioun (**7**) 14.7(9).
consait (**8**) 12.3, 14.3(9); (early **8 > 4**) 12.3.
consave (**8**, early **8 > 4**) 12.3, Fig.13.
consign (**15**) 8.3.
continual [3rd] (**14a**) 6.5.1.
contrite (**1, 2**) 15.
cop 'cup' (**18, 18 > 17**) 16.3.
corn (**18?, 5?**) 14.5(3).
cote 'coat' (**18**) 4.1; (**5**) 3.2, 4.1, 14.5(1), 21.2.2.
couple (**19**) 4.2.2, 16.1; *kipple* (**19 > 15**) 16.1.
course (**6**) 14.6(5).
court (**6**) 14.6(5).
cowp 'overturn' (**13**) 6.0, 14.13(4).
cowp 'trade' (**13**) 17.
craft 'croft' (**18, 18 > 17**) 16.3.
craig 'crag' (**4**) 14.4(2).
craig 'neck' (**4**) 14.4(2).
crap 'crop' (**18, 18 > 17**) Fig.20a.
craw 'crow' (**12**) 18.
creat (**3**) 14.3(6)
creddil 'cradle' (**16**) 14.16(3); (**4**).
crede 'creed' (**2**) 14.2(1).
crese 'grease' (**3**) 14.3(9).
crew p.t. (**14a**) 6.5.1.
crine 'shrink' (**1**) 14.1(13).
crippill (**15, 2**) 4.2.1.
crochet 'hook' (**5, 5 > 19**) 16.2.
croft see *craft*.

croice n. 'cross' (**9**) 12.4, 14.9(1); (**9 > 5**) 12.4, 14.5(4).
cruel (**14a**) 6.0, 6.5.1; (**14 > (/j/) + 6**) 6.5.3.
cruke 'crook' (**7**) 7.1, 14.7(2); (**7 > 14a**) 7.2.1; *crowk* (**14 > (/j/) + 6**) 6.5.3.
cuid 'cud' (**7**) 4.2.2.
cuisen 'cousin' (**6, 19**); (modSc **7, 7 > 15**) 4.2.2.
cuit 'ankle' (**7**) 7.1, 14.7(3).
cuitler 'cutler' (modSc **7**) 4.2.2.
cuke 'cook' (**7**) 7.1, 6.5.3; (**7 > 14a**) 6.5.3; *kowk* 6.5.3 (cf. *pewter*).
cule 'cool' (**7**) 14.7(1).
Culross (**6a**) n.31.
culter 'coulter' (**19 + /l/ > 6a**) 17.
culyie 'caress' 8.1, 8.4; (**19**, modSc **6**) 8.3.
cummer 'godmother' (**19, 19 > 15**) 16.1.
cuntray [2nd] (**2**) 14.2(18); (**8**) 14.8(5); (**8b > 4?**) 22.4.
cunȝe 'coin' 8.4; (**19**) 8.1, 8.2.1, 8.2.2, 8.3.
cure (**7**) 6.5.1, 14.7(9).
curious (**7**) 14.7(9).
'd 'it'(after vowel) 21.2.2.
-d p.t., p.p. (after vowel) 21.2.2, 22.3.2 (*said*, etc.).
daich 'dough' (**12**); (**4**) 6.2.1, Fig.7; *dewche* (**14b(i)**) 6.2.1.
dainty see *denty*.
daith 'death' (**3 > 4**) 20.8.3.
Dalziel 8.1.
dance (**17, 12**) 9.1.
danger [1st] (**12**) 9.2, 14.12(5); (**4**) 14.4(5); (**4 > 8**) 9.2; (**8 > 16**) 9.2. [2nd] (**2**) 14.2(11).
dant 'daunt' (**12, 17, ?4**) 9.1.
dar 'dare' (**17**) 11.1.
David (**4 > 12**) 20.9.

INDEX III: SCOTS WORDS

day (**8**) 6.1.1, 14.8(1), 22.4; (**8b** > **4**) 22.4.
de 'die' (**11**) 6.3.2, 21.2.2; p.t. 21.2.2.
decent (**3**) 14.3(1).
decree (**2**) 14.2(10); p.t. 21.2.2.
decrete 'decree' (**2**) 14.2(10).
dede 'dead' (**3**) 5.2, 14.3, 14.3(2), 20.8.2.
dede 'deed' (**2**) 14.2(2), 21.2.2.
dekine 'deacon' [2ⁿᵈ] (**15**) 20.3.
dele 'deal, the wood' (**16, 3**) 4.1.
dele n. 'deal, share' (**2**) 14.2(19).
dele v. 'deal' (**3**) 14.2(19), 14.3(4).
den 'valley' (**16, 3**) 4.1.
dene 'dean' (**3**) 14.3(9).
denner 'dinner' (**16**) 14.16(5); (**15**).
denty 'dainty' (**8, 8 > 16**) 9.2.
denȝe 'deign' (**16, 3**) 8.3.
depairt 'depart' (**17, 17 > 4**) 11.2; (**4 > 16**).
depe (**2**) 14.2(5).
dere 'injure' (**3 > 2**) 20.8.3.
derene 'challenge' (**3**) 14.3, 20.8.2.
derf 'brave' (**16, 16 > 17**) 11.2.
derth 'dearth' (**16, 16 > 17**) 11.2.
dese 'dais' (**3**) 14.3(9).
desing 'design' (**15**) 8.3; (**2**) 8.3; *desyne* (**1**) 8.2.1, 14.1(9).
dethe see *daith*.
devil (**2**) 14.2(5), 16.5, 21.2.2; (**3, 3 > 15**) 16.5.
devore 'duty' (**9 > 5**?) 14.5(4).
dew 'due' (**14a**) 6.5.1, 6.5.3, 7.2.2, Fig.13.
dew p.t. 'dawned' (**14a**) 6.5.1.
dew n. (**14b(i)**) 6.0, 6.5.2, 6.5.3, Fig.13; (**14b(ii)**) 6.5.2, Fig.13.
dewté 'duty' (**14a**) 6.5.1, 6.5.3; (**6**) 6.5.1..
digne 'worthy' (**15**) 8.3.
dispone 'dispose' (**5**) 14.5(1).
dispose (**5**) 14.5(1).
dissait 'deceit' (**8**) 12.3, 14.3(9); (early **8 > 4**) 12.3.
dissave 'deceive' (early **8 > 4**) 12.3.
dissone see *dousane*.
dissy 'dizzy' (**15, 2**) 4.2.1.
distroy (**9, 10, ?7**) n.26.
do (**7**) 6.5.1, 7.1, 14.7(1); (**7 > 4**) 20.7. + *-is* 12.2.
dochter 'daughter' (**18**) 6.2.2, 14.18(1); (**13**) 6.0, 6.2.2, 14.13(6); *dother* (**5**) 14.5(1).
doit 'the small Dutch coin' (**10**) 14.10(3), 22.4.
dolly, dowie 'sad' (**18, 18 + /l/ > 13a**) n.30.
done p.p. (**7**) 7.1.
donk 'dank' (**17 > 18**) 14.18(7); (**19**).
double (**6**) 14.6(5).
doup 'buttock' (**18 > 13**) 16.4.
dour (**6**) 14.6(6).
dousane 'dozen' (**6, 19, 19 > 15**) 16.1.
dow 'dove' (**6**) 14.6(2).
dowg 'dog' (**18**); (**18 > 13**) 16.4.
draigon 'dragon' (**4**) 4.1.
dre 'endure' (**11**) 1.1, 6.2.1, 6.3.2, 14.11.
drede 'dread' (**2**) 14.2(2), 14.3, 20.8.2.
dreich 'dreary' (**2**) 1.1, 6.2.1.
dreiff 'drive' (**2**) 4.2.1.
dreme (**3**) 14.3(2); (**3 > 4, 3 > 2**) 20.8.3.
drew p.t. (**14a**) 7.2.2; (**14 > (/j/) +**

6) 6.5.3. 7.2.2.
drivin p.p. (**15, 2**) 4.2.1.
drouth 'dryness' (**6**) 6.4.3, 14.6(3).
duik 'duck' (**7**) 4.2.2; (**7 > 14a**) 7.2.1.
duir 'door' (**7**) 4.2.2, 7.1, 14.7(8), 21.1.
duke 'duke' (**7**) 14.7(9); (**7 > 14a**) 7.2.1.
dule 'sorrow' (**7**) 7.1.
dun (**19, 19 > 15**) 16.1.
dung(in) p.p. 'beaten' (**19, 6**) 3.1.1.
dyke (**1, 15**) 14.15(5).
-e 4.1, 4.2.1, 4.2.2, 8.1, 8.2.1, 8.2.2, 13.1, 13.1.1, 13.1.2, 13.2.
-é (**2**) 14.2(17).
-é(e) (**2**) 14.2(18).
e 'eye' (**11 > 2**) 6.3.2; pl. *ene* (**11 > 2**) 14.3, 20.8.2.
egill 'eagle' (**3**) 14.3(9); (modSc /**j**-/) 22.2.1.
egir 'eager' (**3**) 14.3(9).
eild 'old age' (**2**) 3.1.1, 22.2.1; (/**j**-/?) 22.2.1.
eith 'easily' (**3, 2**) 14.2(20).
eke 'also' (**2**) 14.2(6).
eke v. (**2**) 14.2(4).
ele 'eel' (**2**); (/**j**-/) 22.2.1.
ell (**16**); (/**j**-/) 22.2.1.
elyte 'person nominated' (**1, 2**) 15.
ene see *e*.
enew see *ineuch*.
engine [2ⁿᵈ] (**1**) 14.1(8).
ensampill 'example' (**17, 12**) 9.1.
ensew 'ensue' (**14a**) 6.5.1; (/s/ + **14** > /ʃ/ + **6**) 6.5.3.
entray [2ⁿᵈ] (**8**) 14.8(5).
erb 'herb' (**16**); (/**j**-/) 22.2.1.

erd 'earth' (**16**) 11.2; (**2**) 3.1.1, 14.2(7); (/**j**-/) 22.2.1; (**16 > *17 > 4**) 11.2; *yird* (**4 > /j/ + 15**) 11.2. See also *airth*.
-ere < OF (**2**) 14.2.
ere 'ear' (**3**) 14.3(2).
ere v. 'plough' (**3**); (/**j**-/) 22.2.1.
ere 'before' (**3**) 14.3(4); (/**j**-/) 22.2.1.
erl 'earl' (**16, 3**) 4.1; (/**j**-/) 22.2.1.
erlis 'earnest payment' (**16, 16 > 17, 17 > 4**) 11.2.
erne 'eagle' (**16, 3, 3 > 4**) 4.1.
errasy 'heresy' (**16, 16 > 17**) 11.2.
erretike 'heretic' (**16, 16 > 17**) 11.2.
Errol (**16, 16 > 17**) 11.2.
erse 'arse' (**16**) 14.16(3).
Erskine (**16, 16 > 17**) 11.2.
ery 'eerie' (**2?, 3?**); (/**j**-/) 22.2.1.
esch 'ash tree' (**16**) 14.16(3).
eschow 'eschew' (**6**) 6.5.3.
ese 'ease' (**3**) 14.3(9).
este 'east' (**3**) 14.3(2); (modSc /**j**-/) 22.2.1.
-ete (**2**) 14.2(10)
ete 'eat' (**3**) 14.3(1); (**3 > 2**) 20.8.3, 22.1; (/**j**-/?) 22.2.1.
even (**3**) 4.1.
evill (**15, 2**) 4.2.1.
evin 'evening' (**2**) 14.2(2).
exeme v. 'exempt' (**2**) 14.2(13).
expreme v. 'express' (**2**) 14.2(13).
extreme (**2**) 14.2(10).
fader 'father' (**17, 4**) 4.1.
fadome (**17**); (***4**) 4.1; (**4 > 12**) 4.1, 20.9.
failʒe 'fail' 8.4; (**17**) 8.3; (**4**) 8.2.2, 8.3, 14.4(2), 20.4, 22.3.2; (**4 > 16**) 8.3; (**8**) 8.2.1, 14.8(4), 22.3.2.
fain (**8, 4**) 20.7, 22.3.2, 22.3.3.

INDEX III: SCOTS WORDS

faint (**8, 8 > 16**) 9.2.
fair (**8, 4**) 22.3.2, 22.3.4.
faith (**8**, early **8 > 4**) 12.3.
fald 'fold, enclosure' (**4?, 4 > 12, 4 > 13**) 10.
Falkirk (**12**) 17.
fall (**17, 17 + /l/ > 12a**) 17, 20.9.
fallow 'fellow' (**17**) 14.17(4); (**17 > 18**) 14.18(6).
familie (**4**) 4.1.
famyle 'family' [2nd] (**1**) 8.2.1, 14.1(9).
fard 'paint (the face)' (**17, 17 > 4**) 11.1; (**4 > 16**).
fard 'impetus' (**17, 17 > 4, 4 > 16**) 11.1.
farne 'fern' (**16 > 17, 17 > 4**) 11.2.
faucht p.t. 'fought' (**12**) 6.2.2
faut 'fault' (**12**) 6.0, 14.12(4), 21.2.2.
favour (**4, 4 > 12**) 20.9.
faynde v. 'test' (**4**) 3.1.1.
febill (**2**) 14.2(11), 21.2.2.
fecht 'fight' (**16**) 6.2.1, 14.16(1); (**15**) 6.2.1, 14.15(2).
fede 'feud' (**3**) 14.3(9); (**3 > 2, 3 > 4**) 20.8.3.
fee (**2**) 14.2(10).
feer 'cut the first furrow' (modSc **2**) 4.2.1.
feild (**2**) 3.1.1, 14.2(7).
feir 'behaviour' (**3 > 2**) 20.8.3.
fenʒe 'feign' 8.4; (**16**) 8.3; (**16 > 15**) 8.3; (**3**) 8.3, 14.3(1); (**8**) 8.2.1, 8.3, 14.8(4).
fer 'far' (**16, 16 > 17**) 11.2.
ferde 'fourth' (**2**) 14.2(5).
fere 'fear' (**3**) 14.3(5).
ferm 'firm' (**16**) 11.2.
ferm 'farm' (**16**) 11.2.
fernʒere 'last year' (**16, 16 >**

17) 11.2.
ferse 'fierce' (**2**) 14.2(11).
fert 'fart' (**16, 16 > 17**) 11.2.
ferter 'enshrine' (**16**) 11.2.
feste 'feast' (**3**) 14.3(1).
festin 'fasten' (**16**) 14.16(3).
fete see *fuit*.
few (**14b(i), 14b(ii)**) 6.5.2, 6.5.3.
fey 'doomed to die' (**8**) 14.8(2); (**8a > 1**) 22.4.
ficht see *fecht*.
fickill (**15, 2**) 4.2.1.
fidill 'fiddle' (**15, 2**) 4.2.1.
fiftly (**15**); *fayftelie* (**1**) 20.6.
figour (**15, 2**) 4.2.1.
finale (**1**, modSc **2**) 15.
find (**15**) 3.1.1, 14.15(3), 20.3.
finis (**15**, modSc **2**) 4.2.1.
fit see *fuit*.
flaid p.p. 'flayed' (**4**) 20.4.
flatterie [final] (**1**) 14.1(10).
fle v. 'fly' (**11**) 6.3.2.
fleche 'flatter' (**2?**) 14.2(21).
flew p.t. (**14a**) 6.5.1; (**14 > /j/**) + **6**) 6.5.3.
fluid 'flood' (**7**) 5.3, 21.2.3.
fluke 'flounder, the fish' (**7**) n.4.
flure 'floor' (**7, 7 > 14a, 14 > (/j/) + 6**) 7.3.
fochtin p.p. 'fought' (**18, 13**) 6.2.2.
foisoun see *fusioun*.
fold 'the earth' (**18**) 3.1.1.
folk (**18 + /l/ > 13a**) 17.
follow (**18, ??17**) 14.17(7).
force (**5**) 14.5(3).
forfur 'gone amiss' (**7**) 7.1.
Forth (**5**) 14.5(3).
fortune (**7**) 7.1.
foul 'bird' (**6**) 6.4.3, 14.6(3).
foul adj. (**6**) 14.6(1).
found p.p. (**6**) 3.1.1; *fund(in)* (**19**) 3.1.1.

fountain (**6**) 14.6(5).
four (**13**) 6.4.2.
fous 'eager' (**6**) 6.5.1.
fouth see *fulth*
frende (**2**) 14.2(5), 20.4, 20.6.
frendly [2nd] (**1**) 14.1(6).
frere 'friar' (**2**) 14.2(10).
frethe 'set free' (**2**) 4.2.1.
fruit (**7**) 7.1, 14.7(10).
fuird 'ford' (**7**) 3.1.1, Fig.13; (**7** > **14a, 14** > (/j/) + **6**) 7.3.
fuist 'fust' (**7, 7** > **6**) 14.7(9).
fuist p.t. 'fetched' (modSc 7, 7 > **6**) 14.6(10).
fuit 'foot' (**7**) 5.3, 16.1, n.4; (**19**) 5.3, Fig.13, 16.1; (**19** > **15**) 5.3, 16.1; pl. *fete* (**2**) 14.2(3), 20.8.3.
fule 'fool' (**7**) 7.1, 14.7(7); (**7** > **15**) 22.2.3.
full (**19, 19** + /l/ > **6a**) 17.
fulth 'plenty' (**19** + /l/ > **6a**) 17.
fund 'found' (**6, 19**) 14.19(4).
fund(in) p.p. see *found*.
fur 'furrow' (**19**) 6.2.1; (**7**) from inflected forms.
furde 'ford' (**7**) 7.1; (**7** > **14a**) 7.3; (**14** > (/j/) + **6**).
fure 'convey' (**7**) n.4.
Furisday 'Thursday' (**7**) n.4.
fusioun 'foison, plenty' (**7**) 14.6(10), 14.7(9); (**7** > **6**) 14.6(10); *foisoun* (**10**) 14.10(1).
futher 'cart-load' (**19**) 5.3, 14.19(7), 16.1; *fidder* (**19** > **15**) 16.1.
ga 'go' (**4**) + -*is* 12.2, 13.3.
gaberlunzie 8.1.
gadder 'gather' (**17**) 4.1; modSc *gedder* (**16**) 4.1; modSc *gaither* (**4**) 4.1; *gether* (**16**) 14.16(3).

gaine 'befit' (**8**) Fig.13.
gait 'goat, goats' (**8**) 12.3, 22.3.3.
gaither see *gadder*.
gallowbreid 'gallows-bird' (rhymes as **2**) 21.2.2.
gallowis [2nd] (**13**) 6.4.2.
game (**4**) 20.4; *gemm* (**4** > **16**) 21.2.2.
gane 'face' (**4**) 22.3.3.
ganȝe 'cross-bow bolt' (**17, 4, 4** > **16**) 8.3.
gar see *ger*.
gardin (**17, 17** > **4**) 11.1.
gate 'road' (**4**) 12.3, 14.4(2), 20.4, 21.2.2.
gavelok 'crowbar' (**4**) 21.2.2; *gellok* (**4** > **16**) 21.2.2.
gay (**8**) 6.0, 14.8(3); *gey* (**8a** > **1**) 22.4.
gef p.t. 'gave' (**16**) 14.16(3).
geigget 'gigot' modSc (**15**) 4.2.1; (**2**) 4.2.1.
geist see *jist*.
gellok see *gavelock*.
ger v. 'cause' (**16, 16** > **17**) 11.2.
gere 'gear' (**3**) 14.3(1).
gers 'grass' (**16, 16** > **17**) 11.2; *gres* (**16**) 14.16(3); *gris* (**15**) 14.15(8).
get (**16, 3**) 5.2.
gether see *gadder*.
gey see *gay*.
gigot see *geigget*.
girs see *gers*.
give (**15**) 4.2.1; (**2**) 4.2.1, 14.2(15); (**3**) 14.2(15), 14.3(1).
glave 'sword' (**8**, early **8** > **4**) 12.3.
gled 'glad' (**16**) 14.16(3); (**17**).
gled 'kite (the bird)' (**16**) Fig.13.
gleme 'gleam' (**3**) 14.3(4).
gles 'glass' (**17**); (**16**) 14.16(3).
glew 'mirth' (**14a**) 6.5.1.

INDEX III: SCOTS WORDS

gloming 'dusk' (**5**) 14.5(1).
glore 'glory' (**?9** > **5**) 14.5(4); (**5**) 14.5(1).
glorie (**5**) 14.5(1).
gold (**18**) 3.1.1; (**18** + /l/ > **13a**) 17.
golf (**18** + /l/ > **13a**) 17.
gowk 'cuckoo' (**13**) 6.0, 14.13(3).
graid p.p. 'equipped' (**8** > **4**?) 22.3.3.
grain 'seed' (**8**) 12.3; (? near rhyme with **4**) 22.3.3.
graith 'equip(ment)' (**8**) 12.3, 14.8(2); (early **8** > **4**) 12.3, 20.4, 22.3.3.
grand (**17**) 9.1; (**12**) 9.1, 14.12(5).
grant (**17, 12**) 9.1.
grave (**4**) 4.1, 21.2.3; *graff* (**17**) 4.1, 14.17(1).
gray (**8**) 6.1.1; (**8b**).
gre 'satisfaction' (**2**) 14.2(10).
grene (**2**) 14.2(3).
grenge 'grange' (**4, 4** > **8, 8** > **16**) 9.2; (**12**).
gres see *gers*.
grete 'great' (**3**) 14.3(2); (**3** > **1**) 14.1(12); (**16**) 3.1; (**15**) 14.15(8); *gert* (**16, 16** > **17**) 11.2.
greve 'foreman' (**2**) 14.2(11), 21.2.2.
grew p.t. (**14a**) 6.5.1, 6.5.3.
Grew 'Greek, Greece' (**14a**) 6.5.1.
grind (**15**) 3.1.1.
groff 'coarse' (**18**) 16.3; (**18** > **13**) 16.4.
grow 'become larger' (**13**) 6.4.2, Fig.7, 6.5.2, 14.13(1).
grow 'shudder' (**6**) 6.5.1.
grund 'ground' (**19**) 3.1.1,
14.19(2); (**6**) 3.1.1, 14.6(4), 14.19(2).
gryte see *grete*.
gude 'good' (**7**) 7.1, 14.7(1), 20.7, 21.2.3; (**7** > **15**) 22.2.3.
gudly 'goodly' [2nd] (**1**) 14.1(6).
guld 'corn marigold' (**7, 19**) 3.1.1, 5.3.
guttar 'gutter' (**7**) 4.2.2, 16.1; (**19, 19** > **15**) 16.1.
gyle 'wort' (**1, 2**) 15.
habit [2nd] (**1, 2, 15**) 15.
haf (**17**) 4.1, 17; *have* (**4**) 4.1.
haknay [2nd] (**8**) 14.8(5).
hail (**8, 4**) 22.3.2.
hain 'enclose' (**8**) 6.1.1, 9.2, 12.3, 22.3.2; (**4**?) 22.3.2.
hale 'whole' (**4**) 20.3, 20.6, 22.3.2; (modSc **4** > /j/ + **15**) 22.2.2.
half (**17, 17** + /l/ > **12a**) 17.
hals 'throat' (**17, 17** + /l/ > **12a**) 17.
haly 'holy' [1st] (**4**) 20.7. [2nd] (**1**) 14.1(6).
hame 'home' (**4**) 3.2; (modSc /j/ + **4**, modSc **4** > /j/ + **15**) 22.2.2.
hammer (**17**); (**4**) 4.1; (**4** > **12**) 20.9; (**4** > **16**) 21.2.2.
hanche 'haunch' (**17?, 12, ?4, 4** > **8, 8** > **16**) 9.2.
hant 'haunt' (**17, 12**) 9.1.
hard (**17, 17** > **4, 4** > **16**) 11.1.
harm (**17, 17** > **4, 4** > **16**) 11.1.
harnis 'brains' (**17, 17** > **4**) 3.1.1.
harp (**17, 17** > **4, 4** > **16**) 11.1.
hate 'hot' (**4**) 3, 3.2, 14.4(1).
hauch 'haugh' (**17** + /l/ > **12a**) 17.
hauk 'hawk' (**12**) 14.12(6).
hauld 'hold' (**4**?, **4** > **12, 4** > **13**) 10; *haud* (**12** > **17, 17** + /l/ > **12a**) 17.

hautane 'proud' [1ˢᵗ] (**12**) 17. [2ⁿᵈ] (**4, 8**) 22.3.2.
have see *haf.*
havy 'heavy' (**16**); (**3**) 4.1; (**3 > 4**) 20.8.3.
hay (**8**) 6.1.1, 6.3.2, 14.8(1); (**8a > 1**) 22.4.
hecht 'height' (**16**) 5.3, 6.2; (**15**) 5.3, 6.2, 14.15(7); (**2**) 6.2.
hecht 'be called' (**16**) 6.2.1.
-hede '-hood' (**2, 3**) 14.2(19).
heich 'high' (**2**) 1.1, 6.2.1, 14.2(6), 21.2.2, 22.2.1; (/**hj**-/?) 22.2.1; *hey* (**11**) 1.1, 6.2.1, 6.3.2, 14.11.
heid 'head' (**3**) 5.2, 14.3, 14.3(2), 20.8.2; (**3 > 2, 3 > 4**) 20.8.3; *hevid* (**3**) 14.3(2).
heip (**3 > 2**) 20.8.3.
hele 'heel' (**2**) 14.2(2).
hele 'health, heal' (**3**) 14.3(4).
helter 'halter' (**16**) 14.16(3).
here adv. (**2**) 14.2(1).
here 'hear' (**2**) 14.2(4), 20.6.
hering 'herring' (**2**) 14.2(2).
hert 'hart' (**16 > 17**) 11.2.
hert 'heart' (**16, ?16 > 17, 17 > 4**) 11.2.
het 'hot' (**16**) 5.2.
hete n. 'heat' (**2, 3**) 14.2(19), 20.8.3.
heuch 'crag' (**7**) 7.1, (**7 > 14a**) 6.2; pl. *hewis* (**14a**) 7.2.2.
hevid see *heid.*
hevin (**3**) 14.3(1); (modSc **3 > 15**) 16.5; (**3 > 4**) 20.8.3.
hew 'hue' (**14a**) 6.5.1, 7.2.2.
hew v. (**14b(i)**) 6.5.2, 6.5.3; (**14b(ii)**) 6.5.3.
hew p.t. 'hewed' (**14a**) 6.5.1.
hewis see *heuch.*
hey see *hay, heich.*
heynde 'handy' (**2**) 3.1.1.

hicht 'promise' (**15, 16**) 14.15(2).
hicht 'height' see *hecht.*
hing 'hang' (**15, 2**) 3.1.1.
hinnie see *huny.*
hird 'herdsman' (**15**) 4.2.1; (**2**) 3.1.1, 4.2.1, 5.1.
hizzie see *husy.*
hoch see *houch.*
hoffe 'enclosure' (**18, 18 > 13**) 16.4.
holk 'to dig' (**18** + /l/ > **13a**) 17.
holl 'hollow' (**18** + /l/ > **13a**) 17.
hollow (**18, ??17**) 14.17(7).
hop 'hop(s)' (**18, 18 > 13**) 16.4.
hope 'expectation' (**5**) 14.5(1); (**5 > 18, 18 > 13**) 16.4.
hope 'heap' (**5, 5 > 18, 18 > 13**) 16.4.
hope 'valley' (**5, 5 > 18, 18 > 13**) 16.4.
horn (**18?, 5?**) 14.5(3).
horse (**18**) 14.18(1); (**5?**) 14.5(3).
host 'army' (**5**) 14.5(2).
host 'cough' (**5**) 14.5(1).
houch 'hough' (**18, 13**) 6.2.2.
hound (**6, 19**) 3.1.1.
how 'hoe' (**13**) 6.5.2, 14.13(4).
how 'hollow' see *holl.*
hoy 'the type of boat' (**10**) 14.10(3).
huil 'husk' (**7**) 4.2.2.
huird 'hoard' (**7**) 3.1.1.
huke 'hook' (**7**) 7.2.1; (**7 > 14a**) Fig.8; (**14 > (/j/) + 6**) 7.1, 7.2.1; (**7 > /j/ + 19**) 7.1, 7.2.1, Fig.13.
hundreth, hunder 'hundred' (**19, 6**) 3.1.1.
huny 'honey' (**19**) 4.2.2, 16.1; (**19 > 15**) 16.1.
hure 'whore' (**7**) 7.1.
hurt (**19, 6**) 14.19(4).
husy 'hussy' (**19, 19 > 15**) 16.1.
hyne 'hence' (**1**) 14.1(5).

INDEX III: SCOTS WORDS

-ie < OF (**1**) 14.1(10).
Iesu [2ⁿᵈ] (**14a**) 17.
-in p.p. (**15**) 20.3.
increse (**3**) 14.3(6).
indeid (**2**) 20.8.3.
ineuch 'enough' (**7**) 7.2.1; (**7** > **14a**) 1.1, Fig.8, 7.2.1, 6.5.3; (**14** > (/j/) + **6**) 6.5.3; (**7** > (/j/) + **19**) 7.2.1; *inew* (**14a**) 1.1, 6.5.1, 6.5.3, 7.2.2; (**14** > (/j/) + **6**) 6.5.3.
-in(g) 21.2.2; (**15**) 20.3.
Inglis 'English' (**15**) 14.15(9).
ingon see *onʒeon*.
ingyne [2ⁿᵈ] (**1, 2, 15**) 15.
inveit (**2**) 15.
irn 'iron' (**15**) 3.1; (**1**) cf. 4.1; modSc *eirn, airn* imply earlier *ern (**16**) cf. *erne*.
-is 8.2.2, 12.2, 13.3, 22.4.
ischa 'egress' [2ⁿᵈ] (**8**) 14.8(5).
-ise (**1, 2**) 15.
item (**1, 2**) 15.
-itioun '-ition' (**15, 2**) 4.2.1.
ivill see *evill*.
ither see *other*.
jewel (**14a**) 6.5.1.
jist, geist 'joist' (**15, 2, ?16**) 4.2.1.
jo see *joy*.
jogis 'jougs, the instrument of punishment' (**18, 18** > **13**) 16.4. See also *chokis*.
join (**10**) 8.2.1, 14.10(2), 22.4; *june* (**7**) 8.2.1.
jois 'enjoy' (**9, 9** > **5**) 12.4, 14.9(1).
joug 'jug' (**6**) 14.6(5).
journee 'journey' [2ⁿᵈ] (**2**) 14.2(18); (**8**) 14.8(5); (**8b** > **4?**) 22.4.
Jow 'Jew' (**6**) 6.5.3.
joy (**9**) 6.0, 14.9(1); *jo* (**9** > **5**)
12.4, 14.5(4).
joyous (**9**) 14.9(1).
juge 'judge' (**7**) 14.7(9); (**19**) 14.7(9), 14.19(6).
June (**7**) 7.1, 14.7(10).
just (**7**) 14.7(9).
justice (**7, 19**) 14.19(6).
kame 'comb' (**4**) 20.6.
kay see *key*.
kepe v. 'keep' (**2**) 5.2, 14.2(3); (**16**) 5.2, 20.8.3.
kert see *cart*.
kew 'cue' (**14b(i), ?14b(ii)**) 6.5.3.
key (**11**) 6.3.2; *kay* (**8**) 6.1.1; (**8a** > **1**) 22.4.
keyng 'king' (**15**); (**2**) 4.2.1, 5.1.
kill (**15, 2**) 5.1.
kimmer see *cummer*.
kind (**1**) 3.1.1, 14.1(3), 20.3, 20.4.
kipple see *couple*.
Kirkcaldy (**17** + /l/ > **12a**) n.31.
knaw 'know' (**12**) 6.0, 6.4.1, Fig.7, 14.12(1).
kned 'knead' (**16**) 5.2, 14.16(1).
knew p.t. (**14a**) 6.0, 6.5.1, 6.5.3, 7.2.2, Fig.13.
knoll (**18** + /l/ > **13a**) 17.
labour [1ˢᵗ] (**4**) 4.1, 14.4(2); (**4** > **12**) 20.9. [2ⁿᵈ] (**6**) 14.6(5).
laddle 'ladle' (**17, 4**) 4.1.
lafe, lave 'remainder' (**4**) 12.3, 21.2.2.
laft 'loft' (**18, 18** > **17**) 16.3.
laich see *law* 'low'.
lain 'conceal' (**8**) 14.8(2).
laing see *lang*.
lair (**8, 4**) 22.3.2.
laird (**4, ?4** > **16**) 11.1.
laisere 'leisure' (**8**) 14.3(9); (?early **8** > **4**) 12.3.
lait 'search' (**8**) 12.3, 22.3.3.
Laitin 'Latin' (**4**) 4.1.

213

land 'clearing' (**17**) 9.1; (**12**).
lang 'long' (**17**) 3.1.1, 14.17(1); (**4**) 3.1.1.
lard (**17, 17 > 4**) 11.1.
large (**17, 17 > 4, 4 > 16**) 11.1.
lat see *let*.
lauch 'laugh' (**12**) 6.2.2, 14.12(3).
lauch see *law* 'law, low'.
lauchter 'laughter' (**12**) 6.2.2, 14.12(3).
lauté see *lewté*
lave see *lafe*.
law 'law' (**12**) 1.1, 3, 6.0, 6.4.0, 6.4.1, 14.12(1); *lauch* (**12**) 1.1.
law 'hill' (**12**) 6.0, 6.4.1, 14.12(1).
law 'low' (**12**) 1.1, 6.0, 6.4.1, 14.12(1); *lauch* (**12**) 1.1, 6.2.2; *laich* (**4**) 1.1, 6.2.1, 6.4.1; *leuch* (**14b(i)**) 6.2.1.
lawit 'lay, unlearned' (**12**) 6.4.1.
lay (**8, 8b > 4**) 22.4; p.t., p.p. 22.3.2.
layne 'conceal' (**8**) 14.8(2), 22.3.3.
leche 'healer, heal' (**2**?) 14.2(21).
lede n. 'lead' (**3**) 5.2.
lede v. 'lead' (**2, 3**) 14.2(19), 20.8.3.
ledder 'ladder' (**16**) 14.16(3).
leethe, leed 'will to work' modSc 21.2.3.
lefe 'dear' (**2**) 14.2(5).
lefe 'leaf' (**3**) 14.3(2), 21.2.2.
lefe v. 'live' see *live*.
lefe 'permission' see *leve*.
leid 'person' (**2**) 14.3, 20.8.2.
leippie 'quarter of a peck' (**3, 15**) 5.3.
leke 'leek' (**2**) 14.2(6), 21.2.2.
lele 'loyal' (**3**) 14.3(9).

leme 'gleam' (**2, 3**) n.22.
lend 'dwell' (**16**) 3.1.1; (**2**) 3.1.1, 14.2(7).
lendis 'buttocks' (**16**) 3.1.1; (**2**) 3.1.1, 5.3; (**15**) 3.1.1, 5.3.
lene adj. (**3**) 14.3(4).
lepe (**2, 3**) 14.2(20).
lere 'learn' (**2**) 14.2(19), 20.8.3.
lerne (**16, ?2, ?3**) 3.1.1; *lairn* (**16 > *17 > 4**) 11.2.
lese 'lying' (**3**) 14.3(2).
lest 'duration' (**16**) 20.4; (**17**).
leste (**3**) 14.3(4).
let v. 'permit' (**16, 17**) 5.2.
leuch p.t. 'laughed' (**14a, 14 >** (/j/) + **6**) 6.5.3.
leuch see *law* 'low'.
leve, lefe 'permission' (**2**) 14.2(20).
lewed 'lewd' (**14b(i)**) 6.5.2; *lawd* (**12**) 6.5.2.
lewté 'loyalty' [1st] (**14b(i)**) 6.5.2; *lauté* (**14b(iii)**) 6.5.2, 17. [2nd] (**2**) 14.2(17).
libel (**1, 2**) 15.
liberale [1st] (**15, 2**) 4.2.1. [final] (**17, 4**) 14.4(8).
liberte [final] (**2**) 14.2(17).
library (**15?**, modSc **2**) 4.2.1.
licence (**1, 2**) 15.
licht n., adj. 'light' (**15**) 5.3, Fig.13.
licoure (**15**, modSc **2**) 4.2.1.
ligne 'lineage' 8.1; (**15**) 8.3.
like (**1, 15**) 14.15(5).
lilly 'liefly, lovely' (modSc **15**) 5.3.
limit (**15, 2**) 4.2.1.
limon 'lemon' (**15, 2**) 4.2.1.
linth 'length' (**15**) 14.15(9); (**16**).
linyel 'cobbler's thread' (**15**) 8.3.
linʒe 'slender' (**15, 2**) 8.3.
lipper 'leprosy, leprous' (**15, 2**

INDEX III: SCOTS WORDS

5.3.
littar (**15**, modSc **2**) 4.2.1.
littill (**1**) 4.2.1, 20.6; (**15**) 4.2.1; (**2**) 4.2.1.
live, lif v. (**15, 2**) 4.2.1.
liver 'one who lives' (**15**) 4.2.1; *liffar* (**15**) 14.19(9); *luffar* (**15** > **19**) 14.19(9); *levar* (**2**) 4.2.1.
liver 'deliver' (**15, 2**) 4.2.1.
liver 'the organ' (**15, 15** > **19**) 14.19(9).
liveray [1ˢᵗ] (**15, 2**) 4.2.1; **15** > **19**) 14.19(9). [final] (**8**) 14.8(5).
loge (**5**) 14.5(1); (**5** > **19**) 14.19(8), 16.2.
lok (**18**) 14.18(1), 16.4; (**18** > **13**) 16.4.
lone 'lane' (**5**) 14.5(1).
lose n. 'praise' (**5**) 14.5(2).
lose v. (**5**) 14.5(1).
loup 'leap' (**13**) 14.13(3), 17.
love v. 'praise'(**5**) 14.5(1).
low 'flame' (**13**) 6.4.2.
lown 'calm' (**13**) 6.0, 6.4.2, Fig.13.
Lowrence (**13**) 14.13(9).
lows 'loose' (**13**) 14.13(3).
lufe 'palm of the hand' (**7**) 14.7(2).
luif 'love' (**7**) 4.2.2, 14.7(8), 21.1.
luke 'look' (**7** > **14a**, **7** > (/j/) + **19**) 7.2.1; (**14** > (/j/) + **6**) 6.5.3, 7.2.1.
lunȝe 'loin' (**19**) 8.1, 8.2.1, 8.2.2.
lure (**7**) 7.1.
-ly (**1**) 14.1(6).
lyte 'elite' (**1, 2**) 15.
MacKenzie 8.1.
maich see *mauch* 'son-in-law'.
maid (**8**, ? near rhyme with **4**) 22.3.3.
mailȝe 'chain-mail' (**17, 4, 4** > **16**) 8.3.
main 'strength' (**8**) 9.2, 22.3.2, 22.3.3; (**4**) 22.3.2.
mainer 'cultivate' (**17, 4**) 4.1.
mainer 'manner' [1ˢᵗ] (**17**) 4.1; (**4**) 4.1, 14.4(2). [2ⁿᵈ] (**2**) 14.2(11), 20.8.3.
maintene [1ˢᵗ] (**8, 8** > **16**) 9.2. [2ⁿᵈ] (**2**) 14.2(11).
mainȝe 'maiming, maim' (**17, 4, 4** > **16**) 8.3.
mak 'make' (**17**) 6.1; (**4**) 4.1, 14.4(2).
malign (**15**) 8.3.
maner 'manor' (**17**) 4.1.
manger (**17**?, **4**?) 9.2; (**12, 4** > **8**, **8** > **16**).
mart 'fattened ox' (**17, 17** > **4, 4** > **16**) 11.1.
mary 'marry' (**4**) 14.4(2), 20.6.
matere 'matter' (**17**) 4.1; (**4**) 4.1, 14.4(2).
mauch 'maggot' (**12**) 14.12(6).
mauch 'son-in-law' (**12**) 1.1; *maich* (**4**) 1.1.
maugré 'ill will' (**12**) 14.12(4).
maw 'gull' (**12**) 14.12(6).
May (**8b** > **4**?) 22.4; (**8a** > **1**).
may 'girl' (**8**) 22.4.
may v. (**8, 4**) 22.4; modSc *maw* (**4** > **12**).
mede 'reward' (**2**) 14.2(1).
mede 'meadow' (**2**) 14.2(2).
meid 'mood' (**7**); (**7** > **2**) 7.1.
meild see *muild.*
meir 'mare' (**3** > **4**) 20.8.3.
mekill see *mikill.*
mele 'meal' (**3**) 14.3(1).
mele 'tell' (**3**) 14.3(4).
melt 'milt' (**16**) 14.16(5).
memore (?**9** > **5**) 14.5(4).

215

mene 'means' (**3**) 14.3(9).
mene 'complain' (**2**) 14.2(19).
mene 'intend' (**2**) 14.2(19).
menoun 'minnow' (**16**) 14.16(5).
mense 'honour' (**16**) 14.16(1).
Menzies 8.1.
menʒe 'company' 8.1, 8.4; (**16**) 8.3; (**3**) 8.3, 14.3(1).
merchet 'a feudal casualty' (**16, 16 > 17**) 11.2.
mercy [2ⁿᵈ] (**1**) 14.1(11).
meridiane [final] (**4**) 22.3.3.
mers 'the Merse' (**16, 16 > 17**) 11.2.
mes 'mass, the religious service' (**16**) 14.16(3).
mese 'serving of food' (**3**) 14.3(1).
mesell 'leprous' (**3, 15**) 5.3.
mete 'meat' (**3**) 14.3(1), 20.6; (**3 > 4**) 20.8.3; (**3 > 2**).
methe 'landmark' (**15?**) 4.2.1; (**2**) 4.2.1, 21.2.3.
meve see *muve*.
middil (**15, ?2**) 4.2.1.
midding 'midden' (**15, ?2**) 4.2.1.
mikill 'big' (**15**) 4.2.1; (**15 > 19**) 14.19(9); (**2**) 4.2.1, 14.2(15).
milʒeoun 'million' 8.1.
minister (**15**) 4.2.1; (**2**) 4.2.1, 14.2(15).
minute (**15, 2**) 4.2.1.
mirrour (**15, 2**) 4.2.1.
miser (**1**, modSc **2**) 15.
miserable (**15, 2**) 4.2.1.
miserie (**15, 2**) 4.2.1.
mither see *mother*.
mitigat (**15, 2**) 4.2.1.
mittane (**15**) 14.15(6); (**15 > 19**) 14.19(9).

mold see *muild*.
money [1ˢᵗ] (**19**) 4.2.2, 16.1. [2ⁿᵈ] (**8**) 14.8(6).
monument (**5**) 4.5(1).
mony 'many' (**17 > 18**) 14.18(7).
monʒealle 'monial' (**19, 19 > 15**) 8.3.
mother (**19, 19 > 15**) 16.1.
motioun (**5**) 14.5(1); *mudgeoune* (**5 > 19**) 16.2.
moy 'demure' (**9?**) 14.9(2).
mude see *meid*.
mudy 'brave' (**7**) 7.1.
muild 'earth' (**7**) 3.1.1, 7.1, 14.6(10); *meild* (**7 > 2**) 7.1; (**7 > 6**) 14.6(10); *mold* (**18**) 3.1.1; (**18 + /l/ > 13a**) 17.
mudgeoune see *motioun*.
mukill see *mikill*.
mulde v. 'mould' (**7**) 14.7(7).
multure (**19 + /l/ > 6a**) 17.
mune 'moon' (**7**) 14.7(1), 21.2.2; (**7 > 15**) 21.2.2, 22.2.3.
mure 'moor' (**7**) 14.7(1); (**7 > 14a, 14 > /j/ + 6**) Fig.8, 7.3.
muse (**7**) 7.1.
music (**7**) 14.7(9), 21.2.2.
mute 'moot' (**7**) 7.1.
muve 'move' (**7**) 4.2.2, 14.7(8); *meve* (**2**) 14.2(12).
na adj. 'no' (**4**) 20.4, 20.7.
na adv. 'nay' (**4 > 12**) n.37a; (**17**).
narrow (**4**) 4.1; (**17**).
nakit (**4**) 14.4(2); (modSc /j/ + **12**) 16.6.
natioun [1ˢᵗ] (**4**) 14.4(2). [final] (**6**) 14.6(5).
navy [2ⁿᵈ] (**1**) 14.1(10).
nede (**2**) 14.2(4), 14.3, 20.8.2.
neir 'never' (**3**) 4.1.
nete 'neat' (**3**) 14.3(9).
neve 'fist' (**3**) 14.3(1); (**15**) 16.5.
nevel 'a blow with the fist' (**3**)

INDEX III: SCOTS WORDS

4.1, 16.5; (modSc **3** > **15**) 16.5.
never (**3, 3** > **15**) 16.5.
nevew 'nephew' [2nd] (**14a**) 6.5.1; *navow* (**6**) 6.5.1.
new (**14a**) 6.5.1, 6.5.3; (**14** > /j/ + **6**) 6.5.3.
niffer 'barter' (**3**); (**3** > **15**) 16.5.
nobill (**5**) 14.5(1).
nois (**9**) 14.9(1).
north (**18?, 5?**) 14.5(3).
nose (**5**) 14.5(1).
note (**5**) 14.5(1).
noumer 'number' (**6**) 14.6(5); (**19**) 14.19(4).
nout 'cattle' (**13**) 14.13(3), 17.
nowther 'neither' (**13**) 17.
nuke 'nook' (**7, 7** > **14a, 7** > /(j)/ + **19**) 7.2.1; (**14** > /j/ + **6**) 6.5.3, 7.2.1.
nut (**19**) 4.2.2, 16.1; (**19** > **15**) 16.1.
obey (**8**) 14.8(3).
oblige (**1, 2**) 15.
oblis, oblisch 'oblige'(**1, 2, 15**) 15.
odour (**5**) 14.5(1).
off (**18, 18** > **17**) 16.3.
officiale (**15**, modSc **2**) 4.2.1.
officiar (**15, 2**) 4.2.1.
oft (**18, 18** > **17**) 16.3.
oil, olȝe see *ulȝe*.
onȝeon 'onion' 8.1; (**19**) 8.3, 16.1; *ingon* (**19** > **15**) 8.3, 16.1.
opinioun 8.1; (**15**) 4.2.1, 8.3; (**15** > **19**) 8.3, 14.19(9); (**2**) 4.2.1.
oranȝe see *(apill) oranȝe*.
other (**7**) 7.1; (modSc **7** > **4, 19**, modSc **19** > **15**) 16.1.
ou see *(w)oull*.

ouk see *(w)ouk*.
-oun '-on' (**6**) 14.6(5).
ounce (**6**) 14.6(5); (**19**).
-our (**6**) 14.6(5).
our 'over' (**13**) 14.13(8).
-ous (**6**) 14.6(5).
outhall 'udal' (**6**) 14.6(12), 21.2.3.
outwart [2nd] (**17**) 11.2.
owre see *our*.
oxter 'armpit' (**18**) 14.18(2).
paig see *peug*.
paint (**8, 8** > **16**) 9.2.
pair n. (**8** > **4**) 22.3.4.
pair 'impair' (**8** > **4**) 22.3.4.
pais 'weigh(t)' (**8**) 14.3(9), 22.4; (early **8** > **4**) 12.3.
palyas 'palliasse' 8.1.
panch 'paunch' (**17?, 12, 4** > **8, 8** > **16**) 9.2.
pand 'pawn' (**17, 12**) 9.1.
parritch 'porridge' (modSc **18, 18** > **17**) 16.3.
part (**17, 17** > **4, 4** > **16**) 11.1.
Pasche 'Easter' (**4**) 14.4(2).
pat 'pot' (**18, 18** > **17**) 16.3.
pay (**8, 4, 8a** > **1**) 22.4; p.t., p.p. 23.3.2.
pece 'piece' (**2**) 14.2(11).
pele see *pill*.
pepill (**2**) 14.2(12).
perce (**2**) 14.2(14).
pere 'peer' (**2**) 14.2(10).
peril 'peril' (**16, 16** > **17**) 11.2.
perle 'pearl' (**16**) 11.2.
persew (**14a**) 6.5.1; (**14** > (/j/) + **6**, /s/ + **14** > /ʃ/ + **6**) 6.5.3.
pert 'bold' (**2**) 14.2(14).
pertinence (**16, 16** > **17**) 11.2.
pertrick 'partridge' (**16, 16** > **17, 17** > **4**) 11.2.
pese 'peace' (**3**) 14.3(9).
pese 'pease' (**3**) 14.3(9).

217

peth 'path' (**16**) 14.16(3).
peug 'puke, the fabric' (**7** > **14a**) 7.2.1; *paig* (**7** > **4**) 7.2.1.
pewter (**14b(i)**, **?14** > (/j/) + **6**, **?14b(ii)** > (/j/) + **13**) 6.5.2. Cf. *cuke*.
phisik (**15, 2**) 4.2.1.
pil, pele 'peel' (**15, 2**) 5.1.
pind 'impound' (**15**) 3.1.1, 14.15(3).
pité (**15, 2**) 4.2.1.
pitt see *put*.
plain (**8**, ? near rhyme with **4**) 22.3.3.
plaint 'complain(t)' (**8, 16**) 9.2.
plait 'pleat' (**8**) 12.3, 14.3(9).
planching 'planking' (modSc **17?**) 9.2.
plank (**17**) 9.1, 14.17(2); (**12**) 9.1.
planschour 'planking' (**4?, 4** > **8, 8** > **16**) 9.2; (**17?**).
plant v. (**17, 12, 4** > **8, 8** > **16**) 9.2; (**4?**) 9.1.
plaunch 'plank' (**12**) 9.2.
play (**8a** > **1, ?8b** > **4**) 22.4.
plede (**3**) 5.2, Fig.13; (**16**) 5.2.
plenӡe 'complain' (**16, 3**) 8.3.
plese (**3**) 14.3(9).
pleseir 'pleasure' (**3**) 14.3(9).
pleuch n. 'plough' (**7**) 7.2.1; (**7** > **14a**) Fig.7, 7.2.1; (**14** > (/j/) + **6**) 6.5.3, 7.2.2; (**7** > (/j/) + **19**); pl. *plewis* (**14a**) 6.5.1, Fig.7, 7.2.2, Fig.13; (**14** > (/j/) + **6**) 7.2.2.
plew v. 'plough' (**14a, 14** > (/j/) + **6**) 6.5.1.
plewis pl. see *pleuch*.
plouers pl. 'ploughers' (**14** > (/j/) + **6**) 6.5.3.
poind see *pind*.
point (**10**) 6.0, 14.10(1).

poisoun (**10**) 14.10(1), 22.4; (**7**) 14.10(1).
port (**5**) 14.5(3).
pouder 'powder' (**6**) 17.
pound n. (**19, 6**) 3.1.1.
pover see *pure*.
pow see *pull*.
power [1st] (**6**) 14.6(5); [2nd] (**2**) 20.8.3.
powny 'pony' (**13**) 14.13(4).
praise (**8**) 14.3(9), 22.3.4, 22.4; (?early **8** > **4**) 12.3; (**8** > **4**) 22.3.4.
pray (**4, ?8a**) 22.4; p.t., p.p. 22.3.2.
preche (**3**) 14.3(8).
prefe 'proof' (**2**) 14.2(12); *prufe* (**7**).
preist (**2**) 20.8.2.
prence 'prince' (**16**) 14.16(6); (**15**).
prencipall 'principal' (**16**) 14.16(6); (**15**).
press n. (**16**); (**3**) 14.3(1).
presoun 'prison' [1st] (**15, 2**) 4.2.1. [2nd] (**6**) 14.6(5).
preve 'prove' (**2**) 14.2(12); *pruve, prufe* (**7**) 4.2.2, 14.2(12).
proceid (**2**) 20.8.3.
profit [2nd] (**1, 2, 15**) 15.
pruve see *preve*.
pull (**19, 19** + /l/ > **6a**) 17.
pulpit (**19** + /l/ > **6a**) 17.
pultrie 'poultry' (**19** + /l/ > **6a**) 17.
punӡe v. 'prick' 8.1.
punӡoun 'opinion' 8.1.
pure 'poor' (**7**) 7.1, 14.7(7), 21.2.2; (**7** > **4**) 21.2.2, 21.2.3; *pover* (**5**) 14.5(1).
purpose [2nd] (**5**) 12.4.
pusoun see *poisoun*.
put (**19**); (**19** > **15**) 16.1.

INDEX III: SCOTS WORDS

quene 'queen' (**2**) 14.2(3).
quene 'girl' see *quine*.
quere 'choir' (**2**) 4.2(12).
quern (**16, 16 > 17, 17 > 4**) 11.2; (**16 > 15**).
quert 'in good health' (**16, 16 > 17**) 11.2.
quha 'who' (**4**) 12.2, 20.7; (**4 > 12**) 20.9; + *-is* 12.2.
quhais 'whose' (**4, 4 > 12**) 20.9.
quhare 'where' (**4**) 20.6; (**4 > 12**).
quhasill 'weasel' (**3, 3 > 4**) 4.1.
quhele 'wheel' (**2**) 14.2(5).
quhete 'wheat' (**3**) 14.3(4); *quhyte, fyte* (**3 > 1**) 20.6.
quhyne 'whence' (**1**) 14.1(5).
quiet (**1**) 20.7; (modSc **4**) 22.3.2.
quine 'girl' (**3 > 1**) n.13.
quyok, quak 'heifer' (**1, 4**) 22.3.2.
rain (**8, 4**) 22.3.2.
raird see *rerde*.
raise (**8, 8 > 4**) 22.3.4; (?early **8 > 4**) 12.3.
raisin (?early **8 > 4**) 12.3.
rak 'reck, heed' (**16, 17**) 14.17(3).
rane 'rigmarole' (**4**) 22.3.3.
range (**12**); modSc *reenge* (**4 > ?3 > 2**) 9.3; *rynge* (**3 > 1**) 9.3.
rathe 'promptly' (**4**) 12.3.
reconsile [final] (**1, 2, 15**) 15.
rede 'counsel' (**3**) 14.3(5).
rede 'read' (**2**) 14.2(2).
rede 'red' (**3**) 5.2; (**15**).
redeme (**2**) 14.2(13).
reduce (**7**) 14.7(9).
refe 'robbery' (**3**) 14.3(2).
rejose 'rejoice' (**9, 9 > 5**) 12.4.
releve (**2**) 14.2(11).

remede 'remedy' (**3**) 14.3(6); (**3 > 2**) 20.8.3.
remedy [final] (**1**) 14.1(10).
renʒe 'rein' (**16**) 8.4; (**16 > 15?**) 8.3, 8.4; (**8**) 8.3; (**3**) 8.3, 8.4, 9.3, 14.3(7); (**3 > 1**) 8.4, 9.3, 14.1(12); (**3 > 2**) 8.4; (**3 > 4?**) Fig.9b; (**4**) 8.4, 9.3.
repete (**3**) 14.3(6).
rerde 'uproar' (**16 > *17 > 4**) 11.2; (**2**) 3.1.1, 14.2(7).
resait 'receipt' (**3**) 14.3(9).
resave, resafe 'receive' (**8**, early **8 > 4**) 12.3.
resign (**15**) 8.3; (**1**).
reskew (**14a**) 7.2.2.
resoun [1st] (**3**, modSc **3 > 15**) 16.5. [2nd] (**6**) 14.6(5).
respyte [2nd] (**1, 2, 15**) 15.
restore (**5**) 14.5(1).
retyre (**1, 2**) 15.
reule 'rule' (**14a**) 6.5.1, Fig.13; (**14b(i)**) 6.5.2; (?**14** > (/j/) + **6**, ?**14b(ii)** > (/j/) + **13**) 6.5.3.
reveil (**2**) 15.
revert (**16, 16 > 17, 17 > 4**) 11.2.
revife (**1, 2**) 15.
rew v. 'rue' (**14a**) 6.5.1, 6.5.3; (**14** > (/j/) + **6**) 6.5.3.
rew 'street' (**14a, 6**) 6.5.1.
reward (**17, 17 > 4**) 11.1.
rewme 'realm' (**14b(i), 14b(iii)**) 6.5.2; (**14** > (/j/) + **6?, 14b(ii)** > (/j/) + **13?**) 6.5.3.
riches [2nd] (**16**) 20.4.
riddle (**15**) 5.3.
rief 'roof' (**7**); (**7 > 2**) 7.1.
riffin p.p. 'riven' (**15, 2**) 4.2.1.
rind (**1**) 3.1.1, 14.1(3); (modSc **2**) 3.1.1.
ring 'reign' (**15**) 8.3, 8.4; (**16**) 8.3 (n.12).
rissin p.p. 'risen' (**15, ?2**) 4.2.1.

river [1ˢᵗ] (**15, 2**) 4.2.1. [2ⁿᵈ] (**2**) 14.2(11).
roche 'rock' (**18**) 14.18(3).
rok 'rock' (**18, 18 > 13**) 16.4.
rood 'drizzle, chatter' modSc (**7**) 21.2.3.
rose (**5**) 14.5(1).
roth 'land title' 21.2.3.
rouch, ruch, roch 'rough' (**6, 19, 18**) 6.2.1.
roup 'shout' (**13**) 17.
roust 'rust' (**6**) 14.6(1).
ruch see *rouch*.
rude adj. (**7**) 6.5.1, 7.1.
rufe 'roof' see *rief*.
ruke 'rook' (**7**); (**7 > 14a, 14 >** (/j/) **+ 6**) 6.5.3; (**7 >** (/j/) **+ 19**).
ryale 'royal' (**1**) 14.1(8).
ryne see *renʒe*.
safe (**12**) 12.1, 14.12(4), 17; (**12 > 4**) 12.1.
saft 'soft' (**18, 18 > 17**) 16.3.
saiddle 'saddle' (**17, 4**) 4.1.
sail (**8, 4**) 22.3.2.
saim 'grease' (**8**, ? near rhyme with **4**) 22.3.3.
sain 'bless' (**8, 4**) 22.3.2.
-sait '-ceit' (**8**) 12.3, 14.3(9); (early **8 > 4**) 12.3.
saitin 'satin' (**17, 4**) 4.1.
salch 'willow' (**17**) 6.2.1; (**17 +** /l/ **> 12a**).
sall 'shall' (**17**) 17, 20.3.
salt (**17, 17 +** /l/ **> 12a**) 17.
saphire (**1**); (**2**) 20.8.3.
Sapiens (**4**) 20.5.
sark see *serk*.
sauf see *safe*.
saumond 'salmon' (**12**) 14.12(4).
-save '-ceive' (**8**, early **8 > 4**) 12.3.
save (**12**) 12.1; (**12 > 4**) 12.1,
12.3; (**12 > 17**) n.38.
sawure 'savour' [2ⁿᵈ] (**6**) n.4.
say (**8, 4**) 22.4; p.t, p.p. 22.3.2, 22.3.3.
saynde 'messenger' (**4**) 3.1.1.
scharn 'dung' (**17, 17 > 4**, modSc **4 > 16**) 11.1.
scharp (**17, 17 > 4, 4 > 16**) 11.1.
schaw 'coppice' (**12**) 6.4.1.
schaw 'show' (**12**) 6.4.1, 6.5.2, 17; (**14b(i)**) 6.4.1, 6.5.2, 6.5.3, 7.2.2; (**14b(ii)?**) 6.5.3; (**14 >** (/j/) **+ 6**) 6.5.3; (**14b(ii) >** (/j/) **+ 13?**) 6.5.3, 14.13(7).
schepe (**2**) 14.2(2).
schew see *schaw* 'show'.
schew p.t. 'showed' (**14a**) 6.5.1.
scho 'shoe' (**7**) 6.5.1, 7.1; pl. *schone* (**7**) 7.1; (**7 > 15**) 21.2.3.
schow 'shove' (**6**) 14.6(2).
schrew (**14b(i)**) 6.5.2; (**14b(ii)?**) 6.5.3.
schuil 'shovel' (**7**) 4.2.2.
schulder 'shoulder' (**19 +** /l/ **> 6a**) 17.
schute 'shoot' (**7**) 14.7(4); (**2**).
schyrreff [2ⁿᵈ] (**15?**) 20.3.
scrive 'inscribe' (**1**) 15.
scrufe 'scurf' (**7**) 4.2.2.
se 'sea' (**2**) 14.2(9).
second (**3**) 4.1, 14.3(1); (modSc **3 > 4**) 4.1.
sege 'siege' (**2**) 14.2(11).
sein 'soon' (**7**); (**7 > 2**) 7.1.
seke 'sick' (**2**) 5.3.
selch 'seal, the animal' (**16**) 6.2. 6.2.1.
sely, silly (**2, 15**) 5.3.
seme 'seem' (**2**) 14.2(3), 20.8.3.
sempill 'simple' (**16**) 14.16(6); (**15**).
senoun 'sinew' (**16**) 14.16(5); (**15**).

INDEX III: SCOTS WORDS

sere 'separate(ly)' (**2**) 14.2(1).
serk 'shirt' (**16**) 11.2; (**16 > 17**) 11.2, Fig.13.
serop 'syrup' (**2**) 4.2.1; (**15**).
ser(ve) (**16**) 11.2, 14.16(2); *sar(ve)* (**16 > 17**) 11.2; *sair(ve)* (**17 > 4**) 11.2.
sesoun 'season' (**3**) 14.3(9); (modSc **3 > 15**) 16.5.
sete (**3**) 14.3(4); (**3 > 4**) 20.8.3.
Setterday (**16**) 14.16(3); (**17**).
sevin (**3**) 4.1, 14.3(1); (modSc **3 > 15**) 16.5.
sew 'stitch' (**14a?**) 6.5.1, 6.5.3; (**14 > (/j/) + 6**) 6.5.3; *schew* (/s/ + **14** > /ʃ/ + **6**) 6.5.3.
sew 'sue' (**14a**) 6.5.1.
shin see *scho*.
sicker 'sure' (**15, 2**) 4.2.1.
sign (**1**) 8.2.1; (**15**) 8.3.
sile 'sew up the eyes of a hawk' (**1**) 14.1(13).
silly see *sely*.
simmer see *somer, sommer*.
sin see *sone*.
sinder see *sunder*.
sindry (**19, 19 > 15**) 16.1.
sit 'soot' (modSc **7 > 19 > 15**) n.5.
skaith 'harm' (**4**) 22.3.3.
skanʒe 'skein' 8.4; (**17, 4, ?3**) 8.3; (**4 > 16**).
skill (**15, 2**) 4.2.1.
sla 'slay' (**4**) 22.3.2, 22.4; (**8**) 22.3.2.
slate 'incite' (**8**) 12.3.
sle 'cunning' (**11**) 6.3.2.
sleuth 'sloth' (**14b(i)**) 6.5.2, 6.5.3, Fig.13; (**14 > (/j/) + 6?**) 6.5.3; (**14b(ii)**) 6.5.2; (**14b(ii) > (/j/) + 13**) 6.5.2, 6.5.3, 14.13(7).
slew p.t. (**14a**) 7.2.2.

slype 'slide-car' (**1**) 14.1(13); (**15**).
small (**17, 17 + /l/ > 12a**) 17.
snaw 'snow' (**12**) 6.0, 6.4.1.
sned 'lop' (**16, 17**) 5.2.
snivel (**15, 2**) 4.2.1.
sober (**5**) 14.5(1).
soft see *saft*.
sojourn (**5**) 14.5(1); (**5 > 19**) 16.2.
somer 'summer' (**19**) 4.2.2, 16.1; (**19 > 15**) 16.1.
sommer 'pack-horse' (**19**) 4.2.2, 16.1; (**19 > 15**) 16.1.
son (**19**) 4.2.2, 16.1; (**19 > 15**) 16.1.
sone 'sun' (**19, 19 > 15**) 16.1.
sone 'soon' see *sein*.
sop n. 'sup' (**18, 18 > 13**) 16.4.
sopit 'sunk (in sleep)' (**18**) 16.4(18). See also *soupe*.
sort (**18, ?5**) 14.5(3).
souk 'suck' (**6**) 14.6(1).
soum see *s(w)oum*.
sound 'swim bladder' (**6**) 3.1.1.
Sounday (**19, 6**) 3.1.1.
soupe v. 'weary' (**18 > 13**) 16.4.
soupill 'supple' (**6**) 14.6(5).
southern, sutheron, sudron (**19**) 3.1.
soverane [final] (**4, 8**) 22.3.2.
sowder 'solder' (**13**) 14.13(4).
Spanʒe 'Spain, Spanish' 8.4; (**17**) 8.3; (**4**) 8.3, 14.4(2); (**4 > 16**) 8.3; (**8**) 8.2.1.
speche (**2?**) 14.2(21).
speke (**3, 16**) 5.2.
spere 'ask' (**15**) 4.2.1; (**3**) 14.3(1); (**2**) 14.2(15), 21.2.2.
spere 'spear (**3**)14.3(1).
spew (**14a**) 6.5.1, 6.5.3.
spirit (**15, 2**) 4.2.1; *sprete* (**2**) 15.
spit 'roasting spit' (**15, 2**) 4.2.1.

ote (**18**) 4.1; (**5**) 4.1, 14.5(1).
v. (**15, 2**) 5.1.
licoultry (**19 + /l/ > 6a**) n.31.
e (**1, 2**) 15.
'to, too' (**7**) 7.1.
her 'dowry' (**18**) 14.18(5).
iddir (**16, 15**) 14.15(8).
in 'deceit' (**8**, ? near rhyme ith **4**) 22.3.3.
ist 'trust'(**4?**) 20.4.
ivel 'travel' (**17, 4**) 4.1.
sure (**3**) 14.3(1).
te 'negotiate' (**3**) 14.3(9),).8.3.
uth 'truth' (**14a**) 6.4.2, 6.5.1, 5.3; (**13**) 6.0, 6.4.2, 6.5.1; (**7**) .7(5).
w 'true' (**14a**) 6.5.1, 6.5.3, 2.2; (**14 > (/j/) + 6**) 6.5.3.
wly (**14a**) 6.5.1, 6.5.3; (**14 > /) + 6**) 6.5.3.
w 'believe' (**6**) 6.4.3, Fig.7, 5.3; *trew* (**14a**) 6.5.3(5).
bill (**19**) 14.19(4), 16.1; (**19 >**) 16.1.
th see *treuth*.
'tup' (**7, 7 > 15**) 22.2.3.
e 'brawl' 8.4; (**19**) 8.3; (**7**) , 14.7(8); modSc *toolyie* (**6**) 8.4.
'tooth' (**7**) 14.7(1); pl. *teith* 14.2(3).
'two' (**4**) 20.4, 20.7; (**4 > 12**) 9.
(f) 'twelve' (**16, 16 > 17**) 17(6); (**17 > 18**) 14.18(6).
ve see *taw*.
(**1, 2**) 15.
(**7**) 7.1, 14.7(9).
'oil' 8.4; (**17**) 8.3; (**7**) 7(8); modSc *eely* (**7 > 2**) 8.3; dSc *ooly* (**6**) 8.3; *oyll* (**10, 10**)) 8.2.1, 22.4; *oly* (**5?**) 8.1.

THE OLDER SCOTS VOWELS

umast 'uppermost' (**7**) 4.2.2.
une 'oven' (**7**) 4.2.2; (/j-/) 22.2.1.
-ure (**7**) 7.1, n.4.
use (**7**) 6.5.1, 14.7(9), 7.1, 22.2.3; (**7** > **15**, **7** > **4**) 21.2.2, 22.2.3; (**7** > **2**) 22.2.3; (/j-/) 22.2.3; + suffix 21.2.2, 22.2.3.
vailʒe 'avail' (**17, 4, 4** > **16**) 8.3.
valay 'valley' [2ⁿᵈ] (**8**) 14.8(5).
valew 'value' (**14a, 6**) 6.5.1.
verray 'true' [2ⁿᵈ] (**8**) 14.8(6).
vertew 'virtue' [2ⁿᵈ] (**14a**) 6.5.1, 7.2.2; (**6**) 6.5.1.
vois 'voice' (**9**) 6.0, 12.4, 14.9(1); *voce* (**9** > **5**) 12.4; (**10**) 6.0, 14.9(1), 14.10(1).
voyd 'void, avoid, devoid' (**9**) 12.4, 14.9(1); (**9** > **5**) 12.4; (**10**) 14.9(1), 14.10(1).
wab see *web*.
waddir see *weddir*.
wade 'woad' (**4, 4** > **12**) n.32, 20.9.
wadge 'wedge' (**16, 16** > **17**) 14.17(6).
waith 'hunting' (?early **8** > **4**) 22.3.3.
waizel see *quhasill*.
wake (**4**) 14.4(2); (**4** > **12**) 20.9.
waken (**4, 4** > **12**) 20.9.
wall (**17, 17** + /l/ > **12a**) 17.
walt 'welt' (**17, 17** + /l/ > **12a**) 14.17(6).
wame 'belly' (**4**) 3.1.1, 14.4(3), 20.7; *wyme* (**4** > ***3** > **1**) n.13.
wan see *ane*.
want (**17**) 9.1, 14.17(1).
wantoun [2ⁿᵈ] (**13**) 6.4.2.
wapyn 'weapon' (**4, 4** > **12**) 18, 20.9.
war 'worse' see *wer*.

warld 'world' (**16** > **17**) 11.2.
warm (**17**) 11.1; modSc *wairm* (**17** > **4**) 11.1; (**4** > **16**) 11.1.
warsill see *wersill*.
wast 'west' (**16, 16** > **17**) 14.17(6).
wat see *wete*.
wate see *wit*.
watter 'water' (**17, 4**) 4.1; (**4** > **12**) 20.9.
waw 'the measure of weight' (**12**) 17.
waw n. 'wave' (**12**) 17.
way (**8**) 6.1.1, 14.8(1); (**8a** > **1**); (**8b** > **4**?) 22.4; modSc *waw* (**4** > **12**) 22.4.
wean 'child' modSc 22.2.4.
web (**16, 16** > **17**) 14.17(6); (**17** > **18**) 14.18(6).
weddir, wethir 'weather' (**16**) 14.15(8), 14.17(6); (**15**) 14.15(8); (**16** > **17**) 14.17(6).
weird 'destiny' (**2**) 4.2.1, 5.1, 14.2(15).
weke see *(w)ouk*.
wele adv., adj. 'well' (**2**) 14.2(7).
weltir (**16**); (**16** > **17**) cf. 14.17(6); *woltir* (**17** > **18**) 14.18(6).
wer 'worse' (**16, 16** > **17**) 11.2; (**17** > **12**).
were 'doubt' (**2**) n.23.
were 'war' (**3**) 14.3(1); (**3** > **2**) 20.8.3.
were 'wire' (**1, 3**) 14.3(10).
were 'wear' (**3**) 14.3(1).
wersch 'insipid' (**16, 16** > **17, 17** > **4**) 11.2.
wersill 'wrestle' (**16, 16** > **17**) 11.2.
wesch 'wash' (**16**) 14.16(3); (**15**) cf. 14.15(8); (**17**).
wete 'wet' (**2**) 14.2(2), 20.8.3;

strind 'lineage' (**1**) 3.1.1.
strinth 'strength' (**15**) 14.15(9); (**16**).
stude p.t., p.p. 'stood' (**7**) 7.1, 14.7(1).
stupid (**7**) 14.7(9), 21.2.2.
stuth 'stud' (**7**) 4.2.2.
styme 'the least glimpse' (**1**) 14.1(13).
subtil (**19**) 4.2.2, 16.1; (**19** > **15**) 16.1.
succede (**2**) 14.2(10).
suder 'solder' (**13**) 14.13(4).
suffragane [final] (**4**) 22.3.3.
suld 'should' (**19**) 3.1.1.
summer see *somer, sommer*.
sunder (**19, 19** > **15**) 16.1.
sundry see *sindry*.
sune see *sein*.
sunʒe 'hesitate' 8.1.
superflue [final] (**14a, 6**) 6.5.1.
suppar (**19**) 4.2.2, 14.19(5), 16.1; (**19** > **15**) 16.1.
sure (**7**) 6.5.1, 7.1, 14.7(9).
sute 'soot' see *sit*.
swallow v. see *swelly*.
sweit 'sweet' (**2**) 15.
swelch 'whirlpool' (**16**) 6.2.
swelly, swallow v. 'swallow' [1ˢᵗ] (**16**); (**17**) 14.17(4); (**17** > **18**) 14.18(6). [2ⁿᵈ] (**1**) 1.1, 6.3.1, 14.1(7).
swete v. 'sweat' (**2, 3**) 5.2, 14.2(19).
swey 'sway' (**8**) 6.1.1; (**8a** > **1**) (**11**) 6.3.2.
swik 'deceit' (**15, 2**) 4.2.1.
swoul 'swivel' (**6**); *sweel* (**2**); modSc *sweevil* (***15, 2**) 4.2.1.
s(w)oum 'swim' (**6**) 14.6(8); *swim* (**15**).
swoun 'swoon' (**6**) 14.6(9).
s(w)ourd 'sword' (**6**) 14.6(8);

(**16, 16 > 17**) 14.17(6).
wevar 'weaver' (**3**); *wyver* (**3 > 1**) n.13.
wey 'weigh' (**8**) 6.1.1; (**8a**); (**11**) 6.3.2.
widdir see *weddir*.
widow, wedow (**15, 2**) 4.2.1.
wild (**1**) 3.1.1, 14.1(2).
wind n. (**15**) 3.1.1.
wind v. 'turn' (**15**) 3.1.1; (**1**).
windir see *wondir*.
wirry 'throttle' [2ⁿᵈ] (**1**) 6.3.1.
wise (**1**) 14.1.
wit 'know' (**15, 2**) 4.2.1; (**4**) 12.3.
wob see *web*.
woik p.t. 'woke' (**7, 7 > 6**) 14.6(10).
wolf (**19, 19 + /l/ > 6a**) 17.
wolter see *weltir*.
wondir (**19, 19 > 15**) 16.1.
worn (**18?, 5?**) 14.5(3).
(w)ouk 'week' (**6**) 14.6(8), 17 (see OED s.v. *week*); *weke* (**2**) 5.3.
wouk p.t. see *wake*.
(w)oull 'wool' (**6**) 14.6(8); *(w)ou* (**19 + /l/ > 6a**) 14.6(8).
wound n. (**6**) 3.1.1.
wound p.p. (**19, 6**) 3.1.1.
wraith 'wroth' (**4**) 12.3.
wuid 'wood' (**7**) 4.2.2, 16.1; (**19, 19 > 15**) 16.1; (**6**) 14.6(8).
wuisch p.t. 'washed' (**7**) 14.7(1); (**7 > 6**) 14.6(10).
wyver see *wevar*.
-y < OE *-ig* (**1**) 6.1.2, 14.1(6).
-y < OF (**1**) 14.1(11).
yae see *ae*.
yaird see *ȝard*.
yape 'eager' (**4**) 22.2.4; (modSc **12**) n.37a.
yare 'fish-trap' (**4**) 22.2.4.

yean '(of a ewe) give birth' modSc (**3**); (/**j**-/) 22.2.1.
yerth see *airth*.
Yid 'Adam' modSc (**4 > /j/ + 15**) 22.2.2. See SND Miscellanea: personal names.
yill see *ale*.
yin see *ane*.
yird see *erd*.
yit see *atis*.
yix see *ax*.
ȝallow 'yellow' [1ˢᵗ] (**17**) 14.17(4). [2ⁿᵈ] (**13**) 6.4.2.
ȝard, yaird 'enclosed ground' (**17, 17 > 4**) 3.1.1, 11.1.
ȝeild 'barren' (**16, 2**) 3.1.1.
ȝere 'year' (**2**) 14.2(2), 20.8.3.
ȝett 'pour' (**2, 16**) 5.2.
ȝolden p.p. 'yielded' (**18**) 3.1.1.
ȝow 'you' (**6**) 6.5.3.
ȝow 'ewe' (**13**) 6.4.2.
ȝowr 'your' (**6**) 6.5.3.
ȝude, ȝede p.t. 'went' (**7, 2**) 14.2(5).
ȝyrne 'curdle' (/**j**-/) 22.2.1.

www.ingramcontent.com/pod-product-compliance
Lightning Source LLC
Chambersburg PA
CBHW070342100426
42812CB00005B/1395